# The Essential PageMaker® 5.0

The Essential PageMaker

The Essential PageMaker

# The Essential PageMaker® 5.0

Carla Rose with Rita Lewis

**alpha books**

*A Division of Prentice Hall Computer Publishing*
*11711 North College Avenue, Carmel, Indiana 46032 USA*

International Standard Book Number: 1-56761-249-0
Library of Congress Catalog Card Number: 93-71188

96  95  94  93        9  8  7  6  5  4  3  2  1

Interpretation of the printing code: the rightmost number of the first series of numbers is the year of the book's printing; the rightmost number of the second series of numbers is the number of the book's printing. For example, a printing code of 93-1 shows that the first printing of the book occurred in 1993.

Screen reproductions in this book were created by means of the program Collage Plus from Inner Media, Inc., Hollis, NH.

*Printed in the United States of America*

**Publisher**
Marie Butler-Knight

**Associate Publisher**
Lisa A. Bucki

**Managing Editor**
Elizabeth Keaffaber

**Acquisitions Manager**
Stephen R. Poland

**Development Editor**
Faithe Wempen

**Production Editors**
Michelle Shaw
Linda Hawkins

**Copy Editor**
San Dee Phillips

**Cover Designer**
Scott Fulmer

**Designer**
Roger Morgan

**Indexers**
Craig Small

**Production Team**
Diana Bigham, Brad Chinn, Tim Cox, Meshell Dinn, Mark Enochs,
Howard Jones, Tom Loveman, Beth Rago, Carrie Roth, Greg Simsic


Special thanks to Kelly Oliver for ensuring the technical
accuracy of this book.

The Essential PageMaker

# Table of Contents

Introduction      xvii

## 1   From Idea to Finished Page   2

Planning Your Publication ....................................................... 2
Layout ....................................................................................... 3
Typography ............................................................................... 6
Graphics ................................................................................. 10
Printing .................................................................................. 13
Think in Color ....................................................................... 15
Choosing a Printing Process ................................................ 16
Copyrighting Your Work ...................................................... 18
The Bare Essentials .............................................................. 19

## 2   Getting Started in PageMaker   20

Opening or Starting PageMaker ........................................... 20
Starting a New Publication .................................................. 22
Opening an Existing Publication ......................................... 24
Using the Pasteboard ........................................................... 25
Changing Pages in Your Publication ................................... 26
The PageMaker Toolbox ....................................................... 27
The Rulers .............................................................................. 30
    Have you tried . . . resetting the zero point to
      measure the specific size of an element? .................. 31
Working with a Grid ............................................................. 31
    Setting Margins and Columns ...................................... 32
    Changing Vertical and Horizontal Guidelines ............. 33
Taking a Closer Look ........................................................... 34
    Viewing Different Areas of the Page ............................ 36
Saving Your Work (and Your Sanity) ................................... 37
    Have you tried . . . minimizing mini-saves? ................. 39
    The Revert Command ................................................... 40
Quitting PageMaker .............................................................. 41
Getting Help .......................................................................... 42
The Bare Essentials .............................................................. 44

## 3    The PageMaker 5.0 Upgrade                    46

What's New in PageMaker 5? ................................................47
Aldus Additions ...................................................................48
The Control Palette ..............................................................50
Text and Graphics Rotation ..................................................53
New Print Drivers ................................................................54
Multiple Open Documents ...................................................55
System Requirements for PageMaker 5 ................................56
How Do I Upgrade? ............................................................57
The Bare Essentials .............................................................57

## 4    The Birth of the News                          58

Planning Your Publication ....................................................58
Design Considerations .........................................................60
What's in a Name? ...............................................................61
    Banners and Mastheads ..................................................61
    Logo Graphics ...............................................................62
Setting Up the Page .............................................................64
    Defining the Grid Lines ..................................................66
    Adding Columns ...........................................................66
    Numbering Pages ..........................................................68
Defaults and Templates ........................................................71
    Working with Templates .................................................72
    Word Processor Templates .............................................74
The Bare Essentials .............................................................76

## 5    Creating Master Pages                          78

A Guide to Guidelines .........................................................79
    Line Up and Make It Snappy! .........................................80
Lay Down Layers ................................................................81
Creating a Masthead ...........................................................83
    Wave Your Banner .........................................................85
Setting Up a Self-Mailer .....................................................89
Mailing Indicia ...................................................................90
Removing Master Page Elements .........................................91
Adding Pages ......................................................................91
    Have you tried . . . making a template for mailing labels? ....93

The Essential PageMaker

Save Your Work! ............................................................ 93

The Bare Essentials ....................................................... 94

# 6   Working with Text Files      96

Importing Text .............................................................. 97

   Placing Text with the Place Command ........................... 99

   Text Flow Options ...................................................... 99

   Using the Place Box .................................................. 100

Working with Longer Stories ........................................ 102

   Using Semi-Automatic Text Flow ................................ 103

   Using Autoflow to Place Text ..................................... 103

   Threading and Unthreading ......................................... 104

   Replacing a Story ...................................................... 105

   Inserting Text ........................................................... 106

Adjusting Blocks of Text .............................................. 106

Paragraph Specifications ............................................. 107

   Indents and Tabs ...................................................... 108

   Setting Indents on the Screen .................................... 110

   Using Tabs ............................................................... 111

   Leaders ................................................................... 112

   Paragraph Spacing ................................................... 113

   Alignment ................................................................ 113

   Widows and Orphans ............................................... 114

   Paragraph Rules ...................................................... 115

Using the Table Editor in

   PageMaker for Windows ............................................ 116

Specifying Type .......................................................... 118

   Fonts ....................................................................... 119

   Type Measurement ................................................... 120

   Leading ................................................................... 120

   Subscript and Superscript ......................................... 124

   Have you tried . . . setting type that needs to

     be made distinctive in small caps? ........................... 125

Tracking ................................................................... 125

   Manual and Automatic Kerning .................................. 126

   Have you tried . . . kerning type around an inline graphic? ........ 129

Headlines ................................................................. 129

   Placing a Headline .................................................... 130

   Text Rotation ........................................................... 131

The Bare Essentials ................................................... 132

**7   Styles and the Story Editor                           134**

Working with Styles ....................................................... 134
  Applying an Existing Style ........................................ 135
  Changing Existing Styles .......................................... 136
  Creating a New Style ............................................... 137
  Using a Style Sheet ................................................. 138
  Copying a Style Sheet .............................................. 139
  Using Style Name Tags ............................................. 140
  Overriding Styles ................................................... 141
The Story Editor ......................................................... 142
  Assigning a Style in Story Editor ............................... 143
  Opening Story Editor ............................................... 143
  Word Processing in Story Editor ................................ 144
  Placing a New Story ................................................ 145
Find and Change ......................................................... 148
  Viewing Invisible Characters .................................... 151
The Spell Checker ....................................................... 153
  Have you tried . . . adding your name, company name,
    and other frequently used terms to the dictionary? ..... 154
  Checking Spelling .................................................. 154
Hyphenation .............................................................. 156
  Manual Only ......................................................... 157
  Manual Plus Dictionary ........................................... 157
  Manual Plus Algorithm ............................................ 158
  Setting the Hyphenation Zone ................................... 158
Working with Linked Text .............................................. 159
  Getting Link Information .......................................... 160
The Bare Essentials ..................................................... 166

**8   Working with Graphics                                 168**

Paint Bit-Mapped Images .............................................. 169
PICT Object-Oriented Images ......................................... 169
EPS Graphics ............................................................. 172
Scanned Images .......................................................... 173
  Flat Scanners ....................................................... 174
  Hand-Held Scanners ................................................ 174
  Video Digitizers .................................................... 176
  Color Scanners ...................................................... 176
Importing Graphics ..................................................... 177

Positioning Graphics ........................................................ 178
    Placing from a Graphics File .................................. 178
Modifying Images ........................................................... 179
    Repositioning a Graphic ....................................... 179
    Resizing an Image ............................................... 179
    Repairing Distorted Graphics .............................. 181
Cropping ...................................................................... 181
    Electronic Cover-Ups .......................................... 182
Editing a Graphic .......................................................... 184
Inline Graphics ............................................................. 185
    Placing an Inline Graphic .................................... 186
Text Wrap—Getting the Run Around ............................ 189
    Customizing a Graphic Boundary ......................... 191
    Text Flow Options ............................................... 193
Working with Linked Graphics ..................................... 194
    Link Defaults ..................................................... 197
    Printing with Linked Graphics ............................. 199
Creating Graphics in PageMaker ................................. 200
Image Control—Grayscale and TIFF Graphics .............. 201
    Have you tried . . . using a small inline graphic instead
        of a dingbat to indicate the end of a story? ............ 203
    Screening ........................................................... 204
The Bare Essentials ...................................................... 206

## 9  Printing One Copy or a Thousand          208

PageMaker Printer Drivers ............................................ 208
    Installing a Mac Printer Driver ............................. 209
    Installing a Windows Printer Driver ..................... 209
Composing to a Printer in Windows ............................. 210
Changing a Publication's Printer Type ......................... 211
Printing a Proof Copy .................................................. 212
    Have you tried . . . proofreading your work on a hard copy? ..... 213
Looking at the Laser .................................................... 214
    How a Laser Printer Works ................................... 214
    PostScript Printers .............................................. 215
    Non-PostScript Printers ....................................... 215
Types of Type .............................................................. 216
    Font Fundamentals .............................................. 218
    Using Downloadable Fonts .................................. 219

A Printshop on Your Desktop ...................................................... 222
   Have you tried . . . using your laser
      printer to make your copies? ............................................ 223
   Printing Options ...................................................................... 223
   Specialty Papers ...................................................................... 224
   Specialty Inks .......................................................................... 224
   Desktop Binderies .................................................................. 225
   Two-Sided Printing ................................................................ 226
How to Print All the News Without Throwing a Fit ........................ 226
   Offset Printing Methods ........................................................ 227
   Printing Plates ........................................................................ 228
   Press Size ................................................................................ 229
   Choosing a Printshop ............................................................ 229
   The Ten Percent Solution ...................................................... 230
Printing for the Printer ................................................................ 230
   Creating a Laser Master ........................................................ 230
   Using the Right Paper ............................................................ 230
   Treat the Paper and Your Printer Properly .......................... 231
   Printing Larger Pages ............................................................ 231
   When Not to Use Auto-Overlap ............................................ 232
Working with an Imagesetter ...................................................... 233
   Paperless Printing .................................................................. 234
   Imagesetter Concerns ............................................................ 235
Commercial Color Printing .......................................................... 236
   Working with Service Bureaus .............................................. 239
   Preparing Disks for a Service Bureau .................................. 239
   Leave Home Without It .......................................................... 240
   Virus Warning ........................................................................ 241
The Bare Essentials ...................................................................... 242

**10   PageMaker Goes to Work    244**

Using Pre-made Templates .......................................................... 244
   Working with Templates ........................................................ 245
   Designing Functional Forms .................................................. 248
Designing Your Own Forms .......................................................... 250
   Drawing Lines Manually ........................................................ 251
   Drawing Lines Automatically ................................................ 251
   Drawing Lines with Paragraph Rule .................................... 251

The Essential PageMaker

Business Pages .................................................................. 253
    Designing a Letterhead ............................................. 254
    Working with Databases ........................................... 261
The Bare Essentials ........................................................ 264

## 11   Other Kinds of Pages      266

It Pays to Advertise . . . ............................................... 266
    Laying Out an Ad .................................................... 268
Printing Magazine and Newspaper Ads .......................... 272
    Other Kinds of Ads .................................................. 273
    Post It? ................................................................... 275
    Have you tried . . . keeping scanned photos
        of your pets on your hard disk? ........................... 275
    Thoughts on Being Your Own Advertising Agency ...... 277
Overhead Transparencies .............................................. 278
    Have you tried . . . putting your presentation
        transparencies in sheet protectors? ...................... 279
Creating a Transparency ............................................... 280
Multilayered Transparencies ......................................... 283
Greeting Cards ............................................................. 285
Calendars .................................................................... 287
Awards, Certificates, and Diplomas ............................... 290
    Creating Dingbat Borders ......................................... 290
Label Templates ........................................................... 292
    Have you tried . . . finding uses for wasted label material? ........ 293
Facts About Faxing ...................................................... 294
The Bare Essentials ...................................................... 295

## 12   Longer Documents      296

Planning the Book ........................................................ 297
Designing the Book ...................................................... 298
The Annual Report ....................................................... 301
    Preparing Text to Import .......................................... 303
    Handling Pictures ................................................... 306
    Making a Book List ................................................. 306
    Renumbering Without Losing Table of Contents Numbers ........ 308
The Table of Contents ................................................... 309
    Marking Entries for the TOC ..................................... 310
    The Table of Contents Publication ............................. 311

Creating an Index ............................................................. 313

    Indexing Names ....................................................... 314

    Making an Index Entry ............................................. 319

    Viewing the Index ................................................... 320

    Compiling the Index ................................................ 321

    Printing the Book .................................................... 324

    Printing a Book ....................................................... 325

Additional Tricks ............................................................. 325

The Bare Essentials ......................................................... 326

## 13    Working with Color in PageMaker    328

Spots Before Your Eyes? ................................................. 330

    RGB ....................................................................... 331

    HSB (or IILS) .......................................................... 332

    CMYK .................................................................... 333

What You See *Isn't Always* What You Get ...................... 334

    Color Matching Systems .......................................... 336

Putting Color on the Page .............................................. 336

    Working with Spot Color ......................................... 337

    Specifying Colors from a Library .............................. 339

    Specifying Tints ...................................................... 340

    Applying Colors ...................................................... 341

    Copying Colors ....................................................... 341

Creating a Custom Color Library .................................... 341

The Bare Essentials ......................................................... 345

## 14    Tips and Tricks    346

Tricks for Getting Started ............................................... 347

    Create and Use Templates ....................................... 347

    Change PageMaker's Default Setup .......................... 347

    Create a Dummy Document ..................................... 347

Tips That Help You Find Your Way .................................. 348

Tricks for Making PageMaker More Graphically Aware ..... 350

    Grouping Objects in PageMaker .............................. 350

    Controlling Graphic Effects Within Your Documents ... 351

    Aligning the Tops of Two Graphics or Text Objects ... 354

    More Graphic Tips and Tricks ................................. 358

    Making Your PageMaker Document Have More Pizzazz
        Through the Use of Clip Art and Textures ........... 359

Organizing Your PageMaker Tools ...................................... 361
    Converting PageMaker Pages to an Alien DTP System
        and Back ................................................................ 362
    Increasing the Processing Speed in PageMaker ............ 362
    Locating Your Proper Fonts ...................................... 362
Time-Saving Tools of the Pros ...................................... 362
    Using Color Calibrators ............................................ 364
Printing Tips ................................................................ 364
    Hardware Helper ...................................................... 365
The Bare Essentials ...................................................... 366

# Appendix: Installing PageMaker     368

Hardware Requirements ................................................ 368
    Computer Type ........................................................ 368
    Monitor .................................................................. 369
    Memory .................................................................. 370
    Printers .................................................................. 371
Software Requirements ................................................ 372
    Extras .................................................................... 373
Before You Go Ahead, Back Up .................................... 374
Installation ................................................................ 375
    Mac Installation ...................................................... 376
    Installation (Windows) ............................................ 379
Upgrading from Earlier Versions of PageMaker ............ 383
Problems? .................................................................. 383

# Index     386

The Essential PageMaker

# Introduction

The Essential PageMaker

## From Printing Press to Desk

Every office, every group, has one person who's always being asked to put together some kind of printed material. It could be a newsletter or a flyer. It could be office forms, stationery, or catalogs. It could even be a poster, a daily newspaper, or a book. If you're the person who gets that assignment, there are three things that will make your job a great deal easier: a computer, PageMaker 5.0, and this book.

PageMaker 5.0 is the ideal program for creating all kinds of publications in color or black and white. PageMaker lets you produce great-looking documents quickly and inexpensively. Corporations, advertising agencies, book and magazine publishers, and free-lance artists use PageMaker for all kinds of projects, from single-page flyers to entire books. This book was produced on a Macintosh, using PageMaker, with text written in Microsoft Word and art created with Aldus SuperPaint and Inner Media Collage.

Even though PageMaker is the choice of most graphic-design professionals, the program is equally suitable for the beginner. This book will teach you, step-by-step, how to translate your ideas into attractive and functional documents.

## What Is Desktop Publishing?

Publishing comes from a Latin word meaning people. When you publish a document, you put it into a form that can be read by other people. The "desktop" aspect of desktop publishing comes originally from the Macintosh computer. The Mac, and the Windows operating environment for PCs, use the "desktop" as an idiom for their working environment. The point of desktop publishing is that it can be done on the electronic desktop by a single person. It's not a new idea, though.

The first desktop publishers were the ancient Sumerians, writing in cuneiform script on clay tablets with a reed stylus. Close to a half million of these tablets survived, giving scholars a firsthand look at Sumerian newsletters and flyers 53 centuries old. Figure I.1 shows a piece of a cuneiform publication.

Figure I.1
A fragment of
the Sumerian
Daily News.

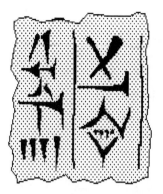

The Hebrew scribes, painstakingly tracing the letters of the
Pentateuch onto vellum scrolls, were also desktop publishers, as were
countless monks in monasteries all over Europe who copied and
decorated psalms and prayer books. At that time, information could be
put together by one person, in a form suitable for sharing with others.
However, with the advent of Gutenberg's movable type and the printing
press, the process changed. It no longer depended on individual effort.
Publishing now required specialists such as artists, engravers, typesetters, and pressmen, and a lot of specialized equipment. Figure I.2 shows
one of the first printing presses.

Figure I.2
An early
printing press.

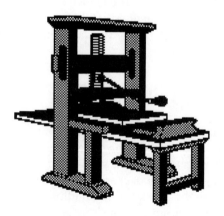

As recently as ten years ago, publishing a four-page newsletter
required the services of many people. Someone wrote the words and
took the pictures. The stories and headlines went to a typesetting
house, and the photos to a photoengraver. Headlines and body copy
were returned separately on long strips of paper called *galleys.* The
photos came back as screened transparencies. After careful proofreading, and assuming the typesetter hadn't made any mistakes, the whole
package of type was sent to a paste-up artist. The paste-up artist would

mark the size and placement of all the elements in blue pencil on big sheets of white cardboard. Next, she would carefully glue everything in place. The paste-ups were then sent to the printer, who would retouch the inevitable spots, strip in the photo transparencies, photograph the pages onto either paper or metal printing plates, and print them. It was a time-consuming, expensive, and frustrating process, especially when a misspelled word or a missing comma meant redoing an entire page of type. Printing more than one color was even more complicated.

Desktop publishing (DTP), as we know it today, has come full circle. It still takes specialized equipment, but we've come back to a system in which one person can easily create and publish a document. You don't have to depend on one specialist to set the type, another to stick it down on paper, and a third to smear ink on the printing plate. With your computer, a word processor, a graphics program, PageMaker, and a laser printer, you can do the whole job. Like the Sumerian scribe scratching his slab of clay, you are in control of the process. If you want to change the words or their position on the page, you can. You can even create a new document any time you have something to say. A simple one-page flyer takes only a few minutes to produce, and a four-page newsletter a couple of hours. With fewer constraints on your imagination, you're able to communicate more effectively as well as more frequently.

Computerized DTP became feasible when the personal laser printer was introduced. Instead of being limited to dot-matrix print that wasn't much better than an ordinary typewriter's, computer users had available to them a range of typefaces and sizes that looked nearly professional. When Adobe Systems introduced a typesetting language called *PostScript,* which could talk to personal laser printers, professional typesetting equipment, and high-resolution devices such as film recorders and plate makers, desktop publishing truly came of age. Now anyone can produce materials with exactly the same look and feel as those of the big publishing facilities.

# Why PageMaker?

Most publications combine text and graphics. For example, newsletters usually have photos or drawings, and financial reports include graphs and statistical tables. Even company letterhead generally has a logo. With a sophisticated word processing program, you can set up a two- or three-column page, and even paste in a graphic or draw a box around a paragraph. Graphics programs allow you to enter and edit text as well. So, why do you need PageMaker? Beyond word processing or graphics programs, PageMaker gives you more control over the look of the finished product and makes the job much easier and faster.

# What You Need to Run PageMaker

PageMaker is versatile enough to be used with almost any current Mac or PC clone. It runs on a Macintosh under System 6.x with MultiFinder as well as under System 7. To run it, you'll need a hard drive with a minimum of 14MB free space. You'll also need a minimum of 5MB RAM under System 6 or 8MB RAM with System 7. A Mac II series, such as a Centris 650 or LC III, or Quadra is recommended, although PageMaker will run on older Macs, such as the SE, as long as there's a hard drive. A color monitor is also recommended.

To run PageMaker for Windows, you'll need Windows 3.1, a 286-based PC (or better), a VGA or SuperVGA monitor, and at least a 40MB hard drive (considering that PageMaker alone takes up almost 15MB of storage). The more RAM you have, the better—but you need at least 4MB.

PageMaker gives you far more flexibility than even the most advanced word processor. You can place your words and pictures with absolute precision. You can also experiment without the risk of losing or damaging your document. If you want to see how a headline would look a point larger, it takes just a couple of mouse clicks to change it. And if you don't like the change, it's easy to undo.

PageMaker is designed to simulate the steps a paste-up artist would use to set up a publication. If you've ever put together a page the old-fashioned way, using PageMaker will seem quite natural. Start by defining borders and pasting the text and graphics electronically on the page. Once the text has been imported into PageMaker, you can:

- Reposition an element by sliding the element until it's where you want it.

- Resize a picture without distorting it.

- Rotate graphics or text to any angle you want.

- Drag elements back and forth from one open publication to another.

- Run type around an irregular shape.

- Link columns, or even whole pages of text, so that a change in format is automatically carried through.

- Shorten or lengthen text, and change the typeface or the amount of space between lines or letters.

- Find out how much space a story will occupy by pouring it into PageMaker and letting it jump to as many columns or pages as it needs.

- Set up a master page and flow text into it.

- Create an index and table of contents, for a book or report, just by selecting the key words to be included. PageMaker will sort, cross-reference, and list the appropriate page numbers for you.

The most surprising thing about PageMaker is that it's not difficult to use. At first glance the package looks complicated. PageMaker comes with six disks and five books. Disk 1 includes an Installer that guides you, step-by-step, through the installation process. (For a detailed explanation of how to load PageMaker onto your hard disk and make backup floppies, see the Appendix at the back of this book.) Before you put the box back on the shelf, however, you may want to flip through the booklet called *Introduction to PageMaker* for inspiration.

# A Word About Version 5.0

Since PageMaker first appeared, each succeeding version has included new features. The current release, PageMaker 5.0, is the most powerful yet. This book was written about PageMaker 5.0, but much of the material applies equally to earlier versions of the program. The basic features haven't changed, although some menu commands and keyboard shortcuts may be different. If you have an earlier version of PageMaker, you should upgrade to the current version to use this book effectively and to take advantage of the innovative new features. Text and graphic rotation, Aldus Additions, multiple open documents, and many other features don't exist in earlier versions. Also, with version 5, Aldus has created a program that works virtually identically on Macintosh and Windows computers. If you get familiar with one platform, you shouldn't have any trouble moving to the other. (That's why this one book could cover both operating systems.)

# Conventions

This book employs several conventions to help you understand certain concepts. To ensure that you don't get stranded, text references act as signposts to point you in the right direction for more information on related topics.

By the Way . . .

*Tips and notes containing extra information are shown in **By the Way** text.*

Watch Out!

*Look for **Watch Out!** for help in avoiding potential pitfalls and solving common problems.*

## Have you tried . . .

Fun, useful projects you can try are spotlighted in these **Have you tried** sections.

Some typographical conventions make referencing easier. New terms appear in *italics*, followed by an explanation. Command, file, and menu names are capitalized.

If you see an instruction to press a key combination, such as ⌘**+D**, hold down the Command key and then press **D**. (Don't type the plus sign between the two keys.) Windows users should substitute the **Ctrl** key for ⌘, so that **Ctrl+D** would mean the same thing. (Macintoshes also have a Control key, but the Mac version of PageMaker ignores it.)

# Acknowledgments

First of all, thanks to the people at Alpha Books who made this book possible, especially Steve Poland. And a big thanks to Windows expert Rita Lewis.

Thank you to Freda Cook and Ashley Hodge at Aldus Corp., for providing *beta* software, manuals, and lots of good advice.

Deep appreciation to Dubl-Click Software for producing the wonderful WetPaint series of Classic Clip Art, which is used throughout this book.

Gratitude to BoShing restaurant for their most excellent Peking Ravioli, Cashew Chicken, and Fried Rice, and to the Yellow Submarine for sustenance of a different kind.

Thanks and hugs to Jay for all kinds of help and support and to Josh and Danny for their patience and tolerance of all those late dinners, and to all three for giving me the time and space I needed to finish this project!

Hi, Robert!

# Trademarks

All terms mentioned in this book that are known to be trademarks or service marks are listed below. In addition, terms suspected of being trademarks or service marks have been appropriately capitalized. Alpha Books cannot attest to the accuracy of this information. Use of a term in this book should not be regarded as affecting the validity of any trademark or service mark.

Macintosh is a registered trademark of Apple Computer, Inc.

Microsoft Windows and Microsoft Word are trademarks of Microsoft Corporation.

PageMaker and SuperPaint are registered trademarks of Aldus Corporation.

PostScript is a registered trademark of Adobe Systems Incorporated.

## Chapter 1

## Chapter Preview

*Planning
your publication*

*Setting up layout*

*Using
typography*

*Designing
headlines*

*Designing
graphics*

*Printing
your publication*

# From Idea to Finished Page

The idea comes first. You have something to tell, something to sell, or something that needs to be printed. Getting the words and pictures into a presentation-quality publication is a multi-step process. Because PageMaker is designed to electronically replicate the procedures that artists and graphic designers have traditionally used, the basic steps are much the same, whether you're using a computer, or scissors and glue. Nothing is particularly complicated, and, as always, the computer makes the job even easier. Once you have learned the steps and the reasons for following them, you'll be well on your way to designing and producing all kinds of printed materials.

## Planning Your Publication

The key to success with Desktop Publishing (DTP) is planning. Before working on a publication, consider the following:

- Who is your audience? Will the publication be distributed only to members of a particular group, or will it introduce your group to a much larger audience?

- Are illustrations needed? What kind? If you are using drawings, how detailed will they be? Will you be using color? How many colors?

- What kind of articles will the publication have? How many? What length? How many pages will you fill?

- How many copies will you need? How will they be printed?

- Will you mail the publication in an envelope, or will it be a self-mailer?

If you know the purpose of your project, you'll probably be able to answer most of these questions right away. Others may take some thought, or even some research. You can learn a lot by looking at other publications. Train yourself to be aware of design; in fact, start right now by taking a look at this book. Notice the running footers at the bottom of each page, and the use of icons to flag special elements that you want to stand out to the reader. Look at the space between the lines of type. Is it the same height as the letters? Look at the width of the margins on facing pages. Is the type actually centered on the page, or is there a wider margin on the outside of the pages? These are things you'll need to think about when you start to design pages.

### By the Way . . .

*When you become a registered PageMaker user, you'll receive a free subscription to* Aldus Magazine. *In addition to providing helpful hints and how to's, the magazine is full of examples of work from other PageMaker users. It's a great source of ideas.*

# Layout

*Layout* is the process of deciding how to put together the jigsaw puzzle of words, pictures, lines, and other elements on a page to convey a meaning to the reader. Layout is also designing each page so that the most important text is noticed first, and so that the whole page is visually pleasing. Laying out pages gives you an opportunity to be creative, to experiment, and to customize your publication to the needs and taste of your audience.

Before you begin to work with PageMaker, use a pencil and paper to make a rough sketch or *dummy,* as shown in Figure 1.1. The purpose is to help you decide what will go where. Whether you're designing a multi-page newsletter, or something as simple as a business card, making a dummy is an important first step. It can be as "rough" as you choose to make it, as long as it contains the elements that must be included in the finished product.

Figure 1.1
A rough
dummy. It's
faster to do
your first
sketches with
a pencil, rather
than with your
computer.

Banner

In the newsletter dummy shown in Figure 1.1, the *banner,* the name of the publication, is at the top of the page. Although this is traditional, it's not necessary. Figure 1.2 shows one of many alternative arrangements.

Figure 1.2
Another
possible layout
with the same
elements.

Banner

When you're designing a newsletter, a flyer, or anything of that nature, there ought to be one lead story or significant element that is noticed first. The usual place to put this is near the upper left-hand corner. Because the English language is read from top to bottom and left to right, the reader's eye automatically goes to this starting point. (If you were laying out a page in Hebrew or Japanese, for example, the rules would obviously be different.) Formal newspapers, such as the New York Times, may put the lead story on the right. The eye tracks across the top of the page and is stopped by the larger headline type. Positioning the story at the edge of the page encourages the reader to turn to the inside pages.

In order to lead the eye down the page and balance the weight of the dominant headline or graphic, you can use a second element, as shown in Figure 1.3. The smaller graphic offsets the weight of the large, black headline at the top of the page, and doesn't fight with the headline for dominance.

Figure 1.3 The headline balanced against a smaller graphic.

You can also use white space as a design element to add emphasis to the story or graphic it surrounds. A well-designed page will create within itself a sort of visual pathway for the eye to follow. The reader sees the main item first, and then follows down to the next and so on, until he reaches the bottom of the page. This is called *eye-leading*. Figure 1.4 illustrates the front page of a newsletter that uses eye-leading successfully. The combination of the margin between the columns and the large, attention-grabbing photograph will bring you to the table of contents beneath.

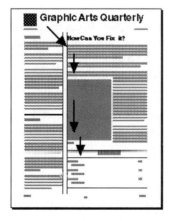

Figure 1.4 Eye-leading used on the front page of a newsletter.

# Typography

Design and layout aren't the only important aspects of publishing. You need words as well. If you are the writer as well as the designer, you have an advantage. If you discover that a story or headline needs to be shortened to fit or needs to be fleshed out a little further to fill up some space, you can do it yourself with a minimum amount of fuss. You can use virtually any word processor and then import the story into PageMaker. Both Mac and Windows versions of PageMaker include filters for all common word processing programs, and for ASCII and RTF (*Rich Text Format*).

Once you have the text, you need to fit it into the layout in an attractive and legible manner. This is where typography comes in. There are hundreds, if not thousands of different *typefaces*. A typeface is a specific design of upper- and lowercase characters, numbers, punctuation, and symbols. Traditionally, typefaces were implemented as fonts—a single size of a typeface. Today, the word typeface and font are used interchangeably in electronic publishing, since most typefaces must be implemented as a series of single-size files.

A *font* is a typeface of a particular style, such as Helvetica Bold 24-pt. Fonts are usually organized into *families*, consisting of four styles: Roman, Italic, Bold, and Bold Italic. An oblique style is also available that is derived by slanting the Roman form of the font. Popular typefaces, such as Helvetica, are generally available in a variety of weights and widths, such as Helvetica Light, Helvetica Thin, or Helvetica DemiBold condensed.

In addition to how fonts are shaped, it is also important to understand a little about how they are displayed. There are two types of fonts: Monospaced fonts, such as Courier and Monaco, are derived from the typewriter's inability to space fonts to fit their shapes; each character uses the same amount of horizontal space regardless of its width. Proportional fonts, such as Helvetica and Times, space the characters horizontally depending on the width of each individual character. For example, a capital W would take up more space than a small i.

Proportional fonts are easier to read, because their variations can be more readily picked up by the eye. Try to use proportional fonts in all of your work and avoid Courier and Monaco, except where you expressly want to illustrate monospacing (such as the depiction of a command-line based computer screen).

Some typefaces have a very casual look, others are quite formal. There are typefaces with *serifs* and without. Serifs are the little finishing strokes on the ends of letters. Most designers find that setting large blocks of text in serif type makes them easier to read. Examples of serif and *sans serif* typefaces are shown in Figure 1.5.

This is 14 point Times.
**This is 14 point Times Bold.**

This is 14 point Helvetica.
**This is 14 point Helvetica Bold.**

Figure 1.5 Times and Helvetica typefaces.

Times Roman is an example of a serif face, which was originally designed for the London Times. Times is a very condensed face, meaning that the characters are narrow and set close together. This was done in order to get as many words as possible per newspaper column, while maintaining legibility. Times Bold is the same face in a *heavier weight.* Using Times for your text gives you a very dense page, perhaps more suitable for a newspaper or technical journal. Bookman is another serif face, less condensed, and often used for books and magazines.

Type without serifs, called *sans serif,* is often used for headlines, advertising, and letterheads. Helvetica, shown in Figure 1.5, is an example of sans serif type. This type has a more modern feel and can be very distinctive. Popular faces, such as Helvetica, are generally available in a variety of weights and widths.

When you are using type to produce camera-ready copy, what you see on the screen and what is printed on the laser printer may not be completely the same. The Mac (or PC) display relies on bitmapped fonts—that is, fonts that are drawn exactly to scale based on the number of bits or pixels on your computer screen. Separate files must be installed for the screen and the printer so that you can see the font on the screen as it will appear when printed. PageMaker can display sizes that aren't installed, but unless you have ATM or TrueType, the results are distorted or blotchy.

PostScript was developed to allow high-resolution laser printers and phototype setters to produce high-quality type without individual files for each size. Letraset, Adobe, Bitstream, and several other traditional typesetters developed outline algorithms to define their original metal-based typefaces. These outlines can be translated by PostScript into information that can be used by the PostScript laser printer to draw the required fonts. These fonts are sometimes called "Type 1" fonts and are stored on your computer or printer as typefaces representing all sizes.

Adobe Type Manager (ATM) lets computer screens and low-cost printers like Apple's StyleWriter use Type 1 files for optimal results, without multiple files. ATM requires only one such file, and uses it and the typeface's PostScript file to create high-quality type at any size without distortion.

Microsoft and Apple developed TrueType as an alternative to ATM. The primary difference is that TrueType doesn't rely on PostScript, so it can be used with the computer's system fonts. TrueType is cross-platform compatible with Windows 3.1, so you can share fonts on both types of computer. It's also slightly slower than ATM, but you probably won't notice the difference unless you're using an older machine.

A third format of outline fonts is called *Multiple Master Fonts.* This is a new technology developed by Adobe to enable you to take your PageMaker documents to any service bureau or alien Mac and print a copy, even if the alien Mac does not have your fonts available. Multiple Master Fonts is a technology that uses Type 1 font algorithms to create a limitless number of font variations from a single typeface. Multiple Master fonts use a criterion called a *design axis* to assist you in generating many different weights and widths for your fonts (from ultra-light to ultra-black and from ultra-skinny to extra-bloated).

Multiple Masters also uses its master design to provide optical scaling and style controls for your font designs to assist you in creating very small or very large font types without distortion. With Multiple Master Fonts, you can create the fonts you want as long as the receiving program, such as PageMaker, can understand Multiple Masters. With Adobe's Super ATM installed, you can use your Multiple Master fonts on any computer running a compatible program. This makes your fonts virtually universal and independent. Multiple Masters do take up more room on your hard disk and require at least 3MB of printer memory to print, making them somewhat clumsy and unwieldy to use.

Even without ATM or TrueType, the Mac and Windows can interpolate styles for those typefaces for which you do not have the screen font styles actually installed. Use the **Type style** command under the **Type** menu to apply bold, italic, outline, underline or shadow styles to simple fonts, such as Helvetica or Palatino to make them appear similar to the actual Type 1 or TrueType versions. You can also expand and condense the letters by using the **Set Width** command on the **Type** menu, as shown in Figure 1.6. When you set width, you can spread out a line or shrink it. Figure 1.6 shows the Set Width submenu percentages. Percentages less than 100% *shrink* the line. Percentages greater than 100% *expand* it.

**By the Way . . .**

*Although you have the option of using outline or shadowed characters, these should be avoided under most circumstances, as they are hard to read and don't reproduce well.*

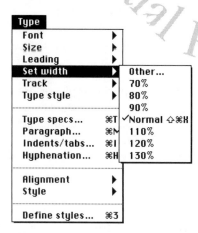

Figure 1.6
The Mac's Type menu with the Set Width submenu highlighted and displayed.

Try to limit the number of typefaces you use in a single document to a maximum of three or four. You'll need a face for the text, one for the titles, and one or two for the headings, captions, and charts or tables. If you use more than four different typefaces, however, you'll run the risk of having your document look like a ransom note. Staying within the four face limit still allows you some flexibility in that you can use bold, italic, and normal *fonts* of each face, as well as different sizes.

Headlines need to be written and typeset in a way that will attract attention. The headline makes the reader decide whether or not to read whatever follows. Bookman and Palatino, both serif faces, and Helvetica and Futura, which are sans serif faces, are frequently used for headlines because they are extremely readable.

**By the Way . . .**

*According to a study commissioned by Adobe Systems, the most legible typefaces for fax transmittal are Bookman, Helvetica, Palatino, New Century Schoolbook, and Courier.*

Harder to read, but fun to play with are the character faces, such as Abeliene, Kells, or London. A few are shown in Figure 1.7. These are often useful for ads or posters, and can work well in a masthead design or logo. Because they are more difficult to read, they shouldn't be used for text.

Figure 1.7
Examples of
character
faces.

**There are round faces**, **funky faces**, **COWBOY FACES**, Fancy faces, **Funny faces**, Old Faces, Familiar faces, *Strange Faces*, *Pretty Faces*, and **FACES** for all kinds of places...

# Graphics

Traditionally, graphics are photographs or drawings produced separately from the text and pasted into the layout. However, the term graphics, as applied to desktop publishing, actually refers to anything that's not set in type. To further confuse you, charts and tables, which are usually typeset, are thought of as graphic elements as well. A box around a piece of copy is also a graphic, as are the thin lines used to separate columns.

Graphics for DTP are generally produced in another program and imported into PageMaker. There are many ways to do this.

- You can use a paint program such as SuperPaint or MacPaint on the Mac, or PC Paintbrush for Windows. (Paint describes images as individual dots or bits, creating a bit-mapped image.) You can also capture similar images from a photograph or drawing by using a Scanner, as discussed in a few pages.

- You can use a draw program such as MacDraw Pro, Canvas on the Mac or Harvard Graphics and CorelDRAW! on the PC, which save images in the PICT format. (PICT describes graphics as objects.)

- You can also use Encapsulated PostScript Format graphics (EPSF)-based illustration programs, such as Aldus FreeHand or Adobe Illustrator that use the PostScript page description language to describe a draw type object.

Many publications use *clip art,* which comes from any of the numerous commercially produced libraries of drawings, scanned images, fancy borders, symbols, and designs. Clip art is commonly presented in PICT, PAINT, or EPS format on the Mac and in BMP, PCX, MSP, EPS, Windows Metafile, TIFF, and PS on the PC and may come on a disk or on a CD-ROM. You can get useful and unusual clip art libraries as shareware from user groups or on-line services such as CompuServe and America Online. Computer clip art can be pasted directly into a PageMaker publication or *customized* in a graphics program. Figure 1.8 shows the before and after of a single clip art image, customized in SuperPaint.

Figure 1.8
A single clip
art image
customized in
SuperPaint.

### By the Way . . .

*Shareware programs are freely distributed by their authors to anyone interested. Users pay a fee to the creator of the program if they use it. Shareware depends on the honor system. If you use shareware, pay for it!*

Customizing clip art lets you use unique images with less work than if you had to create them yourself. Use clip art as a jumping off point for your own creativity. Starting with an existing image, you can add or subtract whatever is needed to make the end result work for you. Combine parts of several different pieces, if you like. Customizing is especially important if you want to adapt a piece of artwork to use as your logo. If you use it directly from the source, you run the risk of having a competitor use the same design.

Using scanned photos successfully depends on how the publication will be printed. Photocopying seldom gives really good results with a scanned photo, but even inexpensive printing reproduces photographic images quite well. The photograph shown in Figure 1.9 was created with a video camera and the Computer Eyes scanner and software package. Later, it was modified in Aldus Digital Darkroom, before being pasted into this PageMaker publication.

### By the Way . . .

*Scanning translates the continuous tones of a photograph into a half-tone. Halftones are fixed patterns of black-and-white dots, which vary in size to create gray areas. The photographic process for turning photographs into halftones places a screen with lines of a specific density over the photograph so that only dots show through. The density of the screen affects the size of the dots and the quality of the reproduction. Figure 1.10 shows a magnified view of a computer screened halftone.*

Figure 1.9
Scanner
photo.

Figure 1.10
400% view of
a halftone.

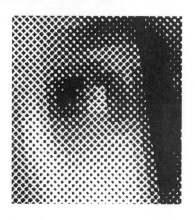

By the Way . . .
*A laser printer needs at least four of its black-or-white dots to make up one grayscale dot, so a standard 300 dpi printer can't give you high-quality halftones. You can approach "magazine quality" with new-generation printers like Apple's 600 dpi LaserWriter Pro and its half-tone-enhancement software. For ultimate imaging, Linotronic printers provide up to 2,500 dpi!*

The limitations of laser printing can also mean that the resulting image will be less than ideal quality. You may want to use a scanned picture to show the size and placement of an image, and then have a commercial printer make a photographic halftone version of the picture to be inserted into a paste-up before printing.

# Printing

After you've placed all the type and graphic elements in the layout, look it over and add any final touches. You may decide, for example, that a drawing needs a line at the top and bottom to keep it separate from the columns of text surrounding it. Now is also the time to do a final proofreading of all copy and to clean up any mistakes. You should look carefully at the design of the pages, both on-screen and on a printed page. Print proof copies often while you're working to spot errors on paper that you may not notice on-screen. Watch out for pages that are too cluttered, too crowded, or lack a focus of interest. If a story has been continued to a second column or another page, verify that the text has flowed across properly. When everything is in its final form and position, you're ready to print.

How you print depends on what you're printing and how many copies you need. If you want only a few copies of a simple one-color publication, it's probably easiest to run them off on your laser printer. Simply enter the number of finished pages you need and proceed.

Photocopying is simple, but not economical for large quantities or appropriate for high-quality work. If you need more copies than you want to run from your laser printer, and higher quality than is possible by photocopying, try instant printing. Instant printers use an inexpensive paper printing plate for as many as ten thousand copies. It's a kind of offset printing, just like the much fancier jobs done by enormous presses at newspapers, magazines, and book publishers. If you're going to be using the services of a commercial printer or a service bureau, it's a good idea to talk to them ahead of time. Find out what your job will cost and what they expect to receive from you. Some printers want camera-ready pages. Other printers may want your publication on a floppy disk. You'll save time and money by checking in advance.

PageMaker makes it easier for you to prepare your publication for printing by including a handy Aldus Addition which generates a list of all the type fonts you have used, as well as styles and linked documents. Give the font list to the service bureau so they can verify that they have the same fonts installed before they attempt to print the pages. To guarantee compatibility, you can use Adobe's Super ATM, which generates missing fonts, or save your publication as a PostScript file. (See the Printing chapter for instructions.)

Service bureaus are equipped with laser printers of various kinds. Many have very sophisticated (and expensive) imagesetting equipment, which can translate your PageMaker files into beautifully set pages at a reasonable cost. Some service bureaus even have computers you can rent by the hour, as well as scanners, photocopiers, binding and collating machines. If you plan to take your publication to a service bureau, consult them first to find out what disk format to use and whether you need to bring your own fonts.

Whether you're photocopying or sending your work to a commercial printer, you'll work from a laser-printed master. Use a good quality copy paper, or a coated reproduction paper for maximum sharpness. You can also take your disk to a larger printing facility, and have them print your publication directly from the disk to a photographic imagesetter. They can even make a printing plate directly from the computer with a laser printer.

If the job involves more than one color, the printing process is more complicated. PageMaker 5.0 can handle both spot color and process color. Spot color uses a particular shade of ink to give you a single color, for instance, lime green. Process color, a different color printing method, uses halftone plates and four colors of ink—cyan (blue), magenta, yellow, and black—to create full-color photos and illustrations. PageMaker 5.0, unlike earlier versions, can create color separations automatically. Figure 1.11 shows a color separation of a two-color flyer.

Figure 1.11 When you select separations, you'll get as many as four or more pages for each publication page.

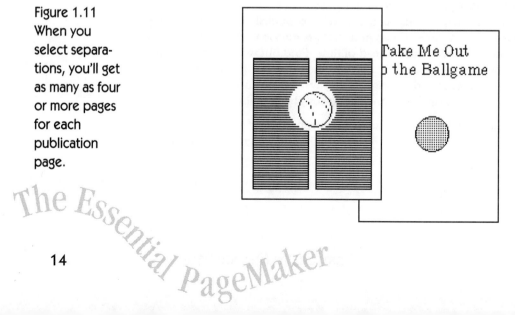

14

If you print using spot colors, PageMaker will separate the color work from the black ink parts of your publication. The paper will be printed twice for a two-color job; once with red, for example, and again with black. There will be two masters and two printing plates, one with only the black ink part of the page, and one with only the red. These are called *spot separations.* They may also be referred to as *overlays*, since one is laid over the other.

If you specify it, PageMaker will add *registration marks* to help the printer keep everything in line. The registration marks have to be in the same spot on all pages. If your publication page is smaller than the print area of the paper you'll be printing on, tell PageMaker to add *crop marks* and registration marks, along with the name of the second color (or colors). Crop marks show the printer where to trim the finished page. If the printed page is full-size, talk to your printer about the easiest way to assure registration.

Sometimes, you may want to print one color on top of another to give the effect of a third. Other times, you want to avoid a second color over the first. In order to keep one color from printing on another, you create a *knockout.* PageMaker 5.0 does this automatically, unless you specify overprinting. *Trapping* is a way of increasing the boundary of spot colors by a small percentage to avoid leaving a thin white line between colors on a slightly mis-registered page. PageMaker 5.0 will automatically compensate for color trapping. Trapping is discussed further in Chapter 9.

# Think in Color

If your publication budget allows for only one color of ink, consider choosing something other than black. The difference it will make to the finished product is generally well worth the small additional charge for press set-up. Consider, for example, brown ink on tan paper, or dark blue on gray. The look is distinguished and tells the reader that you went the extra step. If you are producing a corporate newsletter or another promotional piece for a business, it's especially important to consider the corporate image. With a color monitor, you can preview different ink and paper choices on-screen. Set the background color by opening the **Define Colors** dialog box (from the **Element** menu) and choosing **Edit** and **Paper**. You can either experiment with colors or match a sample. Define your ink color in the same way, and you'll get a pretty good idea what your finished product will look like.

You should be aware that the colors you see on-screen may not exactly match the colors your printer actually uses (especially if you're working on a black-and-white monitor). Colors always look different on-screen and on paper, because while the monitor produces transmitted light, the paper is seen in reflected light. More importantly, what you call cherry red, for example, may not match either your printer's or your client's idea of this color. To avoid unexpected color variations, use a known system of color definitions such as the *Pantone Matching System* (PMS). There are over 700 different colors in the PMS library, and every good printer knows how to match them exactly. PageMaker supports several different color matching standards including US and European Pantone, Focoltone, TruMatch, DaiNippon, and Toyo. Before you choose a color system, ask your commercial printer which color-matching systems they support. For the most predictable results, choose your colors from a printed swatch book, rather than on the screen.

If you are using PageMaker on a Mac with a monochrome monitor, you can still add spot color. You just won't be able to see it until it's printed. PageMaker will use gray tones to approximate the colors on-screen for you. Use a color-matching system chart, such as Pantone PMS colors, to select the spot color(s) you want.

# Choosing a Printing Process

The printing process used depends on the type of job. Four-color process printing requires much more elaborate presses, takes longer, and costs more. Whatever the size of your job, if you need a commercial printing company, talk to them first. You can save a great deal of time and effort by knowing, in advance, that the printer can, for example, make your printing plates directly from your disk. The print shop may advise you to output your final copy at twice the size and let them scale it down on the camera when they make the plates for the offset printing. This will effectively double the resolution of the finished piece from 300 to 600 dpi.

Before you decide on a printer, shop around. You'll find quite a range of prices quoted, even though the specs (the specifications for the job) are the same. You'll also find that some printers do a better job than others, even though they're using the same equipment. Ask to see samples. You can judge whether the image is sharp or fuzzy, or the ink looks even or spotty on any areas of flat color. Look on the back of pieces for ghost images caused by sloppy pressroom work. Examine the samples under strong white light or outdoors, to check color purity.

### By the Way . . .

*Write down all your questions before you go to the printer. If you have a dummy of your project, paper samples to show the stock you want, or anything else that will help the printer figure out what you want, bring it.*

Ask for a written bid but understand that, unless you have a signed contract with the printer, the job may exceed the estimate by up to 10%. Ask about discounts, especially if the job is something like a newsletter that will be produced on a regular basis. If you have several different items to be printed, such as stationery, envelopes, bill heads, and business cards, you may be able to negotiate a better price by bringing in several jobs at once. And, if your job involves a second color, ask if there are plans to use that color on any other upcoming work. You might be able to save on setup charges if the press is already setup with brown ink for someone else's job.

If there is any part of the process you don't understand, don't hesitate to ask for help. Most printers are happy to answer all your questions and provide valuable advice. For example, if there are budget constraints, your printer can often show you ways to do the job more economically.

A good printer will have a selection of various kinds of paper on hand and should be able to special order any paper that you specify. If the stock you want isn't readily available, ask the printer to suggest an alternative. Most print shops can also bind reports, drill holes for a three ring binder, run glue down the edge of a stack of paper to make note pads, or arrange for die-cutting of odd-shaped pieces.

Find out whether your printer wants the job on a disk or as camera-ready pages. If the printer does accept disks, make up one (or as many as needed) with nothing on it but what's required for the job. Make sure your disk is in a format compatible with the printer's computer, and that the printer has any nonstandard fonts you have included in your design.

If camera-ready is specified, it means that the printing plate will be made from the materials exactly as you've submitted them. If there are stray marks or spots on the camera-ready pages, they'll be on the finished work as well. Protect your artwork with tissue overlays, and carry it flat in a folder to protect it from damage.

Be sure that you and the printer agree, in advance, on schedules and deadlines. You should expect to pay more for a rush job, or for any last minute changes. Before you accept the finished job, look it over thoroughly in the shop. Once you've signed for it, it's yours—mistakes and all. If you find mistakes the printer has made such as smeared ink, or the wrong ink or paper was used, calmly indicate what is wrong and ask the printer to reprint it.

# Copyrighting Your Work

When you publish something containing original work, such as a newsletter, you can protect it by placing a copyright bug ©, or the word copyright, along with the year of publication and the name of the owner of the copyright on it. This might be the publisher of a book, the company or group producing a newsletter, or the corporation represented by the flyer or catalog. (The letter (C) in parentheses is not an acceptable substitute.) You must also submit two copies of the work to the Library of Congress within three months. (Failure to do so can result in a fine of $250.) Publishing the notice is sufficient but for further protection, you can register the copyright by requesting the appropriate forms from the Library of Congress. Submit the forms, a fee, and the required two copies of the work to be copyrighted. If you have any questions about copyrights, you may be able to get answers from the Copyright Office at the Library of Congress, or an attorney.

Your responsibilities are different if you're using someone else's copyrighted material. The bottom line here is, don't do it without written permission from the copyright holder, otherwise, you can be sued. For example, suppose you want to reproduce an article called, "Small Rodents and You" from *The Gerbil Journal.* You need a letter from *The Gerbil Journal* giving you permission to use the article in your publication. You must also make a note, on the page in your newsletter, stating the original source and the phrase, *Reprinted by permission.*

If you use clip art files, these are generally safe to reproduce because they were created for that purpose. Copyright, in this case, involves not redistributing the clip art as your own clip art. When in doubt, read the materials that accompanied the art package. It should give you the guidelines for the ways you can legally use the material without infringing on the copyright.

# The Bare Essentials

Before you start to design a publication, you need to consider how the publication will be used:

- Tailor your work to your audience and your budget.

- Make a pencil and paper dummy to help you plan the pages. Among the design considerations are balance and eye-leading. Effective use of white space helps your design as well.

- When you select type, limit yourself to a few faces. Four is the maximum number for most pieces, but you can use different sizes and weights of type within the same family.

- Graphics are everything that is not text. Boxes, lines, logos, charts, diagrams, drawings, and scanned photos are all graphics. Clip art offers an easy way to add images to your pages. Clip art comes in several formats and can be modified in your paint program before being pasted onto the page. Scanned photos can be imported directly into PageMaker, or retouched in a computer darkroom program.

- PageMaker can handle spot color and four-color process separations. It supports five different color-matching systems, including Pantone.

- Always do a final check and proof a hard copy before you take your work to a commercial printer. It's often easier to see mistakes on the printed page than on-screen.

- Work with your printer and don't hesitate to ask questions. Printers can give good advice and help you find less expensive solutions to your problems.

- When you publish something you want to protect, you can copyright it yourself by using the copyright bug © with the year of publication, and the name of the copyright holder. If you reprint copyrighted material, be sure you have written permission from the copyright holder.

## Chapter Preview

*Starting a New Publication*

*Using the Toolbox*

*Viewing Your Work in Different Ways*

*Printing*

*Saving and Quitting*

*Getting Help*

# Getting Started in PageMaker

I f you have never used PageMaker before, or if desktop publishing is new to you, start with this chapter. It will explain the basic terminology and show you how to get started. If you're familiar with the concepts, or are upgrading from an earlier version of PageMaker, you may want to skim this chapter or jump ahead to Chapter 3.

**By the Way . . .**
*If PageMaker 5.0 is not installed on your computer, please refer to the Appendix for installation instructions.*

## Opening or Starting PageMaker

Before you can work with PageMaker (or any program, for that matter), you have to find it on your hard disk and tell it to take control of your computer. In the Mac world, this is called *Opening* a program; in Windows, it's called *Starting*.

When you install PageMaker 5.0 on a Mac, you create a new folder called, appropriately enough PageMaker 5.0. PageMaker 5.0 for Windows works slightly differently, since Windows uses program groups rather than folders. The PageMaker for Windows installation program creates a program group called **Aldus** where the program and its accompanying files reside. Within the folder or program group are a variety of help files, tutorials, "read me's," and other resources, as well as PageMaker itself.

To open (start) PageMaker:

1. Open the folder or program group containing PageMaker.

2. Double-click on the **PageMaker** application icon.

When you open PageMaker, you see the start-up screen with a portrait of Aldus Manutius, said by some to be the father of publishing, and some legal boilerplate about the color-matching utilities. This screen soon changes to show your registration information. When this disappears, the PageMaker menu bar and your Desktop fill the screen, as shown in Figure 2.1.

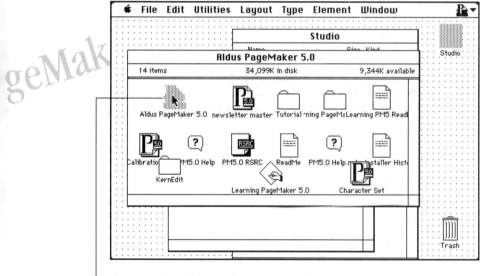

Figure 2.1
The PageMaker
Desktop.

The dotted outline of the icon shows that PageMaker is in use.

By the Way . . .
*For collectors of "Easter Eggs"—those little goodies that programmers hide in applications—hold the **Shift** key as you select **About PageMaker 5.0** from the **Apple** menu (or in Windows, from the **Help** menu).*

It might appear at first that PageMaker closed itself again. However, if you look at Figure 2.1, you'll see that the menu bar is different from the Desktop menu bar, and that the dotted PageMaker icon shows that the program is in use. From this point, you can either open an existing PageMaker publication or begin a new one.

## Starting a New Publication

To set up a new document, select **New** from the **File** menu (or type ⌘+N on the Mac or **Ctrl+N** in Windows).

Selecting New brings up the Page setup box, shown in Figure 2.2. The options in this dialog box tell PageMaker how to set up the pasteboard, on which you'll assemble your layout. These options include:

**Page:** Lets you select the size of your publication. The choices include Letter, Legal, several Magazine formats, Compact Disc (for inserts in CD boxes), or Custom. If you select any of the traditional sizes, the dimensions will appear in the dimension boxes. If you choose Custom, you may type in the size of the pages you want to use.

**Orientation:** Allows you to select Tall, for a vertical page or Wide, for a horizontal page. You cannot mix the two in one publication.

**Start Page #: and Number of pages:** Lets you type in the starting page number and the number of pages to create. If you don't know, guess. You can always add more or remove unused pages when you finish, by selecting **Insert page** or **Remove page** from the **Layout** menu.

**Double-sided**: Double-sided pages are printed on both sides of the page, like a book or pamphlet. Working with double-sided pages is made easier by the use of Facing pages (see below).

**Facing pages**: Facing pages is automatically checked when you select Double-sided; however, it can be deselected if you choose. This option allows you to see both the left and right facing pages at the same time. When Facing pages is checked, side margins will be labeled inside and outside rather than left and right.

**Restart Page Numbering:** Select only when you are working with publications that will be assembled as books, and then only for those publications within the book that are separately numbered, such as front matter or a color plate insert. For most publications, simply ignore it.

**Margin in inches:** Allows you to set the side, top, and bottom margins of your page. The margins are indicated as dotted guidelines within the page, which don't print. You can set margins in thousandths of an inch, millimeters, and picas (a printer's unit of measure, equaling $1/16$ of an inch).

**Compose to Printer:** (Windows version only): You must specify the printer you will use to print the final version of your publication, so PageMaker can resize graphics appropriately for the printer resolution and display the appropriate fonts. (For more information see, "Printing in Windows" in Chapter 9.)

**Target printer resolution:** Select from the popup menu, or enter the number of dots per inch (dpi) your target printer will use for the final printing of a publication. If you're printing proof copies on your home or office laser printer, but intend to have the printing masters created on a high quality imagesetter, use the imagesetter's dpi rather than the laser printer's setting. In this case, the imagesetter is the target printer.

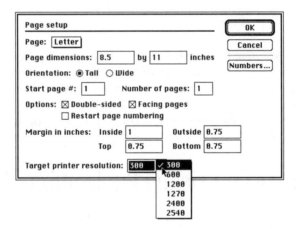

Figure 2.2a
The Page
setup box
(Macintosh).

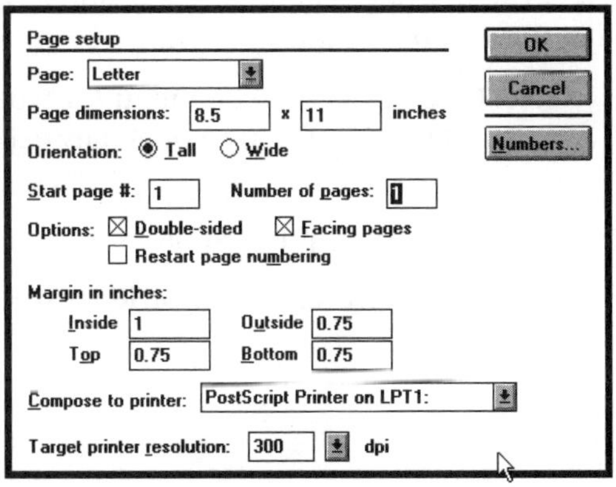

Figure 2.2b
The Page
setup box
(Windows).

**Numbers**: When selected, this button opens the Page numbering box, as shown in Figure 2.3. (The ellipsis (...) after a word indicates that choosing it will give you a dialog box.) This dialog box allows you to select the type of page numbers (Normal, Roman numerals, and so on) you want to use. You can also set a prefix for numbers on the table of contents and index pages.

Figure 2.3
The Page
numbering
box.

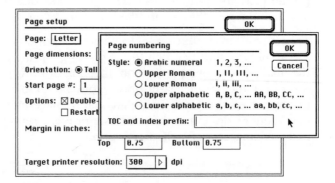

After making your selections, close all dialog boxes to return to the program. To do this, click on **OK** or press **Enter** or **Return** for each box. Or simply press **Option+Return** on the Mac or **Ctrl+Enter** in Windows to accept the current settings and close all the boxes. PageMaker will then create the work area, according to your specifications, on the *pasteboard*.

# Opening an Existing Publication

PageMaker 5.0 can convert and open files created in PageMaker 4, including the 4.0, 4.01, 4.02, and 4.2 versions. (Important: Earlier versions of PageMaker can not open publications begun in PageMaker 5.0.) To open an existing publication:

1. Select **Open** from the **File** menu (or type ⌘+**O** on the Mac or **Ctrl+O** in Windows) to open any existing PageMaker publication.

2. Select the desired publication from the file listing.

3. Click on **OK** or press **Enter** or **Return**.

# Using the Pasteboard

The pasteboard is like a large, slightly sticky drawing board. Anything you put on it will stay there until you move it. The pasteboard surrounds the pages of your publication and extends beyond what's immediately visible in the window. Items you place on the pasteboard before you save and close a PageMaker publication will still be there when you reopen it, unlike those on the artist's real-world drafting board, which have a tendency to disappear. Figure 2.4 shows the PageMaker screen with a new page in place on the pasteboard and some elements not yet placed on the page.

### By the Way . . .

*Items stored on the pasteboard are not printed when you print the publication.*

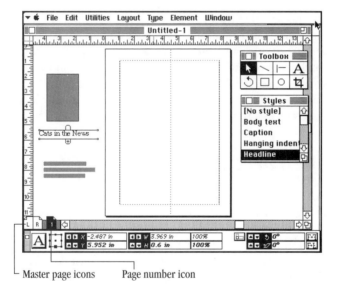

Master page icons    Page number icon

Figure 2.4
A new page
on the paste-
board.

The pasteboard can also be used to store a text block or graphic until you decide where you want to paste it. When you change pages within the publication, anything sitting on the pasteboard will remain there, just like scraps of type or artwork taped to the edges of a drawing board.

By the Way . . .
*You can always see what's stored on the pasteboard by zooming out—type ⌘+0 (zero) on the Mac or Ctrl+0 (zero) in Windows, or select* **Show pasteboard** *from* **View** *on the* **Layout** *menu.*

Items can be placed on the pasteboard several ways. They can be:

- Dragged from an existing publication using the Pointer tool.

- Created directly on the pasteboard for later placement.

- Imported from some other program, such as a word processor or drawing program in which they were originally created.

To move an item from the pasteboard onto the page, simply select the item with the pointer and drag it into position. One of the best features of electronic paste-up is that elements can be moved and repositioned as many times as you want without damaging them.

PageMaker 5.0 allows you to open several different publications at the same time, and each publication has its own pasteboard. To copy an element from one publication to another, select it and drag it to its destination. (Normally, the pages appear stacked in multiple windows, but you can use the **Tile** command from the **Window** menu to view both publications at once.) PageMaker will automatically make—and move—a copy of the item, leaving the original in its original location.

# Changing Pages in Your Publication

The *page number icons,* in the lower left corner of the screen, are dog-eared pages indicating the number of pages in a publication. Clicking on a page number takes you directly to that page. If the publication is longer than the number of icons that can be displayed, PageMaker will add scrolling arrows at both ends of the page list. You can flip forward or backward by clicking on the scrolling arrows. If you hold down the ⌘ key (or Control key, in Windows) while clicking the appropriate arrow, this list will jump directly to the page number for the beginning or end of the publication.

The *Master page icons* are the pair of page icons that appear to the left of the page number icons (if you are viewing facing pages). If you're working on a single-sided page, only one Master page icon appears.

**By the Way . . .**
*If you want a single-sided layout but there are two Master page icons currently visible, select Page setup, and deselect the double-sided box. Then only one Master page icon will show.*

Master pages contain any elements you want to repeat on every page, such as the date, page number, or title of the publication and may also contain a layout grid, column definitions, and other items to make page layout easier. Once these elements are on the master page, they can't be edited or changed on the individual pages. Setting up a master page is discussed more fully in Chapter 5.

# The PageMaker Toolbox

The PageMaker *Toolbox* appears in the upper right part of the screen, as shown in Figure 2.4. You can toggle it open and closed by using the key combination ⌘+6 on the Mac or **Ctrl+6** on Windows. The Toolbox contains eight tools, some similar to those found in graphics programs. Figure 2.5 shows the available tools.

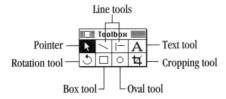

Figure 2.5
The Toolbox.

**Pointer tool:** The Pointer tool is shaped like an arrow. You can use it to select, move, and resize text or graphics.

- To select with the Pointer tool, position the arrow on the text block or graphic and click, as shown in Figure 2.6a.

- To move a selected item with the Pointer tool, hold down the mouse button and drag the item to its new location. Notice that the pointer changes shape when you're repositioning, and becomes a four-headed arrow, as shown in Figure 2.6b. If you hold down **Shift** while you drag, the object will move only on a vertical or horizontal axis.

- To resize an object as shown in Figure 2.6c, click and drag on any of the handles, which are the little black boxes that appear at the edges of the object when it's selected. Notice that the pointer changes shape to show the direction in which the object is being stretched. Holding down **Shift** while you stretch keeps the object in the same proportions.

Figure 2.6
Using the
Pointer.

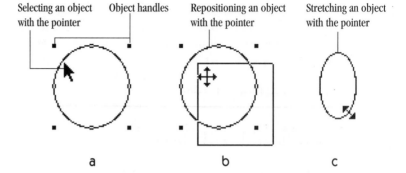

Selecting an object with the pointer   Object handles   Repositioning an object with the pointer   Stretching an object with the pointer

a                                    b                                   c

**Line Drawing tools:** Both tools, shown in Figure 2.5, draw perfectly straight lines. Use the **Diagonal Line Drawing** tool to draw angled lines that can be pointed in any direction. Use the **Perpendicular Line Drawing** tool for lines that automatically snap to perfectly vertical, horizontal, or a precise 45 degree angle. This is especially useful when creating forms and rules between columns. To change the weight of a line, select **Line** in the **Element** pull-down menu, as shown in Figure 2.7. To draw a line, select a line tool from the Toolbox. The pointer becomes a cross. Position the cross hairs on the page, and hold the mouse button down to anchor one end of the line. Now drag the line until it's the right length. When you release the mouse button, the line will remain.

Figure 2.7
Changing the
weight of a
line.

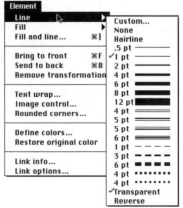

**Text tool:** The letter A, shown in Figure 2.5, represents the Text tool. The Text tool is used to create new text or edit existing text. We'll discuss working with text and the Text tool further in Chapter 7.

**Rotation tool:** New in PageMaker 5.0, the rotation tool lets you rotate any element, text, graphic, shape, or line to any degree you want. Select the tool, and click on the center or whatever corner of the element you want to make the pivot point. That point will remain where it is, while the rest of the element rotates around it. Figure 2.8 shows how a line of type is repositioned at an angle. The rotation tool places a "lever" at the pivot point, which you drag until the object or text is at the desired angle.

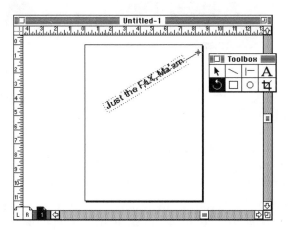

Figure 2.8 Changing the angle of a line of type.

**Box and Oval Drawing tools:** These tools draw enclosed shapes and work like the similar tools you may have encountered in graphics programs. Select the tool, click and hold the mouse down where you want the shape to start, and drag until it looks the way you want. Then let go of the mouse. You can constrain the shape to a perfect circle or square by holding the **Shift** key down before you drag. Choose **Fill** from the **Element** menu to add a tint or pattern inside the box.

**Cropping tool:** The Cropping tool lets you select portions of a graphic to crop. The tool is based on the traditional cardboard frame used by artists and photographers, and can be moved in and out to frame a particular section of a picture. Figure 2.9 shows the traditional tool and the PageMaker Cropping tool. Move the handles (the black dots) to reduce or enlarge the picture area. When you use the Cropping tool, the picture itself remains the same size. You just see less of it. If you decide to change the cropping later on, you can reveal the hidden parts of the picture by sliding it around inside the cropping frame, or enlarging the frame to reveal more of the picture.

Figure 2.9
The Cropping
tool icon.

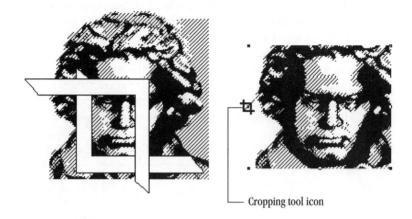

Cropping tool icon

# The Rulers

Vertical and horizontal rulers at the edges of the pasteboard appear automatically. You can turn them off by pressing ⌘+R on the Mac or **Ctrl+R** in Windows, or by selecting **Rulers** from the **Layout** menu.

PageMaker's rulers can be set to measure inches, picas, millimeters, or even ciceros (a European standard for type measurement). The measurements on the rulers are changed in the File menu's Preferences box, as shown in Figure 2.10. Notice that the vertical ruler may be set to a different scale. Many users find it convenient to measure page length in inches but keep the width in picas, to match standard newspaper column widths.

Figure 2.10
The Prefer-
ences box.

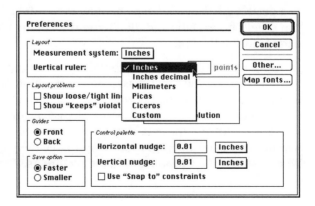

The ruler normally measures distances from the upper left corner of your page: the *zero point*. You can keep it there by *locking* it, or move it around if you want to measure other distances. Select **Zero** lock from the **Guides and rulers** submenu (**Layout** menu) to lock or unlock the zero point on the ruler.

You can reset the zero point (if it is not locked) by clicking on the dotted cross hairs in the upper left corner of the screen, where the rulers intersect, and then dragging the intersection point to the place where you want to set zero.

## Have you tried . . . resetting the zero point to measure the specific size of an element?

For example, if you are creating a flyer with a tear-off postcard and you need to make the postcard exactly 3" x 4", drag the intersection point down to the upper left corner of the postcard and measure it. Reset the zero point when you are done.

# Working with a Grid

When you have many items to place on a page, or when you will be setting up many similar pages, using a layout grid is a tremendous time-saver. A grid is a series of nonprinting dotted or lightly colored lines, which you use as guidelines for placing text blocks and illustrations. Grids usually include margin lines and column guidelines, as well as guidelines for rules (straight lines that do print). Grids can be used on individual pages or as a master page. Usually, you'll do a bit of both: placing grid lines that apply to all pages on a master page, and those for the particular graphics or headlines on the individual page where they're needed.

Grid lines can be identified by their color (on a color monitor). Margins are pink, column lines are blue, and other guidelines are light turquoise. Depending on your monitor, some of these marks might overlap others when you first start the program.

On monochrome monitors, columns, margins, and guidelines are all defined by dotted lines. Column lines have dots closer together, and end at the margins, while other guidelines run from edge to edge, right through the margins. Figure 2.11 shows the grid for a four-column page. Note the difference between the column lines and the margin lines.

Figure 2.11
Layout grid for
a typical
newsletter
page.

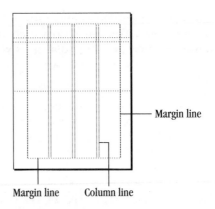

Margin line

Margin line    Column line

## Setting Margins and Columns

The first step in setting up a grid is defining the margins. A page has four margins: top, bottom, left, and right. If you're using facing pages, inside and outside margins take the place of left and right margins. The area between two facing pages is called the *gutter*. If your publication is being bound, leave a wide-enough gutter to accommodate the binding process.

When you opened the publication, you either entered margin measurements in the Page setup box or accepted the default margin settings. If you have text or a graphic that should extend past the margin, such as an icon or a page number, all you need to do is put it there. As long as it's within the print area of the page, it will appear. (The print area is determined by the type of printer used.)

### By the Way . . .

*Margins apply to every page in your publication. You can change the margins at any time by returning to the Page setup box and entering new numbers, but the change will be reflected on every page in the publication. You can't change the margins by dragging them.*

When you set the margins, PageMaker assumes that you want one column, and that you want that column to fill the entire space between the margins. Accordingly, it places a set of column guidelines over the margin lines. You can relocate these column guidelines:

1.  Point to a column guideline.

2.  Hold down the mouse button. A double-headed arrow appears, which indicates in what direction you can move the line.

3.   Drag the guideline to the new position. A dotted line scrolls across the ruler as you drag, so that you can set precise measurements. Figure 2.12 shows a column guideline being re-aligned.

If you want to use more than one column of type, as we did in Figure 2.11:

1.   Open the **Column guides** box under the **Layout** menu.

2.   Enter the number of columns and the distance between them. This will give you columns of equal width. If, for some reason, you decide you want unequal columns, simply drag the column guides to whatever position you want.

3.   Select **OK** when finished.

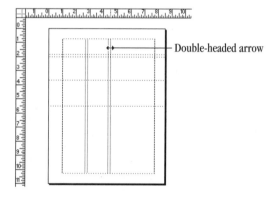

Figure 2.12
Realigning a
column
guideline.

# Changing Vertical and Horizontal Guidelines

*Guidelines*, or ruler guides, will help you position headlines, sidebars, and other items consistently from one page to the next. They save time, because you measure only once instead of every time you position an item.

For example, suppose your photo captions always begin a half inch from the left edge of the photo. You could place a vertical guideline a half inch from the edge of the column, and align photos to the column edge and the captions to the guideline.

Here's how to add vertical and horizontal guidelines.

1.   Place the pointer anywhere on the appropriate ruler and hold down the mouse button. The pointer becomes a double-headed arrow.

2. When you drag the pointer to the desktop, it becomes centered over a dotted line. Drag the line into the correct position. To create precise measurements, watch the rulers as you drag. Figure 2.13 shows the cursor position on the ruler.

Add and remove guidelines as often as you want. To remove a guideline, simply select it by clicking on it, and drag it from the page to the pasteboard. It will disappear.

Figure 2.13
Read the measurements on the ruler as you drag.

Note dotted line on ruler indicating cursor position.

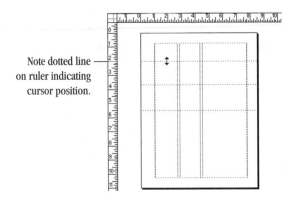

Here are some additional hints for using guidelines, all found on the Guides and rulers submenu of the Layout menu.

- Like any other tool, a layout grid is only helpful if you use it consistently. Selecting **Snap to guides** and **Snap to rulers** will guarantee that items you place align perfectly with the grid.

- If you drag items around on the page to try out different layouts, you may find it helpful to check **Lock guides** so they don't accidentally move.

- If the lines are in the way when you're trying to visualize finished pages, toggle them on and off with the **Guides** option, or by typing ⌘+**J** on the Mac or **Ctrl+J** in Windows.

# Taking a Closer Look

When you open a new publication, you'll see the full page, plus a small amount of the pasteboard. PageMaker always opens in the **Fit in window** view. This view is best for working on the general layout of a page. However, it is impossible to position things precisely or to read small fonts in this view, so you'll need to acquaint yourself with PageMaker's other viewing options. Figures 2.14 through 2.17 show a sample page at various magnifications.

By the Way . . .

*To view the entire pasteboard area, select **Show Pasteboard** from the **Layout** menu's **View** submenu, or type ⌘+0 (zero) on the Mac or **Ctrl+0** (zero) in Windows. This view is useful if you think you've stored something on the pasteboard but don't immediately see it.*

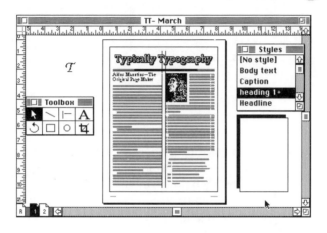

Figure 2.14
A sample page in Fit in window view.

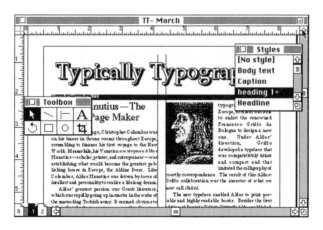

Figure 2.15
A sample page 75% of actual size.

Some sizes are better for editing text, others for aligning graphics and fine-tuning the layout. You can jump quickly back and forth between the Fit in window and Actual size views by pressing **Option+⌘** on the Mac, or **Ctrl+Alt** on Windows, while you click the mouse. If you point to a particular spot on the Full page (Fit in window) view, and press ⌘+ **option** as you click, PageMaker will magnify your view at that spot.

Figure 2.16
A sample page
100% of actual
size.

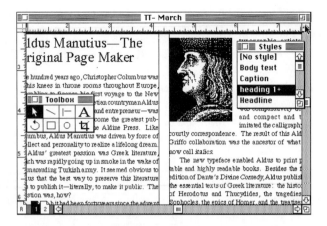

Figure 2.16
A sample page
100% of actual
size.

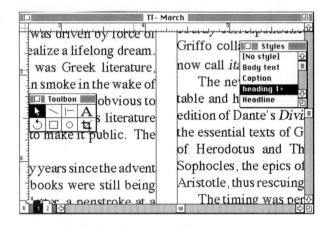

Figure 2.17
A sample page
at 200%
magnification.

# Viewing Different Areas of the Page

Use the scroll bars or the **Grabber Hand** icon to move around the page in magnified view. The Grabber Hand works as it does in graphics programs to take you from one part of the screen to another. Its icon, shown in Figure 2.18, appears when you press **Option** (or **Alt**, in Windows) and hold down the mouse button.

The Grabber Hand is available regardless of what tool is active. When you release the mouse button, you'll return to the tool you were using. This feature is especially useful if you want to create or modify something on the pasteboard, rather than within the page. Use the Grabber Hand to move yourself to a clean spot on the pasteboard, or to locate something stored on the pasteboard that you want to bring into the layout.

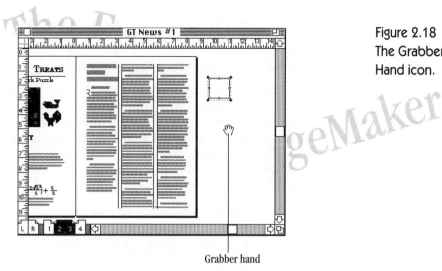

Figure 2.18
The Grabber
Hand icon.

Grabber hand

# Saving Your Work (and Your Sanity)

Saving your work frequently is the best habit you can develop, in PageMaker or in any other application. Computers aren't completely reliable. Systems crash, and power failures can occur unpredictably. If you haven't saved your work, it's gone. If you save frequently, even an unexpected shutdown message is only a minor annoyance, and not a disaster.

Saving in PageMaker is much the same as saving in any other application. The first time you save, you'll need to give your publication a name and decide where to save it. After that, simply use ⌘+S (or **Ctrl+S** in Windows) every time you pause to think.

### By the Way . . .

*Macintosh file names can be any length up to a maximum of 31 characters. Windows file names can be up to eight characters long. PageMaker will add the appropriate extension.*

PageMaker saves publications in either of two ways:

- **Fast save**, which is the default method, saves your work very quickly whenever you press ⌘+S (Ctrl+S in Windows).

- **Save as** always compresses the file to the smallest possible size, but it takes longer to do so.

You can change the saving method from faster to smaller in the Preferences dialog box. Just select Preferences from the File menu and click the appropriate button under Save option.

In addition to saving your publication, the Save As box, shown in Figure 2.19, gives you another interesting choice. You can also save various master layouts or anything else you've created, as a *template*. Templates are publications that automatically open as unnamed copies of themselves rather than originals. The original remains on the desktop to be reused. Because the copy opens as untitled, there's no chance of altering the original by mistake.

Figure 2.19a
The Save
As box
(Macintosh).

Figure 2.19b
The Save
As box
(Windows).

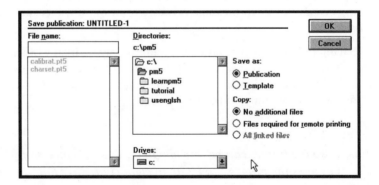

You can use a template as a basis for a series of similar publications. A newsletter template, for example, might contain the masthead and grids for columns. From the desktop, you can easily determine, by looking at the icons, which of your files are templates and which are publications. Figure 2.20 shows the Publication and Template icons. Creating and working with templates will be discussed further in Chapter 4.

Here are the steps for saving a publication.

1.  Open the **File** menu and select **Save As**.

2.  Enter the name of the publication in the text box at the bottom of the box. (In Windows, enter the name in the File name text box.)

Publication icon       Template icon

Figure 2.20
The Template
and Publica-
tion icons.

**By the Way . . .**

*For Windows users: you don't need to add an extension to the publication name. In Windows, PageMaker adds a .PM5 extension to publications and .PT5 extensions to templates automatically. Macintosh names, of course, don't use extensions.*

3.  Change to the drive and folder (or directory) in which you want to save the publication.

**By the Way . . .**

*Mac users can click on the popup menu in the Title bar to move to a different folder. Click on Desktop to save it to a different disk. Use the **Eject** button to change floppy disks. For Windows users, double-click a directory name to change to it, or select a new drive from the Drives box.*

4.  Click on the **Publication** button to save as a publication, or click on the **Template** button to save as a template.

5.  Click on the appropriate **Copy** button to select special files for remote printing, all linked files, or no additional files.

# Have you tried . . . minimizing mini-saves?

PageMaker's mini-save feature can save you some headaches, but it also eats up disk space. Keeping the "mini-saves" as well as the most recent "full-save" requires additional memory. Before you quit a publication, resaving it without the "mini-saves" will shrink the file significantly. To compress the size of the file you're saving, use the **File** menu's **Save As** command, and save your publication with the same name. You'll be queried, **Replace Existing?** Click on **Yes**, and the file will resave without its mini-saves. You can also select the Smaller radio button in the Preferences dialog box to always save with the smallest compression, no matter if you use the Save or Save As commands. Figure 2.21 shows the Save As box. Use the following steps to reduce the size of your publication.

<table>
<tr>
<td>

Figure 2.21a
If you want to replace the existing file with a smaller version of it, click on **Yes**.

</td>
<td>

</td>
</tr>
</table>

Figure 2.21b
The Windows Save As box works the same as the Mac version but looks a little different.

1. Select **Save As** from the **File** menu.

2. Click on **OK** or press **Return**.

3. Click on **Yes**.

## The Revert Command

Once you've saved your publication, you can make changes to it, and then *revert* to the saved version if you don't like the changes. Unlike the Undo command on the Edit menu, which only undoes the *last* thing you did, choosing Revert from the File menu undoes everything you've done since your last save.

In addition to saving your work when you issue the Save command, PageMaker also does what are best described as *mini-saves* every time you perform certain activities. Whenever you add or delete a page, modify the page set-up, or Cut or Paste with the Clipboard, PageMaker stores the previous version. (It also does a mini-save when you Copy to the Clipboard, move from one page to another, switch to the story editor, or print—even though these operations don't affect your publication.) You can revert to the most recent of these mini-saves, instead of to the last full save, by holding down the **Shift** key as you select **Revert** from the **File** menu.

In either case, when you select **Revert**, PageMaker displays an alert box asking you whether you really want to do that. If you have an unsaved, unplaced story in the story editor, reverting will lose it. If mini-saves occur prior to the first real save, since there's no titled file to save, PageMaker creates a temporary file. On a Macintosh, this file is called **ALDTMP01**. (If more than one exists, the rest will be sequentially numbered.) On Windows, temporary files are named with a **.TMP** extension and are placed in the Windows temporary directory. When restoring a temporary file, in the Open dialog box, select the temporary directory, select the temporary file, and then click the **OK** button.

By the Way . . .
*If you're a Windows user, you can set which directory should be designated as the temporary directory by entering a name in the set **temp=** line of the **AUTOEXEC.BAT** file.*

# Quitting PageMaker

When you're done working on a publication, you can either close it and start something else, or quit (exit) PageMaker. Either way, unless you've just saved, you'll get a box asking whether you want to save changes.

In addition to saving as a template, which we described earlier, you have the option of copying *linked files* (see Figure 2.22). This copies any and all external files linked to your document into the same folder to which you're saving.

To quit or exit PageMaker, click on that command in the **File** menu (or press ⌘+**Q** on Macs, or **Ctrl**+**Q** on Windows). If there are no open publications, or any open ones have been saved since the last time you changed them, PageMaker will immediately shut itself down. Otherwise, you'll see the box described in the preceding paragraphs.

Figure 2.22
Copying linked
files isn't
necessary if
you're only
using your own
printer.

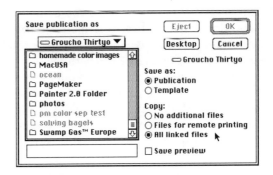

If you're saving a publication on a floppy disk so you can move it to another computer (for example, at a service bureau), you should also copy any *linked files*. A *linked file* is one that PageMaker automatically retrieves from its creator application. After you've pasted a story into PageMaker, if you make changes in the original text in your word processor, the PageMaker version will reflect the changes. When you copy a linked file, a copy of that file is placed with your PageMaker publication. If you make changes in the original file after you've copied it into your floppy, you'll need to update the copy by re-inserting the floppy and re-establishing the links. Linked files and restoring broken links will be fully explained in chapter 8.

# Getting Help

While you are working in PageMaker, if you get stuck or wonder how to do something, on-screen help is available. There are two ways to access a menu of helpful information on the Mac.

- Select **Help** from the **Window** menu to go directly to PageMaker's Online Help files. Click on the button that accesses the general area of the problem, and scroll through the list of topics until you find one that relates to your question.

- Get specific help about any menu item by pressing ⌘+/. The cursor will become a large question mark. Then select the menu item about which you want information.

Getting help on PageMaker for Windows is easy. There are several methods:

- Pull down the **Help** menu and select the type of help you need: Contents to see an alphabetical list of topics; Search to find a specific topic; or Shortcuts to see a list of shortcut keys.

- If you want help about a specific topic, press **Shift+F1** (turning the cursor into a question mark), and then point at the menu or menu item and click. PageMaker goes directly to the help screen that deals with your question.

- In a dialog box, press the **Shift** key while right-clicking on the background to see a help screen about the functions of that dialog box.

The Help system in PageMaker for Windows is fully compatible with the Windows 3.1 Help system, providing you with annotation and bookmark tools to make your searching easier.

In Figure 2.23, we have accessed help about Zero lock. The screen shown in Figure 2.24 explains the function of the Zero lock command.

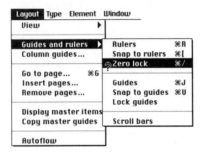

Figure 2.23a Asking for Help about the Zero Lock command (Macintosh).

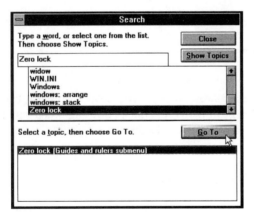

Figure 2.23b Asking for Help about the Zero Lock command (Windows).

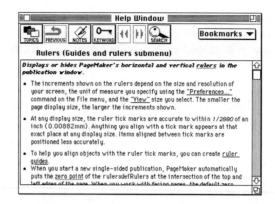

Figure 2.24a
The Zero Lock
Help screen
(Macintosh).

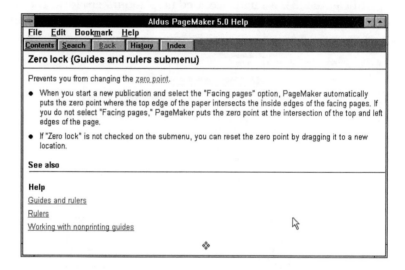

Figure 2.24b
The Zero Lock
Help screen
(Windows).

No matter what PageMaker operation you're working with, the Help screens are available. If you need more help with PageMaker than the Help screens can provide, check your PageMaker manual for information on contacting Aldus Technical Support.

# The Bare Essentials

This chapter taught you basic PageMaker operations. Specifically, you learned about:

- How to open a new publication, set margins, select the appropriate page size, number of pages, and page orientation.

- How to use the Toolbox.

- How to draw guidelines and set the rulers for your preferred unit of measurement.

- How to move around on the page and view the page at different magnifications.

- How to save your work and save disk space by re-saving your publication.

- How to print and make changes for different types of printers.

- How to get help by accessing PageMaker's Help screens.

# Chapter 3

## The PageMaker 5.0 Upgrade

## Chapter Preview

*What's So New About
PageMaker 5.0?*

*Aldus Additions*

*The Control Palette*

*Text and Graphics Rotation*

*Printing—The New Print
Driver*

*Multiple Open Documents*

*System Requirements*

*How Do I Upgrade?*

If you're familiar with earlier versions of PageMaker, you're going to love PageMaker 5.0. Aldus has kept all the best features of earlier releases. It still uses the artist's pasteboard environment. Importing text with styles attached is still simple, as is working with all kinds of graphics. But there are dramatic improvements everywhere you look. In fact, there are over 100 new features and enhancements that will make desktop publishing easier and more satisfying for amateur and professional alike.

PageMaker has been available to Mac users since the summer of 1985. PageMaker for Windows first appeared in 1987. Since then, new or updated versions have been introduced at frequent intervals. But until now, the Macintosh and Windows versions, although compatible—in the sense that you could transfer files back and forth from one computer to the other—were quite different to use. With PageMaker 5.0, Aldus has brought the two versions together. Most dialog boxes are virtually identical in both Windows and Mac formats. If you learn PageMaker on one platform, you'll have little or no trouble using it on the other.

# What's New in PageMaker 5.0?

Much more than a cosmetic upgrade, PageMaker 5.0 represents a significant advance. When PageMaker users spoke out, Aldus listened. The result is a new level of control over all of the elements in your publication. Free rotation of text and graphics is the most requested, and perhaps most spectacular of the new features, but there are many others, including new printing capabilities, process color separations from within the print dialog box, support for more proprietary color libraries, and the list goes on and on.

Part of the big news, for graphic arts professionals, is PageMaker 5.0's new handling of the pre-press process. Preparing publications for commercial printing has been a job for highly skilled technicians and expensive and specialized equipment—that is, until now. With PageMaker 5.0, you can handle some or all of the pre-press process directly from your Desktop. There may be times when you will still choose to go the traditional route, and have pre-press work done by the professionals. But now you have the choice of doing it yourself and maintaining control over every step of the process or of having it done for you.

Since PageMaker 5.0 handles both spot and process color separations, you have more choices in how you use color in your publications. For example, if your publication requires colored hairline rules, these should always be set in a spot color. It's too difficult to guarantee the alignment of the process color separations on a fine line, and your hairline could easily end up as three separate hairlines of cyan, magenta, and yellow—probably not the effect you had in mind.

PageMaker 5.0 also supports *Open Pre-press Interface*, or OPI. It's a PostScript file convention designed to serve as a format for sending files from color DTP applications to separate process color separation applications. The specific purpose of OPI is to handle high-resolution TIFF images for your publications so they can be automatically placed and linked to the lower resolution versions placed within the page. Using lower resolution "place-holders" for your TIFF graphics, since their files are much smaller, will speed up the page-layout process considerably.

# Aldus Additions

They may not be news to users of PageMaker 4.2 for the Mac, but *Aldus Additions* are a new and exciting addition to PageMaker for Windows. They're also new to users of any earlier Mac version of PageMaker. Aldus Additions are program adjuncts that automate certain functions, or combine sets of commands to make your job easier.

Menu Additions can be found under the Utilities menu. They are independent mini-programs that install in your system folder (or in the PM5 directory in Windows). As an example, there's an addition called Edit All Stories. It automatically scans your entire publication and opens every story in it in the Story Editor mode, neatly tiled so that you can switch between them. It will open all the stories in multiple open publications, too. You can then use the built-in spelling checker to check everything at once, or do a global change within a single publication or in all of the open ones.

Another Aldus Addition creates *drop caps*, giving your publications a more elegant and sophisticated look with just a couple of mouse clicks. Figures 3.1 through 3.3 show the steps involved in creating a drop cap. First, select the initial letter to be dropped. Then select **Drop cap** from the list of Aldus Additions. Specify how many lines high the Initial letter should be, and then click on **OK**. That's all you have to do. PageMaker will select the correct size letter, depending on the point size of the rest of the paragraph and the amount of leading between the lines. It will replace the normal-sized cap with the large one and move the lines of type to compensate.

Figure 3.1
After selecting the initial letter, open the Drop cap addition.

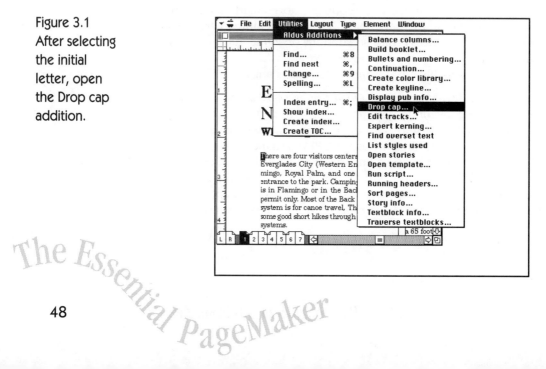

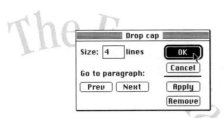

Drop cap

Size: 4 lines

OK

Cancel

Go to paragraph:

Prev    Next

Apply

Remove

Figure 3.2
Set the height
of the initial
letter.

There are four visitors centers in the park. Everglades City (Western Entrance), Flamingo, Royal Palm, and one at the Main entrance to the park. Camping in the park is in Flamingo or in the Back country by permit only. Most of the Back country trail system is for canoe travel. Though the are some

Figure 3.3
And there it is.

There's a convenient Addition called **PS Group It** that lets you combine, and later separate, objects within your PageMaker layout, so you can manipulate them as one unit, and then later separate them again. When you group objects, PageMaker creates an EPS (Encapsulated PostScript) graphic of them and stores their attribute information in a related EPS file. The EPS file keeps track of such things as position, stacking order, and line and fill attributes. The Group Options dialog box lets you decide whether to include bit-mapped fonts, PostScript fonts, or to use the Symbol font. To ungroup objects you have grouped using PS Group It, return to the **Additions** submenu, and select **PS Ungroup It**.

Another helpful Addition prepares a list of fonts used in your publication, linked stories or graphics, and the names of all styles defined in the publication. When you ask PageMaker to **display Pub Info**, you have the option of saving all of this information as a text file, which you can then send as a Read Me with your publication to a service bureau or commercial printer. Doing so helps guarantee that what you see when you look at the screen really will be what you get when you look at the finished page. Otherwise, if there's a problem, like a missing font or one that the service bureau doesn't have, you may not discover it until your nifty Chainlink Bold logo has been printed in Geneva font.

Aldus Additions can also take the form of scripts, similar to macros, which you can create yourself. When you return your registration card, you'll receive a copy of the PageMaker 5.0 Script Language Guide, which explains how you can write and save your own Additions scripts. Scripts can automate such repetitive and time-consuming tasks as applying formatting or setting preferences and defaults for a particular type of publication.

Another type of Aldus Addition is a stand-alone module that runs independently or with another program, such as a database or spreadsheet. These stand-alone modules rely on Windows' Dynamic Data Exchange, Object-Linking and Embedding (OLE), or Macintosh's Apple Events or Inter-application Communications to send information back and forth between programs.

All in all, there are over twenty Aldus Additions that ship with PageMaker 5.0. You can purchase more additions from third-party developers, or download shareware additions from Desktop Publishing forums on on-line services such as CompuServe, America Online and Delphi. Aldus even operates its own user support forum on CompuServe. To access it, CompuServe members need only enter **SBSALDFO** in the Go box. Here you will find answers to many of your questions, along with helpful Additions, templates, and Aldus Technical Notes, a series of bulletins for PageMaker users that explain how to make best use of PageMaker's many features. *Aldus Magazine* is another good source of information on new Additions and other Aldus-related third party software. Your subscription begins when you return your PageMaker 5.0 registration card. *Aldus Magazine* is also available at some newsstands and bookstores.

# The Control Palette

The *Control Palette* was first introduced to Macintosh users in PageMaker 4.2. PageMaker 5.0 has added the Control Palette to the Windows version for the very first time and given Mac users a significantly enhanced version. The Control Palette gives you precise control over graphics and text blocks and lets you make changes without using Command key combinations or going to and from the Toolbox. With the Control Palette, you can position, scale, and crop objects, and you can select the type attributes of individual characters or whole paragraphs. You can also use it for two types of transformation that aren't available on PageMaker's menus: skewing an object and flipping it vertically or horizontally. (PageMaker calls these latter two movements *reflections*.)

If you prefer to drag objects into position manually, you can still use the Control Palette to help you place items precisely, by watching the position readouts as you drag. The Control Palette provides immediate and precise feedback about any selected object, graphic, or text block.

To open or close the Control Palette, choose it from the Window menu, or type ⌘ +' (apostrophe). (In Windows it's **Ctrl + '**.) Like any other window, it can be closed by clicking on its **Close** box in the upper left-hand corner or by deselecting it from the **Windows** menu. If the Control Palette is in the way, it can be repositioned by clicking on its edge beneath the Close box and dragging.

The contents of the Control palette change according to the tool selected. If you select the Pointer, you'll see the X-Y coordinates for the screen location of its *hot spot*. If you select the Box or Circle tools, you will also see the dimensions of the object and the degree of tilt or rotation, if any. When the Text tool is active, the Control palette shows the specifications for the selected type font and lets you change them. It includes a popup font menu, as well as size, style, track, and other convenient controls.

### By the Way . . .

*All Mac and Windows graphic tools have a hot spot. It's the individual pixel at the very tip of the pointer, or in a graphics program, the tip of the pencil or paintbrush. It's the point at which the action takes place.*

Taking a closer look at the various Control Palettes, shown in Figure 3.4, you'll notice that each palette has an icon at the left side of the palette. This represents the tool or function currently selected. PageMaker calls this icon the Apply button. It becomes a three-dimensional button, as in the three lower palette examples, when an object is selected to which the tool may be applied. Use the Control Palette to specify modifications to the selected object, then click on the **Apply** button to apply them. (Pressing **Return** or **Enter** serves the same purpose.)

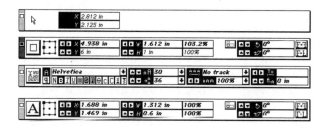

Figure 3.4 PageMaker's Control Palettes for the pointer, box tool, text insertion, and text block movement tools.

The Control Palettes for manipulating objects and text blocks contain an icon of a square with *handles*. In PageMaker terms, this is a *reference-point proxy*. It has several uses. First, the selected reference point is the one about which information is displayed. The position of the proxy point is the one for which the X and Y coordinates are shown (see Figure 3.5). Proxy points can also be used to represent their counterparts on the pasteboard.

Figure 3.5
Positioning the
pointer
precisely at the
edge of the
margin.

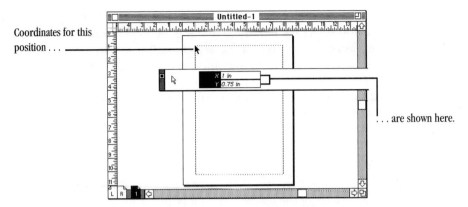

Coordinates for this position . . .

. . . are shown here.

While this may not be terribly important on a small screen, if you're using a large monitor, it will save you a lot of mousing around. Instead of selecting a handle on the actual object you want to move, you can select the corresponding point on the proxy item. If, for instance, you want to change the dimensions of a square, you could do it by selecting a proxy point and entering new measurements in the Control Palette, instead of by dragging the object on the pasteboard. Control Palette manipulations can be accomplished with a degree of precision impossible otherwise.

Double-clicking a proxy point turns it into a familiar PageMaker two-way or four-way arrow, letting you reposition the object or text block by typing new coordinates into the appropriate boxes, or by changing the dimensions of the box, or specifying an angle for skewing or rotating the selected object.

If you want to move something a specific amount—for example one inch to the right—you can either re-enter the position by changing the number in the axis box, or by typing the appropriate math symbol and number. Thus, to move a box one inch to the right, you'd type **+1** after the number already in the box. When you click on the **Apply** button, or press **Return** or **Enter**, PageMaker does the arithmetic and moves the object.

The arrows to the left of the X,Y and W,H boxes are *nudge buttons*. The position nudge buttons will each move the selected object or text block .01 inch in the desired direction. If you press ⌘ on the Mac or **Ctrl** in Windows while you're clicking the mouse, you'll get a "power nudge." Each nudge will be ten times larger. You can also change the default amount of each position nudge from within the preferences dialog box.

On a double page spread, the zero point of the measurements is assumed to be the center top of the spread. All measurements on the left are made in minus numbers.

# Text and Graphics Rotation

You asked for it, and Aldus responded. Now you can rotate any object, line, or type block, by incremental degrees, as much or as little as you want. Rotation is achieved in either of two ways: by using the Control Palette, or by clicking on the rotation tool in the PageMaker Toolbox. Select the object to rotate, and then select the rotation tool. The pointer becomes a starburst-shaped cursor. Click on a handle of the object you want to rotate, and the handle acts as a central pivot point. Then drag a line from the handle, in any convenient direction. The object will rotate to follow the angle of the line. When you let go of the mouse, this line will disappear, leaving the object at the new angle. You can also position the starburst cursor in the middle of an object, if you want it to pivot around its center. (If you're using the Control Palette, the reference point serves as the pivot point.)

In addition to rotation, PageMaker has given users the ability to slant or *skew* any line of type or graphic element by any desired amount up to + 85 degrees. Skewing is accomplished from the Control Palette. Select the element to be skewed, and click on a fixed point on the proxy. Specify a skew angle, and click on the **Apply** button. The equivalent point on the object will remain in place, and the object will skew away from it. (See Figure 3.6.) Positive angles move the top edge of the object to the right, while negative angles (for example, −45 degrees) move it to the left. The nudge buttons for the rotate and skew boxes change the angle by one degree per nudge, if you also hold down the ⌘ (Mac) or **Ctrl** (Windows) key. Without the modifier key, angles change by only a tenth of a degree per nudge.

The Control Palette also lets you flip objects vertically or horizontally. These reflections are accomplished from the Control Palette, again using the proxy to indicate the point across which you want the object reflected. Select the object with the Pointer tool, with the Control Palette displayed. Select the proxy point to flip over, as shown in Figure 3.7. Click either the **Horizontal** reflection button or the **Vertical** reflection button, as needed. Since reflecting an object horizontally is the same as reflecting it vertically and rotating it 180 degrees, PageMaker always adds 180 degrees to the rotation value of any horizontally reflected object.

Figure 3.6
The skewed
rectangle is a
duplicate of
the unskewed
one on the
pasteboard.

Figure 3.7
To make one
diver face the
other, we
flipped a copy.

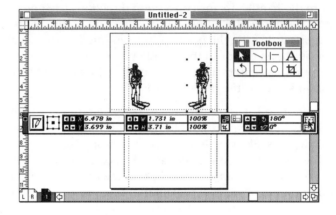

To undo all of these transformations, simply select **Remove transformation** from the **Element** menu. Doing so removes all transformations you have applied to the object.

# New Print Drivers

PageMaker comes with new Printer drivers for both Mac and Windows. You can install them at installation (see Appendix) or before you print for the first time (see chapter 9). These drivers *should* work with your other applications, too, but you may want to leave the old ones on your computer, at least until you're certain that the new drivers work for your favorite programs.

# Multiple Open Documents

PageMaker users are busy people, very often people who do many things at once. They appreciate the power of a system that allows them to use more than one program at a time. When you're working on a publication that uses text and graphics from several sources, it's certainly helpful to have your word processor and graphics program open, as well as PageMaker, as long as there's enough memory to do so. Similarly, if you have several PageMaker publications underway at the same time, or if you are creating a new one based on an older one, it's extremely helpful to have them all available to you at once. Until now, this was impossible. You could move several computers into the same room, open PageMaker on each one and open a different project. You could then copy files onto a disk and walk the disk to another machine. Or you could send a file over a local area network to another project. Either way, it was slow and frustrating. Aldus solved this problem in PageMaker 5.0. Now you can open as many PageMaker publications at one time as your computer's memory can hold. If there isn't enough memory available to open another publication, PageMaker will warn you with an alert box when you choose Open or New.

To open multiple publications from the Mac Desktop, simply hold down the **Shift** key, and click on the ones you want to open. When they are all selected, double-click, and they'll open, neatly overlapped on your screen, with their title bars showing. This display style is called *Cascade*. To view two publications side by side, either manually change window sizes and drag them on the screen, or select **Tile** from the **Window** menu, as shown in Figure 3.8. To stack them again, select **Cascade**. If you have several stories in your current publication open in the story editor, you can use Cascade to stack them, or Tile to display them side by side. To use these commands for more than one open publication at a time, hold the **Option** key (Macintosh) or the **Shift** key (Windows) as you choose **Cascade** or **Tile**.

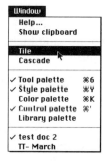

Figure 3.8
The Cascade and Tile options give you two ways to work with multiple publications.

Use this feature to transfer elements from one PageMaker publication to another. Copy and Paste as with any other application, or simply select the object or text and drag from one window to the next. When you drag between publications, PageMaker automatically copies the item from one to the other. The original remains where it was. Links will be preserved.

# System Requirements for PageMaker 5.0

The most important question people ask about PageMaker 5.0 is a simple one: "Will it run on my computer?" Because PageMaker is a complex application, with many necessary program files, it requires a more powerful computer and more RAM than earlier versions in order to let you take full advantage of its capabilities.

To install PageMaker 5.0 on a Macintosh, you must have at least an SE/30. A Mac II series or Quadra, and a color monitor are recommended. Although PageMaker 5.0 will run under System 6.0.7 with MultiFinder, System 7.0 or later is preferred. You'll need approximately 14MB of space on your hard drive to fully install the program; although, if disk space is limited, you can elect to install a minimum configuration that requires only 5MB of disk space. You will need at least 5MB of RAM to open PageMaker under System 7, and 8MB or more is recommended, so you can use your word processor or graphics program at the same time. System 7 users can also create more room for PageMaker and other applications by using *virtual memory*. (System 6.0.7 users can do this, too, with Connectix *Virtual*.) Virtual memory sets aside a portion of your hard disk to be used as a supplement to the installed RAM. Information that's needed occasionally during execution of a program function is stored in virtual memory for faster access. Information that's needed constantly is kept in RAM for immediate access.

On an IBM or other PC, you must first install Microsoft Windows 3.1 or later, and the compatible hardware for Windows, such as at least 6MB of RAM and at least 40MB of storage. Aldus recommends installing PageMaker for Windows only on a 486- or 386-based computer, the faster the better. A color monitor and high resolution graphics adapter card are required, as is a mouse.

In both the Macintosh and Windows formats, Aldus recommends using at least an 80MB hard drive. To print PageMaker publications successfully, you will need a color, grayscale, or monochrome PostScript laser printer, such as Apple's LaserWriter series of printers or QMS ColorScript; or a QuickDraw-compatible non-PostScript laser printer for the Mac, such as the Apple ImageWriter, StyleWriter, or Hewlett Packard

DeskWriter; or a PostScript-compatible imagesetter, such as the Linotronic or AGFA Pro Sets. Windows users can print from such non-PostScript compatible printers as Hewlett Packard LaserJets or PaintJets. For complete instructions for installing PageMaker, consult the Appendix at the back of this book.

# How Do I Upgrade?

Aldus has agreed to ship PageMaker 5.0 free to all registered users of PageMaker 4.2 who purchased their software after January 1, 1993. If you bought PageMaker 4.2 during 1992, or have been using an earlier version, ask your software dealer about the Aldus Upgrade program. You'll be able to upgrade to PageMaker 5.0 for about $150, plus your proof of ownership of any earlier version of the software. Acceptable proofs include the first page of the manual, or a photocopy of the original program disk showing the serial number.

# The Bare Essentials

In this chapter, we looked at the new features and operations available in PageMaker 5.0. You learned about these new functions:

- Aldus Additions: Programs that run within PageMaker to perform repetitive tasks, or to do something useful like assembling a booklet.

- The Control Palette: Keeping precise control over all of the elements of your publication without using dialog boxes and menus.

- Text and Graphics Rotation: How to do these from the Control Palette.

- Printing: The New Print Driver for Macintosh, and new printing methods for Windows.

- Multiple Open Documents: How to work with several PageMaker publications at once.

- System Requirements: The necessary CPU, RAM, and hard disk space to use PageMaker 5.0.

- Upgrading PageMaker 4.2 and earlier versions to PageMaker 5.0.

# Chapter 4

## The Birth of the News

### Chapter Preview

*Creating a Multipage Newsletter*

*Planning and Design Considerations*

*Numbering Pages and Placing Footers*

*Changing and Using Default Settings*

*Formatting a Template*

According to the market research staff at Aldus, more copies of PageMaker are bought by people intending to produce newsletters than for any other reason. Even if your main interest is designing business forms, ads, books, or cereal boxes, the newsletter format is a good way to explore many of PageMaker's features. As you learn to set up the pages and assign page numbers, we'll also look at some planning and design considerations that apply to all kinds of page layout projects, not only to the task at hand.

## Planning Your Publication

The most important part of producing a newsletter (or anything else) happens long before you turn on your computer and open PageMaker. At least, it's *supposed* to happen. The mistake that too many of us make is to plunge right in, figuring that we'll make up a design as we go along. At best, getting everything put together creatively, on time, and within a budget, is a challenge. To try to do it without advance planning is like trying to prepare dinner without looking to see what's in the icebox. Sometimes you get lucky, and all the ingredients come together in a harmonious whole. All too often, you end up with hash—in print, as well as on the table.

Look at the steps in planning, as applied to a semifictitious newsletter. There are four things to consider:

1. **What?**   What materials will you need? How many articles? Of what length? What kind of artwork? What about other graphic elements, charts or diagrams?

2. **Who?**   Who will be responsible for creating or otherwise providing each item?

3. **When?**   When must each of these items be ready in order to be included in the newsletter?

4. **How much?**   Will you need to pay for any of these materials? How many copies of the finished product are needed, and what will the printing cost be? Can you afford to proceed?

For example, suppose your client has decided to produce a four-page newsletter for parents and teachers of gifted children. What will go into this newsletter? With only four pages, there's not much space. Your client wants to use one long article and two shorter ones, plus a fun page of puzzles for various grades. The newsletter won't have room for a great many graphics, but using some bits of clip art can help make it interesting, and the puzzles can be graphics rather than word problems.

Who will provide these items? The articles will be contributed by group members, all of whom have access to computers and will submit their work on disk. One may send text files by modem. Some art will be provided, and you can create the rest in a graphics program. The contributors have agreed to a deadline. The task of laying out the newsletter can begin as soon as all the pieces arrive.

What about the cost? In this case, there's no need to pay the writers or artist. You own the clip art files. There are no photographs, which could add to the printing cost, so the only expenses will be printing and mailing. The newsletter will be printed on single sheets of 11" x 17" paper and folded to make four 8 ½" x 11" pages. In future issues, you may add a separate *middle* page, making a total of six. You have enough information now to sketch out a dummy and talk to the printer, who provides a written estimate.

# Design Considerations

Once you have the materials in hand, or at least an idea of what they'll look like and how much space they'll need, you can begin to design the pages. To do this, you'll make up a dummy of your newsletter with pencil and paper. You might actually make two or three different versions so you can try different arrangements of columns and different story placements.

**By the Way . . .**

*Dummies don't need to be full size, since you're just scribbling in the shapes of pictures and text blocks, and not writing every word. For a tabloid size (11" x 17") newsletter, make the dummy half size on a sheet of typing paper, cut down so that the pages are 4 ¼" x 5 ½". (Just folding the paper in half doesn't give you the right proportions.)*

Be sure that your dummy includes the following:

- Text blocks (columns) for all the stories you're using.

- Picture blocks roughly the right size and shape for all the art you're using.

- Space for the address, postage, and return address if the publication is a self-mailer.

- The banner with the name of the publication, and the masthead.

- Table of contents, if any.

By starting with a dummy, you know you won't accidentally leave out any of the important parts. The dummy can be, and generally is, very rough. Figure 4.1 shows the two double pages of a dummy for a four-page newsletter. There's not much detail.

Figure 4.1
Dummies for a
four-page
newsletter.

When you study a dummy, you can see all the flaws in your design. For example, looking at the two inside pages of the dummy shows that a whole page of type is going to be overwhelming. Using a *pull quote*, a block of copy *pulled* from the text and enlarged, may help relieve the monotony of the page. Fortunately, the page opposite has plenty of white space and will help to balance out the dense text on the right. It's important to design facing pages together, since they're usually viewed together. PageMaker is designed to let you work on both facing pages at once.

You can also see the visual effect of the *gutter*, the double-width margin between the two facing pages. Normally, the inner margin has to be generous, if the publication is a book or pamphlet that is bound or stapled together. Otherwise, the words would be impossible to read. If your newsletter, like the example, is folded, you may decide to make the inside margins smaller, to make the gutter less of a gap.

# What's in a Name?

One of the first things a magazine or newsletter needs is a name. Here's a chance to be creative! The name should fit these criteria:

- It should suggest the subject of the newsletter.

- It should be easy to remember.

- It should attract attention.

Which of these has more appeal: *The Journal of Astrophysical Technology*, or *Skywatcher*? Look for short, catchy names when possible, and when appropriate. If your publication has a serious tone and purpose, a scholarly title, such as *The Pennsylvania Journal of Law* may be more suited to it than something like *Philly Lawyer*.

# Banners and Mastheads

After you've come up with a name for your publication, think about designing the *banner* and *masthead*. On a ship, the masthead is the highest point, up at the top of the mast. This spot is reserved for the "house flag" of the shipping line. On a yacht, the owner's "private signal" banner would fly there. These flags and banners were unique to their owners and helped to identify the vessel from far away. The masthead and banner on a publication are similar to those on a ship in several respects. They sit in a prominent spot on the page, and carry information about the publisher and the publication. A banner should be unique and recognizable at a distance.

Although the terms banner and masthead are sometimes used interchangeably to refer to the design for the title of a newspaper or newsletter, *banner* is the correct word. The masthead is the box that carries the name and address of the publisher and editors, possibly the volume or issue number, and even subscription rates and other information.

## Logo Graphics

Banners often contain a logo or graphic symbol (some examples are shown in Figure 4.2) of some sort, as well as the name of the publication. Your company or group may have a logo that you want to use, or you might decide to create a unique one for the publication. This task is best done in a graphics program, such as Aldus FreeHand, Canvas, IntelliDraw, or SuperPaint on the Mac, and CorelDRAW!, PC Paintbrush, or Harvard Graphics (and soon Aldus Freehand) on the PC.

**By the Way . . .**
*For better resolution, the logo should be drawn larger and reduced. To begin, measure the space available on your pencil and paper dummy, and square it. If the logo is to fit into a one-inch square on the finished banner, create it four times as large or within a two-inch square.*

Figure 4.2
Logo designs.

Since you may be changing the size of the drawing, create a draw-type graphic rather than a paint image. Paint programs create bit-mapped images with a resolution of 72 dots per inch (dpi). Although they look acceptable when printed full size on a 300 dpi laser printer, paint graphics will distort when enlarged or reduced to an inexact multiple of the original dimensions. This is because in order to print correctly, the computer has to translate whole pixels into half pixels, quarter pixels, or some other fraction. Since it can't do this, the fractional pixels are either omitted or left as whole ones, causing lumps

and bumps in outlines, and strange plaids and checkerboards in dot patterns.

### By the Way . . .
*For a complete explanation of the different types of graphic images, see Chapter 8.*

If you create the logo in a draw program, such as MacDraw Pro, Canvas' Draw component, or SuperPaint's draw layer on the Mac or CorelDRAW! on the PC, you can reduce it as a PICT (Mac), CGM (*computer graphics metafile*), or WMF (*Windows metafile*) (PC) object and it won't distort. Or use Aldus FreeHand or Adobe Illustrator and save the graphic as an EPS file or a FreeHand Illustration. PICT, PCX, and EPS formats, as well as Freehand formats, can be placed directly into your publication. Figure 4.3 shows a newsletter logo created in FreeHand and resized to 50%. The type for the banner could be added in the graphics program, but in most cases, it's easier to do it in PageMaker.

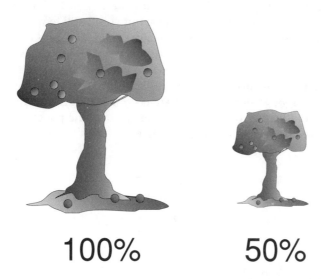

100%    50%

Figure 4.3
Logo at full size and scaled 50% in Aldus FreeHand.

Because much of the overall design of the newsletter will remain the same from one issue to the next, you'll be able to set up master pages and keep them as a template, saving a good deal of time on future issues. You can incorporate the masthead and page numbers into the master layout, and define margins and columns, knowing that you will be able to change them if you want. If you add another two, four, or more pages, they'll appear in the same format, with no additional work needed. PageMaker will allow you to use as many as 20 evenly spaced, equal-width columns per page. This is more than you'll probably ever need unless you're setting financial data, or some kind of catalog format.

As you're setting up the master pages, you can place *hairline rules* between columns; you can even create and save the style sheets—rules about how different kinds of paragraphs or headings should be set—once you decide on the fonts to use. Much of this work can be done well in advance. When it's time to publish the paper, all you'll need to do is place the stories and pictures, and print it.

You need to use margins that will be acceptable to your laser printer, and you also need to be sure to leave a *gripper* for the print shop's press, if you're having the job professionally done. The gripper is a margin, at least three-eighths of an inch wide, on the top or bottom of a page. You need to leave one so the printing press can grip the sheet of paper to move it from the stack to the printing plate, and then off to the pile of finished sheets without smearing the ink.

If you wanted to use a *bleed*, which means there's printing right up to the edge of the paper, you'd have to use a different kind of printer. The Linotronic can print out to the edges, but you'd still have a problem giving the printer his gripper if you chose full bleed, and ran to the edge on all four sides. One way to achieve this would be to use larger paper and cut it down after printing. All you'd need to do, beyond making sure that the right size paper was available and that your printer could handle the job, would be to indicate crop marks at the corners of the pages so the printer would know where to trim the pages. Figure 4.4 shows the use of crop marks and a bleed.

Figure 4.4
The crop marks
mean "cut
here."

# Setting Up the Page

Now you're ready to open PageMaker and get started. When you choose **New** from the **File** menu or press ⌘+**N** (on the Mac) or **Ctrl+N** (in Windows) to start a new publication, you'll see the Page setup dialog box.

If your newsletter will be printed on paper that's 17" wide, you need to specify an 8 ½" x 11" page because that's the size of the individual pages. The orientation is tall, and there are four pages.

If PageMaker's default margin settings (3/4" outside, top, and bottom, and 1" inside) are too wide, you can reduce them by entering new numbers in the boxes. Select the number to be changed and type in a new value. Figure 4.5 shows the Page setup box with the appropriate numbers inserted.

While you're here, open the Numbers box by selecting the **Numbers** button to make sure that Arabic numerals are selected, since you won't need Roman numerals or Alphanumerics for this job.

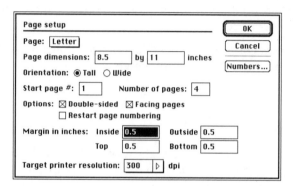

Figure 4.5
Change the margins from PageMaker's defaults to the appropriate newsletter settings.

If you were creating a book with a preface and a table of contents, you would choose some of the other options in the Page numbering box, shown in Figure 4.6. You'll actually place the numbers when you have your master pages open on-screen.

### By the Way . . .
*If you were creating a book or other very long document, you could number up to 999 pages. For the sake of disk space, and to simplify the process of scrolling through long documents, it's easier to divide the material into sections or chapters, and save them as separate documents. The Book command assembles the pieces and keeps the numbering straight.*

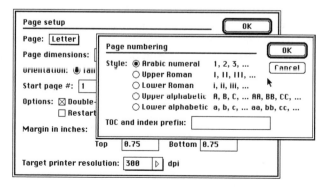

Figure 4.6
The Page numbering box.

To set up a multipage publication, use the following steps.

1.  Start PageMaker from your desktop or from Windows (see Chapter 2).

2.  Select **New** from the **File** menu or press ⌘+N (Mac) or **Ctrl+N** (Windows).

3.  Change the settings as needed. Enter the number of pages and show Facing pages.

4.  Click on the **Numbers** button to verify that the page numbers are correct.

5.  Press **Option+Return** (Mac) or hold down **Alt** while clicking **OK** (Windows) to close both boxes.

## Defining the Grid Lines

Now you can start creating actual pages on the pasteboard. Begin by setting up a grid with the *margin lines*, *column guides*, and *ruler guides*. Grid lines don't print, but they help you to align columns of type and graphics as you place them on the PageMaker page. The margin lines are already in place. You located them when you entered the numbers in the Page setup box. The edge of the page is a solid black line, and the margins are represented by a dotted line inside the page outline. (If you have a color screen, margin lines appear as solid pink lines. Column guides, which are blue lines, are hidden by the side margins on the Mac screen, but appear on top of the pink margin lines on a Windows screen. Thus, in Windows, you'll see blue lines on the sides of the page and pink at the top and bottom until you move the Column guides.)

## Adding Columns

Click on the master page icons to open them. We started this publication with facing pages, so both master pages open at once. If Facing pages is turned off when you start a new publication (or by using the **Page setup** command in an existing one), you can open the left or right master pages individually. Then, open the **Column guides** box on the **Layout** menu, shown in Figure 4.7. The default setting is a single column, or the full page.

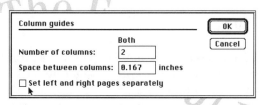

Figure 4.7
The Column
guides box is
found on the
Layout menu.

If you have opened facing pages, the Column guides box will have a check box at the bottom letting you choose to Set left and right pages separately. Click it. Two sets of boxes appear, one for each page, as shown in figure 4.8. You can leave a single column on the left, and change the right page to three columns. You could also change the default spacing between columns to give a little more room. If your publication doesn't use Facing pages, you'll have to set the left and right pages separately (and the check box with that name will be missing from the Column guides dialog box). When you're through making changes, click on **OK**. When the dialog box closes, the changes will be made on the page.

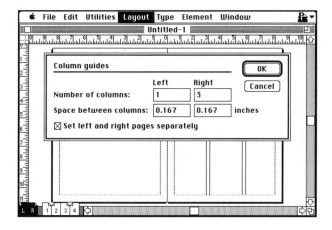

Figure 4.8
Setting left
and right
pages sepa-
rately in the
Column guides
box.

Use the following steps to set columns.

1. Open **Column guides** in the **Layout** menu.

2. To set facing pages differently, click on the Set . . . separately box.

3. If you're changing a setting, type new numbers into the box Click **OK** to close the box and let PageMaker make the changes.

# Numbering Pages

If your publication has only a couple of pages, it's probably not necessary to number them. However, with a longer publication, it's mandatory, particularly if you want to use a table of contents or an index. Without page numbers, there's no way to reference the articles. Even a four-page newsletter will look more professional with page numbers.

Where do the numbers belong? There are several options. You could stick them out in the margin at the side of the page. They could go in a footer at the bottom of the page (as they are in this book) or in a header at the top. Any of these options would be acceptable. Many newsletters include the name of the publication and the publication date next to the page number. You don't have to type in each number because PageMaker will number pages automatically. Use these steps to create a page footer.

1.  On the Master Page, zoom to Actual size so that you can see what you're typing.

2.  Place the cursor at the bottom left edge of the page. Choose **Type specs** from the **Type** menu, or press ⌘+**T** (or **Ctrl+T** for Windows) to open the Type specifications box, shown in Figure 4.9.

Figure 4.9
The Type
specifications
dialog box.

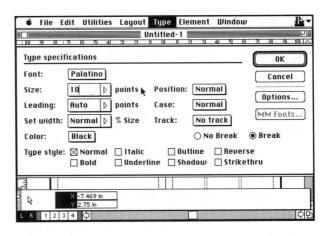

3.  When you click on any of the words in rectangular boxes or the arrows in Windows after boxes, you'll get a popup menu. Select a typeface from the **Font** popup menu. Then set the type size. Since the information will be a single line at the bottom of the page, fairly small type such as 10-point Palatino would be a good choice. Click on **OK**.

4.  Place an automatic page number marker by pressing
    ⌘+**Option**+**P** on the Mac or **Ctrl**+**Shift**+**3** on Windows.
    PageMaker displays the marker **LM** to indicate a page number
    on the left master page, as shown in Figure 4.10. Type in the
    name and date of your publication on the same line, or any
    information you want to put there.

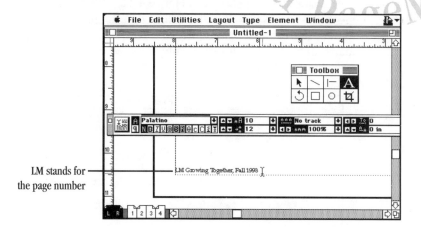

Figure 4.10
A left master
page with
page number-
ing in the
footer.

LM stands for
the page number

5.  Using the pointer, click on the footer you've created. You'll see
    it encased in two parallel lines, with handles at the top and
    bottom, as shown in Figure 4.11. This indicates that it's a text
    element. If you need to move it so that it lines up with the
    bottom of the page margin, use the pointer to drag it around.
    For example, you could move the page/date line to the top of
    the page, if you want.

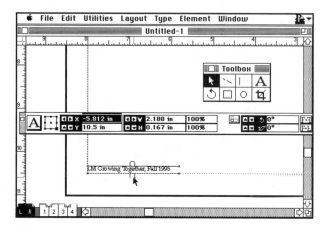

Figure 4.11
The footer has
been selected.

6. To duplicate the footer, press ⌘+C (**Ctrl+C** in Windows) to copy it, and then scroll to the right master page, and press ⌘+V (**Ctrl+V** in Windows) to paste it. Exact positioning isn't possible until it's pasted, so just plunk it down anywhere, and use the pointer to move it. When you position the pointer inside the text box and hold down the mouse button, you get a four-headed arrow, shown in Figure 4.12. This arrow lets you move the box in any direction. Note that the page number marker has changed. Now instead of LM, it says **RM** for right master. (It switched automatically, when you pasted it onto the right hand page.)

Figure 4.12
Moving the
text box.

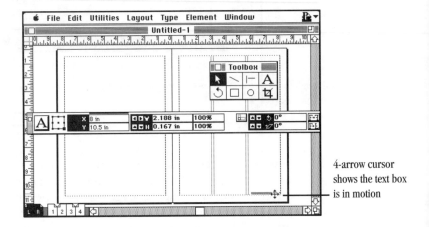

4-arrow cursor
shows the text box
is in motion

Since this block, in the right corner of the page, must mirror the left side, select the type by dragging across it with the Text tool, and then open the **Alignment** submenu of the **Type** menu, as shown in Figure 4.13.

Figure 4.13
The Alignment
menu.

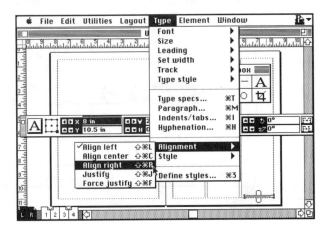

The Essential PageMaker

When you choose Align right, the type scoots over and positions itself against the right page margin. There's still a minor problem, however. The page marker belongs on the outside edge. So simply cut it using ⌘+X (**Ctrl+X** in Windows), insert the cursor where you want the number to appear, and Paste by pressing ⌘+V (**Ctrl+V** in Windows). Figure 4.14 shows the final result.

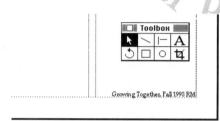

Figure 4.14
The completed footer.

Remember to make frequent saves as you proceed, in case of a power failure, system crash, or other disaster. Since you started a new publication, use **Save As** to give your file a title. Save it as a publication for now, and after you've put the banner, masthead, and other repeating elements in, save it again as a template.

# Defaults and Templates

PageMaker has preset options and settings called *defaults*, for most of its operations. You've already seen the column and page numbering defaults, and the defaults in the Page setup box. You can change any of these defaults while you're working on a particular document, and save the revised settings with the document. They then become publication defaults, specific to that publication. So whenever you start a new document, PageMaker reverts to its original default settings.

If you change default settings from the desktop when no publication is open, you're changing application defaults, and your changes will become the new default settings every time you open a new publication. Customizing PageMaker in this manner can save a great deal of time. For example, if you only use PageMaker for documents to be printed on your laser printer, you can assign the appropriate margins and page setup specifications and not have to think about them each time you start a new project. Or if you have a "corporate identity" typeface that's used on all your printed material, or a "corporate color" that you'll use for accents on your publications, you can set these as application defaults.

# Working with Templates

If there are settings that you want to affect only certain documents, you can create a template containing those settings and apply it to only the documents you choose. When you create a template for a specific purpose, such as a newsletter, you can specify publication defaults to be saved along with it.

In addition to creating your own templates, you can use templates from other sources. Many come with dummy text and graphics place-holders installed, so you need only replace them with your own words and pictures. Your PageMaker package comes with templates for various purposes, including several different newsletter designs, business forms, catalog pages, business cards, and corporate reports. Each also has a Style palette, which defines the type font (face, size, and weight) for each different kind of type used in the publication. (Creating your own Style palette is discussed in Chapter 6.)

You can use pre-made templates just as they come, or customize them by changing their defaults and rearranging the page layouts to suit your needs. Use the convenient Aldus Addition Open Template... to locate and open a copy of any of the supplied templates. If you place your own in the Templates folder, they'll open from the menu, too.

Figure 4.15 shows the PageMaker template identified on the disk as *Newsletter 2*. Notice the filler, or dummy text, used as a placeholder. This dummy text is also called *greeking*, or *Lorem Ipsum*. (I've often wondered why "Greeking" instead of "Latining"?) PageMaker gives you a file of this filler, called SampleText on the Mac, or TEXT.TXT in Windows, with its tutorials, and another called X7 rtf in the folder called Learning PageMaker in the Mac version and TEXT.TXT in Windows. You can use this to fill out your own templates if you choose. (The files are in RTF format, so you can also open them with most word processors.) A sample of Lorem Ipsum is shown in Figure 4.16.

### By the Way . . .
*You can also find useful templates in shareware libraries. If you belong to CompuServe, America Online, or GEnie, you can find templates in their desktop publishing libraries, which you can download to your Mac. If you create a particularly interesting template, and you're in a generous mood, it would be nice to upload it to one or more of the on-line services so others can try it.*

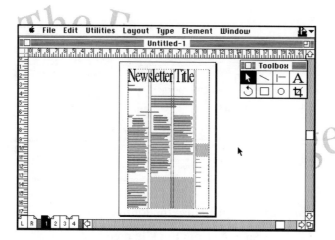

Figure 4.15
PageMaker's
Newsletter 2
format.

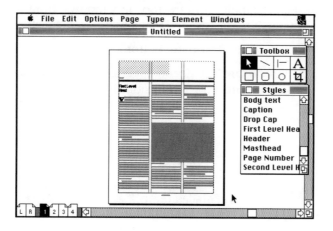

Figure 4.16
It's all Greeking
to me.

When you create and save a template, check the **Template** button in the Save As dialog box, as shown in Figure 4.17. Once the publication is saved in template format, you can use it with **Open template** in the **Aldus Additions** menu. You'll actually be opening a copy, rather than the original template. This protects it so you can't unintentionally erase your work or make unwanted changes. The Template icon looks different from the document icon, shown in Figure 4.18. The copy opens as *Untitled* and you can alter it, add to it, and resave it again as a template or a publication.

Figure 4.17
Check the
Template
button to save
and protect
your template.

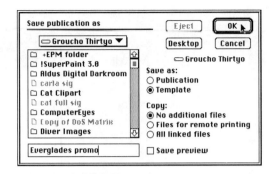

To save your template, use the following steps.

1. Select **Save As** from the **File** menu.

2. Select a folder (or directory, in Windows) from the list. Type a name into the text box that appears in the dialog box.

3. Click on the **Template** button.

4. Click on **OK**. The document is saved as a template icon (on the Mac) or with a .PT5 extension (in Windows).

Figure 4.18
The Template
icon appears
to have
multiple pages.
The Publication
icon does not.

everglades template

everglades

# Word Processor Templates

Ifyou enter your text first in a word processing program, such as Microsoft Word for the Mac or for Windows, WriteNow for the Mac, WordPerfect for the Mac or Windows, or even Windows Write, you can save time by creating a template in that program for text to be imported into PageMaker.

Set up a word processor page with the type style and sizes you'll use for your newsletter copy. Save it as stationery (or a template) if the word processor offers either of those features, with a name like **Newsletter Worksheet** (for the Mac) or **NEWSWORK** (for an IBM-based word processor). Figure 4.19 shows how it's done in Word 5.0.

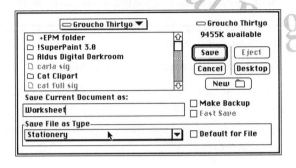

Figure 4.19 Saving a worksheet as stationery in Microsoft Word for Mac.

If your word processing program does not support a stationery or template creation, you can accomplish the same thing from the desktop if you're using a Mac. On the Mac, open the **Get Info** box in the **File** menu, and click on the **Lock box** (In System 6) or the **Stationery box** (In System 7) to lock the document and create a reusable template, as shown in Figure 4.20. Now you can use the document as a template and save your work by giving it a new title.

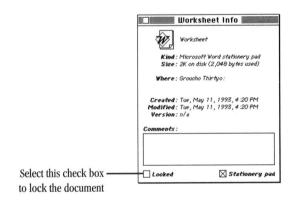

Select this check box to lock the document

Figure 4.20 Lock a document by clicking on the Get info box.

# The Bare Essentials

Planning is the key to a successful publication. In this chapter, you learned:

- How to plan ahead by asking what, who, when, and how much.

- How to make a pencil and paper dummy as a guide for laying out your publication.

- How to set up a multipage publication.

- How to number pages automatically by placing number markers on the master page layout.

- How to change the number of columns per page by using the Columns dialog box.

- How to use and change default settings.

- How to save your work as a publication or as a template.

The Essential PageMaker

# Chapter 5

## Chapter Preview

*Ruler guides
and alignment*

*Working with
layered objects*

*Adding a masthead
and banner*

*Creating a self-mailer*

*Adding and removing pages*

# Creating Master Pages

In the previous chapter, you began to create the master template for a multipage publication. The page number blocks are placed and columns are assigned. In this chapter, you will finish the master page layout grid by placing guidelines and inserting all the elements that will be repeated from one issue to the next.

There's an important distinction that must be made between master pages and the master template. *Master pages* are provided for you in every PageMaker publication you open. They're represented by the **L** and **R** page icons at the bottom left of your PageMaker screen. Every item you place on a master page will be repeated on every (same side) page in your publication. Placing page number markers on the master pages, as you saw in the previous chapter, placed a number on each page of the publication. *Master templates* are files you create (using master pages and customizing individual pages) as a basis for setting up publications with repeating elements, such as a newsletter or a book.

Using a layout grid and master pages helps assure that your publication sticks to the design you've planned out for it. Traditionally, paste-up artists either used preprinted grid sheets or drew the lines they needed in light blue pencil. (Light blue doesn't reproduce when photographed to make a printing plate.) PageMaker makes it even easier to set up a grid. Unlike the preprinted sheets, PageMaker can remove these grid lines when you no longer need them, and, of course, PageMaker can hide them for an unobstructed view of the page.

# A Guide to Guidelines

*Ruler guides* are nonprinting lines that align with the rulers at the top and left sides of the page. PageMaker lets you place ruler guides wherever you need them, to help keep text blocks and graphics in position and to make it easier to lay out forms or other pages that need precise alignment. These guidelines are part of the layout grid, along with the nonprinting margin and column guides. You've already seen the margin lines and column guides defined on the page, which appeared when you assigned columns on the master pages.

On a color screen, you'll see each of the different kinds of guidelines in a different color. The margins are pink, columns dark blue, and ruler guides turquoise. On a black-and-white screen, they'll show up as dotted or dashed lines. To create a ruler guide, select the appropriate vertical or horizontal ruler, and drag a line from it to the exact spot on the page where you want the guide. As you drag the line, you'll see a dotted line move across the ruler indicating the distance from the zero point (the corner of the page, unless you've changed it). Figure 5.1 shows a guideline about two inches down from the top of page 1.

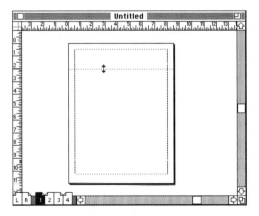

Figure 5.1
Placing a ruler guide.

This guide was placed on the regular first page rather than on the master page because it will only be used on this page. To work on a particular page, go to the lower left corner of the screen, and click on the icon for the page you want to open. Place guides that you'll use repeatedly on the master pages so you won't have to redraw them each time. Then you can add supplementary guides on regular pages later on, as you need them. You can always choose to ignore the guidelines if something needs to be placed close to, but not directly on one.

By the Way . . .
*If you're working on a newsletter or brochure that's going to be folded, place guidelines where the folds will be. They'll help you make sure your fold doesn't cut a headline in half awkwardly, or fall in the middle of an important photo, making it harder to see.*

## Line Up and Make It Snappy!

When you select the Snap to rulers and Snap to guides commands under the Guides and rulers submenu of the Layout menu, it is as if your nonprinting guides become magnetic. As soon as Snap to guides is turned on, anything you place on the page close to a guideline will attach itself to that guideline. Snap to rulers aligns any text, graphic, or tool (other than the Pointer or Text tool) to an invisible grid composed of the tick marks on the rulers. Snapping elements to ruler marks places them with accuracy to 1/2880th of an inch, .00882 of a millimeter, or with similar precision within whatever scale of measurement you are using.

As shown in Figure 5.2, the Snap to commands are selected from the Guides and rulers submenu of the Layout menu or by pressing ⌘ + [ for rulers (use **Ctrl+Shift+Y** in Windows) and ⌘ +U (**Ctrl + U** in windows) for guides. When selected, they have check marks beside their names.

Figure 5.2
Snap to guides and Snap to rulers are on the Guides and rulers submenu.

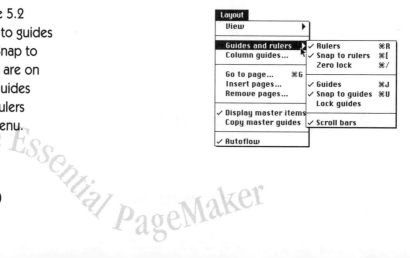

There are times when you might want to place an item close to but not quite on a guideline. With the Snap to feature turned on, it's very difficult to do. Every time you come close to the guide, the item is magically drawn to it, just like a white dog to black slacks. If you turn off the Snap to command either by pressing the key combination again or by deselecting it from the menu, you can position the item wherever you want it. Turning on Snap to again won't move an item once it's placed.

By the Way . . .

*If you place a thin ruled line directly on a guideline, it may be hidden by the guideline. Hide the guidelines to see any missing lines.*

# Lay Down Layers

Other elements often placed on a master page are dot patterns, colored lines, or blocks to accent a block of text. For example, if you'll always place your table of contents in the same spot and want to make it stand out, you might fit a block of color or a dot pattern behind it, as shown in Figure 5.3. The dot pattern could go on the master page or on a regular page of your newsletter template. Then, in each issue, you can add the appropriate text block as a second layer on top of the dot pattern.

Figure 5.3
The dots are a 20% screen, which could be printed in a second color.

Another trick is also shown in Figure 5.3. The picture has been placed over the dots, but they don't show through it as they normally would. We have put a mask over the dot layer to hide the screen pattern in the area where we want to position the art. To create this kind of electronic white out, use the following steps.

1. Assuming the dot pattern is placed on the master page, go to the publication page. Select **Paper** from the **Fill** submenu and **None** from the **Line** submenu under the **Element** menu. This will give you an invisible shape.

2.  Select the appropriate shape tool, and draw a mask to cover the unwanted part of the background. You'll be able to locate it by handles as long as the shape is selected.

3.  If the shape isn't selected, it will be invisible against the background. In case you lose it, click on the approximate area where it is. When you click on the shape, it will be selected again.

4.  Drag the graphic over the mask frequently to check the fit, and move it out to the pasteboard again if the mask needs more adjustment.

**By the Way . . .**
*Try to choose graphics with simple shapes for this treatment, or you'll drive yourself crazy trying to mask them.*

This particular graphic, being an irregular shape, needed several pieces of mask. A close-up with the graphic removed and the masks selected is shown in Figure 5.4. You can also restore a piece of pattern in the middle of the mask by selecting the pattern as Fill and placing it with the appropriate shape tool. Once you've placed an object, you can press **Ctrl+B** to send it to the back layer. Then you can place something else on top of it. Pressing **Ctrl+F** brings a selected object, text block, or graphic to the front layer.

Figure 5.4
The mask is the middle layer and the graphic goes on top of it.

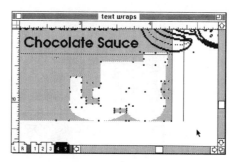

You can use layering to create many interesting effects. What you bring to the front will overlap whatever is behind it. Overlapping lets you simulate shadows and other special effects, and can create a three-dimensional effect on the page. Laying white type slightly offset over black or colored type gives a drop shadow effect. Placing black behind a colored or patterned object brings it forward. Figure 5.5 shows some examples created in PageMaker.

Figure 5.5
Use layering to make pages more interesting and to add emphasis to type.

## Watch Out!

*If you're overlapping blocks of color on the page, be careful how you do it. Colors may mix strangely when printed. Check with your printer shop before you set up a page with overlapping colors.*

# Creating a Masthead

The masthead and banner will remain essentially the same from one issue to the next. Only the date and volume number will change, so these elements can be part of your master publication. Laying out a masthead is simple, because it's really just a block of text. The masthead should include the following information:

- The name of the publication.

- Name and address of the publisher.

- Copyright notice.

- Credits editor, reporters, designer, photographer, and so on.

- Subscription information (optional).

Once you've decided where on the page to locate the masthead, select the **Text** tool, and type the information into PageMaker. Format it so it fits the space available and remains legible. It should either be encased in a box or set in very different type so it's clearly not part of the editorial material (the main text) of your publication.

The masthead is generally placed somewhere near the front of a publication. However, you may place it anywhere it fits; there's no real rule. Newspapers frequently run the masthead with the index on page two or on the editorial page. In the example in Figure 5.6, it's being used as a design element and will be placed on the first page of the newsletter. The table of contents runs down the left side of the page, with the masthead below it. Since the masthead is an area of fairly dense type, it will help balance the other items on the page.

### By the Way . . .

*The arrangement of columns on page one of this sample newsletter could be changed to create a narrow and a wide column. To change the column size, simply click on the edge of the column and drag it to its new position.*

Figure 5.6
The masthead
in position on
page one.

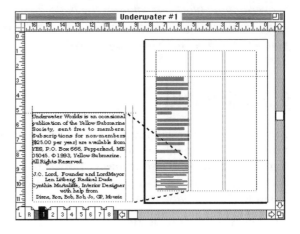

Mastheads and other text blocks that remain unchanged are called *boilerplate.* You can put these items on the master page template, or you can save them as text files and place them as needed. Mac users can also store them in the Scrapbook and simply copy and paste. Retyping them each time is tedious and unnecessary and is practically guaranteed to introduce mistakes at some point.

### By the Way . . .

*Mac users—if you save boilerplate text or graphics as files rather than keeping them in a scrapbook, save them with names beginning with BP/ , or use a distinctive symbol such as * or # at the front of the file name. This way, even if you have many files in your newsletter folder, you'll be able to view by name and find the files you need quickly. (In Windows, most special characters are off-limits for file names, but you can use a dash or underline.)*

# Wave Your Banner

The banner is another page-one element that can be part of a master layout. Aside from inserting a new date for each issue, the banner should remain the same from one issue to the next. Your publication should be immediately recognizable. Keeping the banner in the same place and trying to achieve a consistent look by following the same basic layout and design will help you achieve this goal. Changing the appearance of your publication every time it comes out confuses the reader and makes extra work for the editor.

To create a banner, decide where on the page it should be. Most banners run across the top of the front page, but it could also go across the bottom or even down the edge. In this chapter's example, the traditional top of the page format is used, and a guideline has been placed to show the bottom edge of the banner.

Banners often include a logo. To place a logo, follow these steps:

1. Open the **Place** box by selecting **Place** from the **File** menu or by pressing ⌘+**D** for the Mac, or **Ctrl+D** (Windows). Select the graphic to be placed from the list box, as shown in Figure 5.7.

2. Click on **OK** to close the selection box. The pointer will change to the Place graphics icon, shown in Figure 5.8. Position it approximately at the upper left corner of the area where you want the logo to appear. When you click, the graphic appears (in this example, the tree would appear). Now you can make whatever adjustments are needed.

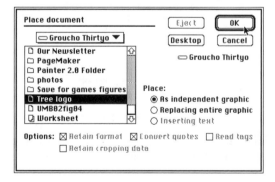

Figure 5.7
Pick the graphic to be placed.

Figure 5.8
The Place
graphics icon.

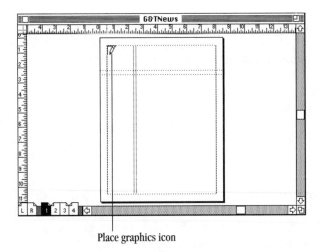

Place graphics icon

The first adjustment you may need to make is done with the Cropping tool. When you transferred the graphic into PageMaker, the whole page was copied in from the paint program. This means there's a lot of blank space around the logo. To avoid confusion, it's best to crop it out. You can use the Cropping tool as a pair of scissors to trim away the unneeded parts of the page. Figure 5.9 shows the Cropping tool in use.

Figure 5.9
Is this crop-
ping, trimming,
or pruning the
tree?

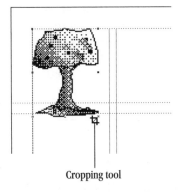

Cropping tool

To crop a logo, use the following steps:

1.  Select the **Cropping** tool and click on the graphic. You'll see little black boxes (handles) at the edges and centers of each side.

2.  Click on any handle and drag to move the edge of the graphic. Dragging the edge in makes the graphic's page smaller. You can drag all four sides of the graphic's page in so the edges are right at the edge of the image.

3.  (Optional) To slide the image around within the box, place the **Cropping** tool in the middle of the graphic box and hold the mouse button down. The tool changes to a hand and lets you reposition the image.

By the Way . . .

*To avoid the need for cropping, Mac users can open their paint program and select only their graphic. Copy it into the scrapbook, and place it into the document from there, or paste it directly from the Clipboard. (You won't be able to maintain links to a graphic pasted this way, however.) In Windows, use the Windows Paint Program. Select the graphic, then select **Copy To** from the **Edit** menu, and give the selected portion its own file name. Another method is to copy the selection to the Clipboard and then save the contents of the Clipboard as a file (through the Clipboard Viewer program).*

After you've placed the logo, you're ready to add some type. PageMaker gives you several options for determining types sizes and fonts. Use the Type Specifications dialog box, the Control Palette, or just select type attributes from the menu. Later on, we'll discuss defining type styles and creating a type style menu.

Remember, banners need to be distinctive, but easy to read. Choose a relatively large type, perhaps 48 points or more, depending on the length of the name. PageMaker lets you choose any type size, not just the ones listed on the menu. If you want to use a different size, choose **Other** and type the size into the little box. You can choose sizes in whole numbers and tenths, so if 48 point is just a bit too large, try 47.5 points. After you've set the attributes for your type, choose the **Text** tool, and type the name into the banner, as shown in Figure 5.10.

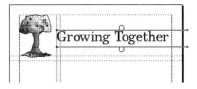

Figure 5.10
Inserting the text for the banner.

Don't be disappointed if the banner doesn't look right the first time you place the type. The illustrations that follow show some of the stages our sample banner went through before reaching an acceptable design.

In Figure 5.10, the banner looks rather crowded, and leaves too much empty space underneath the name. Perhaps we might try moving it to two lines, shown in Figure 5.11.

Figure 5.11
The text looks
better on two
lines.

How about reversing the positions of the name and tree? It's easy to select the elements and try them in various combinations. You can move things around until you're satisfied. In Figure 5.12, we've added other elements to create the final version of the banner. The date, which was added to balance the tree, is in a separate text block making it easier to change from one month to the next.

Figure 5.12
It's beginning
to look pretty
good!

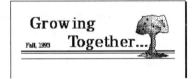

Most publications add a *dateline,* a line of type below the banner that generally contains the date and name of the publishing group sponsoring the newsletter. Since this information is already on the first page of our example, the dateline can be used for other purposes. Figure 5.13 shows one possibility.

Figure 5.13
Placing a
motto in the
space for the
dateline.

If the words you want to place in the dateline don't fit properly, you can adjust them very easily by using the **Set width** menu. To expand them, as we're doing in Figure 5.14, set the width to **100%**. If they're already too long for the space, shrink them by setting the width to something less than 100%.

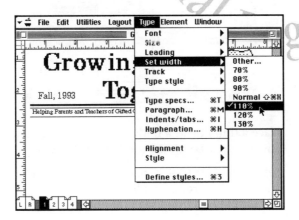

Figure 5.14
Adjusting the
width of a line
of type.

Study your dummy to see what other elements are likely to repeat from one issue to the next. The more you can do to complete a template, the quicker you'll be able to put together the monthly, weekly, or daily news.

# Setting Up a Self-Mailer

A self-mailer, logically enough, is a publication that doesn't get mailed in an envelope. If your publication is to be a self-mailer, you can set aside the addressing area and set up the return address block and mailing indicia on your master page layout. The usual way to produce a self-mailer is to dedicate half of the last page to addressing and mailing requirements. Figure 5.15 shows a self-mailing newsletter. The last page has been divided in half, with copy on the upper half and the return address and mailing information on the bottom.

To add the return address block to the master page layout, use the following steps:

1.  Begin by drawing a ruler guide halfway down the page at 5 ½ inches, the point where the newsletter will fold for mailing.

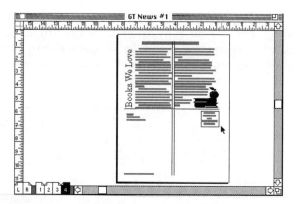

2.   Place a thin line as a folding guide, and to mark the limit for anything placed on the top half of the page.

3.   Select the **Text** tool, drop down to leave a reasonable margin, and insert the return address.

# Mailing Indicia

The United States Postal Service allows bulk rate (third class) mailing of a minimum of 200 pieces of identical mail. Permit mailers must use postage meter imprints, precanceled stamps, or print the bulk rate permit number *indicia* on the envelope. The indicia is a small block that includes the words Bulk Rate, US Postage, and the permit number.

By the Way . . .
*Postal regulations are subject to change without notice. Check with your Postmaster for information on obtaining the necessary permits before planning to use bulk mail.*

If your publication qualifies for bulk mail rates, you can avoid the need for stamps by printing the indicia directly on the newsletter. To create the indicia, use the following steps:

1.   Use the **Text** tool to type the information into a text block.

2.   Draw a box around it with the **Rectangle** tool. Be sure to select **None** under the **Fill** submenu of the Element menu. Otherwise, you'll cover up the text.

# Removing Master Page Elements

Any elements, such as the page number blocks, that were placed on PageMaker's left and right master pages will appear on every page of your publication. If they aren't wanted on a particular page for some reason, you may remove them from that page. To do so:

1. Go to that page and then open the **Layout** menu. There will be a check next to the words **Display master items**.

2. Click on **Display master items** to remove the check mark. Everything that was created on the master page will be removed. There is no easy way to remove only one master page element.

3. If you want to keep some, but not all master elements, open the master page, select all, and then copy and paste to the publication page. Then delete the items you don't want.

If you have placed guides on the master pages, you may choose whether or not to apply them by selecting or deselecting **Copy master guides**, also on the **Layout** menu.

# Adding Pages

The example template is for a four-page newsletter. If your next issue has a lot more material, you might need to make it six pages, or maybe even eight. To insert additional pages, select **Insert pages** from the **Layout** menu, and indicate the number of pages and their position in the box, as shown in Figure 5.16. The pages you insert will renumber themselves automatically. If the next month's newsletter has fewer pages, you delete the unneeded ones by choosing **Remove** pages from the **Layout** menu.

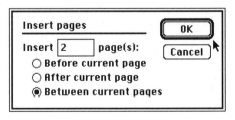

Figure 5.16
Adding
pages to a
newsletter.

When you add pages, remember that your newsletter is printed on both sides of the page, so you are actually adding two pages at a time. You'll want to add these pages in the middle of the existing ones. To add or remove pages, use the following steps.

1.  To change the number of pages in an existing publication, choose **Insert pages** or **Remove pages** from the **Layout** menu.

2.  Type the number of pages to add or page numbers to delete.

3.  If you are adding pages, click on the appropriate radio buttons to add pages before, between, or after the current page. In Windows you can press **Alt+B** for "before," **Alt+W** for "between," or **Alt+A** for "after" to select the appropriate response.

4.  Click **OK**.

5.  If you are deleting pages, PageMaker presents an alert box asking you to confirm that you really want to remove pages. Click on the **OK** button to continue or the **Cancel** button to end the process and return to PageMaker.

If the newsletter is printed on 11" x 17" paper, and folded in half to make four 8 ½" x 11" letter-sized pages, you can add a single, letter-size sheet to make six pages. Tucked into the outer pages, it will stay in place without being stapled. Should you increase the page count to eight, simply print a second double sheet and fold one inside the other. For ten, add the single center page again.

### Watch Out!

*Ten pages is the practical limit for this. With more than ten pages, you need to use some kind of binding, even if it's just a staple in the middle.*

If you're working with more than a couple of pages, it's a good idea to make up an *imposition dummy*, especially if you have a double-page spread (two pages designed to be read as one) in the middle of your publication. The term imposition dummy is an old one, going back to the early days of printing. It's probably called this because the page order is imposed by the manner in which the publication is put together. Make a little book and number its pages. When you unfold it, you may be surprised to see which pages are adjacent! Figure 5.17 shows an eight-page imposition dummy, set up to print on two sheets of 11" x 17" paper.

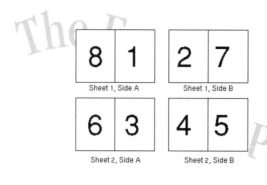

Sheet 1, Side A    Sheet 1, Side B

Sheet 2, Side A    Sheet 2, Side B

Figure 5.17
Pages 8, 1, 2, and 7 are printed on the front and back of one sheet, the others on the second.

**By the Way . . .**
*You needn't worry about arranging your PageMaker pages according to the imposition dummy. There's an Aldus Addition called Build Booklet that will do this step for you. You'll learn how to use it in Chapter 9.*

# Have you tried . . . making a template for mailing labels?

Open a single page publication, and use the master page to place ruler guides the height and width of the label sheet you use. Set your logo and return address at the left side of the label, if there's room. Now, go to the publication page, and enter the names of the people you're mailing to. Position the four line text blocks, and place the comma delimited mailing list in the first block. Keep placing text in blocks until you've filled the page. Add more pages, as you need them, until you've placed the whole list. Run it off on the labels, and apply them to your mailing.

# Save Your Work!

After you place all the elements that will repeat every time you revise the newsletter, stop your work temporarily and save it as a template. Open the **File** menu, and select **Save as**. Name your file, and select **Template**, and then click on **OK**. After saving as a template, you must close the document and reopen it so that you're working on a copy. Otherwise, you could end up creating your newsletter on the template itself.

# The Bare Essentials

In this chapter, you learned how to set up master pages for a newsletter. Master pages hold all the information, graphics, and setup instructions you'll use over and over. Master pages should be saved as a template. Specifically, you learned:

- How to place ruler guidelines.

- How using Snap to guides makes elements attach to the nearest guideline.

- How Snap to rulers creates an invisible grid from ruler tick marks. Elements will snap to this grid.

- How to assemble layers of text and graphics, as if they were printed on cellophane, and how to use masks as electronic white out.

- How to set up a masthead and what should be included in it.

- How to construct a banner.

- How to add and remove pages using the Layout menu.

- How to use an imposition dummy.

The Essential PageMaker

# Chapter 6

## Working with Text Files

## Chapter Preview

*Importing text*

*Linking columns*

*Flowing text into multiple columns*

*Formatting paragraphs*

*Using Table Editor (Windows version only)*

*Choosing type*

*Placing and designing headlines*

A *story*, in PageMaker terms, is any block of text that's considered a single unit. A story can be many pages long, or just one or two words. Headlines are often handled as separate stories, as are picture captions and pull quotes. These may be created directly within PageMaker by positioning the Text tool and typing.

Although you can use the Text tool in Page-Maker to type directly into your publication, you'll find it's easier to use a word processing program for any story more than a few words long. Word processing programs, such as WordPerfect and Microsoft Word, allow you to do more editing, and do it faster, than a page layout program. Most word processors come with built-in shortcuts and key combinations to make editing easier. And, since you're used to using your word processor, typing and editing the text in a more familiar format won't get in the way of creating it.

Using a word processor also gives you the ability to run grammar and spell checking programs before you add the story to your publication. Most word processors include spelling dictionaries, and many feature grammar checkers, as well. Grammar checking programs, in addition to catching common grammar errors, help eliminate the kinds of mistakes spell checking programs sometimes miss. For example, no spell checker can catch this kind of error: "*Sum* people make this mistake *two* often", but a grammar checker will zero in on it.

### By the Way . . .

*PageMaker's own Story Editor can serve as a word processor, if you don't have one readily available. You'll learn how to work with the Story Editor in Chapter 7.*

# Importing Text

PageMaker can import files from all of the popular word processing programs and can accept standard ASCII text as well. When you installed PageMaker on your computer, you selected the proper filters to translate your word processor's documents into PageMaker format. PageMaker's installer created a folder called *Aldus Filters*, which holds the filters that interpret your words into a form that PageMaker can handle.

### By the Way . . .

*To see what filters are installed, press ⌘ as you select **About PageMaker** from the **Apple** menu. You'll see a scrolling list of all the currently installed import and export filters, and Aldus Additions. To see the same information in Windows, hold down the **Ctrl** key while selecting **About PageMaker** from the **Help** menu.*

Once the correct filters are installed, you can forget about them. They work in the background, making no difference at all in the way the program operates. What the filters actually do is to take the formatting commands from your document and translate them into PageMaker's commands. Most of your formatting will come through exactly as you had written it.

### Watch Out!

*A few special word processing text attributes, like double-underlining and hidden text, will not carry into PageMaker, nor will headers and footers.*

PageMaker gives you several options for placing text files. You can use the Place command to locate and import ASCII text or word processor files, spreadsheets, graphics, and charts, from any of dozens of sources, keeping links to the original document. If you're working on a Macintosh with System 7, you can also subscribe to an edition published by another program and insert it into your publication. You can paste text or graphics from the Clipboard or Macintosh Scrapbook. If you're working on a Mac with System 7, you can also subscribe to an edition published by another program and insert it into your publication.

If you are working in the Windows version of PageMaker, you can use the Place command to place linked copies of your text. You can also copy and paste using the Clipboard (and thereby lose any links), or you can use the Object Packager and OLE to link and embed items in your PageMaker document.

The way you choose to import an item into PageMaker affects your ability to edit or update it. Object Linking and Embedding, included in both Windows and Macintosh versions of PageMaker 5.0, lets you share data by creating an active link between the program that creates an object (graphic, text, and so on) and the program into which you paste it. The creator program is called the *source*, and the recipient is the *destination*. The link lets you edit an object at the source and have the edits appear in the destination as well.

OLE linking functions very much like Apple's System 7 Publish and Subscribe feature. Embedding lets you insert an object into your publication and update it from the source application without maintaining a linked original document.

Suppose, for example, you have a spreadsheet created in Excel. You want to use a piece of it in your company's annual report. You can place it using the Place command and create a PageMaker link to it. If you're using a Mac, you could Publish it and have your PageMaker report Subscribe to the spreadsheet's edition. Or you could copy it to the Clipboard and OLE link to it, or embed it. If you've placed it using PageMaker's Place command, you can choose to update the object automatically whenever you open the PageMaker publication, or to update it manually. If you Publish the spreadsheet, and subscribe to it, or OLE link to it, you'll also be able to choose whether or not to update it. All of these links, however, depend on your keeping the original source document available to the destination publication.

Embedded objects, in contrast, exist only in the PageMaker destination. You can edit them in their creator application and save the modifications as part of your PageMaker file. Embedding doesn't require that you keep a copy of the source file available. If you have multiple copies of an object, such as a company logo, in your publication, Linking will allow you to update them all at once. Embedding is best if you need only one copy of the object.

If you are using PageMaker with Windows 3.1 or later, you can use another way to import text into your documents. Select the file you want to import, and drag its icon from the File Manager to an open publication window. When you release the mouse, PageMaker imports the file using the defaults set in the Place document dialog box.

**By the Way . . .**

*Before importing text into PageMaker, prepare the PageMaker pages onto which the text will go. Place columns for as many pages as the text will fill. Making a dummy, as explained in Chapter 3, will help you decide on the position of your elements and the overall layout of your publication.*

# Placing Text with the Place Command

The Place document dialog box can be used to place both text and graphics in Layout view. (As you'll learn in Chapter 7, you can also place text into the Story Editor without placing it on the page.) In the following examples, stories will be placed into a newsletter. Very wide columns have been set on the first page because this section of text is to look like a typewritten letter. For specific information on defining columns and drawing grid lines, refer to Chapter 3.

# Text Flow Options

There's one more thing to think about before placing the text. Do you want to place it a column at a time or all at once? PageMaker gives you three ways to flow text into a publication. You might think of them as three *speeds* of text placement.

- *Manual text flow* is the slowest method. The text stops flowing at the bottom of the column. If there's more to the story, you must click at the bottom of the column to restore the Manual Text placement icon (shown in Figure 6.1). Manual text flow is PageMaker's default. Text flow is manual as long as Autoflow is not checked on the Layout menu.

- *Semi-automatic text flow* fills a column of text and stops. If there's more text to place the icon reappears, letting you fill columns at your discretion. To use Semi-autoflow, select **Auto-flow** from the **Layout** menu. When you begin to place text, hold down **Shift**. This changes the Autoflow text icon to the Semi-autoflow text icon shown in Figure 6.1. After you place the first piece of text, the flow of words stops at the end of the column, and the text icon returns to the screen so you can place more text.

- *Automatic text flow,* or Autoflow is the fastest way. The Auto-flow text icon is also shown in Figure 6.1. As the arrow in the icon suggests, once you position the icon, text keeps on flowing until it's all placed. PageMaker even creates new pages, if the text is longer than the space available. **Autoflow** is turned on by selecting it in the **Layout** menu. Highlighting the command will add or remove a check mark. When Autoflow is checked it's turned on.

Figure 6.1
The Manual,
Semi-
automatic,
and Autoflow
text placement
icons.

## Using the Place Box

Since the first story in our sample newsletter is quite short, we'll place the text manually. To open the Place document dialog box, select it from the **File** menu or type ⌘+**D** (**Ctrl+D** in Windows). The Place document dialog box, shown in Figure 6.2, enables you to select the story you want to place and gives you three other options:

- *Retain format* preserves the same type style and formatting that was used in the word processor's version of the story. When a story has extensive formatting, such as tabs and bulleted lists, various sizes or styles of type, or other formatting that you want to keep, check this option. PageMaker will import the format-ting commands with the story.

- *Convert quotes* changes *straight quotes* to *curly quotes.* One of the things which distinguishes word processors from typewrit-ers are the quotation marks. Typewriter quotes and apostrophes are straight. You use the same set of quotes at either end of the quotation. Typographic quotes, however, are different. You may think of them as "66" and "99" quotes. For professional-looking text, always leave Convert quotes checked.

### By the Way . . .

*In the very early days of typesetting, printers used upside-down commas for the front-end quotes and apostrophes for the rest. When Linotype machines came along, they had the 66 and 99 quotes designed in because that was how the inventors of the machine thought typeset quotation marks were supposed to look. Because of this, the standard for printed (as opposed to typed) copy became curly quotes.*

- *Read tags* enables PageMaker to use style names and attributes you assigned in your word processor. The Read tags option is discussed in detail in Chapter 7.

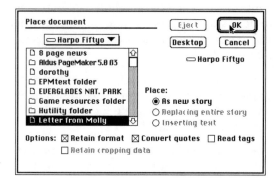

Figure 6.2
The Place document dialog box.

After the appropriate options are checked, use the following steps to place text manually.

1. Verify that Autoflow is not checked on the Layout menu.

2. Press ⌘+D to open the Place box.

3. Select the story to import.

4. Choose whether or not to import formatting, use curly quotes, and read tags.

5. Click **OK** to get the icon. Place it at the upper left corner of the column and click. Text flows into the column.

# Working with Longer Stories

Many stories are longer than a single column. When you have more text than will fit in one column, obviously you need to continue the story into as many more columns or pages as are needed. PageMaker lets you handle long stories as easily as short ones.

When you place text into a column, it comes with what PageMaker calls *window shade handles* at the top and bottom of the text block. The handles are loops at the top and bottom of the block which define the ends of the text selection box. The window shade handles let you change the length of the column by dragging it up or down. If the top handle is empty, it indicates the top of the article. The lower window shade handle will have an arrow in it if there's more text to be placed.

To place additional text, use the following steps.

1. Look at the bottom of the text block. If there's an arrow in the window shade handle, as shown in Step 1 of Figure 6.3, this indicates there's more text to be placed. When you place the pointer on the arrow and click, it changes to the Manual text placement icon.

2. Clicking at the head of the next empty column will place the unpasted text in that column, as shown in Step 2. Again, there's an arrow at the bottom of the column, indicating that there's more text to be placed.

3. The unpasted text can be placed using the steps above to create a third column of text, as shown in Step 3.

Figure 6.3
The steps in placing additional text.

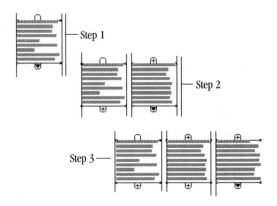

# Using Semi-Automatic Text Flow

There are times when you need to retain some control over the placement of your text, but not so much that you want to stop and pick up the icon again after each column. In this situation, you would use Semi-automatic text flow. To do so, follow these steps:

1.  Turn on **Autoflow** from the **Layout** menu.

2.  Press ⌘+**D** (**Ctrl+D** in Windows) for the Place box, select the story, and choose any options. Click on **OK**.

3.  Position the Autoflow icon at the top of the first column, press **Shift**, and click.

4.  Position the icon at the next column. Press **Shift** and click. Repeat this step until all the text is placed.

You can reflow a text block if you decide, for example, that your page should have been set up as two columns instead of three, or if you want to relocate it to a different place. Simply close up the window-shade handle by placing the pointer on the bottom handle and dragging upward, and then click on the empty top handle. You'll get the Text placement icon again, and you can reposition the text wherever you want it, or store it on the pasteboard until you're ready for it.

# Using Autoflow to Place Text

To place text automatically, turn on **Autoflow** from the **Layout** menu. Open the Place box and select the story. Click any desired options and click **OK**. Position the Autoflow icon at the upper left corner of the first column. Click. That's all. The story will flow neatly into as many columns and/or pages as it needs.

If the text is longer than the number of pages you specified in the Page Setup box, PageMaker will add as many additional pages as the story requires, formatting them like your master pages and flowing the type into them. If you're flowing text automatically, you can stop the flow by pressing **Shift**+⌘ (**Shift+Ctrl** in Windows). PageMaker will automatically revert to Autoflow when you start placing text again. Change Autoflow to Manual flow by holding down ⌘ (**Ctrl** in Windows) and clicking the icon.

**By the Way . . .**

*In Automatic text flow mode the text stops flowing if you manually interrupt it, if the publication reaches 999 pages (its maximum length), or if you run out of text to place.*

If you decide not to place the text you've imported, click on the **Pointer** tool to cancel the placement. If text is already placed, press ⌘+**Z** (**Alt+Backspace** in Windows) to undo the placement or ⌘+**A** (**Ctrl+A** in Windows), for select all, and press Delete. If you decide you'd rather put it on a different page, just drag it to the pasteboard until you're ready to use it.

# Threading and Unthreading

Text that has been flowed into two or more blocks or columns is said to be *threaded*. Threaded text is electronically joined together. If you shorten the length of the first column, the excess words will jump to the head of the next, and so on. It has a sort of ripple effect. This has its good and bad points. A good point is that you're not likely to lose a line from the middle of a story. Text will get pulled back or pushed ahead to the next linked text block. A bad point is that this ripple effect may interfere with formatting, as a change in one line changes all the others.

Threaded text is identified by the plus symbol (+) which appears in both the upper and lower window shade handles when the text block is selected. The text we placed in Figure 6.3 was threaded. Figure 6.4 also shows columns of threaded text. The first column has no plus symbol at the head of the story. That's because the thread starts there. Notice the arrow at the end of the third column. It tells us there's more text left to place.

Figure 6.4
These columns
are threaded
together.
Changes in one
affect all three.

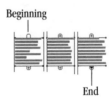

Beginning

End

If you make a change in one block that you don't want to carry all the way through, you can isolate or unthread that particular block. To do so, follow these steps:

1. Select the block you want to isolate with the Pointer tool, and cut it to the Clipboard using ⌘+X (**Ctrl+X** in Windows), or by selecting **Cut** from the **Edit** menu.

2. Now, using ⌘+V (**Ctrl+V** in Windows) or the **Paste** command from the **Edit** menu, replace it where you cut it. The thread is now broken.

Any changes you make in this text block now will affect only this block. To rethread it back into the story:

1. Cut the block to the Clipboard as before.

2. Create an insertion point at the end of the previous text block or at the beginning of the next, by positioning the I-beam cursor and clicking. A blinking vertical line will appear in the text.

3. Paste the block back in. The text will rethread itself into the story starting at the insertion point.

**By the Way . . .**

*When you isolate one text block, the rest of the text remains threaded. If you make editing changes or formatting changes that move lines of text from one block to another, your isolated block could come back in out of sequence. To avoid this, unthread all blocks if you unthread any.*

# Replacing a Story

If you have an existing story you want to replace:

1. First, select the story to replace by clicking on it with the Pointer. Press ⌘+D (**Ctrl+D** in Windows) to open the Place document box, select the replacement story from the scrolling list, and click on the **Replacing entire story** button.

2. Click on **OK** or press **Enter** or **Return**. PageMaker removes the old story and inserts the new one.

If the new story is shorter, any excess text blocks will be deleted. PageMaker adds more text blocks or pages, if the new story is longer, when Autoflow is selected. If Autoflow is not selected, the last text block will have an arrow in the lower handle, indicating that there's more text to place.

## Inserting Text

You can insert new text into an existing story by using the Text tool to create an insertion point, and then following the steps for replacing a story (above) but clicking on the **Inserting** text button instead of the Replacing entire story button. If the Replacing button is grayed out, you haven't selected a story to replace.

Other ways to insert text into an existing story are to position the Text tool and type it in, or to copy if from elsewhere and paste from the Clipboard. Doing so will not break the thread. As long as there's room in the column, the text will reflow to accommodate the added material. If you run out of room, you'll see the arrow in the window shade handle, indicating that you have more text to place.

# Adjusting Blocks of Text

When you click on a block of text, you'll see two kinds of handles. The window shade handles let you adjust the length of a column of type. The black squares at the corners of a selected text block are handles, too, but they're the kind also found on graphics. They let you adjust the width of the column.

To reposition a block of text, select it by clicking anywhere on it with the pointer. As you press the mouse button, the pointer changes to a four-way arrow, indicating that you may move the block in any direction. Here are some other methods for modifying columns and blocks of text:

- To change the length of a block of type, click on the bottom square handle and move it up or down, as if you were raising or lowering a window shade.

- To shrink or expand the width of a column of text, click on one of the windowshade handles at the end of the top or bottom line, (shown in Figure 6.5) and drag the handle in (to shrink) or out (to expand). PageMaker will automatically reflow the text to fit the new column size. If there's more text than will fit, a triangle will appear in the bottom window shade handle.

- To move the whole section of text around within the page, or to drag it out to the pasteboard, click anywhere inside the text, and hold the mouse button down while you reposition it.

Windowshade handle

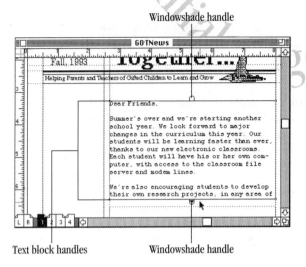

Figure 6.5
Getting a handle on the text block.

Text block handles          Windowshade handle

# Paragraph Specifications

After the text is in place, the next step is formatting it. You may want to adjust the indents. Indents move type in relation to the margin, usually toward the center of the column. You'll also need to determine the alignment—whether to set the type flush left, flush right, or justified. PageMaker gives you a number of options for customizing paragraphs in the Paragraph specifications dialog box, shown in Figure 6.6. To open the dialog box, select **Paragraph** from the **Type** menu or press ⌘+**M** (**Ctrl+M** in Windows). Within it you can change PageMaker's default settings for the options listed in Table 6.1.

**Paragraph specifications**

Indents:
Left `0` inches
First `0` inches
Right `0` inches

Paragraph space:
Before `0` inches
After `0` inches

OK
Cancel
Rules...
Spacing...

Alignment: Left          Dictionary: US English

Options:
☐ Keep lines together   ☐ Keep with next `0` lines
☐ Column break before   ☐ Widow control `0` lines
☐ Page break before     ☐ Orphan control `0` lines
☐ Include in table of contents

Figure 6.6
The Paragraph specifications dialog box.

**Table 6.1**  Default settings in the Paragraph specifications box.

| Option | PageMaker default |
| --- | --- |
| Indents | Left, First, and Right, 0 inches |
| Paragraph Space | Before, After, 0 inches |
| Alignment | Left |
| Dictionary | US English |

You can also select options that will keep lines together, avoid leaving a single widowed or orphaned line in a column, force column breaks or page breaks rather than breaking up a paragraph, and include the specified paragraph in the table of contents.

There are other ways to make these settings, too. You may prefer to set indents and alignment options independent of the Paragraph specifications box. Alignment may be accessed directly from the Type menu. Typing ⌘+I (**Ctrl+I** in Windows) or selecting **Indents/tabs** from the **Type** menu gives you access to the Indents and Tabs ruler described in the next section.

# Indents and Tabs

To indent or not to indent? It's a question worthy of consideration. Many publications are now set *flush left,* meaning that the type is set up against the left hand margin. (You may come across the term *ragged right.* It means the left side is flush with the margin, while the right is not.) Some publications use what's called a *hanging indent* for added emphasis. In a hanging indent, the first word or words of the paragraph hang to the left of the main body of the text. There are *normal indents,* in which the first word of the first line begins a few spaces in. And finally, *nested indents,* commonly used to set apart a piece of text, such as a quotation. Figure 6.7 shows examples of the different styles of indent.

Entering numbers into the Paragraph specifications dialog box with no text selected sets up a format for any additional text you place in PageMaker. To assign any of these indent styles to a specific paragraph, you need to select it first. (Typing into the Paragraph specifications box with text selected affects only the paragraphs selected.) Select the text to be formatted by placing the cursor within it, pressing ⌘+M (**Ctrl+M** in Windows) to open the dialog box, and following these instructions:

- *Flush left:* To set type flush left, simply set indents in the Paragraph specifications box to zero inches.

- *Hanging indents:* The first line of type remains at the margin or to the left of it, with the rest of the paragraph indented. These are produced by making the Left indent a positive number greater than zero. This moves the body of the paragraph in from the column edge the amount you've specified. Next, enter a zero or a minus number for the First line indent. If you enter zero as a First indent, it will hold the line of type at the column edge. A negative number, as shown in Figure 6.8, will move it even further left into the margin.

- *Normal indents:* Enter a number for the indent in the First line field. Leave the other values at zero.

- *Nested indents:* Enter a positive number for the Left indent, again moving the main body of the paragraph in from the column edge, but also use the same number or a larger one, for a First line indent. In addition, as Figure 6.7 shows, the right side of the text can also be indented from the column edge. This is especially effective when the text is justified. *Justified text* is flush with both left and right margins, although the first line may be indented. First-line indents, obviously, apply only to the first line of a paragraph.

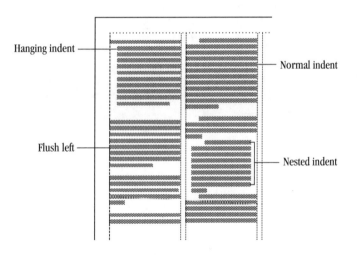

Hanging indent

Flush left

Normal indent

Nested indent

Figure 6.7
Types of
indents.

**By the Way . . .**

*Any time you need to select a single paragraph, place the Text tool cursor anywhere within it and triple-click (just like double-clicking, only three quick clicks). The whole paragraph will be highlighted. Triple-clicking a text block with the pointer will take you into the story editor mode, which you'll learn about in Chapter 7.*

Figure 6.8
The numbers in
the fields
indicate a
hanging
indent.

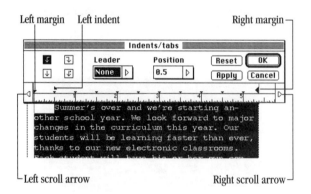

## Setting Indents on the Screen

If you prefer to set the paragraph indents on-screen with a ruler to guide you, PageMaker makes it easy. First, select the text with which you'll be working. Select **Indents/tabs** from the **Type** menu, or press ⌘+I (**Ctrl+I** in Windows), for Indents, to place a ruler at the head of the column of type, as shown in Figure 6.9.

Figure 6.9
The Indents/
tabs ruler lets
you see where
you're placing
tabs and
indents.

At the left side of the ruler, there are two triangles. The lower triangle marks the left margin indent (or the edge of the column), and the upper triangle shows the first line indent. The large triangle on the right side of the ruler shows the right indent (or the right margin). The zero point on the ruler automatically aligns itself with the left corner of a selected text block. (If no text was selected, no insertion point is present, so the ruler simply centers itself on the page.) You can also use the small hollow arrows at the ends of the ruler to scroll left or right as you need to. The ruler may be moved wherever it's needed by clicking on it and dragging it to a new location.

# Using Tabs

PageMaker has default tab settings every half inch (or half centimeter). As many as 40 tab stops may be set on the ruler including left justified, right justified, centered, and decimal tabs. To simplify locating the tabs and indents whenever one is selected, its position can be read in the Position box on the ruler. To rearrange the tabs and indents, use the following steps.

1. Click on the tabs and drag them to a new location. As you drag, the numbers in the Position box change. The Position box gives the exact position of the marker in whatever unit of measurement you've specified in the Preferences dialog box. Use the numbers to guide you in placing markers accurately.

2. You may also place a tab by clicking in the arrow on the Position box to get a menu of tab options, selecting one, and entering a position for it in the box.

3. When you're done, click on **Apply**, and the text will move to reflect your changes.

To cancel your tab settings and return to the defaults, click on the **Reset** button. To remove a single tab, either select it and use **Delete**, or simply drag it off the ruler.

Here are a few things to watch for when you're setting tabs and indents.

- Be sure to select the text to which you want to apply the tab or indent. Otherwise, nothing will move.

- You won't see the position of the words change until you click on the **Apply** button or press **Enter** or **Return**.

- If you imported text that already has tabs or indents applied to it, you must remove them before PageMaker can place its own tab and indent indications.

- You can only set indents within existing page margins or column guides.

- If you add more text to an existing story, PageMaker automatically assigns to it the same indents that were used in the preceding paragraphs.

- Clicking **Reset** on the **Indents** ruler restores the default settings, but may change tab stops defined as part of a paragraph style.

- PageMaker sometimes has problems with imported first line indents. Normal indents and hanging indents can produce strange errors if the first line indent is wider than the column into which the type is being placed. Figure 6.10 illustrates this kind of error.

Figure 6.10
The type gets
scrunched into
whatever
space is
available.

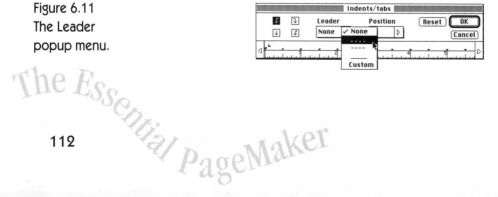

can't afford to replace worn out
textbooks. And the last round of
budget cuts took away even more.

## Leaders

Use the ruler to set the type of *leader* to use between tabs. Leaders are repeated dots or dashes used between tabs in a chart or table to help the reader see the relationship between columns. The leader fills in any space between the end of the text and the next tab stop. Figure 6.11 shows various kinds of leaders. Leaders are set in the Leader box on the Indents/Tabs ruler. Select **Custom** from the **Leaders** menu to invent your own leaders as long as they're standard keyboard characters. For example, **> > >** or ≈ ≈ ≈ can be used for special effects. (You can adjust the spacing of these characters by using the **Tracking** command discussed later in this chapter.) If paragraphs were selected with the Text tool when you created a custom leader or assigned an existing one, the leader applies to the tab location(s) in the selected paragraphs. If the Pointer tool was selected, the leader will apply to the tabs you assign from there on.

Figure 6.11
The Leader
popup menu.

# Paragraph Spacing

Normally, when you typed a page of text with a typewriter, you'd use a double carriage return to leave an extra line between paragraphs. Your choice was one line, or two. One of the advantages of a page layout program like PageMaker is that you are able to specify the exact amount of space between paragraphs, and whether to insert it before or after the paragraph. To set the amount of space between paragraphs, use the following steps.

1. Press ⌘+**M** (**Ctrl+M** in Windows) to open the Paragraph specifications dialog box, or select Paragraph from the **Type** menu.

2. Under Paragraph space, enter the amount of space desired into the Data field for Before or After.

3. Click on **OK**, or press **Enter** or **Return**. PageMaker will insert the space each time you press **Enter** or **Return**.

You can save yourself a great deal of trouble if you always use PageMaker's Paragraph specifications box to set paragraph spacing rather than a double carriage return. Adding extra carriage returns can cause alignment problems, especially if the carriage return accidentally gets tagged with a style different from that of the surrounding text.

# Alignment

*Alignment* refers to the way in which a column of type is placed on the page, relative to the margins on either side of it. PageMaker offers you several alignment choices available as a separate popup menu under the

Type menu, as well as in the Paragraph specifications dialog box. Open the Paragraph specifications box from the **Type** menu or by pressing ⌘+M (**Ctrl+M** in Windows). In Windows, you can press the key combination **Alt+T**, then **A**, and then the type of justification you want (**L, C, R, J,** or **F**). To apply any of these alignment options, first use the **Text** tool to position the cursor anywhere within the block of text to be aligned. Then select the desired option from the menu, or type its command key shortcut listed below. Figure 6.12 shows the effects of the various alignment options.

- *Left-aligned type* (⌘+**Shift+L** on the Mac and **Ctrl+Shift+L** on Windows) is the easiest to read because all the spaces are even. It is the default for PageMaker and virtually every other text handling program.

- *Centered type* (⌘+**Shift+C** on the Mac and **Ctrl+Shift+C** on Windows) is useful for headlines and captions.

- *Right-aligned type* (⌘+**Shift+R** on the Mac and **Ctrl+Shift+R** on Windows) can be used in small amounts as a design element, but right alignment is seldom used for an entire story.

- *Justified type* (⌘+**Shift+J** on the Mac and **Ctrl+Shift+J** on Windows) means that both left and right sides are aligned to their respective margins. Justification automatically adjusts the amount of space between letters and words to make each line the same length. Longer text blocks are often set justified for a more uniform page.

- *Force-justified type* (⌘+**Shift+F** on the Mac and **Ctrl+Shift+F** on Windows) forces justification of the last line of a paragraph. It's not always desirable, as Figure 6.12 shows. You can also force a line break in justified text by using the **Shift+Return** (use **Enter** in Windows) that forces a line break, but does not force the line to go flush left or generate a new paragraph.

## Widows and Orphans

Typographers aren't necessarily mean. They avoid widows and orphans for reasons of design, not economics. *Widows* are the final lines of paragraphs that end up starting new columns rather than being kept with their "husband" paragraphs. *Orphans* are lines that should lead off a new column or page, but somehow get tacked onto the preceding one. They dangle in mid-story looking lost and forlorn, and spoiling the page design. PageMaker lets you control the unsightly effects of widowed and orphaned type on your page makeup. Within the Paragraph specifications dialog box you can set limits for widow and orphan control, as shown in Figure 6.13. Enter a number from 1 to 3 in the boxes for widows and orphans, to define how many lines with which you want to begin or end a column.

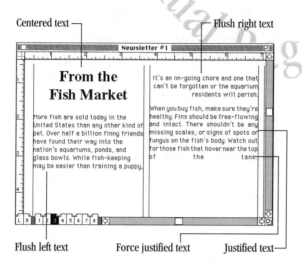

Centered text ─

Flush right text ─

Figure 6.12
The various
types of
alignment.

## From the Fish Market

More fish are sold today in the United States than any other kind of pet. Over half a billion finny friends have found their way into the nation's aquariums, ponds, and glass bowls. While fish-keeping may be easier than training a puppy,

it's an on-going chore and one that can't be forgotten or the aquarium residents will perish.

When you buy fish, make sure they're healthy. Fins should be free-flowing and intact. There shouldn't be any missing scales, or signs of spots or fungus on the fish's body. Watch out for those fish that hover near the top of the tank.

Flush left text

Force justified text

Justified text ─

Figure 6.13
Controlling
widows and
orphans.

**Paragraph specifications**

Indents:
Left [0] inches
First [0] inches
Right [0] inches

Paragraph space:
Before [0] inches
After [0] inches

OK
Cancel
Rules...
Spacing...

Alignment: [Left]    Dictionary: [US English]

Options:
☐ Keep lines together    ☒ Keep with next [2] lines
☐ Column break before    ☒ Widow control [2] lines
☐ Page break before      ☒ Orphan control [2] lines
☐ Include in table of contents

PageMaker can also keep paragraphs together if you select the Keep lines together option. However, if you choose this option, your columns may become uneven in length because paragraphs won't break where the column normally ends in the page.

# Paragraph Rules

Use the Paragraph Rules feature to place thin lines between paragraphs. You wouldn't do this within the body of a news story, but it's nice in a catalog. It can also be used to separate entries in a table of contents or other listing, as shown in Figure 6.14. Rules can be any length you choose to make them. To center a rule in the column, indent both ends by the same amount. If you decide to use color for your paragraph rules, be sure it's a spot color. Process colors don't always overlap correctly on a thin line.

Use the following steps to place rules on the page.

1.  Select the text to have rules applied.

2.  Press ⌘+M (**Ctrl+M** in Windows) to open the Paragraph specifications dialog box, or select it from the **Type** menu. Click on the **Rules** button to open the Paragraph rules box.

3.  Decide whether to use lines above or lines below the paragraph. If you use both, you'll have two rules.

4.  Choose the line style and color by clicking on the popup menus in the appropriate boxes. Click on a button to set line width.

5.  If lines are to be indented, enter indent amounts in the Indent boxes.

6.  Click on the **Options** button to set the lines to a specific height, above or below the baseline of the line of text closest to the rule, or enter Auto in the Top and Bottom boxes to let PageMaker place the lines. (Ignore the Align to Grid option. It's used in setting up a ruled form, which will be discussed in Chapter 10.)

7.  Press **Option+Return** (**Ctrl+Alt+Enter** in Windows) to close all the nested dialog boxes.

Figure 6.14
Placing para-
graph rules.

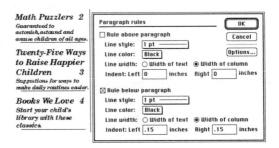

# Using the Table Editor in PageMaker for Windows

Although PageMaker 5.0 for the Mac no longer comes with the Table Editor, PageMaker for Windows 5.0 retains this handy table-generating

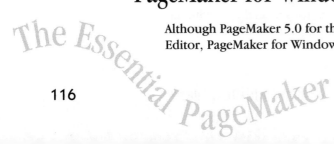

relic from version 4.2. The Table Editor for Windows is a separate program used for creating tables, such as those you can generate in Microsoft Word or Excel. The Table Editor (shown in Figure 6.15) displays a series of cells that you can fill with data and manipulate individually to suit your formatting requirements.

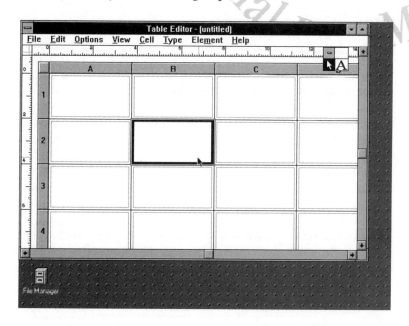

Figure 6.15
The Table Editor is an independent utility used to create tables.

You can access the Table Editor by minimizing the PageMaker window or exiting PageMaker. Then, open the Table Editor 2.1 program from the Aldus program group. Type directly in each cell, and use the **Tab** key to move between cells. You can import data from your word processor or spreadsheet, and any tab-delimited information will be placed in cells as determined by how many tabs you used and where your carriage returns were placed.

The Table Editor exports its tables as .TBL files, Windows Metafiles, or as tab-delimited text files. You can export only part of the file, by selecting text or the whole file. You can also copy and paste cells and rows into the Clipboard for transferring to other programs.

The best way to bring a Table Editor file into PageMaker is as a Windows Metafile. PageMaker considers the file as a graphic, letting you crop and resize it as you would any other graphic. The benefit of using the Table Editor is that you can edit its contents with a keystroke. If you want to make a change in your imported table, switch to the Table Editor and edit the original table. The Table Editor opens to its originating document where you can make your changes.

After you have completed your work, save the file normally using the **Save** command from the **File** menu and reactivate PageMaker. If you have used the Link options box to automatically update linked files whenever you open a PageMaker file, then this file will also be updated.

# Specifying Type

So far, the text we've placed in PageMaker has all appeared in the default type font, 12-point Times. If it's not the look you had in mind, you can specify any typeface that's installed in your computer and select all kinds of style variations. This is done most easily in the Type specifications dialog box under the Type menu. (You can also use the individual options on the Type menu, and you can change most type attributes from the Control Palette.) To use the Type specifications box, open **Type specs** from the **Type** menu or by pressing ⌘+T (**Ctrl+T** in Windows). Figure 6.16 shows the Type specification box which contains the type options as popup menus. To view your options under any category, put the pointer on the word or number in the box, and press the mouse button. A list will appear. Move up or down the list until your choice is highlighted. Use the Type specifications box to define the following choices:

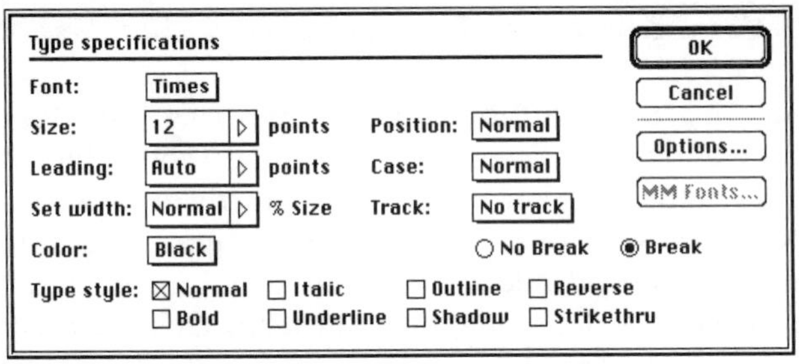

Figure 6.16
The Type
specifications
dialog box.

*Font:* Use this menu to select the name of the typeface you want to use. The selected font has a check mark next to it. If you've selected text in more than one font, nothing will be checked.

*Size:* Type sizes are measured in points. When a box has an arrow, as this one does, click on the arrow to see a list or type your choice in place of the entry in the box. 12 points is the default size.

*Leading:* Leading is the amount of space between lines. Auto, the default setting, adjusts the leading automatically to an appropriate height.

*Set width:* PageMaker will expand or condense the type by a percentage determined in this box. Choose 10% increments from 70–130%. 100% is normal, neither condensed nor expanded. Normal is the default.

*Color:* If you want to set your type in another color or use *reverse* (white on black) type, use this box to change the type color. Black is the default setting for color.

*Position:* This refers to the position of the type relative to the baseline. The options are normal (the default), subscript, and superscript. The latter two are used primarily in scientific notation and footnotes.

*Case:* PageMaker gives you three choices. Normal, the default setting, lets you enter upper- and lowercase letters. All Caps disables the lowercase letters. Small Caps gives you two sizes of capital letters, the smaller being (by default) 70% of the larger. The percentage may be changed in Type options dialog box, which you get by clicking on the **Options** button.

*Track:* This adjusts the closeness of the letters on each line. No track is the default, meaning that no adjustment is made.

*Type style:* Click on the box or boxes for the styles you want to use.

By The Way . . .
*You can determine the type specifications or change PageMaker's default font before you import text. Select the **Pointer**, to be sure no type is selected. Press ⌘+T (Ctrl+T in Windows) to open the Type specifications box. Select the font and settings you want. Click **OK** and then place the text.*

# Fonts

There's often a good deal of confusion about the difference between typefaces and fonts. PageMaker helps contribute to the confusion by identifying the name of the particular typeface to be selected in the Type specifications dialog box as a font. A font is actually the complete character set for a particular typeface, size, and style such as Helvetica Bold 12-point. The font includes both upper- and lowercase characters, punctuation marks, numbers, and any special characters like $ % & π, and so on, which may be included with it. In the Type specifications box, what PageMaker asks you to select as a font is really a typeface. When you click on the **Font** box, you'll see a popup menu listing all the kinds of type currently installed on your computer. Simply select the one you want to use.

## Type Measurement

In the United States, type is measured in units called *points*. PageMaker also supports the slightly larger European type measurement unit called a *Cicero*.

**By the Way . . .**
*The name Cicero comes from the size of type first used in an edition of Cicero's works published in 1458.*

There are several ways to set type styles and sizes in PageMaker:

- Use the Type specifications dialog box on the Type menu to describe your type before you import text into PageMaker.

  Or

- Select the type once it's in position, and either change the specifications in the box, or use the popup menus under the Type menu or the Control Palette to change individual attributes such as point size.

In general you'll use 10- or 12-point type for body copy and larger sizes for headlines. You can use fractional points too. If the point size you want to use isn't shown on the popup menu, choose **Other** and type it into the dialog box.

## Leading

Back in the old, precomputer days of typesetting, words were set in metal type one letter at a time and fastened down into a wooden frame. The typesetter used variously sized strips and blocks of lead to maintain the spaces between the words and lines of type. Although PageMaker does it electronically, the vertical spaces between lines of type are still called *leading,* (pronounced to rhyme with sledding).

Like type, leading is measured in points. The amount of leading used affects both the appearance and the readability of your publication. Too little leading makes a very dense page. The lines are crowded too closely together, and the reader feels cramped and uncomfortable. Too much leading means there's too much space between lines so the reader's eye has a hard time following the flow from one line to the next. There's no clear sense that individual lines of text are related. The reader becomes distracted. Figure 6.17 shows some examples of leading.

This is a block of text in 12 point type. The leading used is 10 points, a *negative* leading. The type is cut off in places, and is hard to read. This is sometimes refered to as 12/10, or "twelve on ten".

This is a block of text in 12 point type. The leading used is 12 points, a *light* leading. The type appears cramped, and is still hard to read. This is called 12/12, or "twelve on twelve".

This is a block of text in 12 point type. The leading used is 14 points, a *normal* leading. The type is easy to read. This is called 12/14, or "twelve on fourteen".

This is a block of text in 12 point type. The leading used is 18 points, a *loose* leading. The type is, once again, hard to read. This is called 12/18, or "twelve on eighteen".

Figure 6.17
When you're reading between the lines, maybe you're looking at leading.

For standard *body copy,* the main text of the story, the amount of leading is correct when it's not noticeable. The casual reader shouldn't be aware of space, or lack of space, between lines of type. In general, the rule is to make the leading 20% greater than the height of the type. As Figure 6.17 shows, the type in the 12/14 example looks best.

### By the Way . . .
*The 12/14 combination of type size and leading height is called twelve on fourteen, not twelve fourteenths. Others might be thirty on thirty-six and so on. Even though they look like fractions, they're not.*

Of course, what's right for one type font and one purpose might not be right for another. Some fonts can tolerate less leading while still maintaining readability. Others need all the help they can get. PageMaker allows you to adjust leading in very small increments, as little as a tenth of a point or 1/720 of an inch. If you needed to squeeze in an extra line of type at the bottom of a column, you could reduce the leading for the entire column or story by a fraction of a point and gain enough space in which to fit the extra line.

### Watch Out!
*It's not a good idea to change the leading for only a few lines of text. The differences, even though small, will be apparent. Uneven line spacing looks sloppy and detracts from the readability and the appearance of the page.*

If you don't change the leading when you enter text, PageMaker's default is to automatically compute 120% leading, which would give you the normal 10/12 or 12/14, and so on. Of course, this doesn't mean that there is a space 12 points high between two lines of 10-point type. It means that the line of type, including its leading, is 12 points high but the characters themselves are 10 points high. To see this, highlight a line of text. Surrounding the letters is a horizontal bar called a *slug*. Figure 6.18 shows what a slug looks like.

Figure 6.18
Anatomy of
a slug.

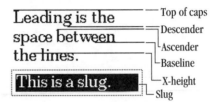

The height of the slug indicates the amount of leading. In Figure 6.18 the slug is 18 points high. Within it the characters are aligned on a common *baseline,* which is a reference line that allows for precise horizontal alignment. To have PageMaker automatically calculate and place leading, use the following steps.

- Select the text and press ⌘+**Shift**+**A** (all together).

  Or

- Select the **Leading** menu under the **Type** menu or from the **Control Palette**, as shown in Figure 6.19, and choose **Auto**.

The type will automatically be leaded to 120%.

Figure 6.19
Leading may
be set on the
Leading popup
menu.

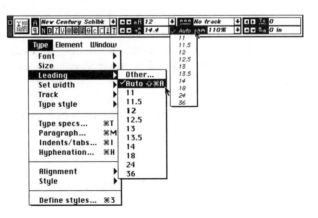

Auto-leading is convenient and is adequate for most layouts. If you wish to specify an exact amount of leading for any section of text, whether it's a paragraph, a whole publication, or a single character, you may do so by:

- Selecting the text and pressing ⌘+T (**Ctrl+T** in Windows) to open the Type specifications box. Select a point size from the **Leading** popup menu, or enter your own setting in the Data field as shown in Figure 6.20.

  Or

- Select **Leading** under the **Type** menu or **Control Palette**, and choose a point size from the list. Or choose **Other**, and enter your setting in the box. Remember, you can specify leading in tenth of a point increments.

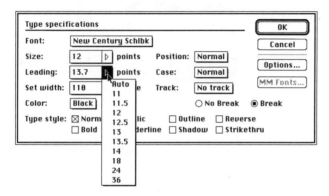

Figure 6.20
Specifying leading in the Type specifications dialog box.

It's important to remember that if you've changed the leading for a character or a word within a line of text, the leading for the whole line will change to the higher number. If the larger character moves to the next line because you've edited the text around it, the leading for the previous line will revert to the smaller amount again. Even nonprinting characters, spaces, tabs, and carriage returns have leading assigned to them. If the text you're working with doesn't seem to have the right leading, you might have a nonprinting character imbedded in the line with the wrong amount of leading. To fix it, triple-click the paragraph with the **Text** tool to select it, and reassign the leading.

PageMaker lets you choose to place leading either proportionally or from the tops of the capital letters. With *proportional leading,* two thirds of the assigned line spacing lies above the baseline, and the remaining third below it. Proportional leading allows you to use different fonts on the same baseline while keeping the overall line spacing the same. This works because all the characters are sitting on a baseline that is always the same distance below the top of the slug.

*Top of caps leading* uses the height of the tallest ascender to position the baseline. The distance from the top of the slug to the baseline equals the height of the tallest font ascender in the particular face, whether it's actually used in the text or not. Figure 6.21 shows the relationship of the letter and its baseline, to the slug in both leading methods.

*Baseline leading* is the method used in traditional typography. The bottom of the slug is aligned with the baseline of a line of text. It works well when you're dealing with metal type but is seldom used for computer typesetting.

Figure 6.21 The relationship of the leading to the baseline. The type in both examples is 24/36.

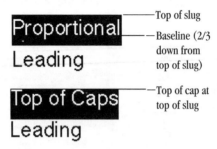

Leading methods are selected in the Spacing dialog box which is accessed by a button in the Paragraph box. Press ⌘+M (**Ctrl+M** in Windows) and then select the **Spacing** button.

By the Way . . .

*The best rule is to stick with Proportional leading unless you have some reason not to. Top of caps may be easier to work with if you're trying for special typographic effects.*

## Subscript and Superscript

The Options box (accessed from within the Type specifications dialog box) lets you define exact positions for *subscript* (words below the baseline) and *superscript* (words above the line). You can also define a percentage size for small caps, and for sub and superscript letters. Figure 6.22 shows the settings and some possible results. If subscripts and superscripts are set in the same size type as the rest of the line, they will affect the leading. If you choose to use them on a tightly leaded page, you can reasonably expect them to force a gap between the lines. The alternative is to let them run into the line above or below, or to use a much smaller type font. PageMaker's default size for subscript and superscript is 58.3% of the point size. In this example, we've increased it slightly for legibility.

**Type options**

| | | | |
|---|---|---|---|
| Small caps size: | 70 | % of point size | **OK** |
| Super/subscript size: | 65 | % of point size | Cancel |
| Superscript position: | 33.3 | % of point size | |
| Subscript position: | 33.3 | % of point size | |
| Baseline shift: | 0 | points | ● Up  ○ Down |

This is an example of <sup>superscript</sup>.
This is an example of <sub>subscript</sub>.
THESE ARE SMALL CAPS.

Figure 6.22
Examples of subscript, superscript, and small caps.

## Have you tried . . . setting type that needs to be made distinctive in small caps?

The normal (default) size for a small cap is 70% of the large cap. If you're setting a company name or headline, you might decide to increase the small cap size to 80%.

# Tracking

No, it's not what a bloodhound does, nor is it the act of leaving muddy footprints on the kitchen floor. *Tracking,* or track kerning, refers to the spacing between the letters and words on the line. Use the Track command to tighten or loosen the space between letters. Track kerning is selected from the Type menu. PageMaker applies predetermined values to each font on your system to determine how much tracking is normal for that font. It then compensates as you specify for "very loose," "very tight," or somewhere in between. You can also specify No track, which means that PageMaker applies no tracking, and letters and words are spaced as the font design dictates. No track usually comes quite close to Normal.

Figure 6.23 shows the effects of different track kerning. Normal track improves the visual appearance of letter spacing by reducing the amount of space on larger point sizes and easing it on smaller point sizes. Generally, at a medium point size, tracking has little or no effect because the type is already spaced properly.

Tracking, like other type modifications, can be applied via the Type menu, the Type specifications box, or the Control Palette. Tracking is helpful when you want to darken, or lighten, the appearance of a page of type. Tighter tracking fits more words per line and makes the page of type denser and darker. Looser tracking opens up a dark page and makes it easier to read. You can also use tracking to make a line of text fit a particular spot on a page, such as a caption. Tracking options interact with other settings for alignment, hyphenation, and spacing. If you've specified force justified type, and then called for especially loose or tight tracking, you may run into difficulty with uneven lines. Adjust as necessary until it looks right.

Figure 6.23
Examples of
tracking.

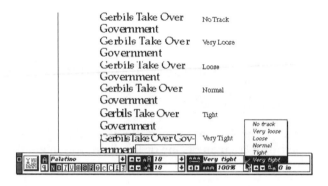

Watch Out!

*If you've specified track kerning, it will take PageMaker much longer to redraw the page whenever you change from one view to another. This is because it must recalculate the tracking each time. To work faster, specify track kerning only for selected lines of very small or very large type such as photo captions or headlines. Apply No track to normal text.*

## Manual and Automatic Kerning

*Kerning* adjusts the space between individual letters. (The word kern actually refers to the little pieces of metal type that hang out over other letters. The bar on top of the capital T is a kern.) Since letters occupy different amounts of space, kerning individual pairs of letters helps them fit together in a more visually pleasing way. At larger point sizes, gaps between letters become painfully obvious. Even a monospaced face, like Courier, benefits from kerning if you use it as a headline font. Kerning has little or no effect on text size type (12 points or less). You'll generally need to kern headlines and other large print. You can either kern type yourself or let PageMaker do it for you.

Pair kerning can be done automatically through the Spacing attributes box shown in Figure 6.24. To open this box click on the

**Spacing** button in the Paragraph specifications dialog box. If you check Auto above, PageMaker will automatically kern specific combinations of letters at any point size larger than specified. Kerning information and tracking information are built into each font of type, and PageMaker can use this information to kern whatever combinations need to be kerned. Such combinations as Tr, Te, WA, We, and Yo all benefit from having the gaps closed up, especially at headline sizes where the open space is even more distracting.

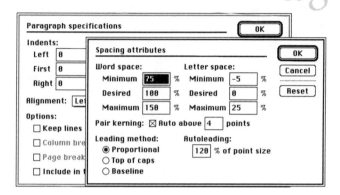

Figure 6.24
The Spacing attributes dialog box.

## Watch Out!

*Kerned text, like tracked text, takes longer to redraw on-screen. If you kern only larger text, such as headlines, your pages will be redrawn faster.*

PageMaker's default for pair kerning is 12 points, but you really won't see much effect at anything under 14 points. You can also adjust letter spacing and word spacing within this dialog box. The space between words, which you insert when you press the Spacebar, is determined by the font design. The "desired" spacing is 100%, but you can change it to anything from zero to 500%, by resetting the minimum and maximum allowable. Letter spacing is also determined by font design. Each letter has a certain amount of space included with it. Here, though, the "desired" spacing is zero. Under ideal conditions, no space would be added to, or subtracted from the individual letter. If you must spread a line of type out, without making it look too loosely tracked, adjusting the letter spacing by a small amount can add width without being too obvious.

You may also kern letters manually. PageMaker adjusts the space by either a large (1/25th of an em) or small (1/100th of an em) increment. An *em*, by the way, is a square the width of the letter m in whatever font you're using. The em is not a fixed measurement since it's related to the particular font. To kern any two letters, place the Text tool cursor between them, and type the keystrokes shown on the table.

**Table 6.2**   Kerning Key Combinations

| Kern amount | Macintosh | Windows |
|---|---|---|
| To increase spacing 1/25 em | ⌘+Shift+Delete or ⌘+right arrow | Ctrl+"+"(Plus on numeric keypad) or Ctrl+Shift+Backspace |
| To increase spacing 1/100 em | Option+Shift+Delete or ⌘+Shift+right arrow | Shift+Ctrl+"+"(Plus on numeric keypad) |
| To decrease spacing 1/25 em | ⌘+Delete or ⌘+left arrow | Ctrl+"−" (Minus on numeric keypad) |
| To decrease spacing 1/100 em | Option+Delete or ⌘+Shift+left arrow | Shift+ Ctrl+ "−" (Minus on numeric keypad) |
| To clear manual kerning from selected text. | ⌘+Option+K | Shift+Ctrl+_ (0 on regular keyboard) |

You can manually kern combinations that have already been automatically pair kerned if you want to change the spacing. Automatic pair kerning doesn't work well for all fonts so you may need to make some adjustments. You can even kern punctuation marks, spaces, or nonprinting characters, such as carriage returns. Since manual kerning is fine tuning, it's generally done as the last step in adjusting letter spacing. If you're kerning type smaller than 25 points, you might not be able to see the effect on-screen unless you're working in an enlarged view. For best results do manual kerning at the 200% or 400% page view.

Figure 6.25 shows how type can be adjusted with manual kerning to give individual letters a more visually pleasing relationship to each other. Automatic pair kerning, since it's done to a mathematical formula, doesn't consider the whole word or the whole page. Letter relationships are affected by the other letters in the word and by such factors as the layout of the page and the leading between lines.

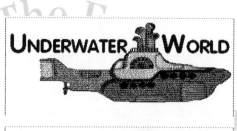

Before
Kerning

After
Kerning

Figure 6.25
Before and
after manual
kerning.

## Watch Out!

*Manual kerning may be inaccurate if you've used odd-sized type without Adobe Type Manager or TrueType. If the type looks jaggy on the screen, don't try manual kerning.*

# Have you tried . . . kerning type around an inline graphic?

Use manual kerning to move the type closer to or further away from the edges of the image.

# Headlines

"It's what's up front that counts" was a popular advertising slogan a few years back. Although the product itself is long forgotten, (the slogan was memorable, but not very effective) the principle it expressed applies wonderfully to the creation of headlines. The headline determines whether or not the reader is going to pay attention to the text which follows. A good headline is bait that hooks the reader and tells, in a few words, what the story will be about. Here are some tips for effective headlines:

- Make your headlines larger than the body text, and set them in a contrasting typeface for maximum clout. Using boldface type also helps.

- A headline has to be brief to fit the space available with large size type. Often you have room for only a few words. That's why you need to make them the right words.

- Ideal point sizes for headlines range from 36 to 72 points, depending on the size of the publication. If you're setting up an ad and the first word is "Sale," it ought to be in big, bold type. Don't overdo it though. Headlines larger than 72 points are hard to read at normal viewing distances.

- Don't capitalize every word of a headline. Capitalize only the most important words and leave the smaller ones in lowercase. Capitalizing every word slows reading comprehension.

- Beware of using fancy typefaces for headlines unless there's a really good reason for it. They're better suited for ads and posters than newsletters or corporate reports.

- Headlines should contrast with body copy. If you're using a serif face for the text, you might use a sans serif face, like Helvetica or Optima, for the headlines.

- In making up pages with several stories on the same page, don't make all the headlines the same size. You should have one obvious lead story per page. The other, less important stories can have more modest headlines. The idea is to keep the stories from competing with each other for the reader's attention.

- Never set headlines in capital letters unless they're only a word or two long. Words set in capital letters are hard to read. Most people read words by recognizing the shapes of their outlines as much as by learning the sounds of the letters. When words are set in capital letters, the reader loses this visual clue, since all the letters are the same height.

## Placing a Headline

When you are placing a headline, always make it a separate text block from the body copy which follows. You can do this in either of two ways:

By typing your headline directly into a new text block.

Or

By cutting the headline from the story you've imported and pasting it into a new block.

Cutting and pasting an existing headline will unthread it from the text which follows so you can work with it without affecting the formatting of the story. Once you have the headline in its own text block, you can extend the block across the page or make it span two columns by selecting it with the pointer, and dragging on a handle. Select it also to change the size and style of type to something suitable for headline use.

Using headlines in a multi-column format can be tricky. Be careful not to place headlines next to each other as they're likely to be read as one continuous line rather than two. This, by the way, is called *tombstoning* because it's reminiscent of the side-by-side stones in old cemeteries. Of course, this can make for some unintentional humor as shown in Figure 6.26.

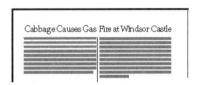

Figure 6.26
Changing the typeface of one headline might help.

The headline should extend over the whole story. If you have a three-column story don't give it a two-column headline. If there's a photo that's part of the story, make sure the headline covers it, too. Conversely, make sure the headline doesn't extend out over a story that's not related to it. To spread a headline across two or more columns, use the following steps.

1.  Separate the text block containing the headline from the rest of the copy by cutting it and repasting it.

2.  Select it with the pointer and drag a corner text block handle as needed, until the text block fits the space available.

To center a headline:

Select it and press ⌘+**Shift**+**C** (**Ctrl**+**Shift**+**C** in Windows), or choose the **Align center** option from the **Alignment** submenu of the **Type** menu.

# Text Rotation

There's a guaranteed way to make a headline get noticed; run it at an angle. You probably wouldn't try this in a newsletter or corporate report, but it can be remarkably effective if you are designing an ad or a flyer. PageMaker 5.0 lets you rotate a text block to any angle you want. You could even break up your headline into individual words or letters and rotate each independently.

Text rotation is accomplished either by using the Text Rotation tool in the Toolbox or by selecting rotation from the Control Palette. First, select the text block. Then select the tool, and click on the corner you want to use as a pivot point. Drag the block to whatever position you want. To rotate to a precise angle, enter it on the Control Palette, and select a pivot point on the object proxy. Then click the **Apply** icon to move the text block (see Figure 6.27). You can still use the Text Insertion tool to click on the rotated text for editing, and you can adjust tracking, kerning, or change the fonts of rotated text, without returning it to normal position.

Figure 6.27 We've rotated individual words and made them part of the design.

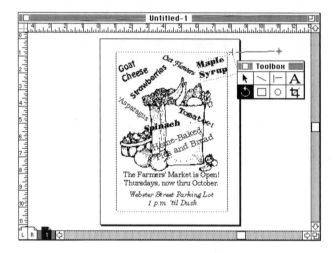

# The Bare Essentials

Many of the skills you need to work with text in PageMaker are skills you've already mastered using a word processor. Formatting paragraphs and specifying fonts aren't all that different, no matter which program you happen to be using. However, PageMaker is designed to handle certain aspects of the job more efficiently and with greater flexibility.

Specifically in this chapter you learned:

- How to import stories into PageMaker. PageMaker accepts text from most word processing programs and ASCII files via modem, or files from PC's linked to the Mac.

- How to place a story, adjust the formatting, define the type and paragraph specifications, and import the text in the designated style.

- How to import longer stories using the Autoflow option to bring in all the text at once. PageMaker will create and fill columns or pages as needed.

- How to import a story into several columns threaded together, and how to break the thread and restore it.

- How to use the Alignment menu to set type flush with either margin: centered or justified. You can force justification to space a headline across a column of text. Use the Indents/tabs ruler or the Paragraph specifications dialog box to set indents and tabs.

- How type heights are measured in points. The space between lines of type is called leading. You can adjust the leading to give more or less space. 120% of the type point size is a good leading size. Thus, 10-point type looks good with 12-point leading.

- How to set the sizes of subscript, superscript, and small caps using the Type specifications dialog box.

- How to adjust the spacing between paragraphs by using the Paragraph specifications dialog box rather than using double carriage returns.

- How to avoid creating widows and orphans, which are misplaced lines of type, by setting a minimum number of lines per paragraph at a column or page break.

- How to track the space between letters and words on a line of type. Kerning is the spacing between individual pairs of letters. PageMaker will kern common pairs automatically or you can kern them manually.

- How to design headlines that are appropriately large and easy to read and how to place headlines over the stories to which they relate.

- How to rotate a text block to any angle.

# Chapter 7

## Chapter Preview

*Using a style sheet*

*Using the Story Editor*

*Finding and changing text*

*Spell checkers and dictionaries*

*Hyphenation*

*Working with links*

# Styles and the Story Editor

In the last chapter, you learned some of the ways to put words on the page and change their appearance. This chapter will teach you about PageMaker's more advanced ways of working with words on the page, such as specifying particular type attributes as a style and applying them to a particular text block or to an entire publication. You'll also learn about the Story Editor and how it can save you time and effort when you need to make changes in a piece of text or check it for spelling errors. Working with linked files is another "advanced" PageMaker skill that can make your page-layout chores much easier.

## Working with Styles

Style sheets may sound like some sort of designer bed linens, but in PageMaker terms, they're much more useful. A *style sheet* contains predefined specifications for headlines, captions, and body copy, called *styles*. Using styles lets you create long documents more easily, and helps you maintain consistency in a publication which uses many different sizes and kinds of type. Following a style sheet is also extremely helpful when there are two or more people working on the same project.

Most word processors let you create and apply styles to paragraphs as you write. You can save time by importing them to PageMaker and using them to format your publication. You can also create style sheets in PageMaker itself, and save them with your templates or publications.

### By the Way . . .

*Be aware that styles refer to more than just a type style, like bold or italic. Style descriptions include everything PageMaker needs to know to format the paragraph, such as type, font and size, indent and tab placement, leading, space before or after, and even color.*

PageMaker maintains a selection of paragraph styles in a *palette.* Select styles from the palette and apply them to your pages, much as you would apply colors to a canvas from a paint palette. PageMaker's Style palette is a small window, like the Toolbox window, and is accessed through the **Window** menu or by pressing ⌘+**Y** (**Ctrl+Y** in Windows). Within this window, you can select from PageMaker's default settings or from styles you've added to the palette. New styles can easily be defined and named within PageMaker, as well as imported from your word processor along with the text.

Use the Style palette to apply styles to text that's already placed in PageMaker. There is really only one rule to remember if you use styles, and that's to be consistent. Apply a style to every paragraph, every headline, every bit of text you type. Otherwise, you haven't really gained any advantage. The purpose of using styles is to insure absolute consistency. If you format your pages with styles, and then decide to make a change, you only need to make it once, in the style definition, and not over and over every time you come to another block of text that's supposed to be in that style.

## Applying an Existing Style

PageMaker has included several default style settings on the Style palette. For example, there's a headline style, one for body text, two styles for subheads, and a style for captions. Even before you learn how to add your own styles to the list, you can practice applying one of these default styles to your text. To apply an existing style:

1.  Use the Text Insertion tool to highlight the text or headline to which you want to apply the style.

2. Press ⌘+Y (**Ctrl+Y** in Windows) to open the Style palette. If the text you arc working with hasn't been formatted with the style sheet, **no style** will be selected, as shown in Figure 7.1.

3. Click on the name of the style to apply. The selected type will change to that style.

Figure 7.1
No style means
none has been
applied. It's
not a criticism
of your page-
design skills.

## Changing Existing Styles

PageMaker automatically keeps a style sheet with every publication (or template). Each new publication that you open has PageMaker's default styles built in. You can use these as they come, or as a jumping off point in creating your own. To change an existing style, use the Edit style box. You can reach this box in one of two ways:

- By selecting **Define styles** from the **Type** menu (or pressing ⌘+3 on the Mac or in Windows press **Ctrl+3**), selecting the name of the style to edit, and then clicking on the **Edit** button.

  Or

- By pressing ⌘ (**Ctrl** in Windows) and clicking on the name of the style to change in the Style palette.

Either way, the Edit style dialog box appears, shown in Figure 7.2. The buttons on the right bring up the Type and Paragraph specifications boxes, the Hyphenation box, and the Indents/tabs ruler that you've already learned to use through the Type menu. The difference between settings you make here in the Edit style box and settings you've previously made in the Type menu is that any settings you make now will apply to the style you're creating, and not to a specific piece of type.

To apply a style, select (with the Text tool) all or part of the paragraph you want to apply it to, and click the name of the style.

The Essential PageMaker

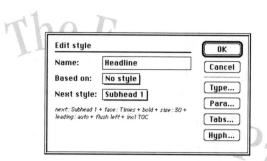

Figure 7.2
Editing a style.

Within the Edit style box, there's a popup menu called Next style. Its purpose is to automate the process of applying styles by letting you specify not only the style you're defining, but the one that will follow it and be applied to the next paragraph. For example, if you define a headline, you can make the next style automatically a subhead. If you've just defined a subhead, you might want to assign body text as the next style. Since the style is applied every time you change paragraphs, you may want to specify same style as next, especially in the case of body text, where you could have many paragraphs of the same style. If you change an existing style after it's been applied to one or more text blocks, the changes will also be applied to those text blocks.

## Creating a New Style

Sometimes, making a minor change or two to an existing style isn't enough. What's really needed is a brand new style. For example, say you want to define several different kinds of headlines. PageMaker's defaults provide you with one which you can edit as you see fit, but you'd like to add two or three new ones. This can be done through the Define styles box. The Define styles dialog box contains a list of all the styles in the Style palette. To base your new style on an existing one:

1.  Press ⌘+3 (**Ctrl+3** in Windows) or select **Define styles** from the **Type** menu to open the Define styles box, shown in Figure 7.3.

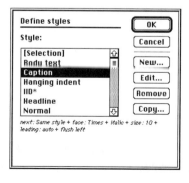

Figure 7.3
The Define
styles box.

2.  Select the style you want to use as a basis for your new one by clicking on it in the scrolling menu.

3.  After the style is highlighted, click on the **New** button. The Edit style box opens (as in Figure 7.2) with the Name box empty.

4.  Enter the name for your new style, and then make whatever changes are needed to the specifications for the new style. Use the **Type** and **Para** buttons to open the Type and Paragraph specifications boxes so you can change the attributes.

If you already have a piece of formatted text that looks good, and you want to apply the same formatting attributes elsewhere in your publication, you can save the formatting as a style. Then, you can apply that style to other text blocks. Here's how to do it.

1.  Select the paragraph or click an insertion point anywhere within the text.

2.  Open the Define styles box (Figure 7.3). The style attributes for your chosen text are listed in the lower part of the dialog box.

3.  Open the Edit style box (by double-clicking **[Selection]** on the list of styles) to make any additional modifications.

4.  Assign the style a name, and click on **OK** to save it to the style sheet.

To create a style from scratch:

1.  Open the Define styles box.

2.  Choose **New**, and then enter a name for your style.

3.  Select the appropriate buttons (Type, Para, and so on) from the Edit style dialog box to change the style's attributes.

4.  Click on **OK** when done. Select it from the Style palette to use it.

### Watch Out!
*Assign style names by function to avoid confusion. You'll have a much easier time telling the difference between styles called Body Text and Caption, for example, than you would if you had to choose between styles called Optima 11 and Futura Demi 12.*

## Using a Style Sheet

Keeping a style sheet helps you avoid using the wrong font for a headline or text block. For example, if you set up a subhead style in Helvetica

Bold 14-point, and apply the style to all subheads, your publication will end up with a more consistent look.

However, there are a few pitfalls in using the style sheet. If you make additional changes (through the Type menus or Type specifications dialog box) in a text block that has style sheet formatting applied, you will lose these changes if you then make any other changes that affect the style sheet. For example, suppose your style sheet definition of subheads is based on the Normal body copy style, using Helvetica as the normal text and subhead face. You then change one subhead to Helvetica Medium italic, using the Type menu. Now you decide that the body copy should be in a serif face, and you change the style sheet to make Palatino 12 your normal font. Suddenly, your Helvetica Medium italic subhead, and everything else in your document with a style based on some variation of normal, turns into Palatino. New styles which are based on existing styles become permanently threaded to a style chain. If you change the style at the head of the chain, all other styles threaded to it will change accordingly.

In PageMaker for Windows, to use the keyboard to assign styles to your document, press the key combination **Alt+T** and then **S**. Then use the arrow keys to scroll down the Style submenu to the style you want to apply. If you give your style alphabetical names, you can use the keyboard even more efficiently by first pressing **Alt+T,S** and then the first letter of the style name. If more than one style begins with the letter, PageMaker will only go to the first such name on the list, so make your names unique. Note that you cannot use a hyphen in a style name.

# Copying a Style Sheet

After you've created a set of styles for a publication, you can reuse that style sheet in your next publication. Just copy them from one PageMaker publication to another. This will save you from having to re-enter the styles again or trying to remember what they were. You can also use the Copy styles feature if you are creating a long document, such as a book or instruction manual, that might be set in several chapters and you need to maintain the same styles throughout. You can copy a style sheet from another PageMaker publication by:

1   Clicking on the **Copy** button in the Define styles box. This opens the Copy styles box shown in Figure 7.4.

2.   Choose the publication whose style sheet you want to copy.

3.   Click on **OK**. PageMaker will copy all of that publication's styles into the current document. If any styles have the same names, an Alert box will appear asking whether you want the new styles

to replace the existing styles. Click on **OK** to continue, and the styles will be copied into your current document, where you can use and modify them.

Figure 7.4
The Copy styles
dialog box.

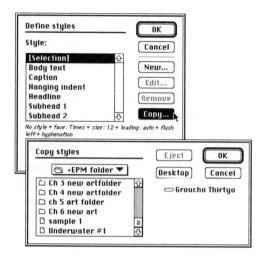

By the Way . . .

*Use the Copy styles feature when your publication is part of a series (like a monthly newsletter or individual chapters of a book) to maintain a consistent look.*

When you import text from a word processing program that uses style sheets (like WordPerfect, Microsoft Word and so on), you can import the word processor's style sheet along with the text. To do so, simply click on the **Retain formats** button in the Place dialog box. When you place the document into PageMaker, the styles will come through along with the words, as long as they're compatible with PageMaker's styles. PageMaker will add the word processor's styles to its style sheet and Style submenu, with an asterisk after the name to distinguish them from PageMaker's own styles.

Watch Out!

*Be careful. If imported styles have the same name as PageMaker's own styles, PageMaker will use its own styles and ignore the imported ones.*

## Using Style Name Tags

If you're working in your word processor and want to save time when placing text into PageMaker, enter the copy as plain text, unformatted,

and put a style name tag at the head of the copy in angle brackets (<>). Be sure the tags you apply exactly the same style names that are listed on the style palette. If PageMaker can't find the style you want to apply, it won't be able to apply it. For example, start a story like this:

<headline> Challengers Sweep Town Election

<subhead> Incumbents stunned at loss

<normal> In a "throw the bums out" mood, local voters elected two new Aldermen, three new library trustees, new school committee members, and a new town clerk yesterday, in the only election in town history in which all of the incumbents lost.

Following paragraphs, as long as they use the same format, don't need additional tags. PageMaker will apply the tag to each subsequent paragraph until it finds another style tag, or until the story ends. When you get ready to place the story into your PageMaker publication, check the **Read tags** option in the Place box. PageMaker locates the tags and applies the designated styles to each paragraph.

You must import tagged stories through the Place box. Using the Clipboard or Scrapbook will not let PageMaker recognize the tags as tags. Instead they'd be brought in as additional text. You can also export stories from PageMaker to a word processor along with their Style Name Tags. To do so, check **Export styles** in the **Export** dialog box, as explained later in this chapter.

### Watch Out!

*Be careful when assigning styles, because you cannot undo them. The only way to return to your previous formatting is to select **Revert** from the **File** menu and go back to the last version saved. It's a good idea to save frequently while you work, and always save before experimenting with styles.*

# Overriding Styles

Sometimes, you'll want to change a single word within a formatted paragraph. There may be a phrase, such as a title, that needs to be italicized or a word that needs to be in boldface for added emphasis. Do this by selecting the word or words to be changed, and modifying them as needed. When you modify a style, a plus sign (+) will follow the name of the style in the Style palette and Style menu, when just those words are selected, to indicate that the style has been overridden. Such overrides are permanent. They'll remain even if you change the format of the paragraph. For example, if you format a paragraph in Helvetica medium and you make a single word bold, when you change the face from Helvetica to Palatino, the emphasized word will switch to Palatino bold.

**By the Way . . .**
*An exception to permanent override occurs when, for example, you've italicized a few words in a paragraph and then decide to set the whole paragraph in a style that includes italics. The previously italicized words will become plain text, since PageMaker seeks to preserve the contrast in styles.*

Type style (italic, bold, and so on) is a permanent attribute, but other changes you might make, such as point size, hyphenation, leading, tabs and indents, are all temporary overrides. If you later apply a style having the same attributes, you'll remove your changes. For example, if you had a line of 12-point type, and you wanted to say **WOW!** in the middle of it in 14-point type, you'd change the word **WOW!** to 14 points. That would be a temporary override. Suppose later that you decided to make that whole paragraph 14-point type, or even 10-point type. The **WOW!**, even though you'd intended it to be two points larger, would change to the same size as everything else. So changing the rest of the paragraph removes the previous change.

**By the Way . . .**
*There's a way to preserve temporary overrides when you change styles. To keep them intact when you apply a new style, hold down **Shift** while you click on the style name in the Style palette. Your paragraphs will change to reflect the new style, but the temporary overrides will remain unchanged.*

# The Story Editor

Although PageMaker lets you edit text while you're looking at page layouts, this isn't always the most convenient way to do it. Most PageMaker users prefer to handle text editing within PageMaker's Story Editor. It lets you focus on the content of the words rather than on their appearance on the page. It also saves you time, because the story scrolls as it would in any other word processor, rather than your having to move from one page to another to see the continuation. Most important, PageMaker's Spelling checker and Search and Replace functions are only available in the Story Editor view.

# Opening Story Editor

To edit a story, position the cursor anywhere within it, and either select **Edit story** from the bottom of the **Edit** menu, or press ⌘+E (**Ctrl+E** or **Alt+E,E** in Windows). Your story will appear in Story Editor format, as shown in Figure 7.5. Story Editor opens as a text-only window on top of the Page layout view, with the first few words of the story as the title. PageMaker considers text blocks that are threaded together to be a single story. Because the story is saved as part of the publication, it doesn't need a separate title. Pressing ⌘+E when you're in Story Editor will take you back to your publication, as will clicking anywhere outside the Story window.

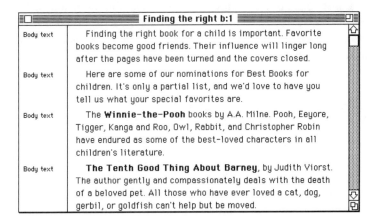

| | Finding the right b:1 |
|---|---|
| Body text | Finding the right book for a child is important. Favorite books become good friends. Their influence will linger long after the pages have been turned and the covers closed. |
| Body text | Here are some of our nominations for Best Books for children. It's only a partial list, and we'd love to have you tell us what your special favorites are. |
| Body text | The **Winnie-the-Pooh** books by A.A. Milne. Pooh, Eeyore, Tigger, Kanga and Roo, Owl, Rabbit, and Christopher Robin have endured as some of the best-loved characters in all children's literature. |
| Body text | **The Tenth Good Thing About Barney**, by Judith Viorst. The author gently and compassionately deals with the death of a beloved pet. All those who have ever loved a cat, dog, gerbil, or goldfish can't help but be moved. |

Figure 7.5
The Story
Editor view.

The Story Editor doesn't show your formatting, except for type styles such as bold or italic. Instead, it uses a generic font like Geneva and lists the names of your assigned paragraph styles, if any, to the left of the story. (You can change the font and point size of the text in the Story Editor by selecting **Preferences** from the **File** menu, and then selecting the **Other** button.)

## Assigning a Style in Story Editor

If you haven't formatted your text, there will be a dot next to each paragraph or headline, and No Style will be highlighted on the Style palette. It means that the text has not had a style sheet attached to it, even though you might have designated a particular face and size using the Type specifications box. Empty lines also have dots indicating No style. If the style has been applied, it will be highlighted on the Style palette, as shown in Figure 7.6.

Figure 7.6
The Style
palette
highlights the
style of
selected text.

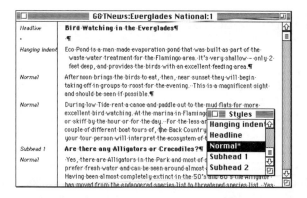

If a style is already defined, you can use the Story Editor to assign it. For example, if you've already designated a style called body copy, it's easy to open your story in Story Editor, select the paragraphs to be put into the body copy style, and click on the style name in your Style palette.

## Word Processing in Story Editor

Once you're in the Story Editor, you can add, remove, cut, copy, and paste text as much as you like, just as you would with any other word processing program. Any changes you make in the Story Editor will immediately be reflected in your copy. You probably won't see them; however, as PageMaker grays out the corresponding text blocks in the Layout window, as shown in Figure 7.7.

Figure 7.7
Text in the
page layout
grayed out
behind the
Story Editor
window.

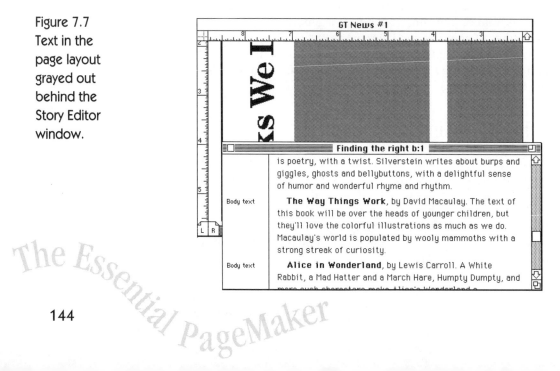

You can toggle back and forth between Story Editor view and Layout view by pressing ⌘+E (**Ctrl+E** in Windows) to see how your changes are affecting the rest of the page. When you leave the Story window, the text automatically reflows back onto the page. Any changes you've made in Story view will appear in Layout view. If you're not finished editing, leave the Story window open. Pressing ⌘+E (**Ctrl+E** in Windows) always takes you to the same point in Layout view that you were at in Story view.

PageMaker lets you open several Story windows at the same time, making it easy to cut, copy, and paste between them. Each window holds one story. To work with several Story windows at once, select the stories you want to edit (one at a time), and press ⌘+E (**Ctrl+E** in Windows) to open them in the Story Editor. The windows will overlap, but you can resize them to see two stories at once, or to conveniently cut and paste from one to another. You can also start a new story by pressing ⌘+E (**Ctrl+E** in Windows) while you're in Layout view with no text selected. An untitled story window opens. Figure 7.8 shows several stories being edited in the Story Editor.

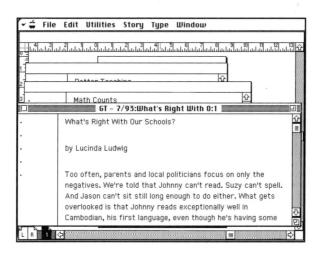

Figure 7.8
Working with
several open
stories.

**By the Way . . .**
*When you have two windows with the same name, the second will be called :2.*

# Placing a New Story

If the story is new, or hasn't been previously placed, closing the Story Editor brings up a dialog box, shown in Figure 7.9, reminding you that the story has not been placed.

- If you choose **Place**, you'll be returned to the Layout view with a text icon ready to place the story.

- **Discard** (obviously) clears the Story Editor without saving the story.

- If you click on **Cancel**, the story will remain in the Story window and will be saved, unplaced, with the publication. Cancel returns you to the Story Editor.

Figure 7.9
The Alert box
forces you to
decide what
to do with the
story.

If you change your mind about placing a story after the Text icon appears, just click on the **Pointer** tool in the **Tool** box, and you'll return to Story view so you can continue to edit. If you want to save the story without placing it in the publication, you could place it on the pasteboard, and it would be saved as part of the publication.

But suppose your answer is "None of the Above." Perhaps you want to keep the story for a future issue. Saving it with this publication is a good way to misplace it. Since it wouldn't have a separate title, you'd have no way to locate it without opening the publication and hunting for it. What you should do, in this case, is save it separately in the folder of newsletter materials. This is easy, thanks to PageMaker's Export function. You can save whole stories or selected blocks of text. The latter is especially helpful if you have a story that's too long for your present publication, and you decide to break it up and run it in two consecutive issues. Follow these steps to export a story.

1. First, make sure the story to save is in the Active window in Story Editor, or select it from the pasteboard.

2. Choose **Export** from the **File** menu. The Export dialog box (called "Export document" in Windows) appears, as shown in Figure 7.10.

3. Locate the folder or disk to save to (in Windows you locate the directory icon from its list and the disk from its list), and give the story a name.

4. Click on the **Export tags** box if the story has been formatted and you want to save style tags with it.

5. Under File format, select the appropriate format in which to save it.

6. Click on **OK** when finished. The story will be saved as a file in whatever folder (or Windows directory) to which you assigned it.

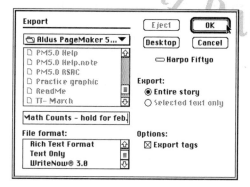

Figure 7.10
The Export
dialog box.

## By the Way . . .

*When you installed PageMaker, you selected import/export filters, which convert your word processor's text into PageMaker and vice versa. If you use several different word processors, you can choose among them or save your file as text only. If you've done a lot of formatting, use Microsoft Word, WordPerfect, or RTF (Rich Text Format) to preserve the majority of all formatting commands. (RTF is an interchange format used primarily to transfer files back and forth between Macs and PCs. Most popular word processors will open files in RTF.)*

*Since PageMaker for Windows does not export files directly into Word for Windows, but rather only into Windows' own Write for Windows, use the RTF filter to retain formatting, and open the saved RTF file in Word for Windows. PageMaker for Windows has filters for MS Word for DOS 3.0, MS Write for Windows 2.0, WordPerfect 5.0, and XyWrite III, so you can export your documents directly into those formats.*

*Although RTF can preserve formatting, it is an unstable format (in Windows) that should be avoided if you have another format available. For instance, Word 5.1 on the Mac will open many alien formats, including WordPerfect, Word for Windows, DOS Word, WriteNow, and MacWrite. Try to save your documents as Word files, if possible, since it is the most accurate format available and doesn't throw in extraneous ASCII codes and tabs as do many other filtering processes.*

Styles and the Story Editor          147

Occasionally you may encounter the box shown in Figure 7.11. A story may fail to import if the computer's memory is already full. This can happen when you are running PageMaker, and one or two other applications, such as Microsoft Word and a graphics program, all at the same time. In such a case, place the story on the pasteboard, or just leave the file open, and close down the other applications. Then try again. It should export without any trouble.

Figure 7.11
If you see this
Alert box,
you're prob-
ably out of
memory.

# Find and Change

On Story Editor's Edit menu (in Windows, look on the Utilities menu), there are two functions familiar to everyone who uses word processors: Find and Change. Find and Change are a big help in editing text. They can help you locate a key word in a long story without needing to read through the entire piece. Change can correct spellings of names, or other words that you don't want to make a permanent part of your dictionary. You can make changes either case by case or globally, meaning at every occurrence throughout your story or publication. Figure 7.12 shows the Change dialog box.

Figure 7.12
The Change
dialog box.

Find, Change, Change all, and Change and Find work exactly as you'd expect. You can also use wild card characters, a caret (^) and question mark (?), to help in your search. The wild card character set (^?)

functions as a joker does in a card game, replacing any other character instead of any other card in the deck. The two characters, the caret and question mark, must be used together to represent a wild card. PageMaker doesn't recognize any other characters or combinations as wild cards. Suppose you wanted to find forms of the verb "to ride" in a long story. In the Find box, you could enter **r ^ ?de**. PageMaker would match the other letters and ignore the wild card, catching both **ride** and **rode** in the same search.

PageMaker also lets you find and change text by its type font, size, style, or formatting. PageMaker lets you look not only in a text block or story being edited, but also in every story in your publication, and in all open publications. It can't, however, search for text that was placed as part of a graphic, because it doesn't recognize the difference between pictures and words within the graphic block.

### By the Way . . .

*The Change box can remain on-screen in the background while you use menu and editing commands. You can move it to an unoccupied corner of your screen and bring it forward when you want to use it.*

Finding and Changing text by its attributes is done through the Attributes box and its popup menus. If you're changing text format attributes:

1. Leave the Find what and Change to boxes empty, and click on **Attributes**.

2. Select the attribute to be changed from the popup menus, and then indicate the changes. In Figures 7.13 and 7.14, we're changing from one subhead style (already assigned) to another.

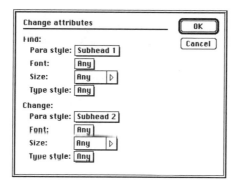

Figure 7.13
The Change attributes box provides an easy way to correct minor formatting errors.

Figure 7.14
The Change
attributes box
in Windows
looks different
but provides
the same
features as the
Mac version.

Change attributes

**Find:**

Para style: Subhead 1
Font: Any
Size: Any

Type style:
☒ Any       ☐ Underline      ☐ All caps
☐ Normal    ☐ Strikethru     ☐ Small caps
☐ Bold      ☐ Reverse        ☐ Superscript
☐ Italic                     ☐ Subscript

**Change :**

Para style: Subhead 2
Font: Any
Size: Any

Type style:
☒ Any       ☐ Underline      ☐ All caps
☐ Normal    ☐ Strikethru     ☐ Small caps
☐ Bold      ☐ Reverse        ☐ Superscript
☐ Italic                     ☐ Subscript

OK        Cancel

### Watch Out!

*If you enter a word in Find what and then select Match case, PageMaker will find only words which appear exactly as you've typed them. A word typed in lowercase will be missed if it happens to be capitalized because it starts a sentence. A search for PageMaker will not find Pagemaker.*

To find and change a word:

1.  Press ⌘+E (**Ctrl+E** in Windows) to enter Story view. (Change and Find doesn't work in Layout view.)

2.  Press ⌘+9 (**Ctrl+9** in Windows) to open the Change box.

3.  Enter the changes in the fields. Choose **Whole word** and **Match case**, if you want. Not choosing Whole word means PageMaker will find your word inside other words. (For example, changing *in* to *out* could give you *outtroduction* or turn *fine* into *foute*.)

4.  Select the text to be searched. You can search a particular block, the active story, or all the stories in your publication.

5.  Press **Enter** or **Return**, or click on **Find** or **Change all**, if you are sure you want to change every occurrence. The searched-for word will be highlighted when it is found.

6.  Click on **Change** or **Find next**. PageMaker takes you to the next occurrence of the word. If a story containing the target word isn't open in Story Editor, PageMaker will open it.

7.  Continue until you are done. Don't forget to save your changes.

PageMaker for Windows and the Mac supports codes for special characters that you can use in the Find and Change boxes to make your life easier. Table 7.1 lists these special character codes and their meanings.

Table 7.1   Special Characters

| Special Character | What It Means |
|---|---|
| ^p | Paragraph end (Enter key) |
| ^n | New-line (Shift+Enter) |
| ^t | Tab |
| ^- | Soft hyphen |
| ^s | Non-breaking space |
| ^^ | Caret |
| ^? | Wild card |
| ^w | White space |
| ^< | Thin space |
| ^> | En space |
| ^m | Em space |
| ^= | En dash |
| ^_ | Em dash |
| ^[Alt+126] | Hard hyphen |
| ^3 | Page number token |
| ^g | Inline graphic |
| ^; | Index entry |

You can also perform a search in PageMaker for Windows using an ANSI character set by typing the character's code into the Find text box. Turn on the **Number Lock** key, hold down the **Alt** key and type **O** and the number of the character. The ANSI character appears in the text box, and the search is performed for that character.

# Viewing Invisible Characters

No, we don't mean seeing pink elephants or even Harvey (the six-foot-tall white rabbit whom Jimmy Stewart brought to life). These invisible characters don't require an active imagination, just a few keystrokes. In PageMaker, *invisible characters* are those that don't print but do affect your text, such as carriage returns, space markers, and tabs. Story Editor lets you see them, which is helpful when you have a line of type that just doesn't seem to be leaded correctly. It could be that one of these invisible characters is upsetting the leading or spacing because it's in the wrong font. Once you find the tab, return, or other invisible character which is messing up your text, you can change or remove it.

To show invisible characters, open the story in **Story** view. Select **Display** from the **Story** menu. The hidden characters will appear. The spaces between words are represented by dots, paragraphs by the ¶ symbol, and tabs by arrows. To solve the leading problem shown in Figure 7.15, isolate pieces of the line and look at the Point size menu, shown in Figure 7.16. If the words selected are in the same point size, they'll be checked. When you find a space and word that isn't checked, you've found the problem. To fix it, delete the space and the letters on either side, and retype them. By replacing a space in the wrong point size with one in the right size, you've solved the leading problem.

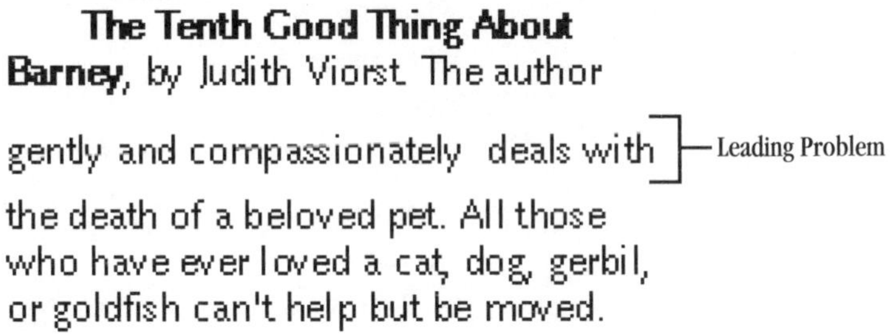

Figure 7.15
Text with a leading problem.

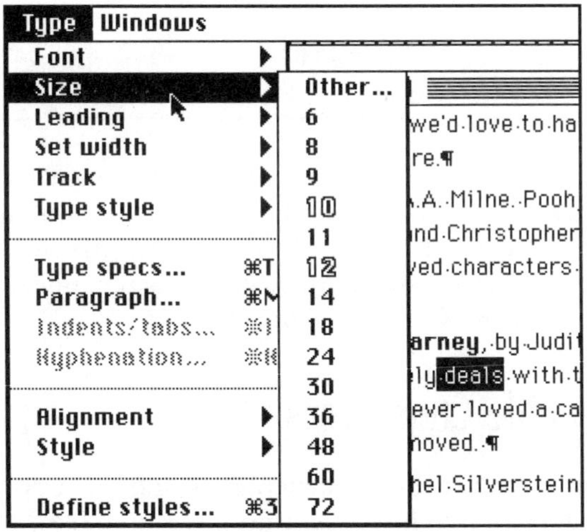

**The Tenth Good Thing About Barney,** by Judith Viorst The author

gently and compassionately  deals with ⎤—Leading Problem

the death of a beloved pet. All those who have ever loved a cat, dog, gerbil, or goldfish can't help but be moved.

Figure 7.16
The Point size menu.

| Type | Windows | | |
|---|---|---|---|
| Font | ▶ | | |
| Size | ▶ | Other... | |
| Leading | ▶ | 6 | we'd·love·to·ha |
| Set width | ▶ | 8 | re.¶ |
| Track | ▶ | 9 | .A.·Milne.·Pooh |
| Type style | ▶ | 10 | nd·Christopher |
| | | 11 | ved·characters· |
| Type specs... | ⌘T | 12 | |
| Paragraph... | ⌘M | 14 | |
| Indents/tabs... | ⌘I | 18 | arney,·by·Judi |
| Hyphenation... | ⌘H | 24 | ly·deals·with·t |
| | | 30 | |
| Alignment | ▶ | 36 | ever·loved·a·ca |
| Style | ▶ | 48 | noved.·¶ |
| | | 60 | hel·Silverstein |
| Define styles... | ⌘3 | 72 | |

Story Editor will also display invisible characters to show the position of inline graphics, page numbers, and index entries. You can cut, copy, paste, and delete these characters, and the elements they represent will be moved or removed on the layout. You can also import pictures into the Story Editor, although you won't see them. They'll appear as inline graphics characters in Story Editor and as the actual graphics in your layout when you place the story. Figure 7.17 shows the different kinds of markers you're likely to use.

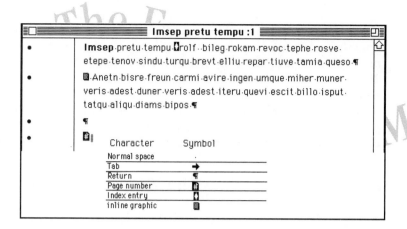

Figure 7.17
Invisible
characters of
all kinds.

# The Spell Checker

PageMaker includes a 100,000 word spelling dictionary, available while you're working in the Story Editor. You can also install dictionaries in other languages if your publications are multilingual. You can check spelling in only one language at a time, however. It is *un poco* nuisance for *todo el mundo* who like to show off their linguistic *savoir-faire*. Dictionaries, if you have more than one, are chosen from the popup menu in the Paragraph specifications dialog box, shown in Figure 7.18. The grayed out dictionaries in the list are not currently installed.

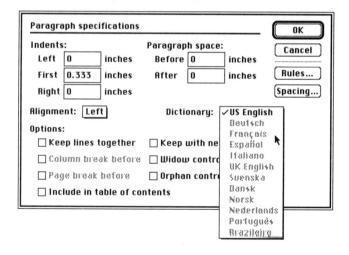

Figure 7.18
Choosing
dictionaries
from the
Paragraph
specifications
box.

Additional dictionaries are available directly from Aldus Corporation or your Aldus distributor. Sets include Central European (French, Italian, German, Dutch); Scandinavian (Swedish, Norwegian, Danish);

Spanish & Portuguese (includes Brazilian Portuguese); American English, and British English. Both English versions include your choice of a free Legal or Medical supplement. The Legal dictionary covers over 28,000 words from law, accounting, and finance. The Medical dictionary contains over 35,000 entries from Webster's Medical Desk Dictionary, including biology and chemistry terms, and abbreviations used in prescriptions. Each dictionary package includes complete installation instructions. Installation is simple and requires only a minute or two.

# Have you tried . . . adding your name, company name, and other frequently used terms to the dictionary?

Proper names, trademarks, and other words PageMaker doesn't already know will be queried each time you check spelling unless you add them to the dictionary. But, once you do so, it will catch mistakes you make when typing them.

## Checking Spelling

To check spelling, choose the **Spelling** command from the **Story** view's **Utilities** menu, or press ⌘+**L**. The Spelling box appears, as shown in Figure 7.19. Check a specific word or paragraph by highlighting it. Use the buttons in the Spelling box to check the story you're working on, or even all the stories in your publication. Click on **Start** or press **Enter** or **Return** to begin the spelling check. PageMaker scans for unrecognized words in the selected text block or stories.

Figure 7.19
The Spelling
dialog box.

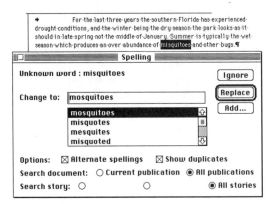

As with most spell checkers, Page-Maker highlights the unrecognized word and displays it in the Change to field. The Edit window will scroll to display the misspelled word, although you may have to move the Spelling box to see it. The questioned word is also displayed in the Unknown word field, and a list of possible substitutes is given.

If your word is correct, click on the **Ignore** button or just press **Enter** or **Return**. Otherwise, select the correct word from the list PageMaker gives you. If none of PageMaker's guesses are correct, type the correct word into the Change to field, and click on the **Replace** button. PageMaker will ignore correct words that reoccur after it has questioned them once.

If you want PageMaker to add your word to its dictionary, click on the **Add** button. PageMaker opens the Add word to user dictionary dialog box shown in Figure 7.20. It verifies the spelling and case of the word and shows you its correct hyphenation, according to grammar rules programmed into PageMaker. (PageMaker uses the same dictionary to check spelling and hyphenation.) You can also choose which dictionary to add it to. If you select **Exactly as typed**, PageMaker will query the word whenever it doesn't exactly match the entry. For example, if the word is capitalized, it will be questioned. Click on **OK** or press **Enter** or **Return** to enter the word and close the box.

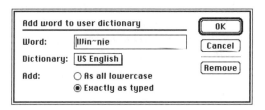

Figure 7.20 Teach PageMaker any words you think it needs to know.

If you tell PageMaker once to ignore a word, it will continue to ignore it for as long as the program remains active. If you quit and then reopen PageMaker, when you do another spelling check, words previously ignored will be queried again. PageMaker will give you an appropriate message if no errors are found.

PageMaker can also catch a few other errors, as Figure 7.21 shows. In this case, a typographical error was made because a sentence was started with **he** instead of **The**. PageMaker queried the mistake. It can also spot repeated word errors, **like like this**. Unlike most dialog boxes, which demand immediate responses, you can leave PageMaker's Check Spelling and Change dialog boxes active while you work on other parts of your publication. You can't resize the boxes, but you can use menu commands and editing procedures while they are on-screen. They may remove themselves to a layer behind the active window, but pressing ⌘+L (**Ctrl+L** in Windows) or ⌘+9 (**Ctrl+9** in Windows), brings the Spelling or Change boxes to the front again.

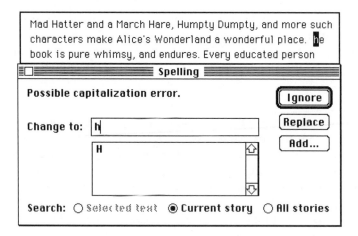

**By the Way . . .**
*When you are working on a compact Mac or any computer with a small screen, you might find it more convenient to move the Spelling box to the bottom of the screen and resize the Story window so you can see both at the same time. Documents which have a lot of spelling errors may need to have their formatting adjusted. Adding or removing even one character can throw off a line of text, especially if the text is justified.*

# Hyphenation

Hyphenation helps your text to flow into nice, even columns by breaking words into pieces where necessary to make lines of equal length. Unfortunately, hyphenation is distracting to read. Ideally, only a few words should be broken up, so your page can look good without putting a strain on the reader. But column widths and word lengths are not always ideal. Hyphenation is a compromise between design and readability. PageMaker offers several ways to handle hyphenating words: you can do it yourself; let PageMaker do it (according to the hyphenation information in its dictionary); or use a set of algorithms built into the dictionary, which can even hyphenate unknown or nonsense words. To apply hyphenation:

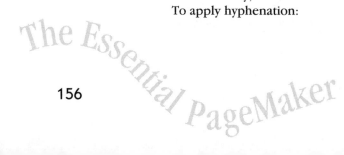

1. Press ⌘+H (**Ctrl+H** in Windows) or select Hyphenation from the **Type** menu. The dialog box shown in Figure 7.22 appears.

2. To turn on automatic hyphenation, click on the **On** button. Automatic hyphenation will remain on until you turn it off. (When you open a new publication, it's on by default.)

**By the Way . . .**
*Algorithms are formulas that a computer uses to compute things like hyphenations. They're rules expressed in an if:then format.*

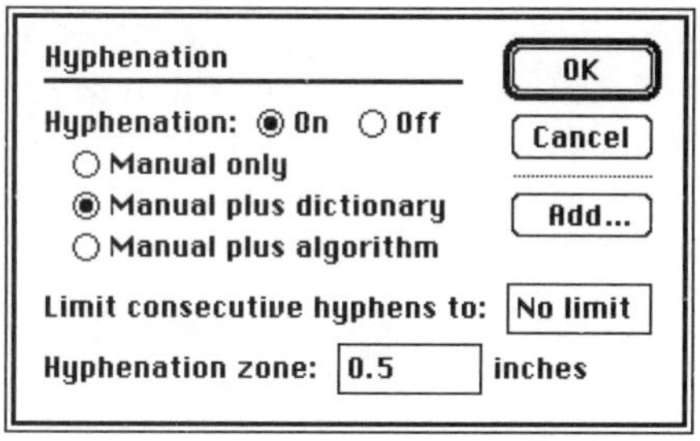

Figure 7.22
The Hyphenation dialog box.

In the Hyphenation box, you can choose any of the following options.

# Manual Only

**Manual only** means that PageMaker will break words only where you have inserted *discretionary hyphens* by typing a hyphen (-). Discretionary hyphens are invisible unless needed. If you reflow the text, you won't end up with a hyphen in the middle of the line, as you would if you simply broke it. Manual only gives you the most control over how your page will look. You can fit copy more accurately than when PageMaker is doing the job automatically. Of course it takes longer, but on the other hand, you don't have to clean up mistakes PageMaker has made. (Algorithms aren't perfect.)

# Manual Plus Dictionary

**Manual plus dictionary** tells PageMaker to use its dictionary for hyphenation. Any discretionary hyphens you've inserted manually will also be used, if needed. The words will be broken based on the priorities given within the dictionary. A word may have several places at which it could be broken. Depending on the space available, PageMaker will choose the most preferred hyphenation first. You can also insert discretionary hyphenation breaks and assign your own priorities, in the PageMaker dictionary.

To assign hyphenation priorities, click on **Add** in the Hyphenation box, or choose the **Spelling** command in the Story Editor. Enter the new word adding one, two, or three *tilde* (Alt+126) symbols where you want a word to break. The single tilde break has the highest priority. If you have a trademark or other word you don't ever want hyphenated, add that word without hyphens and place a tilde directly in front of it, with no space in between. What you're doing is placing a discretionary hyphen in front of the word. PageMaker will never hyphenate any word with a tilde in front of it. Discretionary hyphens you've added to your story will apply only within the publication on which you are working. Words and discretionary hyphens added to the dictionary are part of it, unless removed.

## Manual Plus Algorithm

With **Manual plus algorithm**, PageMaker uses not only the dictionary and your discretionary hyphenations, but goes to the rules programmed into it to see how a word not in the dictionary is hyphenated within the grammar of whichever language you're using. Each PageMaker dictionary contains hyphenation *algorithms* for its language. This choice obviously gives you the most flexibility. You can always override PageMaker's hyphenation by inserting a discretionary hyphen where you'd rather have the word break. You can remove a discretionary hyphen at the end of a line by backspacing over it. This will force the word to the next line. To remove a discretionary hyphen in a word in the middle of the line, select the word, delete it, and retype it.

## Setting the Hyphenation Zone

You may set an amount of space to consider a *hyphenation zone*. In a nonjustified (ragged right) line, the raggedness is a function of how large or small an area you specify. Allowing fewer picas will give you a more even right edge. Justified text is not affected by a hyphenation zone, as all words needing to be broken will be, and the spacing will be adjusted to make them fit. Press ⌘+**H** (**Ctrl+H** in Windows) to open the Hyphenation box. Enter a new value into the Hyphenation zone field. The smaller the number, the less ragged the right margin will be. Click on **OK**, or press **Enter** or **Return** to confirm your settings and close the box.

You may also want to set a limit for the number of consecutive lines PageMaker can hyphenate. When you have a large number of consecutive lines of type hyphenated, the row of dashes at the right of the column tend to look like fringe, or possibly rungs of a ladder. Figure 7.23 shows an exaggerated example. To prevent this, set the limit for consecutive hyphens to some reasonable number such as two, even though PageMaker allows you to have up to 255! You can also type **No limit**, if you don't want to limit the number of hyphenated lines. Typing **0** instead of No limit makes a dialog box appear reminding you that 0 is an invalid number.

Lorem ipsum dolor sit amet, con-
sectetuer adipiscing elit, sed nonu-
mmy nibh euismod tincid laoree-
amm dolore magna aliquam volu-
tpat. Ut wisi enim ad minim venia-
manno nostrud exercitation ullam-
coper suscipit lobortis nisl ut aliqui-

Figure 7.23
Too much
hyphenation!

# Working with Linked Text

Before we explain linking, let's back up a little and think about what PageMaker is. It's a program that you use to combine the text and graphics files you've created in other programs. Pagemaker's purpose is to assemble pages, not to be a word processor or a paint program. To make it easier to use files from your word processor and graphics programs, the authors of PageMaker invented the concept of *links*. They did so several years before Apple came up with System 7's Publish and Subscribe feature, and well before Microsoft brought OLE technology to the PC.

Links are, quite simply, a relationship between the source and the publication in which it's placed. Whenever you import a text or graphics file into PageMaker, the version you see in your publication is linked to its original document. Links serve two useful functions: they let you update PageMaker's version of a file automatically, whenever the original is changed, and they let you work with smaller PageMaker publications by storing imported graphics outside of the publication.

Let's say, for the sake of illustration, that you write a book using Microsoft Word. You create your diagrams and pictures in FreeHand. You plan to use PageMaker to combine them and set up pages in a ready to print format. Now, you open a new file called *Chapter 1* in PageMaker, and you place the text of Chapter 1 from the file you saved in Word. (You haven't trashed the Word file, just basically copied it into PM.) You do the same for the diagrams and pictures. The graphics are still out there somewhere on your disk, but you've copied them into PM and placed them in the middle of text. Now, when you placed the text into PM, it gave itself a little note that said something like this, "Text came from a Word file called Ch.1, in the Book folder, on the Mac's HD disk." Only it did it in shorthand, like this:

**Location: Mac's HD: Book folder: Ch.1.**
**Kind: Text**

**Size: 50 K**

And, for each graphic, it made a similar note. So when you open the PageMaker file called **Chapter 1**, the first thing PageMaker does is to check its notes and take a quick peek at the original files. It's looking to see if there's something new in the Word file called **Chapter 1** that it hasn't been told about. If there is, PM either automatically updates its file or sends you a note on your screen asking if you want to update.

Links are generally handled in exactly the same way, whether they are PageMaker links, OLE-linked or embedded objects, or Apple System 7 editions. The notes PageMaker keeps about which of the stories and graphics you've placed came from its link information. It keeps track of all this automatically, whether you need it or not.

Sometimes, it's unnecessary if you're the only one using PM, entering data for the publication and managing to do all your editing in Story Editor instead of your word processor. On the other hand, if you're editing Chapter 1, while the graphics department is creating the art, and the layout people are doing the page makeup in PageMaker, and everyone's sending files back and forth like crazy, PageMaker's link function is absolutely the only way to make sure that the current version of the words you're editing are going into the book. Because PageMaker is used by people at all levels of publishing, it has some tools that aren't necessary in all situations. But links can be helpful for all kinds of publications, so it's a good idea to learn how to use them.

# Getting Link Information

To get information about linked stories, open the **Links** dialog box in the **File** menu, or press ⌘+= (**Shift+Ctrl+D** in Windows). The Links box shown in Figures 7.24 and 7.25 appears. To get more detailed information on any of your source files:

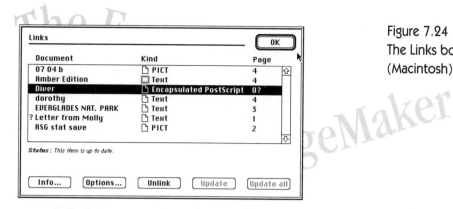

Figure 7.24
The Links box
(Macintosh).

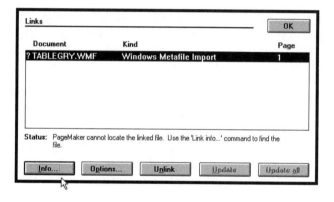

Figure 7.25
The Links box
(Windows).

- Double-click on the file name or click on **Link** button.

  Or

- Select the item itself within your publication (not in the dialog box), and choose **Link info** from the **Element** menu. The dialog box shown in Figure 7.26 appears. (The Windows version is shown in Figure 7.27.) You can get information about linked files of both text and graphics.

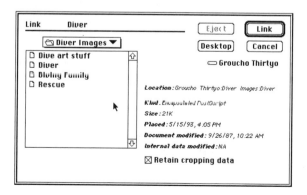

Figure 7.26
The Link
information
box (Macintosh).

Figure 7.27
The Link
Information
box
(Windows).

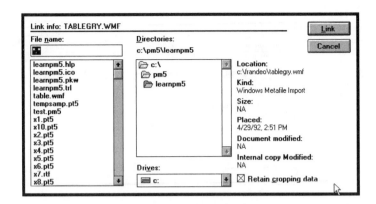

Once the box is open, you can see the status of your links by the presence or absence of the following symbols next to the file name. (If no symbol is shown, either the link is current or no link has been established.)

- A **question mark** means that PageMaker can't locate the file. You've either moved it from its original location, changed its name, or thrown it away.

- A **black diamond** indicates that the file has been modified. You've added or removed something and resaved it. PageMaker will automatically update its version the next time you open your publication.

- A **hollow diamond** means that the file has been modified but you haven't specified that PageMaker can update automatically. The next time you open the publication, PageMaker will ask you for permission to update its version of the file.

- A **hollow triangle** indicates that both the internal PageMaker version and the original word processor or paint version of the element have been modified independently of each other. If you update the internal version, you'll lose any changes you may have made to it that haven't also been made to the external one. In this case, you'll have to decide which version's changes have priority.

The Links box also tells you where in the publication you placed each story or graphic. You'll see page numbers or the following notations:

- **LM and RM:** *Left Master* means you placed it on the left master page. *Right Master* means you placed it on the right master page. Items you placed here would probably be a company logo or small picture of some kind, rather than a text file.

- **PB:** *Pasteboard* means your item is on the pasteboard, not placed in the publication.

- **X:** *X* means the story is open as a new story created in Story Editor but not placed in the publication yet. It's not anywhere except in a Story window. (You won't find it on the pasteboard, Clipboard, or scrapbook, because you haven't put it there.)

- **Page#?:** *Page#?* refers to a linked inline graphic you've inserted into an unplaced story. The story itself has the **X** marker and the linked graphic gets this marker. Once you place the story, you'll be placing the inline graphic as part of it.

- **OV:** *OV* stands for *overset type* and indicates that a linked inline graphic cannot be displayed because it's in a part of a text block that hasn't been fully flowed into the publication. If you want to check the graphic, you could place the overset text on the pasteboard. (The OV symbol would then change to **PB**.)

The reason that PageMaker keeps track of these things is to help you locate specific items within what may be a very large or busy publication. If you think you placed a particular graphic, for example, and you can't remember where, you can use this function to find it.

PageMaker automatically establishes links for every story you import using the Import or Place commands. You can link stories you've created in Story Editor by using the Export command and saving them outside of PageMaker. PageMaker will establish links to both text and graphics created within it and exported from PageMaker. To choose whether to have PageMaker update links automatically or to alert you first, open Link options. (You can open the Link options dialog box by checking the **Options** button in the Link dialog box, or by selecting **Link options** from the **Element** menu. Either way, you'll see the same dialog box.). You can set Link Options for individual imported objects, or as a default setting for all linked objects. To set options for one linked object, select it, and open the **Link options** dialog box. Choose the desired updating method and **OK** to close the box. To set defaults, choose **Link options** with no specific object selected. Set options, click **OK**, and close.

If you are working on a Macintosh with System 7, you can specify whether you want PageMaker to update subscribed files whenever the Edition is revised, or only when you tell it to do so. You can do this either from the Links box, or by selecting **Editions** and then **Subscriber options** from the **Edit** menu. Subscriber options look and act like Link options, allowing manual or automatic updates.

If you make frequent changes in your original documents, it's a good idea not to use PageMaker's automatic updating feature. Otherwise, you could open up a finished layout and find that it has been totally corrupted by the update. For example, if you've added more text, your document might be a page longer than you had intended. If you've cut out a piece, you might find a large, gaping hole in the middle of page one. If you changed a graphic, you might have messed up the text flow around it. Other changes could also undo your formatting.

When you have already applied type or style modifications such as kerning a headline, changing tracking, or adjusting spacing, updating will lose all of these changes as well. Fortunately, PageMaker warns you of the consequences before going ahead and lets you choose not to update. Figure 7.28 shows the Alert box.

Figure 7.28
This box lets
you choose
whether to let
PageMaker
update linked
files.

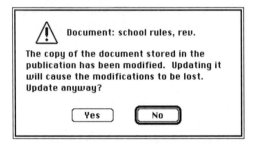

If you like to work on your layout a little bit at a time, you'll have the most success with PageMaker if you make sure your text files are essentially complete before you import them, and then ignore the links. You can still do last minute editing in Story Editor, but the goal is to avoid the need to recompose your layouts over and over because your copy has grown or shrunk. On the other hand, should you prefer to do most of your formatting within a compatible word processor, such as Microsoft Word, and polish and format your pages just before printing them, PageMaker's Link feature can save you a good deal of time and energy.

PageMaker will look for links when you ask it to. It checks them automatically when it opens a publication and when you attempt to print. If it can't find a link or finds one that hasn't been updated, the Alert box shown in Figure 7.29 will appear, asking you whether to print or cancel. What you do next depends on the nature of the text or graphic file involved. If it's a missing link to an original word processing document, which you threw away after you imported it into PageMaker, there's no problem. Go ahead and print. If it's a question of not having the latest version of the document, you'll need to decide whether the changes are important. If so, cancel the printing, update the file, and adjust the formatting before printing.

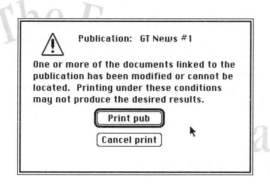

Figure 7.29
Alert box
asking you
whether to go
ahead and
print or cancel.

### By the Way . . .

*Graphics use linking somewhat differently. A missing graphic link can, as the Alert box indicates, produce undesirable results. Linked graphics will be explained in the next chapter.*

In addition to throwing away a file, you can accidentally break a link by moving the linked external file to a new folder or a new directory, changing its name, changing the names of any of the folders or directories in which it's nested, or changing the name of the disk it's on. What happens is that PageMaker keeps a record of the *file path*, the route it must travel to locate that file. The file path of each linked file is shown in the Link Info box as Location. For example, this chapter's file path on the author's Mac IIsi is as follows:

**Mac's HD:Books folder:EPM folder:Ch. 7 stuff:Ch. 7 text**

**Mac's HD** is the name of the hard disk. **Ch. 7** text is the name of the document. All the other phrases, separated by colons, represent folders (and folders within folders). There's a folder called **Books folder** and inside it a folder called **EPM folder**, and so on.

If you change any of the file or folder names, or if you move the document called **Ch.7 text** out of the **EPM** folder, PageMaker would be unable to find it. The changes you make to that file would never make it into the finished book. If a file has been moved or renamed, you can reestablish the broken link by locating the file in the **Link Info** box's scrolling menu and clicking on the **Link** button.

### Watch Out!

*If you bring in text or a graphic from another program using the Clipboard, PageMaker can't track the link and, therefore, can't update its version of the material.*

There may also be times when you want to deliberately break a link. You may, for instance, want to unlink a spreadsheet, to keep if from being updated if you do more work with it. To unlink a file, select it from the **Links** box, and click the **Unlink** button. If you change your mind, at any point, you can click the **Relink** button to restore it. You can unlink any linked file, but you can not unlink an OLE embedded object.

# The Bare Essentials

In this chapter, you explored other ways in which PageMaker can handle text. Style sheets, link capabilities, and PageMaker's built-in word processor, the Story Editor, were explained. Specifically, you learned:

- How to work with styles on the Style palette and how to modify existing styles and create new ones. You also learned how to apply styles to text.

- How to use Story Editor, PageMaker's built-in word processor, the Find and Change feature, and how to save stories you create in Story Editor by pasting them into the publication, or by exporting them as a separate file in your choice of formats.

- How to access PageMaker's 100,000 word dictionary and how to check spelling in a paragraph, a single story, or throughout your publication.

- How to use PageMaker's dictionary to hyphenate words, and how to add words to it. You learned how to tell PageMaker how many consecutive lines it may hyphenate, and how large a gap to leave at the end of a line.

- How PageMaker automatically maintains Links with documents you've imported into it, including OLE links and Macintosh's Publish and Subscribe Links. Links are broken when a file is renamed, moved, or thrown away. You learned how to restore a broken link and when you can safely ignore links.

The Essential PageMaker

## Chapter Preview

*Graphics file types*

*Positioning and manipulating images*

*Working with inline graphics*

*Text runarounds*

*Linked graphics*

*Little boxes and other nonpictorial graphics*

*Image control on halftones and photographs*

# Chapter 8

# Working with Graphics

"picture," it's been said, "is worth a thousand words." That may be a liberal estimate, but pictures and other graphic embellishments can, and often do, make the difference between a bland, boring page and one that's interesting and appealing to the reader. PageMaker supports several different types of graphics: Paint-type images (that is, bit-mapped pictures), including MacPaint (PNT), .BMP (Publisher's Paintbrush and Microsoft Windows format) and .PCX (PC Paintbrush) formats; TIFF files of scanned images (called .TIF on the PC), such as black and white line art, grayscale, halftone, and color photographs; and Draw-type graphics (that is, object-oriented pictures), including PICT, .CGM (Computer Graphics Metafiles), and Windows metafiles (.WMF), and EPS (Encapsulated PostScript) graphics. Each has advantages and disadvantages.

# Paint Bit-Mapped Images

A Paint picture is a *bit-mapped* illustration. This means that it's composed of dots, called *bits* or *pixels*. The first Paint program, MacPaint, was bundled with the early Macintoshes. In the beginning, it was the *only* graphics program for the Mac, just as MacWrite was the only word processor. As other graphics programs came along, they adopted the Paint file format. It is still the standard for the interchange of bit-mapped graphics. All Mac programs that handle bit-mapped graphics can support Paint, including SuperPaint, Canvas, and, of course, MacPaint II. Windows programs that create .PCX images include PC Paintbrush, Harvard Graphics, Micrografix Designer, CorelDRAW!, PC Paint, and Fractal's Painter for Windows. In addition, Publisher's Paintbrush produces PageMaker-compatible BMP files, as does Windows' own Paint program.

Bit-mapped art can be richly detailed and quite effective. The major drawback to Paint images is that the pixels that form them have square corners. Why is this a problem? If you enlarge a paint image, you don't get more pixels. You get a larger pixel. So, if you need to resize a Paint image in PageMaker, you'll see the jagged edges at a greater magnification. PageMaker lets you resize bit-mapped graphics optimized to your printer resolution to minimize the problem, but this means you are limited to certain proportional sizes.

Figure 8.1 shows an example of *jaggies* in bit-mapped art. Seen small, the globe looks reasonably good, but if you blow up the world, you get hit with a ton of bricks! Even at best, the jaggies are obvious, and the higher quality your printer, the more they seem to stand out. The Smooth option (in the Print dialog box) may help a little, but jaggedness is still apparent. You may prefer to use Paint graphics only in their original size.

# PICT Object-Oriented Images

With the introduction of MacDraw, the computer art world gained a second valuable tool—the *object-oriented graphic*. In a PICT image, each object is described by its outline in a series of mathematical vectors. The drawing is saved as instructions, rather than as a bunch of pixels. Because of its precision, its ability to stack elements in layers while maintaining their "separateness," and the ease of modifying line widths and fill patterns, the object-oriented graphic is preferred by engineers and architects. Macintosh drawing programs, such as Claris MacDraw Pro, Aldus IntelliDraw, Deneba Canvas, and multitudes of others, allow you to save a drawing as a PICT file.

Figure 8.1
Jaggies make
some pictures
look like
they're
"drawn" in
bricks.

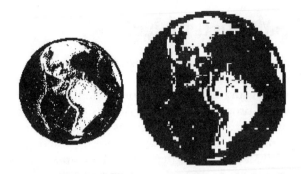

PICT is a Macintosh standard for transferring object-oriented drawings between applications. Some programs can also save files in a slightly modified PICT format called PICT2, which can handle color and more complex formatting. PageMaker can import both PICT and PICT2 drawings. Windows and PC drawing programs, such as CorelDRAW!, Lotus Freelance, Arts & Letters, Micrographfx Designer, and Harvard Graphics, can save object-oriented art as .CGM, encapsulated postscript (EPS), or Windows metafiles (.WMF) formats. Charts and graphs from spreadsheets, such as Lotus 1-2-3, can be imported using the .PIC filter.

CGM, or computer-generated metafiles, is a common format for exporting graphics developed by Harvard Graphics or Lotus Freelance. It is the most common filter used when you want to place these types of graphics into a PageMaker publication in a non-PostScript environment. CGM is very loosely defined, and many different types of PC-based graphics programs support it. Fonts in CGM files degrade when brought into PageMaker. In addition, PageMaker needs to know such information as the number of graphics in a file and how to treat rotated type (if you don't tell PageMaker to make the type a bit-mapped image, PageMaker re-rotates the type back to horizontal). You can specify import options when importing CGM files by holding down the **Shift** key while selecting the **Place File** command from the **File** menu.

WMF is Windows' internal format for all of its graphics. WMF files can contain text, object-oriented images, and bit-mapped pictures as objects. CorelDRAW! and Micrografx Designer can export to this format. WMF is recommended only if you are printing to a non-PostScript printer.

PIC files are the preferred formats of charts and graphs generated in Lotus 1-2-3. Note that text in these graphics is always replaced by a sans serif font with graph titles in bold and the rest of the headings in normal style.

When you create a shape as an object-oriented graphic, the computer needs only a small amount of data. Objects are saved as descriptions of themselves, in the shortest possible terms. The code includes the type of shape, the screen location of a corner of it, and one dimension, generally a radius or diagonal. Fill and/or line width are also saved. Since the representation is based on math, rather than a dot by dot description of the object, it's easy for the computer to resize or reposition it. Distortion isn't a problem, because the computer simply recalculates things in their original proportions. You don't have to deal with jaggies.

On the other hand, Draw-type programs simply don't have the flexibility that Paint programs have. There are object drawing tools similar to the architect's triangles and t-squares, but no pencil, brush, or eraser. You can draw only lines, shapes, or Bèzier curves. A Bèzier curve (pronounced "bez-ee-ay") is one that's mathematically described as a series of control points. FreeHand drawing is difficult, although geometric figures and straight lines are simple. Figure 8.2 shows illustrations for a newsletter in the PICT format.

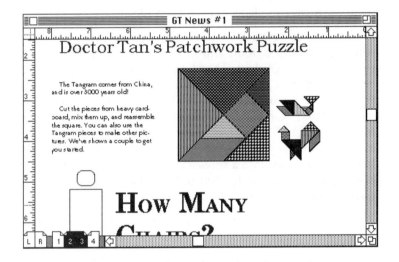

Figure 8.2 Geometric shapes are simple to draw in PICT.

There are ways to get the advantages of both Paint and PICT. One way is to use a program the incorporates both painting and drawing layers, such as Aldus SuperPaint, or Deneba's Canvas, as your Macintosh graphics program. SuperPaint can handle both Paint and PICT files, but in an interesting way. The program has a split personality. It can be both an artist's drawing board and an engineer's drafting table, and can copy from one to the other. You can create a drawing in SuperPaint's Paint layer, and then copy it to the Draw layer to resize it. When you save it as a PICT file, all the dots in the Paint image become parts of the PICT shape. It can then be scaled without added distortion. In Figure 8.3, the largest cat in the group was created in the Paint layer, copied to the Draw layer, and reduced several times.

Figure 8.3
To help
eliminate
jaggies, always
start big and
reduce.

# EPS Graphics

*EPS* stands for Encapsulated PostScript, a way to describe graphics in the PostScript language used by imagesetters and most desktop laser printers. Adobe Illustrator, Aldus FreeHand, CorelDRAW!, and AutoCAD arc among the graphics programs that can create EPS files. (Most scanning programs also can create EPS files.)

Like Paint programs, EPS drawing programs give you great flexibility with a wide range of tools and special effects, including fine lines, curved text, and graduated shadings. Because these programs "speak" PostScript, there's never a problem making the image compatible with a PostScript-compatible printer. The PostScript interpreter is built into most Mac and PC-compatible laser printers, including high-resolution Imagesetters such as the Linotronics. The image will print at the maximum resolution of whatever printer you're using, whether it's a desktop laser printer at 300 dpi; a service bureau's 600- or 1,200-dpi laser printer; or the Linotronic L300 at 2,540 dpi, which gives you magazine-quality images in your publication.

PostScript images are stored as text files. The lion in Figure 8.4 is a string of commands including:

**pop true setstrokeadjust /% x1 y1 x2 y2 x3 y3 c -**

These can be read and edited, if you know how to do so. (Of course, if you do, it's more likely that you're programming computers than pasting up a newsletter. . . .)

The PostScript image alone, although it "talks" to your printer with no difficulty, doesn't give you a picture on the screen. Luckily, the *encapsulation* in an EPS file allows a PICT or bit-mapped version of the image to be appended, so you can have a screen representation as well. Some drawing programs support EPS but will give you only a gray box, rather than the actual image, when you import the file into PageMaker. You can use the box to position and resize the graphic, but you won't see the picture until you print it. Figure 8.4 shows examples of EPS files placed in a PageMaker publication. One has a screen version; the other does not, so you see a gray box where the graphic should be.

Figure 8.4 Both pages contain EPS graphics. The lion picture includes a PICT. The other graphic doesn't, so it can't be shown on the screen.

PageMaker 5.0 also supports color EPS files. You can import a color EPS file into your publication, from any source that can create one. The colors will import with it and will appear in the Color palette so that you can also apply them to other items in the publication. In Chapter 13, you'll learn more about the color palette and how to use it.

### Watch Out!

*When you are working in Windows or on the PC, remember that PageMaker uses the three-letter suffixes on file names to properly identify filterable formats. Be sure to name your files using standard file name extensions. For example, CorelDRAW! files will have an extension of .CDR or .WMF. When you place a file with a nonstandard file name, a dialog box appears in which you specify the file type. The on-line help system lists accepted file formats under the keyword "filters."*

# Scanned Images

Although the computer is capable of producing some very nice art, there will be times when you'll want to use a photograph or a piece of art from some source other than a computer. How can you bring these images into your Mac? The answer is to use a scanner. There are various types of scanners, but essentially, they all work in a similar fashion to translate your photo or artwork into a set of digital signals that produce a bit-mapped version of the original.

The image type a scanner captures depends on the software used to run the scanner. Some scanning software lets you choose among several formats.

## Flat Scanners

One type of scanner, called a *flat* (or *flatbed*) scanner, looks and works like a photocopying machine. The original is placed face-down on a sheet of glass. When you turn on the scanner, a bright light moves across the document and 2,500 or more photo sensors capture the changes from light to dark as *ons* and *offs*.

High-resolution scanners can see up to 256 shades of gray, and some can handle color scans, too. Files are generally saved as TIFFs (Tagged Image File Format), and can be edited in a digital image processor, such as Aldus Digital Darkroom or Adobe PhotoShop, before being placed in PageMaker. Figure 8.5 shows a typical TIFF File created by scanning a photograph. (PageMaker also accepts Color TIFF and compressed TIFF files.)

Flat scanners are highly accurate and provide good to excellent resolution. You can now get a desktop color model with as much as 800-dpi resolution, adequate for many tasks, for around $1,500. Commercial printers and service bureaus may have scanners with a much higher resolution, but these machines are priced accordingly and are out of the reach of most small businesses and individuals.

A variation of the flat-bed scanner is a single-sheet one. It works the same, but the page feeds through past the stationary sensor rather than the sensor moving across the page.

## Hand-Held Scanners

Hand-held scanners are quite inexpensive and can do some amazing things. ThunderWare's LightningScan Pro 256, which looks something like an overgrown electric razor, scans at 400 dpi! You can join the files from several passes of its four-inch wide scanner into a full-page picture. It scans bound books, textured surfaces, even tattoos!

Figure 8.5
Never get in a
TIFF with a
tiger!

Caere's Typist scans graphics at 300 dpi, but its primary use is as a text scanner. It will input up to 500 words per minute into a word processor or spreadsheet program. The Typist includes OCR (Optical Character Recognition) software that can translate a bit-mapped image of a letter into an ASCII character, which can be imported into virtually any application that accepts text files, including PageMaker. If you have large amounts of material that have been hand typed or created on a noncompatible word processor, the Typist could save you many hours of retyping. It scans at two inches per second and is remarkably accurate on clean, typed or printed copy. It can recognize eleven Western-European languages, and scans nonstylized fonts from 6 to 72 points. The Typist scans images into TIFF or PICT formats and can separate graphics from text.

Hand-held scanners require patience, especially when you're just learning to use them. The scanner must be rolled across the text at a steady pace, neither too fast or two slow, and not at an angle. Side to side motions or jerkiness will result in an uneven scan. With an OCR program, you'd get unintelligible text. Once you've mastered the technique, though, these devices can solve many problems, especially if you're working on a newsletter or similar publication with text from many sources.

# Video Digitizers

Another alternative for low-cost scanning combines a little box called a video digitizer with a portable VHS camcorder or other video source. You'll need a steady still frame, such as from a video disk player, one of the new hand-held video snapshot cameras, or an ordinary TV camera pointed at a still image. The video source must be one that can provide a steady, flickerless still frame. (A VCR deck is not a good source, unless it has built-in digital editing, because VHS still frames jiggle too much.) The digitizer translates the video signal into digits, specifically ones and zeros, which translate into pixels on the computer screen.

The two most popular Macintosh video digitizer packages, Digital Vision's Computer Eyes and Koala's MacVision, come with hardware and software. (Computer Eyes also sells a color version on a Mac II expansion card.) If you're using a digitizer with your camcorder, all you do is plug everything in, open the scanning program included, and capture an image. You can crop the photo, set brightness and contrast, and convert it to a Paint document or save as a TIFF, PICT2, or EPS file to go directly into a PageMaker publication, or go first through Digital Darkroom or Photoshop for retouching. How good are they? A lot depends on the quality of the image you're scanning. Most of the photos in this book were produced with Computer Eyes and a VHS camcorder.

For IBM-compatibles, Truevision makes a line of special video cards (of which Targa is the most famous) into which you can plug a video camera directly. You can save images in TIFF or its native TGA (Targa) format, and then crop or retouch the image directly using Truevision's own software.

# Color Scanners

Color scanners let you put color photographs and colored art into your PageMaker document. Even though they cost about four times as much as gray scale scanners, they are well worth it to the printing and publishing industry.

When you need a color scan, look for a service bureau or printer who uses the Barneyscan system. Barneyscans can handle either flat art or 35mm slides and can produce four-color separations for the printer. You may need to do some retouching on the scan. If your scanned image needs editing, Adobe PhotoShop can do any necessary color retouching on scanned color images. Color TIFF files can take up a great deal of memory. You'd need a Mac II with 4 or 5 meg of RAM to view your work while scanning a color photo, and you'd want to save it as a linked file with your PageMaker publication, rather than within the PM file itself. Otherwise, you could end up with a publication too big to fit on a disk.

Speaking of file sizes, you can save disk space by scanning your images at the lowest acceptable resolution. Detailed art is best scanned at the resolution of your printer, 300 dpi if you're using a LaserWriter or similar. If your art is very simple, though, you may be able to get away with using a lower resolution scan, which will give you a much smaller file. Scanning images at the size you want to print them saves time and helps avoid distortion. If you must deal with especially large files, you can place linked documents on a different disk and restore the links before printing by opening the publication in PageMaker and verifying them.

### Watch Out!

*Since TIFF, like PCX (Paint), is a bit-mapped format, you risk distortion if you scale a TIFF image, unless you plan your enlargement or reduction to a percentage of the resolution. For instance, if you intend to reduce the scanned image by 50% when you move it into PageMaker, and you'll print it on a 300-dpi laser printer, scan it full-size, at half the desired resolution, or 150 dpi. You'll have a smaller file, and when you shrink the image, you'll be back at the desired 300-dpi resolution.*

# Importing Graphics

PageMaker supports the placing of graphic images with special programs called *filters*. Several bit-mapped image filters come with the program, including PCX, BMP, PNT, and TIFF; these can be placed directly into your publications, but sadly in the PC world, there are many more graphic formats than any software manufacturer could possibly support.

The best way to ensure compatibility with PageMaker is to save the images from your graphics program in a format for which PageMaker provides a filter (such as PCX, BMP, WMF, PNT, PIC, PICT, EPS, or TIFF). The complete list of compatible formats and their uses is available in PageMaker's on-line Help system under the keyword "filters."

### By the Way . . .

*If you use a format that PageMaker recognizes, you can use the graphic even across platforms; for example, you can create the graphic on a Mac and then use it in PageMaker for Windows.*

If your graphics program does not allow you to save images in any of these formats, you'll need to convert your graphics to one of these formats so that PageMaker can recognize it and place it correctly. To convert Windows formats to Mac formats, use Adobe Photoshop. Windows users can convert images using Harvard Graphics' The Graphics Link Plus+, Inset Systems' HiJaak, or SymSoft's HotShot Graphics.

The alternative way of importing alien graphic formats is to avoid the use of the Place command and bring the graphic in directly. Perhaps the simplest way to accomplish this is to copy it to the Clipboard (Mac or Windows) or Scrapbook (on the Mac only), and paste it into the publication. In addition, on a Macintosh with System 7, you can use Publish and Subscribe. In Windows, if your graphics program supports it, you can use OLE.

**By the Way . . .**
*Windows 3.1 lets you place a file in PageMaker for Windows by dragging the file's icon from the File Manager to an open publication window. When you release the mouse, PageMaker imports the file using the default settings in the Place document dialog box.*

# Positioning Graphics

When you have created a graphic, scanned one, or taken one from a clip art file, you need to put it into the PageMaker publication. The way to do so is to use the Place document dialog box, just as you did to import text. Graphics can be placed from their own files or from the Scrapbook on the Mac. There are several different Place graphic icons, shown in Figure 8.6. Which one you'll see depends on the source of your graphic.

Figure 8.6
In order: Paint, PICT, TIFF, EPS, and Scrapbook icons.

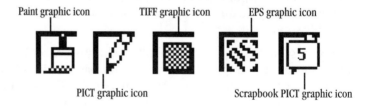

Paint graphic icon    TIFF graphic icon    EPS graphic icon

PICT graphic icon    Scrapbook PICT graphic icon

## Placing from a Graphics File

Placing graphics in PageMaker is a simple task. Just select the item by name, from within the Place document dialog box. Select the option to place **as independent graphic**, and click **OK**. The icon that appears will reflect the type of image you're placing: bit-mapped image (such as PNT, BMP, and PCX formats), object-oriented image (such as PICT, WMF, or CGM formats), EPS, or TIFF. Position the icon where you want the upper left-hand corner of the picture, and click to place it.

Whenever you place a graphic in this way, you establish a link between PageMaker's copy of the graphic and the original file, just as you do with linked text files. The link allows PageMaker to automatically update its copy whenever the original is updated, if you've allowed it to do so. It also lets you store graphics files outside of your PageMaker publication, to help keep your files in a more manageable size. (For more information about links, see "Working With Linked Graphics" later in this chapter.)

# Modifying Images

PageMaker lets you modify the graphics you import in several ways. You can crop them, and resize and reshape them to suit your needs. You can also move them around within the publication, just as you could if you were laying out pages the old-fashioned way, with bits of paper and rubber cement.

## Repositioning a Graphic

Moving an image is simple. Just hold the mouse button down anywhere on it. The pointer will change to a four-way arrow, indicating that you can drag it in any direction.

If you want to place it on a different page of your publication, the easy way is to drag it from the old page out to the pasteboard. Make sure none of it is touching the page. Then, click the page number icon at the lower left for the page you want to move to. It will open, and you can drag the image back onto the new page and place it where you want it. If you want to move it to another open publication, drag it from one to the other. It will be copied (not cut) to the new location. If you don't want it in the original one any longer, select it, and press delete to remove it.

## Resizing an Image

When you select an image, you'll see resizing *handles*. Use the Pointer tool to grab one of the handles and drag it. The pointer will change to an arrow indicating which direction(s) that handle may move. A side handle will stretch the picture in that direction. A corner will stretch both dimensions. To keep the picture in its original proportions, hold the **Shift** key down as you drag.

A more precise way to resize an image uses the Control palette. Enter the dimensions you want the object to be, or the percentage you would like to enlarge or reduce it. To enlarge or shrink by a small amount, click the arrows (nudge buttons) on the control palette as shown in Figure 8.7. To preserve the proportions of an object, turn on **Proportional Scaling** on the Control Palette before you resize the selected object. To resize a monochrome bit-mapped image to a size that won't distort on your target printer, turn on **Printer-resolution scaling**.

Figure 8.7
Resizing on the
Control
Palette.

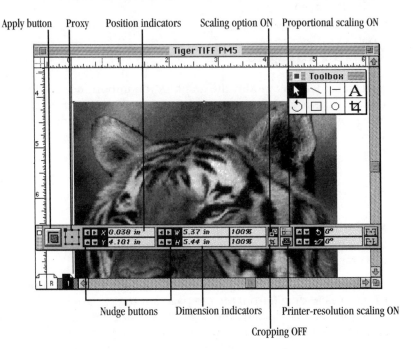

By the Way . . .
*You can set the amount of horizontal and vertical "nudge" PageMaker adds or subtracts when you click a nudge button. It's done in the Preferences dialog box. The default setting is .01 inch. If you're not using the Control Palette, the arrow keys also nudge a selected object by the same amount.*

You can also resize a bit-mapped graphic to match your printer's resolution by holding down the ⌘ key (Mac) or the **Ctrl** key (Windows) as you drag. PageMaker will check to see what type of printer is indicated in the Page setup dialog box and will scale the graphic appropriately for the printer or imagesetter. To preserve its original proportions while matching printer resolution, press ⌘+**Shift** (Macintosh) or **Ctrl+Shift** (Windows) while you drag the corner handle. PageMaker calls this function *magic stretch*. The graphic may possibly look distorted on your screen, but like magic, it will print properly if you've followed the instructions.

## Repairing Distorted Graphics

Everybody makes mistakes. Sometimes you may forget to press the Shift key or the ⌘ key while you drag a graphic, or you may resize one from the Control Palette without clicking the appropriate buttons. PageMaker has kindly given us a way to "rescue" distorted graphics. Figure 8.8 shows the steps in this process.

Figure 8.8
A tall ship can
be too tall.

The first picture shows a graphic of a tall ship. It got stretched too tall when we attempted to move it. (This happens *a lot*!) In the second picture, it's selected. With the pointer on any handle, hold down the **Shift** key and the mouse button. It takes a second or so for the pointer to change; then a boundary box appears in the original proportions of the ship. The final picture shows what happens when the mouse button is released; the ship jumps back into its boundary box.

To return a distorted picture to its original proportions:

1. Use the Pointer tool to select it. Hold down the **Shift** key, point to any handle, and hold down the mouse button.

2. When the pointer changes to a double-headed arrow, release the mouse button. A boundary box will appear in the size of the original graphic. The graphic then snaps back into shape

# Cropping

The Cropping tool is used to get rid of unwanted parts of a picture. As explained in Chapter 2, the Cropping tool's "real world" analogy is not scissors or a knife, but rather a moveable cardboard frame. When you crop a graphic, you needn't be afraid that you're throwing away a piece of it that you might need later. PageMaker's electronic cropping is far superior to the traditional method of throwing away what you don't want to see. If you change your mind in PageMaker, it's easy to reposition the graphic. Just point to it with the Cropping tool, and slide it around inside the frame.

To use the Cropping tool, select it from the Toolbox. Then click on the graphic you want to crop. You'll see handles, as you do with any selected object. When you point to a handle with the Cropping tool and hold the mouse button down, the tool changes to the double-headed arrow, and the handles are replaced by a boundary box, just as if you were stretching the picture. But when you move the box, only the boundary box moves; the picture stays put. When you crop, you *only* change the shape of the boundary box.

To crop a graphic:

1. Select the Cropping tool from the Toolbox, and click on the picture. Handles will appear.

2. Point to a handle, and hold the mouse button down. The Cropping tool becomes a double-headed arrow, and a boundary box will be drawn around graphic.

3. Use the arrow to drag the boundary box down to the desired size. The picture will not change size or shape, but now the box should frame the wanted part of it.

4. Release the mouse button, and the box will disappear.

Once you've trimmed away the excess, you may find that you need to reposition the picture so that more of one side of it shows, and less of another. Again, click inside the graphic, not on a handle with the Cropping tool, and hold the mouse button down. The Cropping tool will turn into a grabber hand, and a boundary box will frame the picture. Use the hand to slide the picture around inside its frame. When you've positioned it as you want it, release the mouse button, and the boundary box will vanish.

Figure 8.9 shows several stages of cropping. Three dolphins were too many, and the picture was too wide. Cropping it to the right size gave an awkward design. Sliding the dolphins back into the frame results in a much better-looking graphic.

## Electronic Cover-Ups

It sounds like something from the plot of a high-tech thriller, but an electronic cover-up is really a simple trick that can solve a lot of problems when you're working with graphics. Sometimes, you bring in a piece of clip art and then discover that cropping it to size isn't enough. As you can see in the dolphin picture in Figure 8.9, there's something in the frame that shouldn't be there. Cropping lets you shrink the rectangle that your picture is in, but doesn't let you notch out that little bit of something else that's in the way.

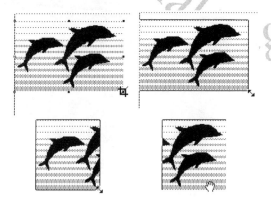

Figure 8.9 Cropping a picture from large to small and repositioning the picture inside the new, small frame.

Follow these steps to remove anything you don't want to show:

1. Choose an appropriate shape tool. (You may need to repeat these steps several times to cover an oddly shaped intrusion.)

2. Before you draw the shape, select **None** from the **Line** submenu and **Paper** from the **Fill** submenu under the **Element** menu. (See Figure 8.10.) This is the electronic equivalent of pasting a piece of paper over the offending object.

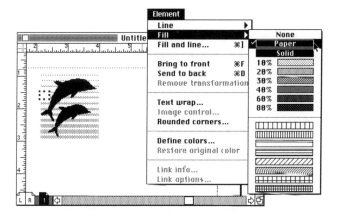

Figure 8.10 Covering the third dolphin's nose gets him out of the picture.

3. If your artwork has a pattern behind it, as this example has, copy a piece of the pattern or duplicate it from the fill menu, if possible, to cover the white shape. Figure 8.11 shows the result.

Figure 8.11
Adding some
pattern to the
background
hides the
mask.

When an object is oddly shaped, you may need several cover-up boxes to blot it all out. If you're working on the pasteboard, or if you need to move the art once it's been covered, be sure to select the cover-up boxes along with it. Otherwise, you'll have to slide them back into place afterward. If the boxes get "lost" on the page, it's most likely because they've gotten behind the graphic they're supposed to be in front of. If this happens, select the graphic and type ⌘+**B** (Mac) or **Ctrl+B** (Windows) to send it behind. ⌘+**F** (or **Ctrl+F** in Windows) brings anything selected to the front.

### Watch Out!

*A lot of cover-ups on complicated graphics may make the PageMaker file unnecessarily large. If your artwork needs a lot of work, edit it in a graphics program instead.*

# Editing a Graphic

Electronic cover-ups are fine for minor changes. However, if you import a graphic and then discover it needs a lot of work to make it fit, you'd be much better off editing it in a real graphics program. There are several reasons why. Graphics programs, such as Aldus SuperPaint and FreeHand, give you many more tools with which to work. The task will be easier if you have the right tools. Also, each object you add to a PageMaker page adds to the size of the publication file and slows down screen redraws. Also, the more complex a publication becomes, the longer it will take to print, and the better your chance of generating a PostScript error. (PostScript errors are strange anomalies that make certain objects print incorrectly or not at all.)

Fortunately, PageMaker 5.0 has made editing a graphic easy. After the graphic has been placed, if you decide you want to change it, PageMaker will reopen the original file in its native application, as long as the original graphics program and file are available on your hard drive or network file server. To do this, either select **Edit original** from the bottom of the **Edit** menu, or simply hold down the **Option** key (Mac) or **Alt** (Windows) as you double-click on the selected object.

Of course, the graphic must be linked to its original file. The Edit original command will not work if PageMaker can't locate the original. You may be able to re-establish a broken link in the Links Info dialog box. Graphics created in a paint or draw program can also be edited by copying them and pasting them onto a new page in the creator program, and then recopying and repasting them in PageMaker once they are edited.

### By the Way . . .
*You can also do this with a block of text, a spreadsheet, or other imported object. In the case of an OLE object, the object format will appear on the Edit menu; for example, "Edit Works Object." You can also double-click an OLE object to open its native application.*

If you have more than one graphics program, or if you don't have access to the program that created your graphic, but do have another one that can open it, you can still edit the graphic. If you select the graphic object to edit, and hold down the **Shift** key while you select **Edit original** from the **Edit** menu, or press **Shift+Option** (Macintosh) or **Shift+Alt** (Windows) while double-clicking on the selected object, you'll open a dialog box like the one in Figure 8.12. (The Windows version looks a little different but works the same.) The Select the application you want to use to edit the object. The notes in the box will tell you whether the chosen application can open that file, whether or not it's running, and whether it will update automatically, or if you'll have to update the link manually. Click on **Launch** (or **OK** in Windows) to open the application and the file.

# Inline Graphics

So far, you've learned about *independent* graphics, those that stay where they're placed. The opposite of an independent graphic is one that moves in response to the movement of other items on the page layout. It's not called a dependent graphic, although it could be, since its position depends on the text around it. This type of graphic is called an *inline* graphic, because it stays "in line" with the text on either side of it.

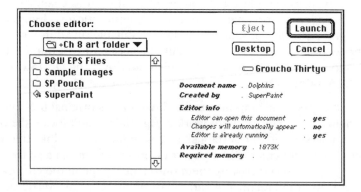

Inline graphics always remain in the same position relative to the words. This feature is especially useful if you're dealing with a chart or an illustration that needs to stay with its explanation. If you were to simply place it as an independent graphic and flow text around it, and then decided to add a paragraph at the beginning of your story, you'd have to do extensive reformatting of one or more pages to keep the chart together with its explanation. Inserting it as an inline graphic, however, means that no matter how much you add or remove to the beginning of the story, the words on either side of your chart will remain with it. PageMaker treats the graphic as a single character, no matter how large or small it is.

By the Way . . .

*Inline graphics are also an ideal solution for those times when you need to use a symbol, icon, or trademark in your text that's not available as a regular key character. Copy the symbol you want to use to the Clipboard, and paste it into the text whenever you need it. You can also use inline graphics as design elements to add interest to a page. Figure 8.13 shows some examples of ways you might use inline graphics.*

## Placing an Inline Graphic

Graphics are automatically placed inline whenever you use the Place command after using the Text tool to select an insertion point. If you forgot to select an insertion point, the graphic will appear as an independent graphic. If this happens, place it anywhere on the paste-board, then copy or cut it to the Clipboard, use the Text tool to select your insertion point, and paste it back at the insertion point. You can also copy a graphic from the Scrapbook to the Clipboard, or from its creator, and paste it inline. Once the graphic is in place, you can resize it, stretch it, scale it to your printer, or crop it as needed. Inline graphics may also be OLE-linked, embedded, or Subscribed to (Mac System 7 only.)

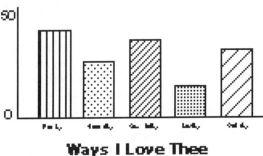

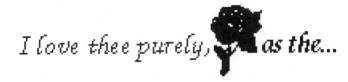

Figure 8.13 Inline graphics can be little spots of color, big charts, or anything else that needs to remain in a specific position.

To place an inline graphic:

1. Select the Text tool from the Toolbox, and put the I-beam cursor where the graphic should be. This creates an insertion point for the graphic.

2. Type ⌘+D (Mac) or **Ctrl+D** (Windows). The Place document dialog box opens, as shown in Figure 8.14.

3. Select the graphic and click **OK**. When the box closes, the graphic will appear where you put it.

Figure 8.14
Using the
Place docu-
ment dialog
box is one of
several ways
to import an
inline graphic.

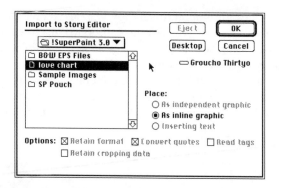

Inline graphics have a baseline that lines up with the baseline of the adjacent text, if any. By default, the baseline is two thirds the distance from the top of the bounding box to the bottom. Adjust this, if necessary, by dragging the graphic up or down with the pointer. You might need to do this if the graphic is something like a mathematical formula that needs to be aligned with the rest of the line. You can also apply paragraph attributes such as track, kerning, and leading to the graphic as needed.

Yet another way to place an inline graphic requires drawing a text box with the Text tool, and then pasting the graphic from the Clipboard or using the Place document dialog box. If you do this, be sure to make the text box large enough to accommodate the graphic, otherwise it will not be shown completely.

If you've placed an inline graphic and then switch to story view, you won't see the graphic. All you'll see will be a marker indicating its location. Figure 8.15 shows inline graphics markers in story view. If you want to bring in an inline graphic while you're working in story view, choose **Place** from the **File** menu. The procedure is the same as placing something in the Layout view, except that you'll only be able to see the marker until you return to the Layout view.

You can use text alignment to position an inline graphic. Make it a separate paragraph and select left, right, or center alignment from the Type Alignment menu. You can also apply manual kerning, tracking, and leading to an inline graphic, just as you would with text. You can't, however, apply other character attributes such as type style, width, or point size to an Inline graphic. If you want to change its size, treat it as you would any other graphic. PageMaker lets you crop, resize, and transform an inline graphic just as if it were an independent graphic.

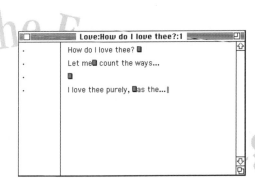

Figure 8.15
The markers
don't reflect
the size of the
inline graphic.

You can also apply transformations to the text block containing the graphic. For example, suppose you had placed a small inline graphic and wanted to skew its text block by 10 degrees. If you select the entire text block, the graphic will be skewed with it, by the same amount. You could also select the graphic separately from the text block, and skew it back 10 degrees in the other direction to restore it to normal, or skew it independently of the text block to a different angle. To remove an inline graphic, select it, and delete it. To make it an independent graphic, select it with the pointer, cut it to the Clipboard, and paste it back into the publication outside of a text block.

# Text Wrap—Getting the Run Around

Text wrap is PageMaker's name for the function that makes text run around a graphic. Up until computer typesetting programs came along, getting this effect meant painstakingly setting each word by hand to match a tissue tracing of the graphic. It was an effect that was used only rarely, because it was very expensive to do. Now, you can do it yourself with just a couple of mouse clicks.

Text can be wrapped around an independent graphic, making it look as if it has been set inline. However, you can't wrap around inline graphics. If it were possible to try to do so, the picture would move whenever PageMaker tried to recompose the words around it. This would confuse the computer. Cleverly, Aldus designed the text wrap function so that it's disabled whenever an inline graphic is selected.

When you choose Text wrap, you'll get a dialog box that shows your wrap and text flow options (see Figure 8 16). First select the graphic that you want the text to wrap around. Then open the **Text wrap** dialog box from the **Element** menu. Click on the icons that look the way you want your finished column to look.

Figure 8.16
The Text wrap
box lets you
run type
around or over
a graphic.

The following are your Text wrap options:

 **No boundary:** Text will flow over the graphic.

 **Rectangular boundary:** The text will flow up against the rectangle surrounding the graphic.

 **Custom boundary:** This option lets you create an irregularly shaped boundary around the graphic.

These are your Text flow options:

 **Column break:** Choosing this option tells PageMaker to stop flowing text when it reaches the graphic. Text flow will be continued in the next column.

 **Jump over:** Text flow stops when the text reaches the graphic and begins again beyond it, leaving white space on either side, if the graphic doesn't exactly fill the column.

 **Wrap all sides:** This option flows text all around the graphic as long as there's room enough for it to do so. This gives you the most complete text wrap.

Standoff is the distance between the edge of the text block and the graphic's boundary box. PageMaker's default settings are shown. To change them, simply type new numbers into the standoff boxes.

As soon as you close the Text wrap box, a dotted line with diamond-shaped handles will appear around your chosen graphic. This is the Text wrap boundary box. The way the text flows around the graphic is determined by the shape of the graphic's boundary box.

To use Text wrap with a rectangular boundary:

1. Select the graphic around which the text will wrap.

2. Choose **Text wrap** from the **Element** menu to open the Text wrap dialog box.

3. Select the middle Text wrap icon. This wraps words around a rectangular boundary.

4. Click a Text flow icon to set the desired pattern of text flow.

5. Type the desired values into the standoff fields. Values will be set in whatever measurement system you've selected.

6. Click **OK**. The text will wrap according to your specifications.

# Customizing a Graphic Boundary

The boundary box is rectangular when you turn on Text wrap, even if you've chosen the Custom wrap option. You can reshape it by selecting it and dragging its diamond-shaped handles. Place handles wherever you want them by clicking on the boundary line. You can fit it as closely to the graphic as you want. To remove an unwanted handle, drag it over an adjacent one. Figure 8.17 shows the Text wrap boundary box being reshaped. Figure 8.18 shows the result.

Figure 8.17
The Text wrap boundary box in place and enlarged to show the handles.

Figure 8.18
The finished
product.

Be careful not to drag the boundary line over itself. If you do, you create a loop, and the text will not wrap properly. If you change your mind about using a custom text wrap after you've seen the results, open the Text wrap box again, and click on the rectangular boundary. When you click on **OK** and close the box, the text wrap will revert to its original rectangular shape again.

### By the Way . . .

*Since PageMaker redraws the page each time you change the boundary on a graphic, reshaping a boundary near a lot of text can be time consuming. You may find it quicker to shape the boundary before you pour in text.*

Obviously, if you don't want type following the shape of the artwork, all you need to do is change the text flow boundary to whatever shape you want. In Figure 8.19, we created a box with no outline into which we set the headline for the story. The ball was created in SuperPaint, brought in and overlapped on the headline's box.

Figure 8.19
You can flow
text around
empty space,
too.

# Text Flow Options

The previous examples have used the Wrap all sides option. Other options have their uses, too. If you select the Column Break icon, as shown in Figure 8.20, PageMaker will stop flowing text when it runs into a graphic and will start the flow again at the start of the next column. This option can be handy if you're doing something that uses a lot of single column pictures, such as laying out a catalog or a school yearbook.

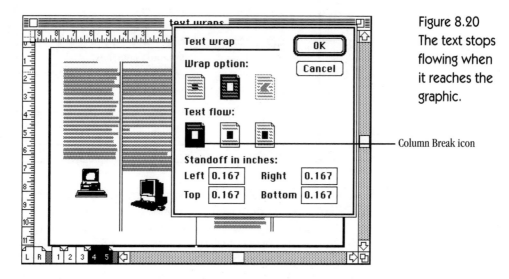

Figure 8.20
The text stops flowing when it reaches the graphic.

Column Break icon

The "jump over" icon, shown in Figure 8.21, indicates that the text will jump over the graphic and continue below it, leaving white space on either side. Changing the amount of standoff in the Text wrap box lets you control how close the text comes to the graphic. When you're placing a picture in the middle of the column of text, as was done in Figure 8.21, you might want to increase the standoff on the top and bottom to give the page better composition. Placing the text too tightly against the picture can be awkward. To change the distance between the text and the graphic, enter new standoff numbers in the Text wrap dialog box.

If you want the text to overlap one side of the graphic, enter a negative number to indicate just how much. Entering –.25 in the left box, for instance, would give you a quarter inch of text over the left side of the art. Entering zero brings the text right to the dotted line of the boundary. If you resize the graphic, PageMaker will keep the same standoff values. To wrap text around only one side of a graphic, place the other side next to a column guide, or increase the standoff on that side so there's no room for text between the graphic and the margin.

Figure 8.21
The text will
keep on
flowing on the
other side of
the graphic.

Jump Over icon ————

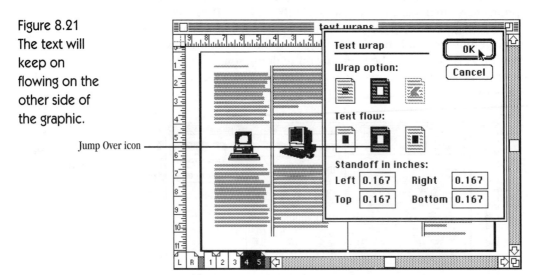

When your picture has a caption, be sure to extend the graphic boundary far enough that the caption (and its handles) can be placed inside it. Otherwise, when the text wraps around, the caption will flow with the text and may get carried away. Figure 8.22 shows how captions can be treated. Notice that we've extended the bottom standoff enough to leave room for the caption, and that we've placed the caption well inside the gap.

# Working with Linked Graphics

As you know, PageMaker can automatically keep track of everything you place into your publication. It does so by maintaining a list of file path information, which it calls *links*. The links tell PageMaker where each placed item came from, and how to find it again. It also checks the date and time you placed the item, and the date and time the original was most recently changed. It compares these two, and if the original file has been changed since PageMaker's copy of it was placed, you have the option of automatically updating it, or of being asked whether you want to update the changed item.

PageMaker will automatically establish a *hot link*, which updates your publication copy every time you save the original file, if the original document was created in any of the following applications:

194

- Aldus FreeHand 3.1 (Macintosh Only)

- Aldus Persuasion 2.1

- PhotoStyler 1.1

- PrePrint 1.5 (Macintosh Only)

- Table Editor 2.0 (Windows Only)

- ColorStudio 1.5 (Macintosh Only)

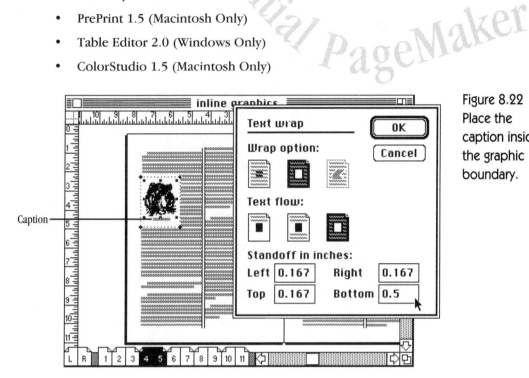

Figure 8.22
Figure 8.22 Place the caption inside the graphic boundary.

Hot links may be risky, if you are working with certain kinds of files. Spreadsheets are an example. You may need to place a particular version in your publication and then continue to work with the original. In this case, either save the spreadsheet again with a title such as **Hold for publication** on the Mac or **HOLDFOR** in Windows, and be sure you're linked to that version rather than the original, or open the **Link info** dialog box under the **Element** menu, and click the button to unlink that file.

Linking has another use, too. Since graphics files tend to be large, PageMaker gives you the option of storing either a complete copy of the graphic or only the screen version in the publication. Storing linked graphics outside the publication keeps your file small, conserving disk space and saving time when you open it. When you place a large graphics file, 256K or more, you'll get an alert message (see Figure 8.23) asking you if you want to store a complete copy of the graphic in the publication. If not, PageMaker keeps a low-resolution copy of the graphic and links to the original, so the publication file can be smaller. You must, however, be sure to have the external linked file available when you print the publication. If you send the file to a print shop or service bureau, be sure that you include linked graphics files. Otherwise, PageMaker will print the low resolution copy of the graphic instead. (See chapter 9 for more information about printing.)

Figure 8.23
To keep your
publication
small, store
large graphics
outside it.

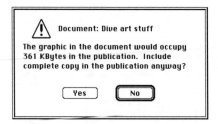

EPS files are a special case. They are always automatically linked. The PostScript file includes a screen image, which is what you see in your PageMaker document, and a PostScript language description of the picture, which is what goes to the printer. PageMaker always stores a copy of EPS files with the publication. You don't have a choice. The check box is checked and grayed out when you look in the Link options dialog box, shown in Figure 8.24.

Figure 8.24
The Links
dialog box.

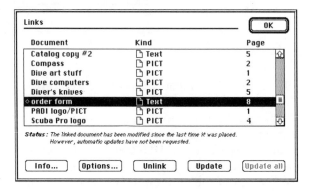

By looking at the list in the Links dialog box, we can easily see all the pieces that make up our publication. We can find out at a glance what kind of file it is, where in the publication it's been placed, and whether or not PageMaker's linked version is up-to-date. We can even use the Link info box, shown in Figure 8.25, to find out where the original is filed, how large it is, and when it was most recently modified.

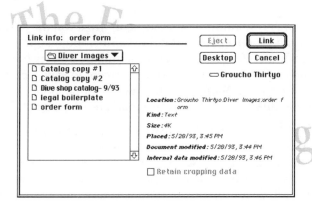

Figure 8.25
Checking the
Link info dialog
box to get
information
about a file.

PageMaker will check each of these files whenever you open a
publication and will notify you if any of the linked items have been
changed since you last saved the publication. You can then update them
without having to replace them.

# Link Defaults

In the Preferences dialog box, you have the option of deciding how to
view graphics in your publication. If you select grayed out, you'll see a
gray box called a placeholder in place of your graphic. This option saves
a great deal of time when there are frequent page redraws. You can go
back at any time and select normal or high resolution to see the graphic.
Figure 8.26 shows graphics placeholders in use. The darker box indicates a tint we're placing over a photograph.

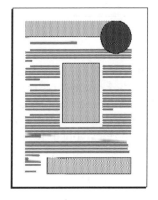

Figure 8.26
Graphics
placeholders
are gray
rectangles. You
can treat them
just like the
graphics they
replace,
wrapping text
around them
and adding
tints.

The high-resolution view supposedly gives you the best image your screen can produce, instead of the "normal" bit-mapped version. Screen redraws under the high-resolution setting take a very long time, though, so you won't want to use this option except to view a particularly critical piece of art. Note: With a Mac IIsi and 13" Apple hi-res monitor, there's no visible difference between "normal" and "high-resolution" viewing.

Links allow PageMaker to use the original graphics files for printing, even though they're not technically part of the document. Any changes that you've made to the screen version within your publication, such as cropping or resizing, will be kept. If you've gone back and redrawn the original art, your cropping or other changes might not look right. Whenever you open a publication, PageMaker checks all the linked documents. If a file has been moved, PageMaker will warn you that it can't find it and will ask for help in locating the original. Figure 8.27 shows the Cannot find dialog box. Use the menus to locate the file, and click the **Link** button to re-establish the link. If you're not planning to print or the links aren't critical, you can just click the Ignore button and PageMaker will open the document without updating the links.

Figure 8.27
If you move a file from one folder to another, you'll break its link, and PageMaker won't be able to find the original.

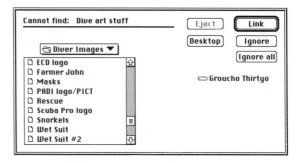

Because PageMaker keeps track of links by file names and folder location, changing either one breaks the link. If you modify a file, and save it under a different name, PageMaker isn't aware of the modification and will use the original. If you then delete the original, PageMaker loses the link. You can re-establish these links in the Link info dialog box. Find the new version, and click on the **Link** button to change the link to the new document.

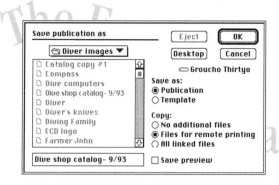

Figure 8.28
This is the easy way to make sure you've copied all of your linked files onto the disk for the service bureau.

Figure 8.29
PageMaker will let you decide whether you want to proceed with a missing link.

# Printing with Linked Graphics

If you're doing your own printing, either from a hard disk or from a floppy, there shouldn't be any link problems unless you've moved or thrown away your original files. The publication and all of its source files should be in the same place, so PageMaker can find the information it needs to send to the laser printer. When you send a publication out on a disk for printing at a service bureau or commercial printer, be sure that you include the source files for all your linked graphics. The easy way is to resave your publication, using the Copy All linked files option in the Save publication as box, as shown in Figure 8.28. If PageMaker has lost a link, it will warn you, with the box shown in Figure 8.29. If you proceed, it will print from a bit-mapped version of the graphic, giving you a much lower quality image.

### Watch Out!
*It's possible that a link could accidentally get broken when the publication is copied. After you've copied your publication onto a blank disk, re-open the publication from the floppy to verify the links.*

# Creating Graphics in PageMaker

PageMaker also lets you add quite a few graphic elements without going anywhere near your draw or paint program. PageMaker's Toolbox includes a set of line and shape tools, sometimes referred to as LBO for Line, Box, and Oval. You can use these tools to create some fairly complex graphics, as well as adding boxes and rules around text. The box, oval, and line tools work just like the ones in a graphics program. Choose line weights and styles from the **Line** submenu and fill patterns from the **Fill** submenu of the **Element** menu, or type ⌘+] (Mac) to open up a Fill and line attribute dialog box in which you can set both at once. Using the dialog box also allows you to add color to a line or a fill pattern, and to determine whether it overprints something else. Figure 8.30 shows how the popup menus in the Fill and Line box let you choose a fill pattern.

Figure 8.30
There's also a popup menu for line attributes.

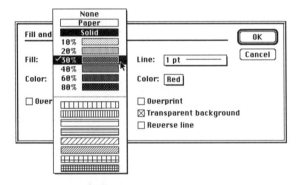

Use lines and boxes to add interest to your pages. A thin line between columns of type often helps make the pages more readable. Add a tint behind a particular block of copy to make it stand out. However, since PageMaker's Fill palette is less comprehensive than those found in a typical graphics program, you may want to create more complex filled shapes in your favorite graphics application. You'll be amazed at what a difference a few lines or shapes can make to a publication. Figure 8.31 shows how a box sets off a block of type. We chose a double line from the line menu, then added a second box in a heavier line around the first. Choosing **None** from the **Fill** menu allowed the type to show through the box.

Use the line tools to create thin lines between columns of type and to add rules between stories. You'll also find these tools very handy for laying out forms. Figure 8.32 shows an order form designed and created in PageMaker. Using combinations of thick and thin lines helps define the different areas on the form and adds some visual interest, too.

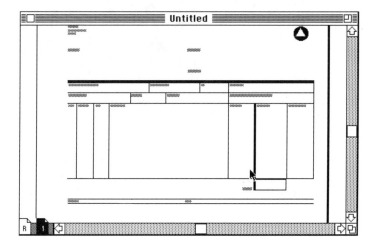

Figure 8.31
A box around the copy makes it stand out.

Figure 8.32
The perpen-dicular line tool makes jobs like this easy.

Notice to Customers
This bank will be closing its doors on April 1, 1993.
We regret the inconvenience.
For inquiries about deposited funds, please contact the State Banking Commission or the Federal Deposit Insurance Corporation.
*Thank you for your Patronage*

### Watch Out!

*If you use the Perpendicular line tool to draw lines and then move them with the pointer, PageMaker will "forget" to keep them perpendicular. To keep things in line, hold the **Shift** key down while you move them.*

# Image Control—Grayscale and TIFF Graphics

If you're using a scanned photograph or halftone in the TIFF format, PageMaker has a special feature that lets you alter the appearance of the image. Increase or decrease the contrast, change a dot screen to a line screen and vice versa, and even convert a negative to a positive or posterize a photo, breaking it down to a black and white picture or one with only one or two shades of gray.

The magic takes place in the Image control dialog box, shown in Figure 8.33. Select the graphic to modify and choose the **Image control** command from the **Element** menu. There are three modes to chose from, and all three can be applied to TIFF files.

Figure 8.33
We can't change the tiger's stripes to spots, but we can turn them from gray to black.

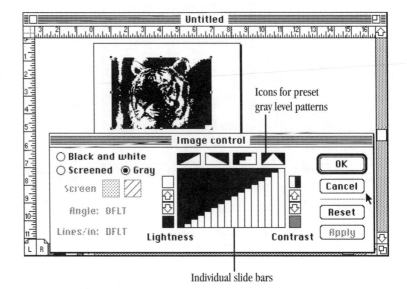

Icons for preset gray level patterns

Individual slide bars

**Black and white:** Applies to line art and also can be used to convert grayscale photographs to high-contrast black and white images. Choosing this removes the rays from the gray-scale picture. Everything becomes either black or white depending on whether it was originally darker or lighter than 50% gray.

**Screened:** Breaks the gray image into a pattern of black dots or lines, depending on which you've chosen. PageMaker also lets you change the lines per inch and angle of halftone screens, and choose between dot and line patterns. Screening a photo lets a black and white monitor or printer produce an acceptable image.

**Gray:** Is only available when you are using a grayscale or color monitor that supports grayscale images. If your monitor is capable of grayscale display. PageMaker selects it automatically when you select a TIFF graphic.

The best way to learn how to use Image control is to play with it. If you haven't saved, Revert will restore your original graphic. Within the dialog box, you'll see four preset gray-level patterns. If you saved, and then changed your mind, choosing the first preset pattern icon will restore the even gradations from light to dark. The second gives you a negative image, evenly graduated from dark to light. The third reduces everything to four shades of gray (actually black, white, and two grays), while the last emphasizes the middle grays instead of the blacks and whites. Figure 8.34 shows the four possibilities.

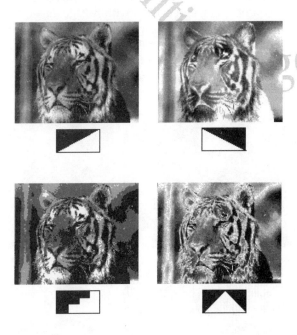

Figure 8.34
The four views correspond to the four Image control icons below them.

All the settings in the box affect the entire graphic. It's not possible to bring out just one area in PageMaker. To do so, you'd need to use a "darkroom" program such as PhotoShop or Aldus Digital Darkroom.

The scroll bars let you adjust the values from light to dark, and the contrast from stark black and white to foggy gray. The sliding bar graph will change as you scroll up and down, or you can change individual bars to bring out particular values. Each bar represents between 4 and 16 shades of gray, depending on how the original was scanned. Again, the best way to learn what these do is to play with them. Click on **Apply** to see the effects of your changes, and reset to return the TIFF to its original appearance. When you've reached a setting you like, click on **OK**.

# Have you tried . . . using a small inline graphic instead of a dingbat to indicate the end of a story?

*Dingbats* are those little stars and other shapes commonly used at the end of a book chapter or a magazine article. You can create your own dingbat in a draw or paint program and paste it as an inline graphic, so it will remain at the end of the story even if you edit the text.

# Screening

*Screening* means transforming the gray tones of a photo into a pattern of dots or lines. You can do this within PageMaker, by using Image control's screen settings. Figure 8.35 shows several different screen settings along with the original TIFF image, as a reference. Print proofs of your screened photos as you go along. PageMaker can't show you the details on your 72-dpi computer screen.

Figure 8.35
Experiment
with screens
until you find a
combination
that looks
good.

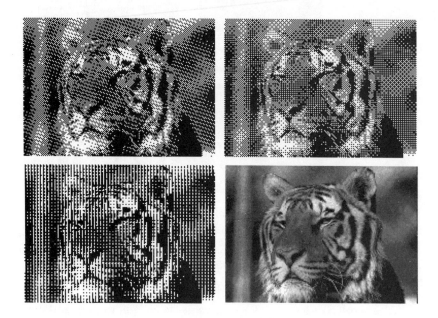

## Watch Out!

*One word of warning should be included here. Because of the size of the files and the complexity of translating TIFF images into PostScript, printing such a picture may tie up your computer for several minutes. In creating the sample pages here, we needed at least two minutes to process a single tiger. (And that's with a Mac IIsi, which is a fairly fast computer.) Don't assume your system has crashed, just because nothing seems to be happening. Sharpen your pencils, walk the dog (or feed the tiger), and then, if nothing's happening, consider that you may have asked your computer for more than it can handle.*

If you're using Windows, the dialog box you'll see (Figure 8.36) is different from the Mac version. You won't be able to choose between the three modes, but you can adjust the appearance of the graphic. You can change the lightness and the contrast of the graphic, and you can alter the printing parameters if you're using a PostScript printer. Note that these changes are limited to black and white TIFF graphics; you can't change a color graphic.

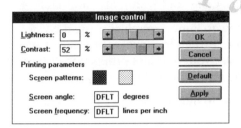

Figure 8.36 Windows' dialog box for Image control.

Type in a percentage or use the scroll bars to change the Lightness and Contrast of your image. A higher Lightness percentage will make your entire image lighter. A higher Contrast percentage will make the blacks and whites more intense. If you set the Contrast percentage very low, you'll get a lot of gray.

When the dialog box is first displayed, the printing parameters will be disabled. However, you'll be able to use them as soon as you change the lightness or contrast. You can change the screen pattern from dots to diagonal lines, change the screen angle to alter the grayscale, or change the screen frequency to adjust the dot screen.

The letters DFLT in the text boxes represent the default values. The printer default for the line screen is usually 45 degrees, but you can change the angle if you want it to print in a different grayscale. The default number for lines per inch (lpi) varies according to the printer you have. The lower the lpi, the more dotted your image will appear.

The Default and Apply buttons also come in handy. If you've previously changed some of the printing values and you want to switch back to the defaults, just click on the **Default** button. The **Apply** button allows you to experiment with lightness and contrast without having to close the dialog box. You can change the numbers, then click on **Apply** and see how your graphic is adjusted on-screen. If it's not what you want, change the settings and click Apply again. When you finally have everything right, click on **OK**.

# The Bare Essentials

In this chapter, you learned about PageMaker's graphics capabilities. Specifically, you learned:

- That PageMaker handles graphics in four different formats: bit-mapped (PNT, BMP, and PCX), object-oriented (PICT, PICT2, PIC, CGM, and WMF), EPS, and TIFF.

- How to import graphics using the Place document dialog box. You learned to move, resize, and crop and how to choose to resize your graphics proportionally and in a size that will match the resolution of whatever printer you have selected to use.

- How to hide unwanted parts of a graphic with "electronic cover-up."

- How to place Inline graphics as part of the text, so they will move when the text reflows, and how to use inline graphics to keep charts and illustrations with the copy they're meant to be seen with.

- How to wrap text around a graphic and how to use text wrap options to flow text over or closely around irregularly shaped objects.

- How to keep track of linked graphics using PageMaker's Link options.

- How PageMaker can create some types of graphics right within the application. You learned how to draw lines and shapes of varying thicknesses and to fill shapes with a choice of patterns or screen tints.

- How to use Image control to adjust the relationship of blacks, whites, and grays in a photo or a piece of art, and add a line or screen pattern.

The Essential PageMaker

## Chapter 9

## Chapter Preview

*Setting up your Mac printer*

*Setting up your Windows printer*

*Printing a no-frills proof copy*

*Getting the most from a laser printer*

*Working with down-loadable fonts*

*All you need to know about offset printing*

*Creating print masters on laser printers and imagesetters*

*Color separations*

*Dealing with service bureaus and print shops*

# Printing One Copy or a Thousand

Printing is absolutely the most important step in publishing. Until you actually print it, all you have are points of light on a screen. By now you've created some beautiful, persuasive pages on-screen. But *publish* shares the same Latin root as *public*, and you won't persuade anybody until you put those pages in your public's hands. That means getting them off the screen and onto paper in quantities large enough to distribute. This chapter deals with the best and most cost-effective ways to print your work.

## PageMaker Printer Drivers

Both the Mac and Windows normally supply the printer driver information to their applications automatically, so the user doesn't have to worry about setting up the printer separately for each program. PageMaker, however, comes with updated versions of these drivers and requires that you use them rather than your existing

drivers. Installing the new drivers is a one-time procedure that you
should perform before you print for the first time.

## Installing a Mac Printer Driver

Setting up the new Mac printer driver is easy. When you installed
PageMaker on your Mac, you installed a new LaserWriter Printer Driver
(version 8.0) that talks to your PostScript printer. To set up a Macintosh-
compatible PostScript laser printer, just use the **Chooser DA** in the
**Apple** menu to select the **LaserWriter** driver, as shown in Figure 9.1.

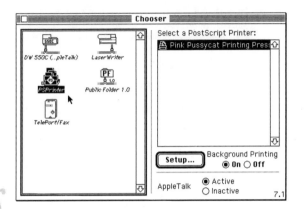

Figure 9.1
You needn't
remove the
older
LaserWriter
driver when
installing the
new one.
Some older
applications
may not work
with it.

## Installing a Windows Printer Driver

In Windows, PageMaker requires you to install a new printer driver
manually. PageMaker 5.0 comes with the latest version of the Windows
PostScript printer driver, as well as a new Universal driver for non-
PostScript printers. You'll need to install this driver using the Printer
control panel procedures described below.

1.  Minimize the PageMaker program window (or close it entirely),
    and then open the **Control Panel** window from the **Program
    Manager's Main** program group.

2.  Click on the **Printers** icon.

3.  When the Printers dialog box appears, click on the **Add>>**
    button, and the List of Printers appears (Figure 9.2).

Figure 9.2
The Printers
dialog box in
Windows.

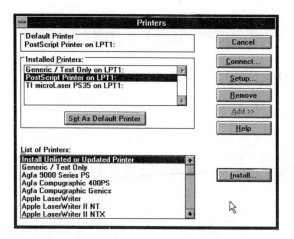

4. Choose **Install Unlisted or Updated Printer** from the List of Printers, and then select the **Install** button.

5. Windows will ask you to insert a setup disk in the drive. Insert the PageMaker disk containing the updated drivers into your floppy disk drive.

6. Type the drive letter in the box, then select **OK**. A list of printer drivers on that disk appears.

7. Select the printer driver you want to install from the list, and then choose **OK**.

8. Highlight that printer on the Installed Printers list, then click the **Set As Default Printer** button.

9. Choose **Close** to exit the Printers dialog box.

10. Reopen the PageMaker window, and select **Page setup** from the **File** menu.

11. Choose the new printer from the Compose to printer drop-down list.

# Composing to a Printer in Windows

Macintosh users can set up their publications without worrying too much about how the end result will be printed, as long as the resolution is specified. Windows users, however, must perform an additional step. The first time you run PageMaker for Windows, you must select **Page Setup** from the **File** menu and choose the printer you'll use to print the final copy from the Compose to Printer drop-down list (see Figure 9.3).

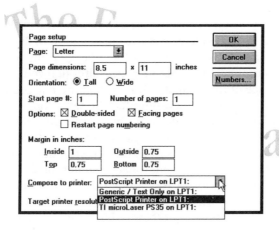

Figure 9.3
Select your
final printer
from the
Compose to
Printer drop-
down list
before begin-
ning your
layout in
PageMaker for
Windows.

Selecting the printer up front is important because as you work in Windows, PageMaker formats the publication you create for the default printer set up on that PC. If that's the printer on which you'll eventually print the final proof, fine. But if not, when you attempt to print the publication on the final printer, you may see a message like this:

**Recompose entire publication for PostScript Printer on LPT1?**

If you answer no, the document won't print. If you answer yes, PageMaker attempts to reformat the publication for the new printer, and your beautifully crafted document's layout may be ruined by font substitutions, line width changes, and character spacing problems.

If you are printing proof pages on your own printer, but taking the completed publication to a commercial printer, you'll specify the print shop's imagesetter or film recorder as the target printer. You'll still be able to print to your desktop printer, provided you have installed both printers in Windows. If you are working with a non-PostScript printing device, such as an HP PaintJet, you'll need to make sure that you have installed both the Windows PostScript printer driver and the new Universal Printer driver that shipped with PageMaker 5.0 for Windows, as you learned in the previous section.

# Changing a Publication's Printer Type

Suppose you've set your publication up for a particular print shop's imagesetter, and then you decide to take the job somewhere else, where the equipment is different. What must you do to compensate for the change in target printers?

First, you may need to adjust your publication to fit within a smaller print area than it was originally set for. A larger print area, obviously, doesn't require recomposing the pages, although you can if you want to take advantage of the smaller margin requirements. Second, you need to be sure that the new target printer has the same fonts available. If not, you'll have to change your fonts to those available, and adjust tracking, kerning, and other spacing attributes if necessary. If you ignore this step, the target printer will substitute its own fonts, with what may be unsatisfactory results. Different fonts use different letter spacing and word spacing. In a "worst-case" scenario, your headline requires an additional line, and the story that follows is auto-flowed to a previously nonexistent page, throwing off everything else that's part of the publication.

# Printing a Proof Copy

To print a file on either the Mac or Windows, select **Print** from the **File** menu. A dialog box appears, as shown in Figure 9.4 and 9.5. At the top of the Print document dialog box is the name of the selected printer.

Figure 9.4
The Print
document
dialog box
(Macintosh).

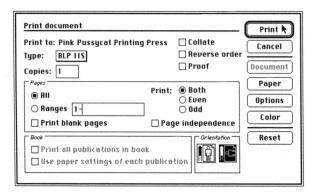

The Print document dialog box offers you a great deal of control over the printing process. You'll use it to define how the document will be printed, how many copies will be created, whether or not they should be collated, and whether the pages should be printed to read vertically or horizontally. You can also choose whether you will print a single page, a few pages of a multipage publication, or perhaps print all the even sides first, and then turn them over to print the odd sides, making double-sided pages. Use the following steps to print a copy of your publication.

1. Make sure your Printer is correctly chosen in Chooser or Print Manager.

2. Select **Print** from the **File** menu, or press ⌘**+P** (or **Ctrl+P** in Windows).

3. Select the appropriate options.

4. Click on **Print** or press **Enter** or **Return**.

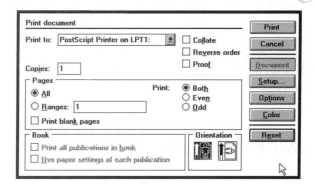

Figure 9.5
The Print document dialog box (Windows).

# Have you tried . . . proofreading your work on a hard copy?

Don't wait until your publication is finished to print it. Print draft copies often while you're working on page layout and text editing.

It's often easier to proof a printed copy instead of proofreading directly on-screen. Printing drafts gives you a better sense of the appearance of your chosen typeface and leading. When you see the whole page in print, for example, you may decide that the type blocks are too dense and need to be opened up more, or changed to a lighter face. A printed copy can also show design flaws you hadn't noticed on-screen, such as a crowded headline, too much space between elements, or margins that are too big or too small. If you print and check your work at various stages, you'll be able to make changes that affect other pages without having to completely redo everything. Even if you don't have access to a laser printer, printing a proof will be somewhat helpful.

# Looking at the Laser

Desktop laser printers are capable of good, relatively high-quality output. They break your page into tiny dots, (most typically, 1/300th of an inch in diameter) and form letters and graphics from combinations of these dots. This is usually good enough for most business applications, but can cause noticeable patterns in photographs and gray areas. Each shade of gray requires at least four dots, so a 300 dot per inch (dpi) laser printer is really capable of only 75 dpi halftones, about the same quality as an old-fashioned newspaper photo. Some of the newer laser printers can give higher resolution, up to 600 dpi, but professional typesetters and publishers rely on photographic imagesetters or film recorders with even smaller dots (as small as 1/2,400th of an inch) to get fine curves in their type, and high-quality grays in their photographs. But they also rely on desktop laser printers for their proof copies.

## How a Laser Printer Works

Yes, there really *is* a laser in the box. Laser light can be tightly focused and controlled by computer chips, so it can be shined at any one of the approximately eight million tiny locations (at 300 dpi) that make up a typical printed page. The laser scans each of these locations in turn, blinking on and off to create patterns of type and graphics. These patterns are projected onto an electrically charged drum similar to the one in an office copier. Essentially, the drum makes a photocopy of your page, depositing black ink particles in the same pattern on the paper. Figure 9.6 illustrates, in simplified form, the laser printing process.

**Figure 9.6
Laser printing.**

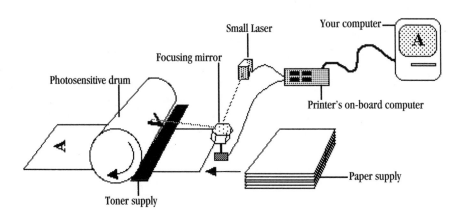

Photosensitive drum
Focusing mirror
Small Laser
Your computer
Printer's on-board computer
Paper supply
Toner supply

## PostScript Printers

Laser printers come in two types. The difference is how they get instructions from your computer. The type shown in Figure 9.6 has a small computer of its own, and receives relatively simple instructions sent from your computer in the PostScript language. PostScript describes pages in terms, such as *put a 14-point bold Times 'A' right here*, and the printer translates that into the pattern of dots you see as **A**. This type of printing is called *PostScript printing*, and has several advantages:

- Since the page descriptions are relatively simple, they can be sent over simple networks. This makes it possible for many computers to share a single printer on a network.

- Most of the work is done by the printer's computer, so printing can be optimized for a specific hardware design.

- Almost all professional typesetting devices share this same language, so you can proof a page on a 300 dpi laser printer and be reasonably certain of the final output on a 2,400 dpi imagesetter.

# Non-PostScript Printers

PostScript printers require an on-board computer and a license to use Adobe's copyrighted PostScript computer language. These things can add more than a thousand dollars to the printer's price tag. Non-PostScript printers, such as Apple's Personal LaserWriter LS, GCC's Personal Laser Printers, and Hewlett-Packard's DeskWriter, skip both language and computer, and rely on the Mac's internal brains instead.

The final printed page can look just as good when printing text as a PostScript page because these companies use the same print mechanisms in their high-end printers, but without the PostScript license and chips the equipment costs much less. On the other hand, because these printers lack the sophisticated software they do not have the capability to create graphic images with the same precision as a PostScript printer, since they draw exactly what is on the page.

Macintosh's non-PostScript printers communicate through the Mac's high-speed SCSI port and are often called *SCSI Printers*. (SCSI, or Small Computer Systems Interface, is pronounced *"SKUZ zy"*) Special software is supplied with the printer to figure out which dots go where. The software uses the Mac's built-in QuickDraw graphics language, so these printers are also sometimes called *QuickDraw Printers*. Most non-Postscript laser printers for the PC use a page description language called PCL, and are called, logically, *PCL printers*. They usually hook up to a PC via a Centronics (parallel) or RS-232 (serial) interface.

While non-PostScript printers can give you excellent printouts at a reasonable cost, they do have a few disadvantages:

- QuickDraw is anything but quick; your computer is tied up a lot longer to print the page.

- SCSI connections are electrically complex, so the printer can't be shared with other computers or even be located more than about ten feet away.

- Both QuickDraw and PCL need special type fonts, plus Adobe Type Manager (ATM) or TrueType, for high-quality text. Neither can handle Encapsulated PostScript images well.

- Because of minor inconsistencies between QuickDraw and PostScript, SCSI printed proofs from the Mac won't accurately preview imagesetter pages.

- Printing to a PCL printer monopolizes a great chunk of the available memory in Windows. While you can perform other tasks while printing, the other programs often run sluggishly because they are sharing the processor's time with the resource-greedy printer.

- PCL printers contain only one or two typefaces in a few sizes. Other fonts must be supplied by a plug-in cartridge or down-loaded from the PC's hard disk as needed. Downloaded fonts (*soft fonts*) take up many megabytes of valuable hard disk space and require a few seconds to download each time they're needed.

Even with these disadvantages, however, the price difference can make a non-PostScript printer a good investment for some users. Both the Apple and GCC versions for Macintosh can be upgraded to full PostScript printing by installing an accessory computer card, and many non-PostScript printers for the PC can be converted to PostScript with special cards or cartridges.

# Types of Type

PostScript printers usually include a few type fonts in their built-in computer—most often Times, Courier, and Helvetica. (Many higher-quality printers also include Avant Garde, Bookman, Helvetica Narrow,

New Century Schoolbook, Palatino, Zapf Chancery, and Zapf Dingbats.)
While it's certainly possible to create a good-looking page with just
these faces, many designers prefer to work with a wider palette.

Downloadable fonts can be sent, via PostScript or TrueType, to the
printer. Hundreds of typefaces are available, representing a good slice of
the history of typography. They can be purchased on floppy disk from
software dealers, or you can buy CD-ROMs preloaded with hundreds of
faces. Some excellent fonts (in PostScript and/or TrueType formats) are
also available as shareware from user groups or computer bulletin
boards.

Figure 9.7 shows a very few of the hundreds of TrueType fonts
available from America Online. Downloading a list of the TrueType fonts
available from AOL (with a brief description of each) took over six
minutes, and took up 147 pages when printed! There are as many or
more for PostScript fonts, and these don't include the thousands of
commercial fonts. TrueType fonts, like PostScript fonts, are scalable and
look good on the computer screen as well as on all kinds of printers.

By the Way . . .
*If you don't have access to a PostScript printer, or if you expect to see
PostScript type looking good on the screen, you need a type manager
utility, such as Adobe Type Manager (ATM). Both ATM and TrueType
smooth the letters to their maximum possible resolution.*

```
┌─────────────────────────────────────────────────┐
│ ▦▦▦▦▦▦▦▦▦═══════ MDP - TrueType Fonts ═══════▦▦▦ │
├─────────────────────────────────────────────────┤
│      UpId  Subject                      Cnt Dnld │
│   🖫 05/16 Maginot Font (True Type)      350 05/23 ⇧│
│   🖫 05/16 Averoigne Font (True Type)    359 05/23 ▓│
│   🖫 05/09 Sinaiticus TrueType           179 05/23 ▓│
│   🖫 05/09 Visage Font (True Type)       255 05/23 ▓│
│   🖫 05/09 Wet Paint v2 (TrueType)       720 05/23 ▓│
│   🖫 05/09 Capel-Y-Ffin TrueType         238 05/23 ░│
│   🖫 04/20 Porter Li'l Kaps (TrueType)   332 05/23 ░│
│   🖫 04/18 Futhark Font (True Type)      397 05/23 ░│
│   🖫 04/18 Castiglione Font (True Type)  554 05/23 ░│
│   🖫 04/18 Octavian Font (True Type)     443 05/23 ⇩│
│   ┌─────────────┐ ┌──────────────┐ ┌───────────────┐│
│   │Get Description│ │ Download Now │ │ Download Later ││
│   └─────────────┘ └──────────────┘ └───────────────┘│
│       ┌─────────────┐     ┌──────────┐              │
│       │ Upload File │     │ More...  │            ▣ │
│       └─────────────┘     └──────────┘              │
└─────────────────────────────────────────────────┘
```

Figure 9.7
Make prettier
pages for less
money with
shareware and
freeware fonts.

PCL printers contain two kinds of built-in fonts: PCL bitmap fonts and
Intellifont scalable fonts. PCL-4 printers support only the bitmap fonts
that come in particular sizes, while PCL-5 printers support both types.
The type of fonts you choose determine whether or not you will be able
to use all of PageMaker's type manipulation features. Both PostScript
and TrueType fonts, including PostScript fonts handled with ATM on

non-postscript printers, will let you transform type in any way you see fit, including rotation and reflection. Intellifont and Bitstream Speedo fonts (for Windows) will not. These two types of fonts can be scaled but not otherwise manipulated. PCL-4 fonts print only at their specified point sizes and cannot be manipulated in any way.

# Font Fundamentals

Fonts have to be installed somewhere. As noted earlier, a few come installed in your PostScript printer. You must install their *screen fonts*, or bitmapped versions, on your computer's hard disk so you can see the fonts correctly on your screen. Downloadable fonts live entirely on your hard drive, both the screen and the printer portions. Whether it's in your printer or on your hard disk, fonts take up space, so you must be judicious in choosing which fonts you really need to have.

Which sizes and styles should you install? That depends on whether you use Adobe Type Manager to help draw characters on-screen. Here are some practical considerations:

- If you're using a PostScript printer but not ATM, and you've got enough room on your hard disk, install all the font sizes and styles available. This will help insure that What You See is, indeed, What You Get. (If space is limited, sacrifice the bold or bold/italic versions first.)

- If you are using ATM, then install just the smallest sizes you're likely to use for body text (usually 9-, 10-, and 12-point). This will let ATM create its own, more accurate versions of the font for larger sizes.

- If you're not using either ATM *or* a PostScript printer, TrueType will look much better in print than a PostScript font.

Windows recognizes several kinds of fonts: the *resident* fonts in the printer's computer, cartridge fonts, and *downloadable* fonts that reside on your hard disk. You can customize your font strategy in Windows by manipulating the WIN.INI file to best employ all the font types available to you. Read your Windows manual to learn how to use WIN.INI to change font pathways and identification numbers.

ATM's Control Panel also updates WIN.INI for the inclusion of any new soft fonts, as does the Windows Fonts control panel for TrueType fonts. The WIN.INI file must have an entry for every printer port to which a PostScript printer is connected. In addition, every soft font must be listed by value so that PageMaker knows where to find them for downloading.

218

On a Macintosh running System 7, TrueType fonts and bitmap versions of PostScript fonts are stored in the System suitcase. The more fonts you add, the slower and larger your system file will be. One of the best ways to manage a great many fonts is to use them from a CD-ROM disk and download them as you need them. You may also want to invest in a font manager such as Master Juggler or Suitcase 2.0, keeping your fonts in suitcases and opening them only when you need them. Figure 9.8 shows my font suitcases.

Figure 9.8
You can stuff as many fonts as you wish into a suitcase, and only install the ones you need.

One difficulty that often arises when you have a great many fonts is that you forget which is which. On the Macintosh, the solution is simple. Font utilities such as Eastgate's Fontina give you WYSIWYG (What You See Is What You Get) menus. You can see your fonts as they'll appear rather than in the Mac's usual Chicago menu font. Or if you use Suitcase, its Resources window, shown in Figure 9.9, will give you a small sample of any open font. You can also set Suitcase to give you a WYSIWYG menu in any application when you press an option key, but it's slow. In Windows, you can open the Fonts dialog box (from the Control Panel) and see each font displayed in the Sample window as you highlight it on the Installed Fonts list.

# Using Downloadable Fonts

Once downloadable fonts are properly installed, you can use them freely in your layout. PageMaker will automatically send the proper information to your printer's memory each time you print. This takes about twenty seconds per font. When the program thinks it won't need the font information anymore, it tells the printer to forget it (but don't worry; the font still lives in your computer). Unfortunately, PageMaker doesn't look ahead to see if a typeface is used on subsequent pages, and will erase a font it might need a moment later. A multi-page document can end up using quite a few of those 20-second downloads.

Figure 9.9
Use Suitcase to see what your fonts really look like.

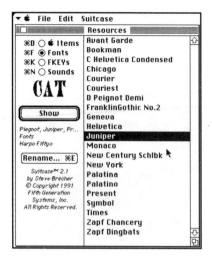

Windows provides three ways to download soft fonts to your printer: automatic/temporary, manual/semipermanent, and manual/permanent. In the automatic method, PageMaker sends the fonts you previously selected in the Compose to printer drop-down list to the printer whenever you select the Print command. These fonts are not permanent, since the Printer has limited memory and PageMaker must flush out old fonts to retrieve new ones if you are using a large quantity of fonts in your document. This can take a long time. The Windows Font control panel lets you install TrueType fonts permanently (although this takes up memory) or temporarily by selecting the appropriate button. Figure 9.10 shows the Font control panel.

If you are using a PostScript printer, you must set up the WIN.INI file so that PageMaker can automatically download fonts to the PostScript printer. You must change the Softfont line so that it includes the location and name of numbered .PFM and .PFB files (the PostScript printer and bitmapped font files) under the entry for the printer port to which the PostScript printer is connected. Check your Windows manual for more information on how to modify the WIN.INI file successfully.

You can also manually download popular PCL fonts so that PageMaker does not have to flush fonts each time it downloads another. These manually downloaded fonts will remain in the non-PostScript printer's memory until you turn it off. The number of fonts you download is limited by the capacity of the printer's memory. Use Windows

Printer Control Panel's Setup dialog box's Font button for the specific PCL-based printer you are using to download fonts to the printer either permanently or temporarily. Figure 9.11 displays the Fonts dialog box for a Hewlett-Packard LaserJet printer.

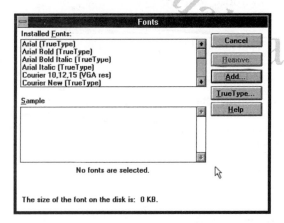

Figure 9.10 The Font Control Panel manages soft TrueType fonts in Windows.

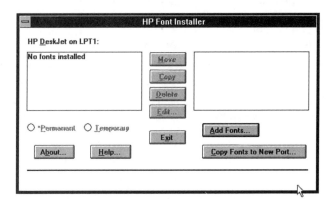

Figure 9.11 Download PCL fonts using your Printer's setup routines, including the Fonts dialog box.

On a Macintosh, you can eliminate the download waiting time by "permanently" downloading to the printer with a *Font Downloader*. Font Downloader is a utility that looks at the printer's memory, sees how many outline fonts the printer can hold at once, and sends you a dialog box with a list of the fonts you can move into the printer's memory for faster printing. You choose the ones you'll need to use and download them. Adobe's version is shown in Figure 9.12.

Apple's Font Utility is similar. Both programs find the specific laser printer you've selected in Chooser, determine its downloading capability, and then present you with a dialog box similar to the Font/DA mover. Both can also print a catalog of available fonts. Apple's Font

Utility is sometimes supplied with third-party fonts and is available from user groups. Adobe's Font Downloader is included with Adobe font disks but won't work with fonts from some other publishers. (When asked how to get around this, Adobe's technical representatives said, "Just buy only Adobe fonts.")

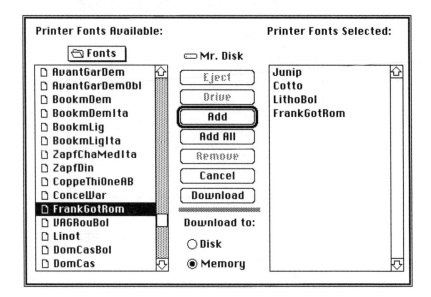

Not all permanent downloads are truly permanent. If you download a font to the printer's memory, it will disappear when you turn off the printer. Even so, this downloading to memory will save you time if you're going to be using the same font a lot. To permanently download a font, you'll have to use the Hard disk option available with some laser printers. It's possible to attach a hard disk to some laser printers, which the printer can use as a memory bank to keep all the outline fonts available to it, without having to download them for each page. Whether or not this can be done depends on the model of printer in use. Both Apple and Adobe's font utilities search for a printer hard disk, and let you download to it instead of the printer memory. A cheap 20 megabyte hard disk can store hundreds of font files, saving lots of time in a busy design shop.

# A Printshop on Your Desktop

Some projects require only a few copies. If you're preparing a report, a proposal, or a certificate that'll be seen by only a few people, you can get surprisingly good final copies from the same printer you've been using for proofs. With a few tricks, you can produce multicolored, two-sided, professionally bound documents easily and inexpensively.

# Have you tried . . . using your laser printer to make your copies?

Laser printed final pages usually look better than photocopies of laser printed pages and frequently look better than offset printing, so the key question is cost. If you're using your own laser printer rather than renting time on one at a service bureau, you may find it economical to run four or five copies of a multi-page report (or a few dozen copies of a single-sided flyer) directly.

# Printing Options

When you open the Print dialog box, you have many choices to make. You can print many copies of your publication or just one. If you have a multipage document, and you're making multiple copies, you can choose to have them collated. Ordinarily, PageMaker would print the determined number of copies of one page, and then go on to the next, and so on. If you select the Collate box, it will print one complete set of pages, in order, and then repeat the process until it has made the number of copies requested. However, collating takes longer to print, since each page must be loaded into the printer's memory all over again.

The *Reverse order* option allows you to tell the printer to print the last page first, and the first page last. Normally, a printer adjusts itself to end up with a stack of pages that has the top page on top. However, on older printers, the first page printed is on the bottom and the last page is on top. In this case, Reverse order allows you to lift a stack of pages off the tray in the correct order, with no paper shuffling.

The *Scaling* option allows you to tell the computer to rescale the entire publication proportionately. You'll find it in the Paper dialog box on the Mac or in the Options dialog box in Windows. This is helpful if, for example, you've designed your layout to print on a Linotronic 300, which can print right to the edge of the paper. However, you're proofing it on a LaserWriter II, which leaves a margin. To fix this, you can simply scale down the publication a few percent, until it fits into the LaserWriter's print area.

The *Print area* is shown in the dialog box (Mac only). Printing Thumbnails is another helpful option. Use it to save paper when you're checking on page layouts, by asking PageMaker to print miniature pages just under two inches high. Because type smaller than 18-point is virtually illegible to the average eye, you won't tend to get caught up in the content of the words and can focus on the weight of the type and the flow from one page to the next.

## Specialty Papers

So far, you've probably done most of your proof printing on standard, low-cost office copier paper. If you're using anything more expensive for PageMaker proofs, you're wasting money. Ordinary 20-pound white paper, available from most office supply stores, is fine for general purpose laser printing. It should cost about $5 a ream (500 sheets). You don't need anything special; just look for a paper grade suitable for Xerographic office copiers.

For direct printing of signs, proposals, and mailers, use a slightly heavier weight paper. Most large office or printing supply houses can sell you Offset weight papers in a variety of colors for around $10 a ream. A 70-pound offset paper is roughly equivalent to 24-pound bond weight paper and usually includes a polished finish on both sides that handles laser toners very well.

Specify a polished, calendared or super-calendared finish, which smooths out the paper itself, rather than a coated finish, which might not react well to the heat generated by a laser printer. (Laid or textured surfaces usually don't print well. Preprinted sheets with raised letter thermography can damage your printer.) Calendaring may also be described as *Lustre*, a reflective finish excellent for flyers and brochures, or *Vellum*, a softer finish that lends weight to proposals and correspondence. Postcards can be printed directly on 110-pound index stock with varying degrees of success, depending on the type of printer and how large the black areas are. Anything heavier will probably jam your printer.

## Specialty Inks

Most affordable desktop laser printers are a little bit like Henry Ford's Model T: "You can have any color so long as it's black." But an inexpensive desktop process can convert your laser printer's print into any color of the rainbow! Letraset's ColorTag system uses sheets of specially colored dry ink that, when heated, bonds to the toner. Where there was toner, you get color. Where there was plain paper, the color peels away. The system comes with a small electrically-heated wand. To use this system, you make a sandwich of the ink sheet and a standard laser (or copier) page, and rub it with the wand to transfer the color. This can be a time-consuming process since the ink sheets have to be carefully aligned with the printout, and you have to rub with just the right pressure. On the other hand, the results look as good as professional foil-stamping and are excellent for short-run certificates and package dummies.

A similar system that uses your laser printer as a heat source has you cut out foil in the right sizes to fit the parts of the page you want colored, and attach them with removable stickers. After you run the page through the printer, and remove the foil and stickers, you have colors where there was black toner.

Of course, you can also duplicate your black and white laser pages in an office copier equipped with a colored toner cartridge. There are color PostScript printers available, but those with desktop prices use inkjets or thermal processes rather than lasers, and most require special paper to produce an acceptable image. A non-PostScript inkjet printer, like the Hewlett-Packard DeskWriter 550C (for Macintosh) can give you a reasonably good color print, as long as you use TrueType or ATM.

# Desktop Binderies

Professional reports and presentations look a lot more effective in a professional binder. Thermal binding systems use an electric heater to melt a thin strip of glue, trapping your pages in a plastic report cover. The result is far less messy than it sounds, and resembles a commercially bound magazine. Mechanical binding systems twist little plastic strips through holes punched in your pages. They can resemble the bent wire binding of some software operating manuals or just appear as a plastic strip along the left edge of your publication. These binding systems can cost as little as $50.

### Watch Out!

*If you are binding a publication, be sure to leave enough gutter space (inner margin) so that you'll be able to read the words close to the inside margin. If the gutter is too narrow, when you open the publication, the text and pictures closest to the inside of the pages will be hidden by the adjacent page.*

## Two-Sided Printing

If you're taking the job to a print shop, they'll take care of getting the pages properly lined up so that page two appears on the back of page one and not on the back of page three. If you're publishing a short run at your desktop, you'll have to do some extra thinking. PageMaker lets you select Print Odd (or Even) side only from the Print document dialog box, so it is possible to run one side of a stack of paper, flip it over, and then run the other side. A few warnings are in order, however:

- Don't try to print more than one copy of the document at a time. PageMaker's Print Odd doesn't work properly if you select multiple copies in the Print document dialog box.

- Make sure the first print run (usually the odd-sided pages) is collated upside down.

If you're using an original LaserWriter, it spits its pages out right side up. Since page three, right side up, lands on top of page one in the output stack, it's automatically collated upside down. (This is a nuisance when printing ordinary reports but handy when printing two-sided documents.) Put the stack (of one-sided printed pages) in the paper tray, and you'll be able to print page two on the back of page one, and page four on the back of page three, just as it should be. Most modern printers flip the pages as they exit, so they're collated properly for reports. If this is the case, select Reverse order in the Print dialog box of the Print menu when you print the odd-sided pages, and then deselect it before you print the even-sided pages.

You'll also have to figure out which side is up in the stack and which end is top. Mark a sheet of paper with an X at what you think ought to be the top, right side up, when it's printed. Then run it through and verify your guess.

A few printers, notably the HP LaserJet 4si, let you print on both sides of the paper at once. If your printer supports double-sided (duplex) printing, on the Mac, you choose **Long Edge** or **Short Edge** from the **Paper** box. In Windows, you choose **Long Edge** or **Short Edge** from the **Options** box. Tall or Wide is on the Print document dialog box in both.

# How to Print All the News Without Throwing a Fit

Chances are, you'll need more than a few copies of your finished project. This generally means you'll have to deal with a commercial printer, whether at a copy shop or at a large, full-service printing plant.

Most printers are knowledgeable, dedicated to their craft, willing to take the time to answer questions and help you get a good job. (If you encounter one of the exceptions, look for a different print shop.) Take advantage of their experience when you're initially planning the job. A good printer will help you choose colors and formats that can avoid expensive custom work. And by all means, talk to the printer before you prepare the final output of your PageMaker design. A quick phone call or visit can make a big difference in the finished piece.

You should be thinking about printing techniques from the first day you start a project. While you're still in the planning stages, you and your printer should pay attention to the following:

- *Finished size:* A stock size or easily cut variation will be much cheaper than a custom size. Depending on the printing process, bleeds (colors that extend off the edge of the page) may change the desired size.

- *Paper type, finish, and color:* Special effects work better on some papers than others. Screened photographs generally work best on smooth white papers. Coated or cover stocks may have different characteristics on different sides.

- *Printing method:* Offset printing's capabilities can vary, depending on how the printing plate is made. Sizes, bleeds, paper choices, and cost will be influenced by how the paper is fed to the press. Some of the different options are discussed later.

- *Binding:* Different methods require different gutters (the area that becomes difficult to read because of the stiffness of the binding). This can have a profound influence on your design, especially if you have layouts that spread across two pages.

- *Coverage:* Large areas of ink adjacent to fine details might print properly in some directions, and badly in others, depending on the type of press and how the paper is fed. If you're planning any large areas of black or colored ink, show a pencil sketch to your printer before you begin.

# Offset Printing Methods

The printing plate is the most important part of the offset printing process. This is ironic since the plate never touches the paper. Offset printing is so named because the plate prints an image on a rubber blanket, which is then pressed against the paper. The image *offsets*, or transfers itself, much like a comic book page being transferred with a piece of Silly Putty. Offset just means the plate doesn't touch the paper. This process is illustrated in Figure 9.13.

Figure 9.13
Offset printing.

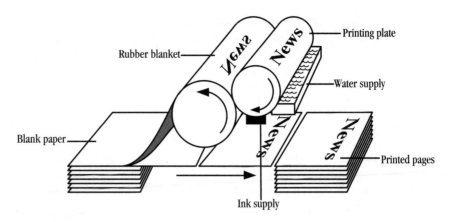

## Printing Plates

All offset plates used to be made of thin metal and were photosensitive. They were exposed through a specially prepared negative, and the resulting positive images could be inked and printed. Metal plates were durable, so the same plate could be used for hundreds of thousands of copies. The negative could be changed (or spotted) by the printer, to correct minor errors. Negatives of screened photographs could be stripped or spliced in to the main negative for extra precision and control.

Today some high-quality offset printing jobs still use negatives, but most use paper-plate printing (often called *Itek* printing). The paper plates can't print more than 10,000 copies, tend to distort or stretch, can't hold as detailed an image, and are impossible to strip or spot (what you shoot is what you print). On the other hand, Itek printing is much less expensive than metal-plate printing. There's no negative, the plate is made directly from the original. These days, most small print shops can't make metal plates. They have to subcontract some of the work to a specialty shop.

The quickest and cheapest paper plates can be made on a large office photocopier or one of the high-end laser printers like a Linotronic. This is done when specially prepared plates are run through the unit, and the deposited toner does a fair job of repelling water when the page is printed. Most desktop laser printers (and small office copiers) can't handle these plates, but some service bureaus and corporate printing departments can.

## Press Size

The other important consideration is the size of the printing press. Most copy shops can't print an image larger than 11" x 17" (and many can't print larger than 10" x 13"). Larger presses cost more per hour to operate, but printing prices are based on the total length of time a press has to run. So even if your finished page will be only 6" x 9", it may be cheaper, depending on the number of pages, colors, and printed copies, to print all the pages at once on a three- or four-foot-wide piece of paper, fold them so the right pages end up in the right places, and then trim the edges to make separate sheets.

Large printing presses may also be web-fed, printing giant images sequentially on a long roll of paper. There's more work involved cutting and folding, but since the paper runs continuously, very large jobs use less press time than if they were sheet-fed. Some presses can handle only one color of ink at a time, others two or four. If you have a print job that requires process color, you may save money by finding a print shop with a four-color press.

## Choosing a Printshop

Obviously, there are many different ways to offset print a given project. And *letterpress*, (using raised, photographically etched plates) or *gravure*, (using plates that hold ink in tiny grooves) might be more appropriate for very large, high-quality jobs. Your local copy shop may provide the most convenient (and in some cases, the cheapest) way to print a simple newsletter. But a large commercial printer with magazine, advertising, or corporate report experience, can offer you a dazzling (and still affordable) range of printing options.

If you haven't already built a relationship with one particular printing company, it's important to shop around. Ask to see samples of similar printed pieces they've done. Decide if you're comfortable with their working style. Then prepare a careful list of specifications including paper, ink, and binding choices, the number of halftones or other special effects, trim size, and number of copies, and ask for a written estimate. Comparing estimates from two or three different printers can be very revealing.

## The Ten Percent Solution

Unless you make changes in the specifications or start changing the design after the job is started, the finished printing bill should match the estimate with one exception. Printers frequently run more copies of the job than you ask for to perfect the ink distribution, and to give them spare copies in case some get damaged. If they don't need the extra copies, they'll give them to you. But even if you don't want the extras, the printer is traditionally allowed to charge you for them, up to ten percent over the agreed cost of the press run. If you're uncomfortable with or unsure of this arrangement, talk to the printer about overrun costs before you give them the job.

# Printing for the Printer

Now that you've picked a printer and printing method, probed potential printing problems, and perfected your pages, it's time to print the master copies of the pages the printer will produce. This can be as simple as putting the proper paper in your laser printer, or it can involve service bureaus, mechanical paste ups, and photographic effects. The choice is determined by your design, printing methods, and quality standards.

## Creating a Laser Master

A 300 dpi laser printer can produce masters that are more than adequate for simple, Itek printing jobs with no photographs or fine type sizes. The process is no more complicated than printing proof pages, which you learned to do earlier in this chapter. There are just a few special considerations.

## Using the Right Paper

Ordinary copy paper is fine for laser proofs. But for final masters, use a special laser output paper. These papers have fibers that hold a smoother line, are particularly opaque and white for maximum contrast, and are designed to stand up to the heat and pressure in laser printers without distorting or curling. Hammermill Laser Plus is preferred by many desktop publishers. It features a special coating on the back that prevents rubber cement or paste-up wax from bleeding through (the back of the paper is marked Paste-Up Side in light blue letters). Laser Plus is available at large office supply stores for about $15 a ream.

If you can't get a true laser output paper, use the smoothest, whitest paper you can find. 70-pound offset white, lustre finish will do an acceptable job. Avoid rag bond papers. Although these high-quality papers are excellent for correspondence and certificates, they have an irregular texture that can cause slight blurring of the tiny toner dots.

## Treat the Paper and Your Printer Properly

Leave laser paper in its original box or ream wrapper until you're ready to use it. Open stacks of paper can accumulate moisture, causing curling and distortion. Fan out the paper before loading it in the paper tray to prevent static cling. After you've printed, put the copies in a flat heavy envelope so they don't pick up any moisture.

You should also make sure your printer is clean. Dry toner is dusty stuff, and it can accumulate on the edges of rollers and in other unfortunate places. Run a test sheet, and examine it carefully for gray smudges (especially along the edges). If you see any, try the following:

- Set up a page with just a single dot or small letter on it, (something that won't require much toner) and print a dozen copies of it. Chances are, the later copies won't have the smudge.

- Feed a Cleaning Sheet through the printer. LaserKleen has a special surface that sucks up loose toner. It costs about $1 a sheet.

- Check your printer's owner's manual for cleaning instructions.

## Printing Larger Pages

PageMaker 5.0 lets you design pages as large as 42" square. But then you run into the question of what to do with them. Some service bureaus might have laser printers capable of tabloid (11" x 17") output, but most laser printers can't create an image wider than eight inches. Larger pages will require tiling to break the image up into printer-sized pieces. You (or the print shop) can then assemble the pieces by hand with scissors and tape. Figure 9.14 shows a page broken up into four tiles. Notice the white margins around each printed piece. The white margin appears because the laser printer can't print up to the edge of its page. When you tape these pieces of a page together, cut the white borders off to make an unbroken image.

**By the Way . . .**

*Taping tiled pieces of a page together is a lot easier if you use a light table, available at most print shops and some service bureaus. These glass-topped tables shine a bright light up through your pages, so you can align them and then cut them with a razor blade.*

*Tiling* is set up through the PageMaker Print document dialog box. Select **Print** from the **File** menu to open the dialog box. If you're using a PostScript printer, click on **Paper** (**Options** button in Windows) to open the box shown in Figure 9.15. Select **Tile Auto** and specify an Auto overlap of at least half an inch, to compensate for the unprintable borders around the edges of most laser printed pages. If yours is not a PostScript printer, click on **Options** to bring up a similar dialog box. When you click **Print**, PageMaker starts tiling from the upper left corner of the publication and prints as many pages as are necessary.

# When Not to Use Auto-Overlap

Most laser printers can't draw a straight line. If you hold a straight edge along the baseline of a full line of type in the middle of the page and look closely, you'll probably notice tiny hills and valleys in the line (shown somewhat exaggerated in Figure 9.16). These are caused by mechanical or paper inconsistencies as the mirror scans the laser beam across the page. Usually, these variations are hardly noticeable. But if the overlap between two tiles falls in the middle of a large graphic or a column of type, and the two tiles don't line up properly, you might see a seam that looks like badly applied wallpaper.

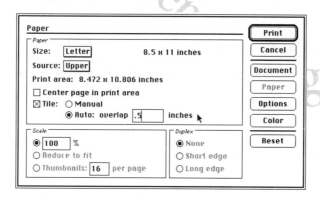

Figure 9.15
Selecting Tiling
in the Print
Paper box.

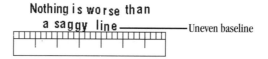

Figure 9.16
Laser printers
rarely draw a
straight line.

You can avoid this kind of tiling problem. If you select **Tile Manual** (on the Paper box on the Mac and on the Options box in Windows), PageMaker will print just one tile with its upper left corner at the zero point. Then you can locate a safe place for the next tile and print it, and so on. To control what part of the image is tiled during manual tiling, reset the ruler zero point on your page to where you want the upper left corner of the tile to start. Place the ruler, then open the **Print document** dialog box. If you're using a PostScript printer, click on the **Paper** button (**Options** button in Windows) to open its dialog box. If you're using a different printer, you'll see tiling options in the Print document dialog box. Click on the **Tile** box and select **Manual**. PageMaker prints just one file at a time this way. Click on **OK** to print the file. Then move the ruler, and repeat the procedure for each tile. If there are no safe places to put the boundaries, you may have to print text and graphics separately on the laser, and manually glue them together just like the pasteups we had to do before desktop publishing was invented.

# Working with an Imagesetter

The best way to get large page images, finely cut type, and good-looking halftones is to print your final copy photographically on a high-resolution imagesetter. These devices, usually available at service bureaus or large print shops, use photographic papers and negatives instead of the office copier drum found in desktop laser printers. The resulting dot pattern is up to eight times more precise, and individual dots can be invisible to the naked eye.

ImageSetters speak the same language as desktop printers. So, you can print accurate proof pages on a PostScript laser printer to check your layout, and be reasonably certain the final photographic output will match. (You can't do this with SCSI, PCL, or QuickDraw laser printers.) In fact, many service bureaus require you to print a proof on their laser printers before you can send a job to their imagesetter. There are, as you might expect, some special considerations for working with imagesetters.

Page dimensions are different for imagesetters. If you are planning larger custom-size pages, you will need to talk to your print shop about the maximum sizes their imagesetter and presses can handle.

In Windows, you need to know the type of printer on which your pages will be printed. Fonts, paper sizes, and resolution (dpi) vary from one brand of printer or imagesetter to another, and you must set up PageMaker with the correct printer driver for the target printer, by selecting it from the Compose to printer drop-down list. Otherwise, you could waste time laying out unprintable pages with fonts that are unfamiliar to the target printer.

On a Mac, you don't need to specify the brand of printer, but you do need to know its resolution in order to resize graphics proportionally. Again, ask your printer to recommend a resolution for the imagesetter or laser printer. Color separations should be printed at a high resolution, preferably 2,540 dpi. Black and white pages and spot colors can be printed at lower resolution, perhaps 600 – 1,200 dpi, with good results.

# Paperless Printing

Imagesetter output is usually on lightweight, high-contrast photographic paper, similar to the paper snapshots are printed on. This copy becomes the master that is then photographed directly onto a paper printing plate, a plastic printing plate, or a negative for a high-quality metal plate. A cheaper alternative for high-quality printing is to create imagesetter output directly onto a film negative. This usually costs slightly more than paper output, but skips the photographic negative step entirely. Scanned halftones can be screened and combined with the image at the same time, eliminating the expensive stripping step at the print shop.

Many publications require one of these composite negatives, including text and halftones, when you submit an ad. However, not all printing jobs (or print shops) want a negative, so check first. In most cases, you'll be asked for a *right-reading emulsion down negative* to make the highest-quality offset plates. A right-reading emulsion down negative is a piece of photographic film with clear letters on a solid, black background, designed for direct contact with the printing plate.

Before you print to a negative, select **Negative** in the **Color** options box. *Emulsion down* means you should also select **Mirror**. PageMaker's default is a positive image, emulsion side up. Some types of imagesetters make these selections from their front panel. Make sure you haven't set up contradictory information in the Print box.

### Watch Out!

*On the Mac, if you set the imagesetter switches to positive, right reading, and the Print Color box to negative and mirror, you'll have a conflict, and possibly a crash.*

## Imagesetter Concerns

Imagesetter output might not match LaserWriter output perfectly, because the image is so much more finely detailed, and the internal computer takes fewer PostScript shortcuts. Here are some things you need to watch out for when you're making the transition from Laser printer to imagesetter:

- Hairline rules are considered by most drawing programs to be one dot high. On a laser printer, this is 1/300th of an inch, a nice size for ruling forms or music staves. The same rule on an imagesetter, 1/2,400th of an inch high, virtually disappears. Whenever you can, define your rules and lines in point sizes in PageMaker.

- Grays at both ends of the scale will fool you. A 10% gray on a laser printer, because of its nice, round dots, is a fairly usable background pattern. On an imagesetter, it virtually disappears. Similarly, a laser's 90% gray has noticeable white dots. Anything darker than 70% on an imagesetter appears almost black.

### Watch Out!

*PageMaker's fill patterns are not true PostScript grays. If you need absolutely accurate gray-scale tones, import them from a PostScript drawing program.*

- Very complex graphics are likely to confuse an imagesetter because the system pays more attention to the PostScript commands that create them. Even scraps of text or graphics left outside the printing area on the pasteboard can throw off an imagesetter. If the printer won't handle your job, make sure the pasteboard is clean. If this doesn't help, try printing one page at a time. If you still have problems, you might have to go into a drawing program and simplify your graphics. This may be advisable anyway, since service bureaus charge by the minute for imagesetter time.

# Commercial Color Printing

Black and white pages are inexpensive to produce and are fine for some purposes, but if you're serious about desktop printing and graphic design, you are going to have to get into color. Color printing is a much more complex process. Instead of one ink, you have anywhere from two to a half dozen. *Process color* uses four different inks: Cyan, Magenta, Yellow, and blacK. It's sometimes called CMYK printing. (Yes, K stands for black, so it's not confused with blue, which, in process terms, is Cyan.) Process colors are printed by overlapping halftone screens of the three translucent colors—cyan, magenta, and yellow. Although you could, in theory, make black from equal parts of the three, printers use a true black for better results.

It's quite common to use one or more *spot colors,* in addition. A spot color is a specific ink color, which is premixed as an opaque or semi-opaque ink, rather than being composed of individual dots like process colors. Spot colors are used when you must match exactly a predetermined color, as in a corporate logo, or when only one or two colors are needed rather than continuous tone blends. *Tints* are made by screening spot colors. Tints are often used to add color behind a block of type.

To print colored artwork, the colors must be broken down, or separated into the four process colors. A separate film or paper print is produced for each, hence the term color separations. PageMaker 5.0 can print spot and process color separations on a PostScript imagesetter. The printer uses these separations to prepare the plates for color printing. When you look at the Edit color dialog box, you will see the process colors specified, along with any spot colors you may have used in your publication (see Figure 9.17).

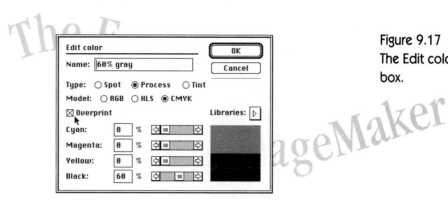

Figure 9.17
The Edit color
box.

PageMaker supports several different color-matching systems. If you intend to use spot color, be sure to check with your printing facility to see which color matching system they prefer to use. Always choose colors according to printed samples since colors look different on a computer screen than they do when printed.

You can convert spot colors to their process color equivalents for printing, or print them as spot colors. You can also specify whether a spot color prints over another color that it overlaps, or knocks out the color behind it. This is important, since printing inks are seldom totally opaque. You may want to deliberately lay one color over another to produce a third, or you may decide to knock out the first color so the second prints on the paper and retains its original characteristics. This is done in the **Define Colors** dialog box, on the **Element** menu. Spot colors knock out by default. To overprint, select the name of the color to overprint and open the **Edit color** box as shown in Figure 9.17. Click on the **Overprint** check box to overprint that color. Otherwise the color beneath it will be knocked out. Click **OK** to confirm and close the box.

To print spot color separations, open the **Print document** dialog box, and then the **Color** box (Figure 9.18). Click on **Separations**. Select the name of each spot color ink to print, and click on **Print this ink**, or double-click it on the menu, so that it's checked. Uncheck any that you don't want to print. On the Mac, you can change the default screen angle from 45 degrees to some other angle for a special effect. When done, click **Print** to create your separations. Be sure to leave Registration checked (on the color separations list), whenever you're printing more than one color. It puts registration marks on every page, so the separations can be properly aligned.

Figure 9.18
The Color
dialog box.

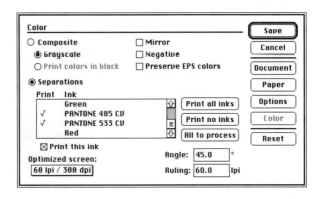

When you process color separations, you still have the choice of printing all inks or only specific ones, and what screen ruling and angle to produce best results (on the Mac) when printed. As a general rule, unless you have reasons to do otherwise, accept PageMaker's default settings for screens and angles. Doing so avoids the rosette and moirè effects that can otherwise occur when screens overlap badly. PageMaker's PPD files contain the information for the best screen angles and rulings for various kinds of printers. That's why it's important to verify that you have chosen the correct printer type in the Print document dialog box.

### By the Way . . .

*PPD stands for PostScript Printer Description. Each PPD file describes the standard features for a particular printer, including the amount of memory available, the predefined paper sizes it handles, the resident fonts, and optimized screens for color separations. If you install additional fonts or memory in a printer, you'll need to create a custom printer file for it. (See PageMaker's documentation for instructions.)*

To print process color separations, choose **Print**, and be sure the proper target printer is selected (Windows) and the proper printer type. Click on **Color**, and then select **Separations**. If desired (ask your print shop!), select **Mirror** and **Negative** options (on the Mac). Select the process colors and verify their screen angles. Usually they are as follows: black, 45 degrees; magenta, 75 degrees; yellow, 90 degrees; and cyan, 105 degrees. Double-click on the Process colors you want to print, or click on **Print All Inks**. Then, go ahead and print it.

*Trapping* is a concern for both spot and process color printing. When separations are printed slightly misregistered, they can leave gaps where a spot color hasn't completely filled its knockout, or a color shift where two process colors haven't completely overlapped to make a third.

Trapping compensates by deliberately overlapping colors by a small amount, anywhere from about a twentieth of a point up to as much as two points. Trapping errors are one of the most frequent reasons for reprinting a job, and one of the more easily avoidable ones. Traditionally, trapping is handled by the commercial printer, and it's often done using a desktop printing utility like Aldus TrapWise, to set precise trap values.

Be sure to talk to your commercial printer about trapping your color separations. Ask whether they'll do it, or if it's your responsibility. If you are doing it, find out exactly what needs to be trapped and what size traps to specify. Process color trapping is done by creating a shared color or third color trap for objects that share some common colors. If you have, for instance, an orange square on a purple background, both the orange and purple contain a good deal of magenta. So the trap would be magenta, and you'd notice it much less than a white gap where the colors missed. If the objects don't share a common color, make one by combining the colors they do contain. Thus, if one object was a mix of 50 yellow and 50 magenta, and the other 75 cyan and 25 black, your trap color would be 75C, 50M, 50Y, and 25K. The darker line will be less obtrusive than a light one.

# Working with Service Bureaus

Service bureaus charge for their time, usually at a flat fee per hour for the use of their Macs, plus a small charge per laser output page (currently about $8 a page in the Boston area for Lino output). So, if you're going to use a service bureau, you want to do it quickly and with as few mistakes as possible. A little preparation will help a lot.

# Preparing Disks for a Service Bureau

Naturally, you'll want to make up a floppy disk with a copy of your PageMaker document to take to the service bureau. Even though PageMaker embeds TIFF graphics in its documents, it's also a good idea to copy any graphic files you've used in the document. Be sure any linked files are copied. Call the service bureau to make sure they have outline fonts to match all the screen fonts you've used in your layouts. If they don't have the ones you need, check your own system folder and put copies on your disk.

In fact, as a general rule of thumb when going to a service bureau, when in doubt, bring a copy. Some users bring their entire hard disk. (If you're planning to do this, check the virus warning later in this chapter.)

Some Macintosh programs used to cause trouble at service bureaus because they described fonts by number instead of by name. If the service bureau's Mac assigned the number to a different font, the results would be unpredictable. Fortunately, you probably won't encounter these font conflicts, both because Apple has changed the way it assigns font numbers and because PageMaker 5.0 refers to fonts by name instead of by number. However, you can still get some surprises. Classic type families (like Garamond) are frequently available from multiple publishers. One publisher's screen version might not line up with another publisher's outline version, affecting column alignment and justification. There are even slight differences between the screen version of Times supplied by Apple with their systems and the one supplied by Adobe with ATM.

By the Way . . .
*You can avoid most spacing problems by borrowing copies of the screen versions of the fonts your service bureau uses, before you start the design. This isn't considered software piracy; it's the outline versions that count (and are usually copyrighted).*

## Leave Home Without It

If you want to save as much time as possible at a service bureau or print shop, don't bring a PageMaker file at all. Select **Print** from the **File** menu and open the Print Options dialog box, as shown in Figure 9.19. Under Postscript, click the **Write Postscript to File** box. This lets you *print to disk*, which means you can save your entire publication on floppy disk as a PostScript file, which can be sent directly to the printer with no intervening software. You can even send the resulting file to the printer by modem, if you want, or store it on a removable SyQuest cartridge or other medium. Check with your print shop or service bureau to see what format(s) they accept. If you check **Normal** in the PostScript box, you'll get a pure PostScript text file, the standard for most printing operations.

If you check **EPS**, you'll get an Encapsulated PostScript image of a single page attached to a low resolution screen image, which can then become part of an even larger PageMaker document. If you have the outline fonts in your System folder and want to guarantee compatibility at the service bureau, check Download PostScript fonts; this will build copies of the fonts into your PostScript file. If you check **Separations**, the file will be saved as a set of color separations, which the printer or service bureau can output directly to film.

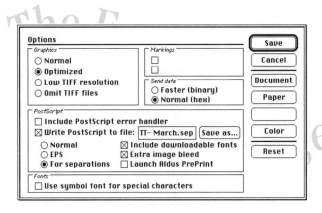

Figure 9.19
PageMaker will
automatically
assign a file
name to the
print file.

One advantage of printing PostScript to disk is that you needn't send
the printer all of the linked graphics files. They're incorporated as part
of the PostScript page description. Another is that you needn't worry
about whether the printer or service bureau is using the same version of
PageMaker, or whether they have the same version of Windows or the
Macintosh System and Finder that you use. PostScript files on disk are
always compatible. And, if you've downloaded the fonts you've used,
your type will print correctly whether or not the print shop has installed
the same fonts.

Again, use the telephone first. Some print shops prefer PostScript
files to PageMaker files because they use less computer time to print.
Some service bureaus would rather get PageMaker files to guarantee a
chance to refine the proof.

# Virus Warning

Computer *viruses* are little sections of self-copying computer code that
can jump into otherwise useful software, with frequently destructive
results. Service bureaus, unfortunately, are one place they've been
known to spread. Innocent (or malicious) users bring infected floppies
with their applications for printing, and a copy of the virus jumps onto
the service bureau's hard disk. If you're not careful, it can then jump
onto your floppy and back to your hard disk when you get home.
Fortunately, viruses are fairly easy to avoid, if you follow these simple
tips:

- Don't bring public domain (or illegally copied) applications or
  HyperCard stacks home from the service bureau. Most
  Macintosh viruses are carried by the resource forks found in
  applications and stacks, rather than by the data forks found in
  PageMaker files. (*Forks* are a way of organizing stuff in a Mac

application. There are resource forks and data forks. The data fork is the "what," and the resource fork is the "how to.")

- Lock your floppy by moving the plastic tab over the little hole before you go to the service bureau. No known virus can jump to a locked disk.

- Follow the same rules to avoid contamination when taking materials to and from your PC as you would from your Mac. PCs have their own brand of viruses, and although they do not cross-pollute Macs, they are just as dangerous to your PC and to Windows. Be sure to install a virus detection and protection program and scan any floppy for potential viruses that you insert into any drive on your computer. Lock your floppy disks and never use the master disk of any program, but only a copy.

- To be extra careful, don't put the disk back into your machine when you get home. Viruses are spread by inserting your floppy disk into your computer.

- Install a virus detection program into your Mac or PC. Programs such as Symantec Anti-Virus for the Macintosh (SAM), Virex, or Disinfectant (or the Norton AntiVirus for the PC) continuously scan for viruses and when detecting any suspicious activity, fix the problem by either forbidding the activity or repairing your disk and computer. Symantec and other virus prevention software manufacturers keep their products continuously updated for the newest virus strains via on-line bulletin boards.

# The Bare Essentials

In this chapter, you learned all about the printing part of desktop publishing, and how to handle printing jobs that can't be done on your own desktop. Specifically, you learned:

- Desktop laser printers sell for a wide range of prices, deter-mined (primarily) by whether or not they use the PostScript printing language. This affects printing speed and compatibility with other printers.

- Paper quality affects printing quality. Papers range from very cheap (for everyday proofing) to very fancy for desktop reports, individually printed flyers, and high-quality printing masters.

- Cheap desktop processes can add color and professional bindings to your laser output.

- Offset printing methods vary greatly in price, quality, and capability. Choose carefully before you begin the design process.

- Your desktop laser printer can create bigger pages or effectively higher resolution output, with a few simple tricks.

- You can create spot color and process color separations directly from PageMaker. Color knockouts are created by default. Trapping can prevent problems caused by misregistration of colors.

- For the highest quality output, make a positive or negative image with an imagesetter, available at service bureaus. If you prepare your material carefully for the service bureau, you can avoid expensive disappointments.

- Some reasonable, common-sense precautions can protect you from most virus infections when you bring your disks to another machine.

## Chapter 10

## Chapter Preview

*Using pre-existing templates*

*Designing your own forms*

*Invoices, order forms, and ruled forms*

*Letterheads, logos, and business cards*

*Catalogs*

*Sales reports and annual reports*

# PageMaker Goes to Work

Now that you've mastered the basics of working with PageMaker 5.0 and newsletter design, it's time to take a look at some of the other tasks PageMaker can make easier. Businesses, artists, and design shops use PageMaker for laying out and creating all kinds of forms, stationery, and reports. If you look at the contents of an average desk drawer, virtually everything that's printed could have been done in PageMaker, and it's likely that much of it *was*. PageMaker has been the choice of graphics professionals ever since it first appeared, but it's so simple to use that even the beginner can create invoices, business cards, appointment slips, labels, letterheads, package designs and much more.

## Using Pre-made Templates

Grandpa used to say, "There's no point in reinventing the wheel." What he meant was simply that there's no good reason to redo something that's already done well. He had a point. Basic business forms, like purchase orders, invoices, and receipts, needn't be recreated each time you need them. The form itself is standard issue. All that needs to be customized is the name and address of the company.

This brings us to the real point of this section. When you purchased PageMaker, the package included a set of templates. These basic layouts, for all kinds of business forms and documents, can save you hours of design time and effort. However, you still need to know how to use PageMaker to customize them. You have to insert your own company's name and address, and change the logo to yours. You should also make sure the form either fits the procedures your business already follows, or will make them more efficient.

PageMaker comes with a selection of predesigned templates, ranging from letterheads, envelopes, and purchase orders to multipage catalogs, brochures, and even Avery labels. If you belong to a user group, a local group, or an on-line information service, such as America Online, CompuServe, or Delphi, you have another good source for templates. There are many generous people who are happy to share their designs, either for free or for a small shareware fee.

# Working with Templates

There are two kinds of templates you may encounter. PageMaker 5.0's templates are provided in a special format, as scripts, which you'll find under the Aldus Additions submenu. Templates from earlier versions of PageMaker and templates you create yourself are saved as template publications. To convert a script into a template, you must open it with the Open template Addition. Here's how:

1. Open the **Utilities** menu, and pull down the **Aldus Additions** submenu, as shown in Figure 10.1.

2. Select **Open template**, and then select the name of the template you would like to use from the list of installed template scripts. When you click on the name of the template script, you will be able to see a thumbnail view of the template it creates. Figure 10.2 shows an example.

3. If you want the template in a size other than the one shown, use the Page size popup menu to set an appropriate page size for your publication.

Figure 10.1
Click on Open
Template to
open the
Template
Script selec-
tion box.

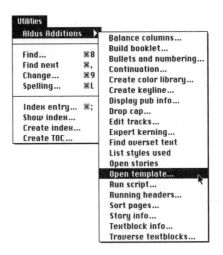

Figure 10.2
The box shows
a thumbnail of
the template
the script
creates.

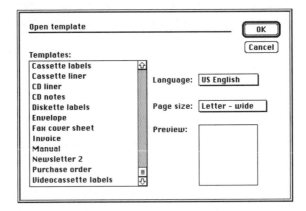

4.   Click **OK** when done, and PageMaker will create the template you've requested as an untitled publication. (In a few cases, PageMaker may prompt you to supply more information. After you respond to the dialog boxes, the template will be created.)

After you've created a template from a script, you should save it as a regular publication template. Doing so lets you open it from the regular menu using the Open command, and eliminates the time it takes PageMaker to convert an Additions script into a template. To save a script template as a template publication, choose **Save As** from the **File** menu, give the template a name, and click the **Template** button, as shown in Figure 10.3.

If you know you'll only be using a template once, you might want to save it as a regular publication instead. No matter how you save it, your modifications don't affect the Additions template script; you can use it again and again in its original form.

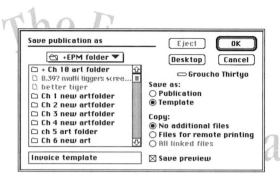

Figure 10.3
Click the Template button to save the file as a template.

When you want to base a new publication on a template, first start PageMaker, and then open it by selecting **Open** from PageMaker's **File** menu. When you open a template in this way, you actually open an untitled copy of the template. (Note that the Copy button is automatically selected.) If you start PageMaker by clicking on a Template icon in a folder (on the Mac), you'll open the original template instead of a copy. Any changes you make will be made to the template itself. On the Macintosh, templates can be identified by their icons, as shown in Figure 10.4; in Windows, they're distinguished by the .PT5 file extension.

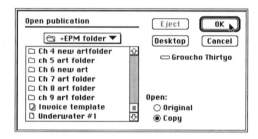

Figure 10.4
Opening a copy of the Invoice template.

### By the Way . . .

*If you're not sure whether you've opened the template or a copy, look at the title bar of the open document, or watch the screen as the publication opens. A copy will open as **Untitled**, and the legend on the opening thermometer will say, **Opening a copy of....** If you accidentally open the template itself, close it and open a copy.*

Once you've opened a copy of the template, you can customize the form to suit your needs. You can name and save it, and do anything to it that you'd do to any other PageMaker publication.

# Designing Functional Forms

A famous architect, Le Corbusier, observed that, "Form follows function." He was referring to buildings, of course, but it's also true of business forms and other documents. In fact, it's the function that determines the format of the form. If you're designing a business form, either from scratch or from a template, you need to think about how to make the form as functional as possible. How do you know what you really need? Ask yourself and the people who regularly use the form these questions:

- Who uses this form? When? How many copies are needed? How is it filled in; typed, handwritten, or by computer?

- Why are we replacing the present form? Is there a problem with the current version, or is this a cosmetic change? If this is a brand new piece of paperwork, will it solve a problem? Provide needed information? Make a process easier?

- Assuming this replaces a previous form, were there parts of the old one that were never filled in? Was additional information needed with no place to enter it?

Now you can take a more educated look at the form itself. Figure 10.5 shows a typical purchase order form, one of PageMaker's templates. It could be used as is, after replacing the logo, company name, and address with your own. Or, based on the information you gathered by talking to the people who would be using the form, you could make some changes that would make it even better.

Figure 10.5
PageMaker's
Purchase
Order
template.

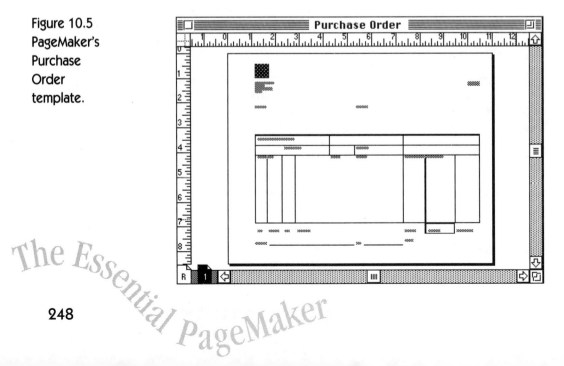

For example, one problem with this particular form was that users tended to get confused and enter the vendor's name in the area that was intended for the shipping address. They would then insert the form in a window envelope meant for a different form, and end up mailing it to themselves. The close view in Figure 10.6 shows the problem and the reason. The solution: simply switch the two address boxes, an easy job in PageMaker.

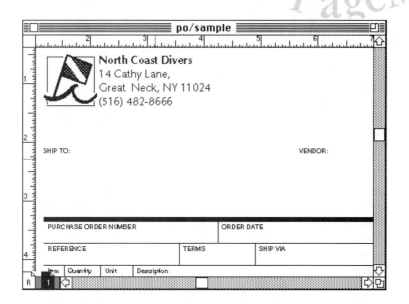

Figure 10.6
The Vendor box and the Ship to box need to be reversed.

To customize a template, you'll need to remove the placeholders Aldus has inserted for a logo and company name. On some PageMaker templates, these are on the master page rather than on the working page, so you'll need to go to the master page in order to delete them. Delete the contents of the text block and type in your own information. Use the Place command to place your company logo, or copy it and paste it in from the Scrapbook (Macintosh) or from the Clipboard (Windows).

After making any other revisions to the form, print a proof copy. Don't forget to save your work. If you like what you see in the proof version, think about the next step. If this is a brand new form, it may be a good idea to run off a dozen pages on the office copier and try them out in daily use before you go to the expense of having hundreds printed.

For a small business and a low-use form, such as a purchase order or an employment application, photocopying might be the most cost efficient way to continue. If your bookkeeping system requires multiple copies of invoices and other forms, have the forms printed on multiple-part NCR (No Carbon Required) paper. These are available as pinfeed forms for dot-matrix printers as well as separately. NCR forms can't be run through a laser printer, but can be written on, typed on, or used in any dot-matrix or daisywheel printer. The printshop can also number forms sequentially, or you can purchase a hand operated numbering stamp to do the same job.

# Designing Your Own Forms

It could be there's no template readily available for the form you need, or perhaps you'd just rather have the fun of doing it yourself. Designing forms with PageMaker is simple. The biggest problem, that of drawing straight lines, is already taken care of for you. In this section, you'll see several different ways to lay out forms.

The considerations in designing a useful form are the same as those for improving an existing one. Consider the purpose and decide what information must be put into the form. Make a pencil and paper dummy—or two or three—until you find an arrangement that seems to make sense. Then open PageMaker and place guide lines, and then text and graphics as needed, just as you would for a newsletter or any other project.

Figure 10.7 shows the grid for a form listing various items with check-off boxes. This particular page has been set up with three columns. Later, the company name, address, and logo will be added to the page.

Figure 10.7
Begin by
setting up a
grid of column
guides and
ruler guides.

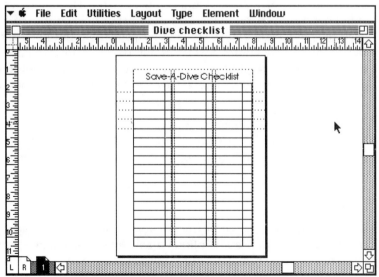

# Drawing Lines Manually

To draw the lines individually, select a line weight from the **Line** submenu under the **Element** menu. Using the **Perpendicular** line tool, simply begin at one margin and drag a line across the page to the opposite margin. Use the ruler guides to space the lines. Be sure that Snap to rulers is selected. It makes your ruler guides act as if they're slightly magnetic. The lines you draw will automatically be attracted to them, making precise placement much easier.

# Drawing Lines Automatically

Another way to place ruled lines equally spaced is to draw one, copy it, and select **Multiple paste** from the **Edit** menu, as shown in Figure 10.8. Multiple paste lets you paste as many of an item as you want, at predesignated offsets. Define the spacing you want, click **OK**, and the lines will snap into place.

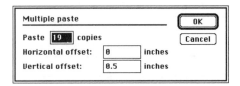

Figure 10.8 If the page is 11 inches, it can hold a total of 20 lines a half inch apart, allowing for the margins.

# Drawing Lines with Paragraph Rule

You can also let PageMaker draw the horizontal lines as part of the text formatting. To do so, follow these steps:

1. Create your list, either in Story Editor or in your favorite word processor. Set it up so each item is on a separate line with a single carriage return, as shown in Figure 10.9.

2. Place the list on the page, and adjust the type size and leading as needed to correctly position the various list items within the grid.

3. Select everything to be underlined. Open the **Paragraph specifications** dialog box and within it, the **Rules** box. Choose a line width and color, and click on **Rule below paragraph**.

4. Open the **Options** box (as shown in Figure 10.10) and select **Align to grid**. In the Grid size box, enter the amount of leading as the grid spacing. Close all the boxes at once by pressing **Option+Enter or Return** (use the **Alt** key **instead of Option** on the PC). A line appears between each pair of words. Figure 10.11 shows the finished form.

Figure 10.9
One item per line, followed by a carriage return, makes each item a separate paragraph.

Figure 10.10
Ask PageMaker for a rule below each paragraph.

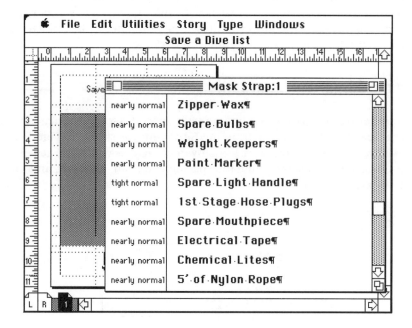

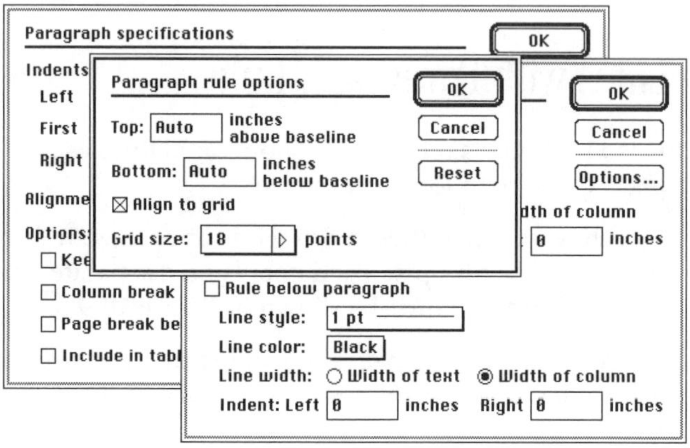

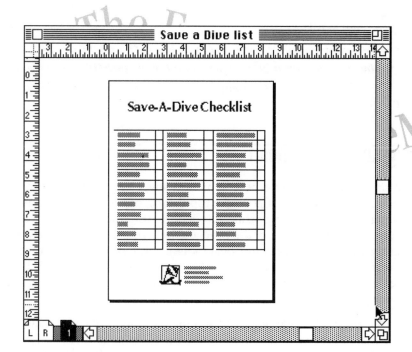

Figure 10.11
Add the vertical lines to make check boxes.

# Business Pages

Quite often a business needs not just one form but a whole package including letterheads, business cards, fax transmittal forms, invoices, purchase orders, and all the other paraphernalia of a small corporation. In order to achieve a corporate look, these pieces should contain common elements so that they have a similar look and feel. Using the same type font and placing the same corporate logo on each piece will help. Choosing a corporate color scheme for ink and paper colors on stationery, business cards, annual reports, and brochures will also help create your corporate image.

The greatest challenge in designing related pieces lies in finding combinations of type that look good in a variety of sizes, and logos that are simple, yet striking, in both large and small versions. Using a graphics program on the Mac, such as SuperPaint or FreeHand (or on Windows using CorelDRAW! or Harvard Graphics), allows you to experiment with scaling a logo to different reductions. Of course, you can use PageMaker to experiment, too. Place your logo as a graphic on a blank PageMaker page, copy it a dozen times, and scale each copy differently. Print the page so you can see what happens at various sizes.

**By the Way . . .**
*Create the logo as a PICT (CGM, CDR, or WMF on the PC) or an EPS graphic, rather than a bit-mapped (Paint, PCX, or BMP) file. As you learned in Chapter 8, bit-mapped images often become jagged-looking when they're resized.*

# Designing a Letterhead

Although the word letterhead somehow suggests that anything you place on the page must go at the top (head), this is an old-fashioned design rule that you may choose to ignore. Letterheads can have type running along the side of the page and/or across the bottom, as well as at the top. PageMaker is the ideal tool for this type of task, as you have a great deal of flexibility with type placement. Just remember to leave at least ¼-inch of margin so your design will fall within the imaging area of your printer.

A *formal* letterhead generally has the company name and address, either centered or set flush left at the top of the page. The logo, if any, is small, neat, and dignified. A more casual one might have the address block across the bottom or at the side of the page, and would have a larger and perhaps less serious logo. Using PageMaker's Text rotation feature can help you produce unusual effects. Figure 10.12 shows some examples of various styles of letterhead.

Stick with standard 8 ½" x 11" paper and number 10 envelopes. Other sizes will cost more and look less professional. They're also more likely to jam in your laser printer. Envelopes should use the same type style as the stationery, in letters small enough to make a neat corner block. Use of a logo on the envelope is optional.

**Watch Out!**
*Avoid thermographic (raised letter) printing on letterheads, envelopes, or any other printed item that might be run through your laser printer or photocopier. The heat will melt the raised letter ink and gum up the printer, possibly requiring a new drum or other expensive repair.*

Business cards can be printed as a page of ten and cut apart. The correct measurements are 3 ½" x 2", or 21 x 12 picas. Set the page up so cards are two across and five down. The grid for a page of business cards is shown in Figure 10.13. Design one card and copy it into the other nine positions. You can change the names on each card if you want. Have business cards printed on a heavy stock. (100-pound cover is a minimum weight for cards.) Ask the printer about embossing the logo or adding a second color to the card. Don't forget to add crop marks to show the printer where to cut the cards apart. Figure 10.14 shows the proper position for the crop marks.

If you're having something else printed on heavy stock and trimmed to size, you can often sneak business cards in on the cropped area. Similarly, if you're having shipping labels printed and trimmed on crack & peel paper, place other odd size labels in the margins. Figure 10.15 shows a page of labels arranged to get maximum value from a single sheet of paper.

Figure 10.12 Letterheads may be formal, funky, or simply functional.

# Have you tried . . . using a single negative for several items?

Here's a tip from the pros. If you're laying out a letterhead, place the business cards, envelope block, or whatever else will fit on the same page. Have the printer or service bureau make one negative of the whole page. Ask them to mask it or cut it up as necessary to make the printing plates for the other jobs. You've saved the cost of several negatives.

Figure 10.13
A grid for a
page of
business cards.

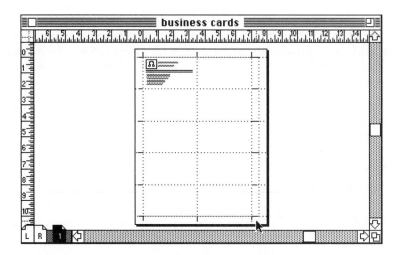

Figure 10.14
The thin, black
lines at the
margins of the
cards show the
printer where
to cut.

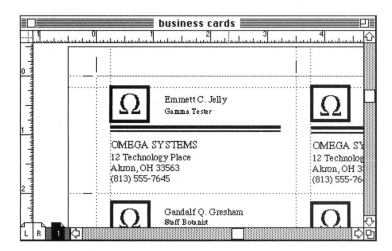

Figure 10.15
Five cuts give
you six differ-
ent kinds of
labels.

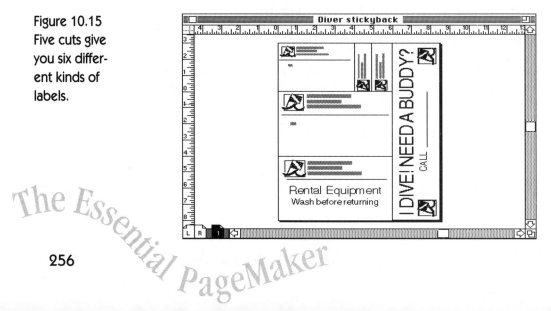

# Catalogs

Catalogs are one of the more complicated jobs a layout artist ever has to handle. PageMaker can make producing a catalog a good deal easier, and you can save additional time and effort by standardizing your layout.

A catalog is a multipage publication, and since most of the pages can be identical in terms of layout and design, creating a master page layout is the best way to proceed. Think also about how the catalog will be printed and bound, and how many pages you'll need to produce. As always, make a dummy before you proceed.

Usually, the outer covers of a catalog are printed on a heavier weight paper or even card stock. They generally contain the name of the company and a logo, or other illustration. The covers may, but not necessarily, include pictures and descriptions of merchandise. You may decide to make the catalog a self-mailer by leaving an area for an address label and mailing indicia.

Will there be an order form bound in? If so, it may be wise to let this fall on the center pages of the catalog. This way it's possible to remove it without tearing the whole catalog apart. Setup the catalog pages with a grid, perhaps mirroring left to right, as shown in Figure 10.16.

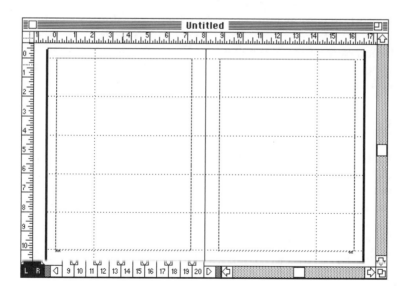

Figure 10.16
A grid for catalog pages.

For catalog work, you'll need access to a scanner of some kind. To maintain a more consistent look, decide on a single type of illustration, such as line drawings, photos screened as halftones, and so on. If you're using pictures from the manufacturer's catalog sheets, trim away extraneous backgrounds, and try to scale all the illustrations to the same relative size. Use the same typefaces and sizes throughout. If you keep graphics and text linked to the publication, the inevitable last minute updates will be easier to manage. Figure 10.17 shows an example of a catalog entry.

Figure 10.17
A typical
catalog entry.

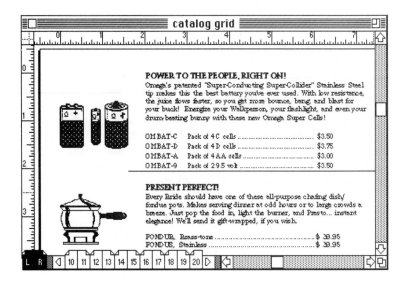

Most catalogs include an index to help users find specific items more easily. PageMaker can produce the index for you. Highlight the words to be indexed, and the list will be automatically assembled with appropriate page numbers. Chapter 12 explains in detail how to make index entries and assemble the index.

## Sales Reports and Annual Reports

Large corporations often spend many thousands of dollars to produce their annual reports. These documents, sent to stockholders and potential investors, detail how well the company is doing, usually with the aid of charts, graphs, balance sheets, long blocks of copy, and lavish illustrations. Many reports include letters from the Chairman of the board or CEO. These reports generally have two things in common: they look expensive and they were (mostly) produced in PageMaker. Even if you're working on a shoestring budget, your presentation can be thoroughly professional.

On the Mac, tables can be imported from any program that creates them, such as Microsoft Excel or Word. The easiest way is to save the table as a text file, tab-delimited. This means that the columns are separated by tabs, and the rows by carriage returns. When you import the text file, the characters take on your publication's default attributes. You can then reposition the tabs with PageMaker's tabs ruler, change the font and size if you want, and apply any other changes. If the table's columns don't seem to be correctly aligned in your publication, It may be that the space between the tabs is too narrow for the font size you are using. Try a smaller font, or choose a tighter track.

You may decide to use rules between the rows and columns in the table. If so, insert them as we did in the ruled form above. As an alternative, try putting a block of tint behind the middle column of a table, as shown in Figure 10.18.

| Hand | Number of combinations | Odds - #of hands played |
|---|---|---|
| Royal flush | 4 | 1 in 649,740 |
| Straight flush | 36 | 1 in 72,193 |
| Four of a kind | 624 | 1 in 4,165 |
| Full house | 3,744 | 1 in 694 |
| Flush | 5,108 | |
| Straight | 10,200 | |
| Three of kind | 54,912 | |
| Two pairs | 123,552 | |
| One pair | 1,098,240 | |

**Lucy's Lemonade**          May, 1990

| | Actual Income | Percent of totals |
|---|---|---|
| Current Assets - | | |
| Cash on hand | $ 43.75 | 68 |
| Inventory - cups, sugar | 12.50 | 19.5 |
| Fixed Assets - Pitchers, ladle, signs, etc. Current Assets - | 8.00 | 12.5 |
| Total Assets | $ 64.25 | 100 % |

Figure 10.18
A chart and a simple balance sheet.

Although PageMaker for the Macintosh dropped the use of the Table Editor program from version 5.0, PageMaker for Windows has retained its use. This nifty little program consists of a series of cells into which you can enter your information (see Figure 10.19). You then can manipulate the cells, changing their size and shape, fonts, styles, and shading, as well as line up cells so that the text wraps appropriately. To import information into the Table Editor, save it as a tab-delimited ASCII text file. Open up the Table Editor, and place the data as you would into a PageMaker document. The different sections of tabbed data fall into the appropriate cells ready for your manipulation.

Figure 10.19
Windows Table
Editor 2.0
makes generat-
ing tables easy.

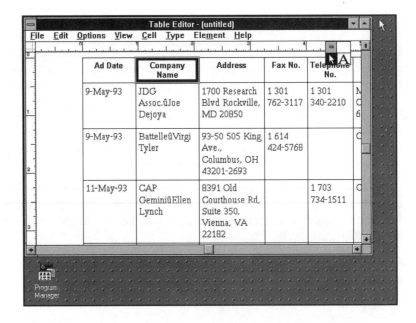

When you're finished creating your table, choose **Export** from the **File** menu. In the Export to file dialog box, choose **Windows Metafile** under **File format**. That way, your table will be saved as a graphic. Give your table a name, and then click on **OK**. It will be automatically saved with the Windows Metafile extension.

You can choose **Text only** as the file format, but you will lose a lot of your formatting that way. An advantage to choosing **Text only** is that you'll be able to edit your table's text from within PageMaker instead of having to go back to Table Editor.

To import the table into PageMaker, use the **Place** command. From the Place document dialog box, select your table from the file list. It should have a **WMF** extension. Click on **OK**, and then place the graphic as usual. You'll be able to crop, size, and apply colors to the table just like you can with a regular graphic.

If you change the original table through Table Editor, make sure to export it in Windows' Metafile format again so the links are up to date.

You can also import graphs and charts to use in your publications. PageMaker supports a wide variety of formats on both the Mac and PC/Windows platforms. Some spreadsheet formats, such as Microsoft Excel, can be imported directly as text files with the Place command. You can then adjust the formatting of the columns and cells in PageMaker and edit the contents if you want. You can also place Excel documents as graphics, preserving the original document's formatting.

260

Any item, including spreadsheets, graphs, and tables, that can be imported as a graphic can also be handled as an inline graphic, allowing you to keep the item with the text that relates to it. This is especially helpful if you're likely to be editing or updating the text after you've placed the spreadsheet or graph. Otherwise, the text would flow but the graphic would remain where you originally put it, which might be anywhere from a paragraph to several pages distant.

When you elect to import spreadsheets as text, PageMaker converts each row in the spreadsheet to a paragraph and separates columns with tabs, matching the column widths of the original spreadsheet. PageMaker allows you to import selected areas of your spreadsheet by range (with a limit of 40 columns or tabs). After you have imported your spreadsheet, PageMaker creates a style for the data, calling the style W*KS for Lotus 1-2-3 and XLS for Excel.*

### Watch Out!

*Before you place an Excel chart as a graphic from Excel for Windows, make sure you have the following setup procedures completed. You must have Excel installed on your hard drive, since PageMaker for Windows must run Excel to place the chart. If you are using Excel 3.0, the directory in which it is installed must be listed in your DOS path statement. The fonts used to create the chart should be installed and available for use by PageMaker, and the same printer should be targeted in both programs to avoid unexpected font substitutions. Allocate as much memory as you can to PageMaker to avoid any low memory alert messages.*

You can edit a spreadsheet placed as a OLE object by selecting it and double-clicking to open the original applications, or on the Macintosh by using System 7's Publish and Subscribe features. If you import an Excel, Lotus 1-2-3, or Symphony spreadsheet as text, PageMaker converts it into tab-delimited text as if it had come from a database, but matches the width of the spreadsheet columns when it sets tabs. If you intend to use a larger font than the spreadsheet originally used, you may need to widen the columns in the spreadsheet to leave room for the larger font.

## Working with Databases

Any collection of organized data is a *database*. Many publications, such as phone books, address books, business directories, and such, are, in reality, large databases that have been cleaned up for publication. PageMaker supports the importing of databases (for instance, any file in

Windows with the extension .DBF) via the Place command. The most prevalent type of database using the .DBF extension is dBase IV. Placing this information in your PageMaker document is relatively simple, as long as you have done your homework and selected the fields you want to copy prior to performing the task.

The dBase filter lets you place your database information in the form of either a *directory* (meaning a table with fields represented by columns and the records by rows) or as a *catalog* (where each field or cell takes up a separate paragraph with two lines between records). You can also apply styles to each type of layout.

To import a dBase file, follow these steps:

1. Select the **Place** command from the **File** menu.

2. In the File name list, select a file with the **.DBF** extension, and click on **OK**.

3. In the Place dBase file dialog box, select the fields you want to use by selecting a field in the **Fields available** box and clicking on the **Add** button to add it to the **Fields selected** box. You must select the fields in the order you want them to appear in your document. You can remove unwanted fields by selecting the names from the **Fields selected** box and clicking on the **Remove** button.

4. Click on either the **Directory** or **Catalog** radio button to generate either a tabular layout (the default) or a paragraph-based layout.

5. Click on one of the **Directory style name** radio buttons to name your style either **DBF** (if you have selected the Directory option) or **Test** if you have selected the Catalog option. Catalogs are formatted so that a separate style is applied to each column or field of the database. Style names are the names of the columns.

6. To apply specific formats to your fields, select a field in the right-hand Fields selected box, and click on the **Style** button. If you have selected the **Directory** option, the Choose type style dialog box lets you select a font style and alignment for each field as named in the dialog box's title. If you have selected the **Catalog** option, the Style dialog box lets you select an existing style to apply to the catalog's field, as well as the placement for each field (for instance, you can keep a field on the same line as the previous field.

7. Click on **OK** to place the data.

PageMaker's native filter for dBase is very good at placing relatively small databases but is not good at placing really large amounts of data from databases. Luckily, Elseware Corporation has designed DataShaper to clean up data that comes from an alien database. In addition, another program, called PageAhead, lets you import queries from SQL databases into Pagemaker.

### Watch Out!

*PageMaker does not read date formats directly from your database, but instead uses the date formats set by your Windows program. Use the Control Panel in Windows to change your date format to fit your requirements.*

*In addition, if you have used a DOS-extended character set in your database, be aware that Windows ANSI character set does not support all of these characters. Be sure to convert spurious characters to an equivalent ANSI item before using the Place command.*

Corporate annual reports frequently include color photographs or other artwork, and may be printed on slightly larger than letter size stock. A common size is 9" by 12", meant to stand out from the usual mail and attract attention to itself.

## Directories and Address Lists

Because PageMaker can import data from databases and arrange it neatly in columns, it's easy to create company phone directories, parts lists, and other similar materials. Figure 10.20 shows a sample page from a directory.

The data for the phone book was imported from the employee database, in HyperCard on a Macintosh, into PageMaker. You could just as easily use a PC database to import the data into PageMaker for Windows. Whenever you import data as a text file, you'll see a dialog box like the one in Figure 10.21, giving you options for how PageMaker imports it. Since you're bringing in tab-delimited lists, be sure not to change the tabs, or else you'll have to reformat the data once it's pasted into the publication.

The original file (shown in Figure 10.22) included several other data fields that were inappropriate for this listing, so we wrote a script to export only the data we needed for the phone directory. At another time, it would be easy to write a different export script to send all of the employee names and addresses to mailing labels on a PageMaker template, or to create full directories with home addresses, or whatever else was needed.

Figure 10.20
Use your
database to
make up
phone lists and
directories.

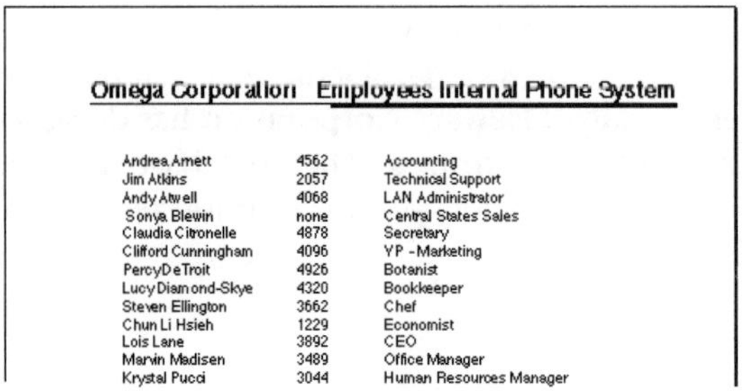

**Omega Corporation   Employees Internal Phone System**

| | | |
|---|---|---|
| Andrea Arnett | 4562 | Accounting |
| Jim Atkins | 2057 | Technical Support |
| Andy Atwell | 4068 | LAN Administrator |
| Sonya Blewin | none | Central States Sales |
| Claudia Citronelle | 4878 | Secretary |
| Clifford Cunningham | 4096 | VP - Marketing |
| Percy DeTroit | 4926 | Botanist |
| Lucy Diamond-Skye | 4320 | Bookkeeper |
| Steven Ellington | 3662 | Chef |
| Chun Li Hsieh | 1229 | Economist |
| Lois Lane | 3892 | CEO |
| Marvin Madisen | 3489 | Office Manager |
| Krystal Pucci | 3044 | Human Resources Manager |

Figure 10.21
Check the text
import options
appropriate
for the job.

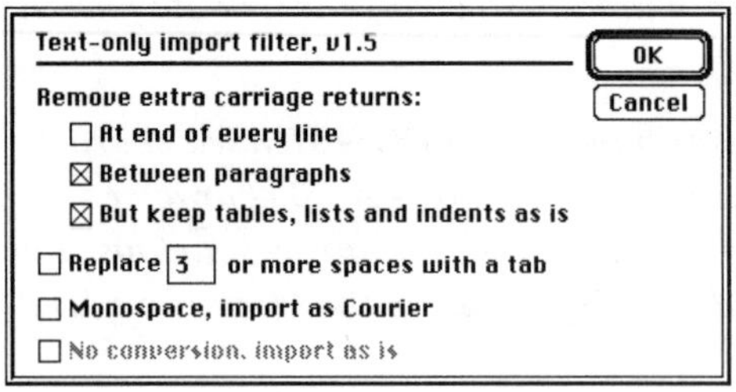

**Text-only import filter, v1.5**   [ OK ]   [ Cancel ]

Remove extra carriage returns:
☐ At end of every line
☒ Between paragraphs
☒ But keep tables, lists and indents as is
☐ Replace [ 3 ] or more spaces with a tab
☐ Monospace, import as Courier
☐ No conversion, import as is

Figure 10.22
The original
HyperCard
database.

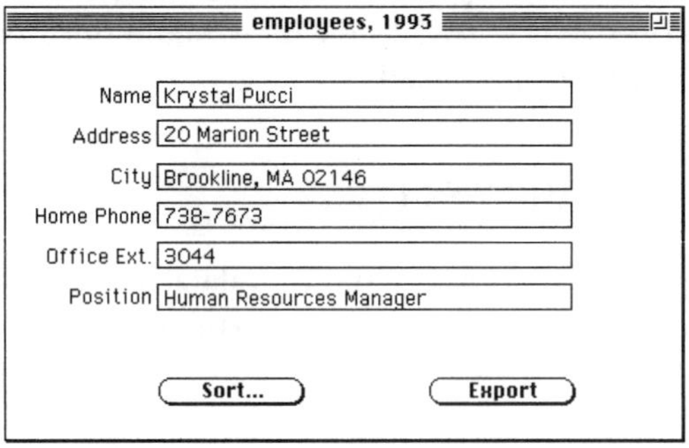

**employees, 1993**

Name [ Krystal Pucci ]
Address [ 20 Marion Street ]
City [ Brookline, MA 02146 ]
Home Phone [ 738-7673 ]
Office Ext. [ 3044 ]
Position [ Human Resources Manager ]

( Sort... )    ( Export )

# The Bare Essentials

In this chapter, you learned how to create business forms and reports in
PageMaker. You learned how to work with PageMaker's template scripts
and with templates you created yourself or got from other sources.
Specifically you learned:

- How to use and customize PageMaker's predesigned templates.

- How to design a custom form, and several ways to create evenly spaced ruled lines.

- How to design letterheads, and other business and social stationery.

- How to set up pages of business cards and labels to save money on printing.

- How to design catalogs and how to set up a grid for type and graphics, to make catalog pages more uniform.

- How to import tables, spreadsheets, and databases into PageMaker as text files or as graphics, and the pros and cons of each.

# Chapter 11

## Chapter Preview

*Ads "R" You*

*Handbills, flyers, and self-mailers*

*Overhead transparencies*

*Greeting cards*

*Awards and diplomas*

*Calendars*

*Using label templates*

*Faxing*

# Other Kinds of Pages

So far, you've seen PageMaker's capabilities as a tool for newsletter production and for designing business forms, stationery, and catalogs. However, there are many other kinds of pages and publications you may have to work on. Whatever you need to design, PageMaker can help. This chapter looks at some of the other things you can do with PageMaker, and your laser printer or a service bureau.

## It Pays to Advertise . . .

If you've heard that once, you've heard it a hundred times, or at least a dozen or so. Sure, it pays. The advertising industry is a multibillion dollar business. Interestingly, many advertising agencies, as well as newspaper and magazine publishers, have turned to PageMaker. Being able to produce beautifully set type and accurate paste ups right in the computer has meant tremendous savings in both time and money.

Even if you're not quite ready to be the ad agency for InterGalactic MultiFoods or Ree-verse sneakers, with PageMaker and a flair for copy and design, you'll be able to put together your own ads a little more effectively and a lot more easily.

## By the Way . . .

*Copy is the newspaper and advertising business' word for text. Advertising writers are called copywriters. The person in an advertising agency who does the graphic part of the ad is variously called the art director, layout artist, or designer.*

The very first newspaper ad appeared in the *London Weekly Newes* in 1622, and called for the return of a stolen horse. A few years later, print advertising was firmly established. In 1661, Robert Turner's *Dentifrice*, complete with trademarks, started the trend for display advertisements.

A *display ad*, by definition, is anything that's not a classified ad. It can be as little as an inch high by a column wide, or can be a whole page, or even a double-page spread. Ads are frequently defined as a quarter page, a half page, an eighth, and so on. Obviously, you have to know the size of the page in order to set the ad up correctly. You should find the actual dimensions of the page on the publication's rate card, along with prices and other important details, such as deadlines and format specifications.

Typically, an ad contains the following elements:

- A headline: something to grab your attention.

- A picture: usually, but not necessarily, of the product.

- Some text (copy) describing the product, service, and so on.

- Who makes it, where to buy it, or who paid for the ad.

It doesn't matter whether you're selling shoes or insurance, soap or politicians—the basics are the same. One of the great advertising gurus has pointed out that the only effective ads are the ones that you remember when you're reaching for the product. (Well, you might not reach for the Mayor, but you'd reach for the lever under her name, or the square on the ballot next to it.) In order to have this effect, the advertisement has to: first, get noticed; and second, evoke a response.

PageMaker can help you design ads that get noticed. PageMaker's flexibility lets you experiment with different placements for copy and art, and you can edit and recompose copy until each word is perfect. The response comes from the reader, who makes a mental connection with the words and/or image. Many people, when they reach for a can of soup on the grocer's shelf, subconsciously hear, "Mmm good," and pick up the one with the red and white label.

The basics of layout and design that you've already learned for newsletters and other publications apply to ads, too. Remember to:

- Avoid clutter.

- Keep headlines readable.

- Follow the principles of eye-leading.

- Proofread carefully before you print!

## Laying Out an Ad

One of the first things to consider in designing an ad is where it will be placed. If it's a newspaper or magazine ad, will it have a page to itself, or will it compete for the reader's eye with other ads and stories? If your ad occupies only part of the page, what else is likely to be on that page? Figure 11.1 shows a fairly typical magazine format. Each of these pages combines text and advertising, the latter in a single column. If you were to design an ad for this publication, you'd need to make it different from everything else on the page to get noticed.

Figure 11.1
A small ad could get lost in here.

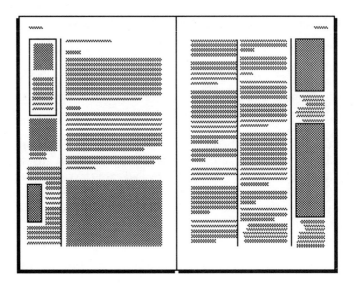

By the Way . . .

*It's probably safe to say that every possible layout has already been used many times over. But, once you come up with a design that seems to work, your choice of copy and illustration can make it unique. Of course, no one formula works for every product every time. You need to experiment.*

When you design an ad in PageMaker, start with the dimensions of the page it's going on, to help you visualize your ad against the rest of the page. You may not be able to specify *position*, where the ad is placed on the page. However, if you know what publication the ad is going to, you can probably make an educated guess as to where it will land. For instance, if you're buying a one column ad in the *New Yorker,* it's a pretty good bet that it will be on the outside of the page, and that the rest of the page will be two columns of justified type, approximately 11 points high. Cartoons and ads never appear on the same page. Set up a page dummy with greeking so you can see the impact of the ad against the surrounding material, as shown in Figure 11.2.

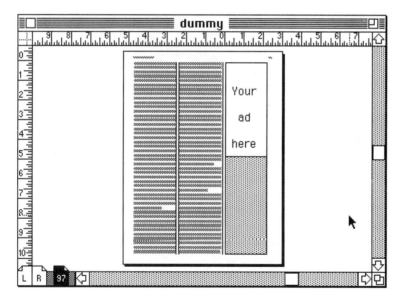

Figure 11.2
The page dummy lets you see what you've got to work with.

By the Way . . .

*If you can specify position, ask for the upper right corner of a right-hand page. It's the most visible spot on the page and will catch the eye of those who just flip through the magazine.*

To create a page dummy, use the following steps.

1. Start a new publication with the correct dimensions for the page the ad will go on. Measure to be sure. Verify the number of columns and gutter width, too.

2. Set the number of columns and pour text into them. Use any text file you have handy, or type in some random words and copy and paste them until the column is full.

3. Measure and define the boundary for your ad. If there are other ads on the same page, put them in as 20% gray boxes.

Now you can see what space you have to fill, and how it will relate to the rest of the items on that page. In the preceding example, the ad will fill a sixth of a page. Figure 11.3 shows an ad that works well in that space.

Figure 11.3
This ad follows the rules: an attractive illustration, a headline that gets you involved, and some very simple copy.

*Put yourself in this picture...*
*at*
*Newhart Lodge,*
*Vermont's finest Bed and Breakfast*
*South Maple Rd.*
*Petersglen, Vermont*

*For reservations, call*
*1-800-NEWHART*
*(1-800-639-4278)*

**By the Way . . .**
*When you're dealing with small space, don't try to say too much. In copywriting, the one rule is to use as few words as possible. A tiny image in a sea of white space gained attention for a certain auto maker a few years back. The accompanying headline simply urged car buyers to, "Think Small." The campaign won dozens of awards and sold a lot of cars, too.*

Sometimes, you can be most effective by breaking the rules. In the example in Figure 11.4, we've broken at least a half-dozen different rules: too many typefaces, too many words, no picture, it's crowded, and so on. But the ad still works because each rule was broken for a good reason. The type is the illustration, so no picture is needed. All those different faces represent different voices, and it's not afraid to laugh at itself. (This ad was designed to go into one of those yearbooks in which most of the pages just say "compliments of " or "greetings from.")

Figure 11.4
Humor helps.

The kind of ad you design is going to depend on what you're selling. Obviously, an ad for a product like stereo speakers or mayonnaise isn't going to look like an ad for a bank or a hotel. Identify the most important point about your product or service. Make that point your headline. Follow with subheads and copy that explain and support the headline.

Some products do best with dignified advertising. Others may decide to scream a little louder. One way to call attention to your headline is to use a *blat*. Blats are blotches of color or gray tone behind your text. You could create a smooth-edged one in PageMaker, but most blats are irregularly shaped and should be done in a draw program and imported. Blats are especially effective if the type inside them is rotated. In fact, you may decide to rotate blat and type together. PageMaker makes that simple. Just select the blat and the text block, and use the rotation tool to swing them around to a good angle. Figure 11.5 shows an ad that uses blats.

The magazine cover in Figure 11.5 uses another trick that's easy in PageMaker. We've put drop shadows behind the magazine title and the large blat, by copying them, changing the color of the copy to "paper" and pasting them behind the original, just slightly offset. Hint—Use the Aldus Addition **Group it** to group the objects so they'll be easier to move around the page.

There are numerous other tricks you can use in your ads. One is to create a background for a page by using the company logo, or the name of the product, repeated over and over in a wallpaper effect. This looks best if you set it in a very light gray or color tint. It's also effective to do this with rotated type. Experiment with negative leading, tight tracking, and forced justification to make "solid" blocks of type for the wallpaper. Try offsetting the same block in white for an embossed effect.

Figure 11.5
Blats don't just
stand out—
they jump out.

## Printing Magazine and Newspaper Ads

Find out from the publication in what format they want the ad delivered. Most will ask for it *camera-ready*. If you've done all the work in PageMaker, just give them a good quality print of the ad, same size. Some publications are now requesting film negatives. Your service bureau can prepare film negatives from your PageMaker files.

### By the Way . . .
*You may not even need to go to the service bureau or print shop. Many publications now accept PageMaker files by modem. If yours does, be sure that you send the advertisement as a file and not as a fax. Check with them first, of course, to make sure they have PageMaker 5.0. (You can open PageMaker 4 files in PM 5, but not vice versa.) Also ask if they want the file compressed, and if so, by what method. StuffIt and CompactPro are the two most popular compression utilities for the Mac, and for PCs: PKZIP. A compressed file won't tie up the computer, or the phone, for as long.*

## Other Kinds of Ads

Of course, newspapers and magazines aren't the only way to advertise. You may need to put together a brochure or flyer. The easiest, and least costly of these is a *threefold,* a single-page flyer printed on two sides and folded in thirds. Such flyers are known variously as self-mailers, hand-outs, or stuffers, depending on how they're distributed. A *stuffer* goes in an envelope with other items. Banks often include stuffers with your monthly statement. *Handouts* are stacked on the counter or placed in displays. *Self-mailers*, like the newsletters and catalogs previously discussed, have a place for an address label and stamp, and are meant to be sent without an envelope. Figure 11.6 shows dummies for a typical threefold.

Figure 11.6
The brochure on the left could be a stuffer or handout. The other is a self-mailer.

The most critical part of designing a threefold is to make sure it can be folded evenly and that the type inside won't land on or across the fold line. The easy way to do this is to place hairline guides for folding, as shown in Figure 11.7.

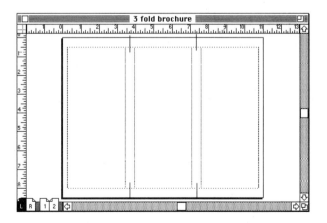

Figure 11.7
Fold on the line.

To set up a threefold with hairlines, use the following steps:

1. Open a new PageMaker publication.

2. In the Page setup box, choose the **Wide** orientation and click on **Double-sided**, but not Facing pages, as shown in Figure 11.8. Select the target printer (Windows) or resolution (Mac and Windows). Set the inside and outside (left and right) margins to **0**. Click on **OK** when done.

Figure 11.8
The Page setup
box, setting up
a threefold.

Page setup       OK

Page: Letter      Cancel

Page dimensions: 11   by 8.5   inches

Numbers...

Orientation: ○ Tall  ◉ Wide

Start page #: 1     Number of pages: 2

Options: ☒ Double-sided   ☐ Facing pages
         ☐ Restart page numbering

Margin in inches:   Inside 0     Outside 0
            Top 0.5     Bottom 0.5

Target printer resolution: 1200 ▷ dpi

3. Open the left Master page by clicking the **L** icon.

4. Select **Column guides** from the **Layout** menu. Divide the page into three columns. Specify **0** space between columns. Click on **OK**. The page will be divided vertically into thirds.

5. Select **Hairline** from the **Line** submenu of the **Element** menu, and draw a vertical line over the guidelines extending in about 1/2" at top and bottom. These are your folding guides. A machine-folded brochure won't need them, but if you're hand folding a few laser printed samples, they'll help you keep the panels even.

6. Now, go back to the Page setup box, and set your side margins. Then open the Column guides box and set the gutters between the columns to whatever seems right— usually 1/2" or so.

7. If you don't want to print the hairlines, but want to use them to help you layout the page in equal thirds, either change them to a color that you won't print, or draw ruler guides over the three-column lines instead of placing hairlines on them.

By the Way . . .

*If you're using heavy paper or light card stock to print your brochure, place your text blocks, gutters, and fold guides to make the left side just slightly wider, to compensate for the thickness of the paper when it's folded.*

# Post It?

Posters are yet another form of advertising, and one of the oldest of all. Posters for circuses and gladiator matches were found in the ruins of Pompeii, and were known to have decorated walls in Rome and Carthage well over 2,000 years ago. Posters can be an inexpensive and very effective advertising medium, especially for nonbusiness ads. When you have to put together a poster, PageMaker is ready to help.

The least expensive way to make up a poster is to design it in PageMaker and have the master photocopied or Itek printed onto whatever stock is most appropriate. Look for bright colors, particularly if the poster is the kind that gets stapled to telephone poles or stuck on the laundromat bulletin board. Both of the posters in Figure 11.9 were low-budget ads that got fast results.

Figure 11.9
Low-budget
Advertising.

# Have you tried . . . keeping scanned photos of your pets on your hard disk?

If you're a pet owner, you can put together a poster like the one in Figure 11.9 in a matter of minutes, alerting the neighborhood and safely returning Rover before he gets in trouble.

Since you can set pages of various sizes, PageMaker is just as handy for creating a theatrical poster or a window sign as it is for a photocopied flyer. You can go as big as 42 x 42 inches if you need to, although printing something that large might be a problem. Typical poster sizes are 20 x 30 inches, 24 x 36 inches, or 30 x 40 inches. Again, check with your printer first, to find out what sizes they can handle, and in what form they want the PageMaker files.

For something this large, you may be able to supply the file on a floppy disk or removable SyQuest cartridge, and let the printer deal with tiling it and assembling the tiled masters or film negatives. Some print shops even have imagesetters capable of printing film negatives that large. If you want to print proof copies of the poster, you can either tile the output of your laser printer or scale the publication to fit the paper size.

Scaling is done in the Paper dialog box on the Mac and in the Options dialog box in Windows. The simplest way is to select **Reduce to fit**. PageMaker does the arithmetic for you and scales the poster down to a size that will fit on whatever kind of printer you have specified. Pages can be reduced or enlarged anywhere from 5% to 1,600% of their original size. Pages will print centered on the paper. You can design a poster in a large size and then shrink it down to use as a flyer as well. Figure 11.10 shows a theatrical poster that was printed in several sizes; 20" x 30" for use outside the theater and around town, 8 ½" x 11" as a flyer, and 10" x 15" for store windows and posting on lamp posts. It worked equally well in all sizes, thanks to PageMaker and Adobe Type Manager.

Figure 11.10
Decorative
fonts and clip
art give this
poster a style.

By the Way . . .

*If you want to get the best possible result from a laser printer, leave liberal margins on your pages. Scale the camera-ready prints a little more than 100%, just enough larger that they'll still fit on the page. Have the printer scale them back down to the original proportions, when shooting the film for the printing plates. Doing so will reduce the size of the individual dots, giving you better resolution than your actual 300 dpi.*

# Thoughts on Being Your Own Advertising Agency

It's true. PageMaker makes it possible for you to produce your own newspaper and magazine ads, brochures, flyers, and other advertising pieces so you can, literally, be your own ad agency. Should you be? That's another question and one that bears some thinking.

Just as owning your own home video camera doesn't turn you into Steven Spielberg or George Lucas, having the tools to lay out an ad doesn't mean you're instantly ready to go head-to-head against the biggest names on Madison Avenue. Ad agencies know a lot more than this book, or any single book, can teach you. They have teams of experts who do everything from redesigning your corporate image to figuring out who your customers are by age, income, gender, what newspaper or magazine they read, and what radio or TV station they tune to. An advertising agency can make sure you get full value from every dollar you spend.

On the other hand, your computer and PageMaker *can* turn out professional-quality pages, if you use them properly and if you start with good copy and good design. The choice, really, is yours. If you want the know how and years of experience that an advertising agency brings to your business, hire one. The background you've gained from using PageMaker yourself makes you a better informed client and gives you an advantage in the agency-client relationship. If you feel comfortable doing your own ads, or if there's no money in the budget to hire an expert, you have the tools to do a fine job. Apply the skills you've learned and have fun!

# Overhead Transparencies

Not really in the realm of advertising, but incredibly useful in a business presentation, the classroom, or when speaking to any kind of a group about a topic, producing *overhead transparencies* gives you another opportunity to put PageMaker to work. Overhead transparencies are sheets of transparent, clear, or colored film, which can be run through a laser printer. When placed on an overhead projector, like the one shown in Figure 11.11, they give a large, very legible image. Light shines through the glass plate on which the transparency is placed. It then passes through a lens, onto an angled mirror, and bounces forward onto the screen.

Figure 11.11
The projector is usually placed at an angle to raise the image higher on the wall over the speaker's head.

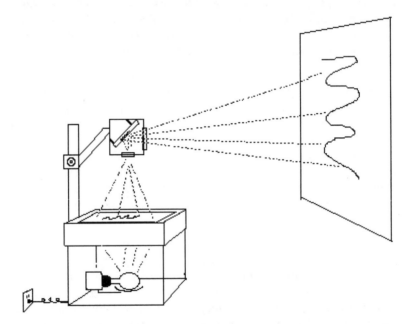

One advantage to this type of projector is that, unlike a 35mm slide show that needs darkness or a very elaborate projection system, overhead transparencies can be viewed with the room lights on. Another advantage is that the transparency reads correctly for both the speaker and the viewer. The lecturer can draw on the transparency with grease pencil or marker as he or she speaks, and elaborate, multilayered graphs and charts can be prepared with a little bit of Scotch tape.

To create overhead transparencies you need a laser printer and one or more packages of transparency film. 3M is the popular brand. Look for 3M type PP 2950 for best results. The film comes in clear and assorted colors. If you find a different brand of transparency film, don't buy it unless it says "for use in high-temperature plain paper copiers." The operant words here are *high-temperature*. If you get the wrong kind of film, it could melt inside your laser printer, turning the printer into a very expensive paper weight.

### Watch Out!

*Don't even think of trying to copy on other kinds of acetate, plastic report covers, or anything other than high temperature transparency film! It will ruin your printer.*

Although they're not mandatory, a package of cardboard transparency frames is helpful. Just stick the sheets of printed film into them. They'll help prevent damage to the transparencies from wrinkling and scratching. The frames also provide a convenient place to number your transparencies.

# Have you tried . . . putting your presentation transparencies in sheet protectors?

You can keep your entire presentation—a copy of the speech, transparencies, and even masters for photocopying the handouts—in clear plastic sheet protectors and store them in a 3-ring binder when not in use. You'll have them all together when you're ready to give a speech, and you won't even have to remove the transparencies from the sleeves. They'll project perfectly, if you've used clear, clean sheet protectors.

Even if you're planning to use frames, you can save yourself a good deal of trouble by numbering each page. Create the whole batch of transparencies in PageMaker, and place them in the correct order as one long publication. Place a page number marker near the edge of the master page, and let PM handle the numbering for you.

If you have a color or black and white inkjet printer, you may also be able to print transparencies. (The HP DeskWriter 550C and DeskJet 550C require HP LX JetSeries transparency film.) Read the printer manual to find out whether your printer will accommodate transparency film, and if so, what type to use. Transparencies printed on inkjet printers may take a long time to dry. To avoid smearing, remove each transparency from the print tray as it's completed and lay on a flat surface to dry. Do not mount them until they're fully dry.

When you're using PageMaker to lay out overhead transparencies, here are a few things to think about:

- Projection screens are usually horizontal. Design your pages so they'll fit the horizontal format.

- Overhead projectors may not have the best quality lenses. Anything near the edge of the screen could distort. Plan to put important headlines, charts, and illustrations in the middle of the screen where the image is sharpest.

- Creating your transparencies in PageMaker lets you use high-quality TIFF and EPS images, including screened photographs and elaborate line art. Illustrations can perk up your presentation, too. Use them generously.

- You can use PageMaker's Print Thumbnails feature to print out a numbered reference copy of the visuals. Keep one with the speaker's notes.

- You might even have the thumbnails photocopied as a handout for the audience. Experiment with different numbers of thumbnail pages per page, until you find a combination that's legible and efficient.

- Extremely thin lines sometimes tend to break up when printed on transparency film, even though they look fine on paper. Either use thicker lines, draw them in with india ink and an artist's 00 technical pen, or use a thin line of Chartpak tape instead of the printed line.

## Creating a Transparency

To set up a transparency, use the following procedure:

1. Open PageMaker and start a new publication, specifying the **Wide** page orientation. Do not choose Double-sided or Facing pages from the options available since you'll be working with one page at a time.

2. The projected area of a transparency is 8" x 9 ³/₄" inches. Set your margins to .25 inch at the top and bottom of the page, and .625 inch at the sides. This will give you the correct frame size, centered on the page. Click on **OK**, or press **Enter** or **Return** to see the page.

3. Open the master page. Place a page number just outside the margin, as shown in Figure 11.12. To place a page number

marker, create a text block, and press ⌘+**Option**+**P** (Mac) or **Ctrl**+**Shift**+**3** in Windows. Add the company logo, or anything else that will be repeated on every transparency, as an element on the master page. Save your work, and then go to the first page and start creating your presentation.

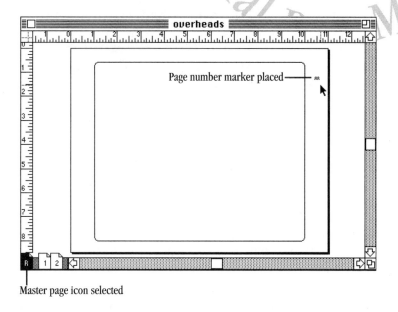

Master page icon selected

Figure 11.12
Lay out your transparency within a border.

In Figure 11.12, you'll notice that we've drawn a rounded corner box as a border for our transparencies. This shape echoes the cutout area of the cardboard transparency frames and is a nice-looking way to define the screen area.

Use legible type sizes for projection. Anything between 18 and 90 points may be acceptable, depending on the font. Look for medium weight type in larger sizes and bold in smaller sizes. Big, heavy type can be hard to read when projected. Figure 11.13 shows an overhead transparency set up as a type test. As you can see, different faces have different degrees of readability at 48 points. Using bold face at smaller sizes is recommended. Be sure to kern headlines as needed and to space the lines of type so they'll look good on-screen. If your page has only one or two words on it, place them about a third of the page down, not exactly in the middle.

### By the Way . . .
*Transparencies are one of the places where you can use the Mac's outline and shadow type styles. (Outline and shadow styles are not available in Windows.) They project quite nicely, although they're hard to read on the printed page.*

Figure 11.13
If you're not
sure how well
type will
project, make
a type test
sheet and
experiment.

Helvetica Bold 24
Helvetica Medium 30
Helvetica Bold 30
Helvetica Medium 36
**Helvetica Bold 36**
Helvetica Medium 48
Helvetica Medium 60
Helvetica Med. 72
Helvetica Med.Shadow
Times Bold Shadow 48
Dom Casual 48 Optima 48
Dom Cas. Bold Ital. Shad.48
Bookman 48 Palatino 48
Avant Garde 48 **Hobo 48**

If you set up a series of transparencies in numbered order, and then decide to switch two pages, you needn't worry about messed up numbering or having to make the changes by hand after the sheets are printed. An Aldus Addition called Sort Pages makes changing the order of pages in your set ridiculously easy.

Open the **Utilities** menu and select **Sort pages** from the Aldus Additions submenu. You will see a dialog box like the one in Figure 11.14, with grayed out thumbnails of your pages. To see the page in greater detail, click on it, and then click on the **Detail** button. Use the magnifying glasses to zoom in and out if you need to read the text on a page before you swap it. To rearrange the pages, select one by clicking. Drag it to a position in between the two pages you want to move it between. You'll see the icon in the figure and a black bar to indicate the page. When it reaches its destination, the page numbers will show its new position and its previous one.

Figure 11.14
Swapping
pages.

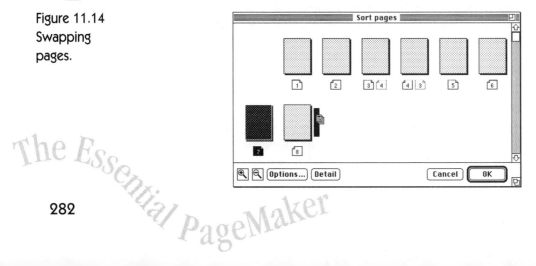

In this example, we've already swapped pages 3 and 4, and are switching 7 and 8. If you placed the page number marker on the master page, it will renumber the pages automatically. When you've done all the page swaps you want to make, click on **OK**, and they'll reshuffle accordingly.

# Multilayered Transparencies

You can achieve a sort of animated effect by starting with a headline and adding subheads below it, or bringing in the various elements of a graph or diagram one at a time. You could simply recreate the headline on each page and add first one subhead on the second, and two on the third. An easier way is to place only one add-on on each page, and attach them to the main page with cellophane tape hinges, so you can flop these overlays on top of the first page as you need them.

### Watch Out!

*You can build up to three layers of overlay on a single page. More than four thicknesses of transparency causes problems, however. Even though the material looks clear, it absorbs some light. By the time you've added the fourth layer, the image is getting dimmer and harder to see.*

Figure 11.15 shows a sequence of overlays on a main page. In the first view, the overlays have been flopped back. The speaker introduces the topic, then adds the left overlay and explains the subtopic. Then the right overlay is added to bring in the next subtopic, as indicated in the second view. If desired, a third overlay could be added at the bottom of the frame.

### Watch Out!

*Use overlay sheets full size, even if there's just a small amount of printing on them. Cut edges will show as jagged black lines on the screen.*

To separate the layers of a multilayer transparency like the one in Figure 11.15, use the following steps.

1. Create the page as a unit with all the layers in position.

2. Select the items to be on the overlay, or on the first overlay, if there are two or three.

3. Select a color other than black from the Color palette, and apply it to the overlay items, as shown in Figure 11.16. Any color will do.

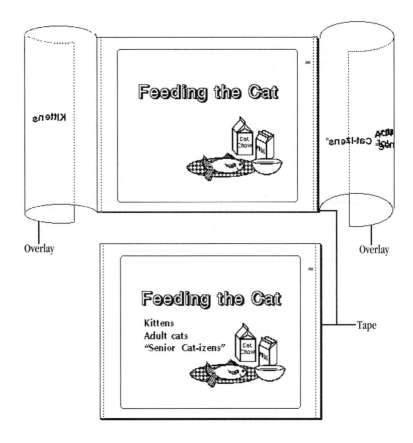

Figure 11.15
The overlays
are taped to
the cardboard
frame.

4.  If there's a second overlay, select the items to go on it, and apply a different color.

5.  When you print, select the colors you assigned to the overlays from the Print Colors dialog box. PageMaker will prepare the overlays for you, exactly as if they were color separations.

6.  Insert the main page in the frame and place the overlays on it. Tape only one side of the overlay to the frame so you can fold it back for the first step of the presentation.

### By the Way . . .

*If the transparencies are handled a great deal or rolled up, you may have a problem with little bits of toner flaking off or smearing, especially on fine lines in a graphic. To overcome this, buy a can of artist's matte-finish spray fixative. It's the same stuff used to preserve charcoal, pastel, and pencil drawings. Spray the transparencies lightly with fixative as soon as they're printed. Use only a small amount; too much spray will leave streaks on the toner.*

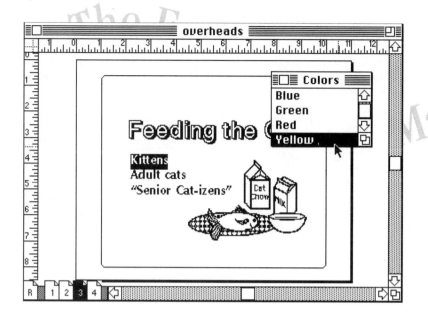

Figure 11.16
By designating the type as a spot color, you will get a separate page with just the selected words, perfect for an overlay.

You can add color to your presentation by using transparencies in colors rather than clear ones, by hand coloring them with marker (use special transparency markers for this), or by applying colored overlay sheets. These are slightly sticky sheets of evenly colored film, which are also available at your local art supply store. Letraset is one of several brands of transparent overlays. They come in a full range of Pantone PMS colors. You can colorize areas on the screen to preview the effect and then print out the transparency with black outlines on your laser printer, and add areas of the same color you applied on-screen.

# Greeting Cards

If you have a clip art collection, or the time and patience to draw your own pictures in a graphics program, PageMaker can help you produce beautiful greeting cards. You might even personalize them with the name of the recipient as well as your own name. When you design and print your corporate holiday greeting card, you can be sure that none of your clients will get the same card from someone else. You can even work your company's logo into the design, as has been done in Figure 11.17.

The simplest kind of card to create is called a *French fold.* Use a regular 8 ½" x 11" page, but print the card on a fairly heavy weight stock. If you only need one or two, print them on the laser printer and hand color them. A 70-pound weight paper will run through your laser printer quite well and will fold easily, but is stiff enough to stand up so your card can be displayed. Look for paper before you plan your card design. Often the color of the paper will suggest a theme for the art. Your stationery store will have 4 ³/₈" x 5 ³/₄" envelopes in which to mail the cards.

Set up the page for a greeting card by following these steps:

1.  Open a new publication. Set up a single letter-size page either **tall** or **wide**.

2.  Position ruler guides halfway across and down the page to divide it into quarters. These guides are simply for your own convenience in laying out the page. (You won't need to add folding guide lines since this is an easy fold.)

3.  Place your text and graphics in the appropriate quarter pages according to the sample in Figure 11.17. Select the **Text rotation** tool from the **Toolbox** to turn the type upside down.

Figure 11.17 PageMaker makes holiday greetings more fun.

Obviously, if you're printing more than a few, it's more reasonable to have them done by a commercial printer. Use colored inks and colored stock for a more festive (and professional) appearance.

You may also want to design a tall, thin, *contemporary* style card, like the ones in the rack at your local card shop. Typically these cards are about 3 ¹/₂" x 8" and could fit in a #10 envelope. These would obviously not be folded in quarters. Instead, you'd print on both sides of a sheet of card stock and cut it down to size after printing. When you're doing this kind of a card, don't forget to add crop marks, and be sure that the front and back sides of the card will line up properly. If you set the card dimensions as the margins and call for a two-sided page, PageMaker will automatically shift the second side to align with the first. Figure 11.18 shows a thumbnail of a contemporary card. Chapter 9 discusses printing for a two-sided page.

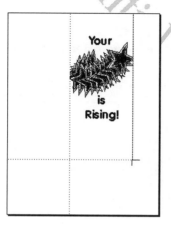

Figure 11.18 Make a card for any occasion. Inside, this one will say "Congratulations on your promotion."

# Calendars

Customized calendars are a nice handout for businesses, a good holiday gift for the family (especially with birthdays and anniversaries noted), and a wonderful fund-raising tool for school and community groups. You can design your own calendar template and plug in the dates and data you want to include. Or you can use PageMaker's calendar template from the Aldus Additions template scripts. It's shown in Figure 11.19. Aldus has included a set of PageMaker scripts to update this calendar with correct dates for any month from January 1993 through December 1994. To use them follow these steps:

1. Open the **Aldus Additions** menu in the **Utilities** menu, and select **Open template**. Open the calendar template to create a blank calendar page. Return to the **Aldus Additions** menu, and choose **Run script**.

2. Locate the directory containing the calendar update scripts, shown in Figure 11.20.

3. Choose the correct script for the month you want to print, and click on the **Run File** button on the Mac (**OK** in Windows). The dates and month will be placed correctly on the calendar page. You can then insert your own special days or other text, if you want.

The path to the script directory should be:

- On the Macintosh:
  **System Folder:Aldus:Additions:Templates:Calendar update scripts**

- On a Windows PC:
  **\aldus\usenglish\addition\template\caldates**

Figure 11.19
The Aldus
Additions
calendar
template.

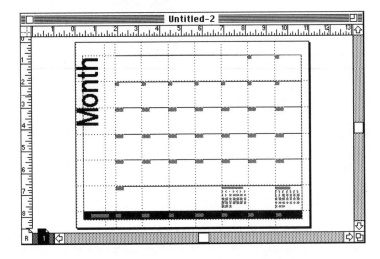

Figure 11.20
Choose the
month to
number, and
click OK.

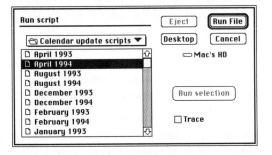

Of course, the first thing you have to do is to open a copy of the calendar script and save it as a template. Add your company logo, school name, or greeting on the master page. If you select **Trace** from the Run script dialog box, you can see exactly how Aldus's programmers wrote it, and you can write your own for 1995 and beyond.

If you'd rather design your own calendar, that's fine too. Place the dates by using tabs, as shown in Figure 11.21. The page numbers can be entered most easily in PageMaker's Text Editor. For example, if the month begins on a Sunday, start with one tab, to place the date at the right side of its block and then just place date, tab, date, tab, and so on to the end of the first line. Leave a space after the last date on the line, then another tab, and the second row of numbers, and so on. When the dates are placed into the PageMaker calendar and the style applied, the tab spacing changes to the correct amount for the distance between two calendar numbers. Use the same principle to create your own text files of dates for other months, placing two tabs to start a month on a Monday, and so on.

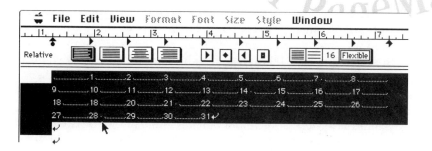

Figure 11.21 The dates are simply spaced with tabs. To align them, set appropriate tabs across the calendar page.

There are lots of calendar styles you might use. Instead of a month per page, how about a week at a glance? Figure 11.22 shows a different kind of calendar page. To create this page, use several shortcuts. Rather than figuring out exactly how much space to leave between the lines, simply set the day names in a column, with two carriage returns in between each line, and adjust the position of the text block until it sits nicely on the page. Then draw the lines under each word. The date numbers are set in a different text block. Here, instead of spacing between them, just take a good guess at the appropriate leading, and then increase it until they fall in the right spot. You could borrow a set of small calendar dates from the Calendar files, and adjust the type size and tabs to fit. Finally, add the graphic elements like the gray stripes, the logo, and the month at the bottom.

Figure 11.22 A weekly calendar listing classes and special events is a good way to promote them.

# Awards, Certificates, and Diplomas

Everybody deserves a little recognition. Maybe an "Employee of the Week" certificate isn't as rewarding as a raise, but it still goes a long way toward improving company morale. Teachers know the value of praise. Attendance awards, SuperSpeller, and Math Marvel certificates are powerful motivational tools for young students. Not all awards are serious, of course. How about a "Hazardous Waste" warning on the door of a teenager's room? Or "Duffer of the Year" for the golfer who's just shanked his 1,000th ball into the adjacent fairway? If you can think of a reason for an award, PageMaker can help you put together all sorts of certificates for all occasions. Figure 11.23 shows what can be done with a clip art border and a handful of type. Clip art collections have all kinds of borders, some more fanciful, others more ornate than what's shown here. You may find only one corner of a certificate, but you can copy and flip to complete the square.

Figure 11.23 You could use the same border for a stock certificate, diploma, or license.

By the Way . . .
*There are some very specific requirements for what appears on a stock certificate. Among them is the provision that the certificate must include "a human face or likeness." Consult an attorney before you design stock or bond certificates.*

## Creating Dingbat Borders

Certificates and awards are a great place to use some of the more fanciful clip art borders. This is also the ideal spot to use the fonts you wouldn't use for more ordinary jobs. There are a number of faces that imitate hand lettering, including Zapf Chancery, included with most laser printers. The symbol set that comes with it, Zapf Dingbats, may also give you some ideas for certificate embellishments. The dingbats could even be used as a typeset border, produced quickly and easily right in PageMaker. In Figure 11.24, we've drawn some dingbat borders. The row of pencils might be used for a classroom award, the daisies and stars for more generalized applications. Use the following steps for creating dingbat borders.

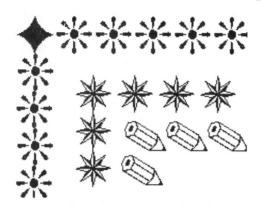

Figure 11.24 Dingbats are little symbols that can be used for all sorts of purposes.

1. Type a row of your favorite dingbat (not Edith Bunker). Use the KeyCaps DA (in the Apple menu on the Mac or the Fonts Control Panel in Windows) to see what's available.

2. Adjust the tracking so the row is nicely spaced, and place it at the top of the page.

3. Copy it for the bottom. Make it a separate text block.

4. Copy it again, and use text rotation to make the sides of the frame. You may need to add or subtract dingbats to adjust to the length of the page.

### Watch Out!

*Dingbats are fun to play with. Please use restraint if you're placing them in a book, newsletter, or other publication. Try not to use more than one or two styles per document, lest your publication look as if it's coming down with measles.*

# Label Templates

It wasn't so very long ago that labels had glue on the back, and you needed to lick them or run them over a wet sponge to apply them. And as soon as the glue dried out, the label was likely to fall off. Self-sticking labels made the job easier. They were more apt to stay on, and you didn't have the taste of glue haunting you all day long. But they were hard to write on and tended to gum up the typewriter. Finally, somebody realized that labels could be made on standard size sheets and fed through a photocopier or laser printer. Now, you can label anything that needs identification, with appropriately sized die cut labels. And if you have lots of labels to print, PageMaker can help.

If you look at **Open Templates**, an **Aldus Addition** under the **Utilities** menu, you'll find a selection of label templates, for everything from standard Avery address labels to VCR labels. These templates will help you set up mailing lists, product labels, and all sorts of sticky little things with the greatest of ease. Your label kit includes the following:

| Purpose | Avery | Size |
| --- | --- | --- |
| Address | 51 | 1" x 2 $^5/_8$" |
| Cassette | 5198 | 1 $^5/_8$" x 3 $^1/_2$" |
| Diskette | 5196 | 2 $^3/_4$" x 2 $^3/_4$" |
| VCR spine | 5199 | |

Labels come in both white paper and clear acetate. The latter is a good choice when you're doing a mailing with colored envelopes, or a self-mailer brochure or catalog. The transparent labels aren't completely invisible, but they show up a lot less than white ones against a colored background. Avery is not the only label maker, but probably the best known. You'll find Avery labels in most stationery and computer stores. Figure 11.25 shows a piece of the 5160 template with some design suggestions.

### By the Way . . .
*The best way to handle mailing lists on the Mac is with Avery's MacLabelPro. For under $50, it includes templates for every kind of label Avery makes, plus a small clip art library. Most important, it has a mail merge function that lets you bring in your mailing lists and data files from Microsoft Works or Word.*

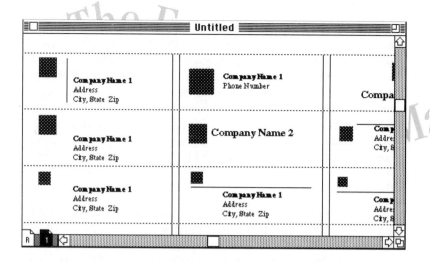

Figure 11.25
Some of the
ways to use
the label
template.

The only difficulty you might encounter using PageMaker's label templates is that they're not very detailed. Figure 11.26 shows the Aldus cassette label template on the left and a custom one on the right. The page on the right was set up for a different brand of cassette label, so the spacing is a bit different. More important, though, it shows the cutout area in the middle of each label. You need to know this if you are putting more than a few words on the label, or designing it with type at the sides as well as top and bottom, as in the example. Templates like these can often be found in the DTP area of online services or in user group.

# Have you tried . . . finding uses for wasted label material?

Print your company logo, a name tag, or any small label you need on the cut out area in the center of the cassette label. You'll get an extra set of labels for free.

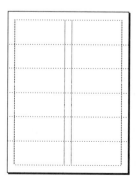
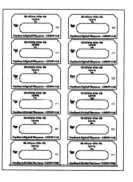

Figure 11.26
You may
decide to
prepare your
own label
templates.

Printed labels are handy for a great many tasks. For example, you can import a list of names of conference attendees or party guests, and prepare elegantly printed name tags, complete with the organization's logo or a suitably festive party design, on #5163. (PageMaker numbers refer to Avery labels.) #5161 could be used to label your output of homemade grape jelly, or those mysterious packages in the freezer. You could print friendly—or not so friendly—reminders to stick on unpaid invoices. My son Josh, an avid cartoonist, prints sheets of transparent labels with PageMaker's various fill patterns and percent tones to use instead of the expensive, and virtually identical, shading sheets sold in the art supply store.

A dedicated electronics hacker prints up labels with the schematics for modifications he makes to amplifiers, and other pieces of high-tech electronic gear. He then pastes one copy on the back page of the instruction book and the other inside the chassis of the equipment. Six months later, when he thinks of a new modification or when he decides to sell the stuff and upgrade his system, he's able to see what he's already done to it.

You may find templates for additional label sizes and shapes at your local computer user group, on a bulletin board, or in an online service such as CompuServe or Delphi. If you can't find a template for a particular label size, design your own. Then post it on your local user group's BBS (Bulletin Board System). If you ask for a postcard from everyone who uses it, you'll probably get mail from all over the world. There are laser-printable label pages for virtually anything you can think of. Some are tricky to find. The cassette labels, for instance, are generally available only through the kind of places that sell professional audio equipment and large quantities of tapes to recording studios. Still, if you have a need for any of these less common labels, you'll probably also know where to look to find them.

Once you have the labels in hand, what should you do with them? The only limit is your own creativity. Avery even makes full-size sheets of label paper. You can use PageMaker to set up a page of bumper stickers, print them on full sheets and cut them down to size. Set the page for wide orientation, and divide it into three or four stickers. A squirt of Krylon spray, available at your local art supply store, will make the bumper sticker reasonably weatherproof.

# Facts About Faxing

These days, most computers have modems, and most modems have built-in faxing capability. You can lay out pages in PageMaker and fax them directly from the program, without ever printing them. You can also use PageMaker to design custom cover sheets. Many fax programs let you import your own custom cover sheets. If yours doesn't, set the entire fax in PageMaker, and send the whole thing as a multipage fax with your custom cover sheet at the head.

Customized cover sheets can include clip art and scanned photos if you want. Sent from the computer instead of a stand-alone fax machine, they'll look much better, even if they're received on a separate fax machine instead of another fax modem. That's because fax modems send at 200 dpi, in high-quality mode, and with TrueType or ATM, pages are composed at the correct resolution so you get perfectly straight, properly aligned letters. By the way, there's a line of Macintosh modems, from PSI, which include OCR software so you can read and edit incoming faxes.

If there's a one-page fax you send often, like the map that shows how to get to your office, the corporate capabilities chart, or a one-page blurb about your hottest product, save it as a cover sheet in your fax folder. Then, select **Quick Fax**, and send it whenever you need to.

# The Bare Essentials

In this chapter, we looked at other uses for PageMaker. Specifically, you learned about the following:

- How to use PageMaker to put together ads for newspapers and magazines.

- How to create flyers and brochures.

- Using PageMaker to design posters of all kinds.

- Advantages and disadvantages of being your own advertising agency.

- Creating overhead transparencies and how to make multilayer transparencies. How to use PageMaker's thumbnail printing capability to produce handouts for your presentation.

- Designing your own greeting cards and how to set up a French fold or a contemporary format card.

- How to make calendars in PageMaker using the calendar templates, or starting from scratch.

- Using the Avery label templates to create all kinds of labels and ideas for label uses you may not have thought of.

- How to use PageMaker to create custom Fax cover sheets.

# Chapter 12

## Chapter Preview

*Book design and layout*

*Managing large documents*

*Creating a table of contents*

*Creating an index*

# Longer Documents

PageMaker can do more than make elegant pages. Aldus might have just as easily named it BookMaker, except for the somewhat negative connotations in the law enforcement world. But there's nothing negative about PageMaker's ability to handle longer publications. In fact, it's used by many professional publishing houses to create books of all kinds.

Experts in the field of book design like PageMaker because it lets them create publications with a consistent "look." Page design must remain the same page after page, chapter after chapter. Because PageMaker lets you design a master page and autoflow a whole chapter's worth of text into it in one pass, it's not only consistent—it's quick. Editors enjoy working with PageMaker because it can automate the previously exhausting chores of assembling an accurate table of contents and index. The production department prefers

PageMaker because it can organize the chapters and print them one at a time or as a whole book, even doing the time-consuming chore of imposition easily, quickly, and accurately.

# Planning the Book

Whether the book in question is a novel, instruction book, technical manual, or an annual report, the process of designing and producing it begins almost as soon as the author starts to think about writing it. Creating a book length publication demands a lot of advance planning.

PageMaker can assemble a book from separate chapters, a capability that can save you a great deal of work, especially if you rearrange chapters frequently. It also lets you deal with files in manageable sizes—a definite advantage. Therefore, it's helpful to think of the text in sections. Call them chapters if you like, or whatever division seems most appropriate. Use the same paragraph styles and formatting throughout to make indexing easier.

If the publication in question is a corporate report, you may be dealing with between twenty and fifty pages of material. If it's an epic novel, you may have hundreds of pages to contend with. PageMaker lets you manage up to 999 pages in one publication, and you can link publications together to maintain automatic page numbering, indexing, and printing in order for up to 9,999 pages.

### By the Way . . .

*The longest "important" novel ever published, according to the Guinness Book of World Records, was Men of Good Will by Jules Romains. Published by Peter Davies, Ltd. in 1933–46 as a 14-volume "novel cycle," the work would have been an easy job for PageMaker at 4,959 pages plus a 100-page index.*

When you break down the text in chapters or sections, create a separate section for the front matter: the title page, acknowledgments, copyright statements, and table of contents. The preface or foreword, if any, should also be a separate section, as should each chapter and each appendix. Keep the index separate, too. These divisions will be convenient for design and page numbering as well as for printing.

Although novels may not be profusely illustrated, reports and manuals usually are. As you've learned, PageMaker can handle illustrations and charts with ease. You've already learned how to import graphics into PageMaker and how to manage inline graphics, keeping charts and diagrams with the text that describes them.

## Watch Out!

*Be sure to keep graphics with their chapters for convenience in printing. Save each chapter and its associated graphics in a separate folder (on the Mac) or in a separate directory (for Windows).*

# Designing the Book

In book design, perhaps more than in any other task in which you'll use PageMaker, you'll come to appreciate the program's capabilities for using templates, master pages, and style sheets. The way to assure consistency is to create a master page for the text and a master style sheet with the fonts and spacing attributes you'll use throughout the entire publication, and then to not deviate from these.

Begin by considering a single page of text. What size will the page be? Although normal pages are 8 ½" x 11" and this is the paper size that your laser printer most readily handles, few books are printed at standard size. More commonly a book will measure something like 6 ½" x 9", or maybe 7 ³/₈" x 9¼", or some other similar proportion. This is often referred to as the *trim size*. Pages are first printed and then trimmed to that size as part of the binding process. A magazine or an annual report may even use a larger size paper than normal to make it stand out from the usual stacks of stuff on a busy desk. Annual reports are frequently printed on extra heavy stock, with a textured or other special surface, and may be designed in a 9" x 12", or 11" x 14" size as well as in the more common formats.

Of course, you can set up a standard page so the margins give you an area about the right size for the book's page, but it's far better to tell PageMaker to use Custom pages and to make them the size you want them. Figure 12.1 shows a typical book page setup. When you print on standard 8 ½" x 11" paper, you can have PageMaker add the appropriate crop marks for your real page size automatically just by clicking on the **Printer's marks** box in the **Print Options** box. Crop marks will show the printer where to trim pages to get the right size. If you also click **Page information**, as shown in Figure 12.2, your pages will show the name of the file, page number, and the date and time they were printed.

You'll also need to think about binding the book so you'll know how much margin to assign. If you're not sure, take a look at other books or publications that use the same type of binding you're planning to use. Measure their margins. See whether they're generous enough to make reading the words at the middle of the book easy. The book should open enough that you can see the whole line of type.

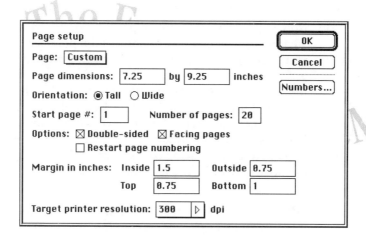

Figure 12.1 When you set up pages this way, the screen page reflects the numbers you've entered, not the size of the paper in the printer.

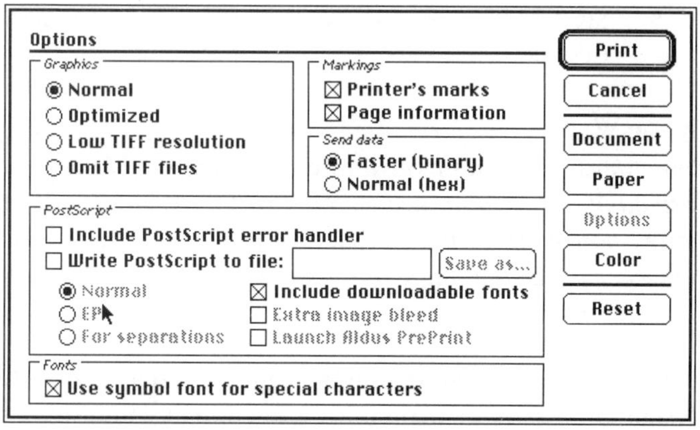

Figure 12.2 Click both Printer's marks and Page information to print the name, page number, and date of the file, as well as crop marks and registration marks.

In order to see what your pages are going to look like, follow these steps to create a dummy:

1. Open PageMaker and set up your page to the size and margin setting you think will work for you. Ask for several pages, and be sure to select facing pages and double-sided pages.

2. After you've set up your pages, open the master pages, create guidelines as needed, and place page numbers. Do this by creating a text block on the left master page and pressing ⌘+Option+P (Ctrl+Shift+3 in Windows) to add page numbers. Copy this text block and drag it to the right master page. Add a chapter header if you intend to use one and any rules or other repeating graphics on the page. Remember, you can override the master pages for the first page of a chapter. Be sure to save your work.

3. Now pour some text into the page. It doesn't particularly matter what kind of text you use as long as the point size is correct. If you're going to set the book in 12-point type, use 12-point greeking. The Lorem Ipsum greeking file, called **SampleText** on the Mac and **TEXT.TXT** in Windows (on both, it is found in Lesson1 subdirectory/folder of the Tutorial subdirectory/folder of the Pagemaker5 directory/folder), is fine if you don't already have text written and waiting to go. If the text file isn't long enough to fill two facing pages, copy and paste. Create styles on the Style palette for the text and for headlines or header/footer text blocks.

4. Add gray boxes to represent graphics if there will be a great many of them, as you'd expect to find in a technical manual or a book like this one.

5. Study what you've done, and make whatever changes are needed.

### By the Way . . .

*Sometimes, it's easier to evaluate your design by looking at a thumbnail instead of at the computer screen. Print thumbnails of just the pages you've poured text into, as well as full-size dummy proofs. Greeking the text lets you see the shape of it on the page so you don't get hung up on the content.*

Look carefully at these dummy pages and decide whether the page design looks right or wrong. Is there enough white space to set off the text properly? Too much white space so it looks lost? Is the header in the right place? Would a footer be more effective? Figure 12.3 shows a pair of dummy pages for a text book. The two diagonally striped boxes represent small graphics. The page number markers have been placed in the side margins, but the dummy reveals that they should either be moved or made much larger.

Experiment with different concepts and layouts until you find one you're satisfied with. Then remove the text from the dummy layout by selecting it all and deleting it. Remove any specific headers you've put in, and leave simple place holders, such as the *chapter name*, *topic*, and *text*, with your style sheets applied to the appropriate place holders. Save this publication as a template. You can use the template to begin each chapter of the book or each section of the publication.

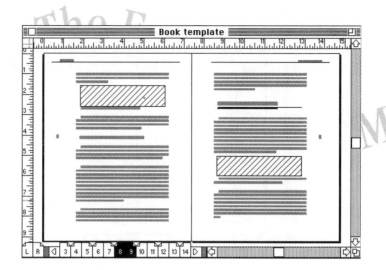

Figure 12.3
Place all elements that repeat on the master pages, and then open two facing pages and import some text.

# The Annual Report

In an annual report or other publication of this nature, you may wish to vary the design of the page layout. You can do this exactly as you would in a newsletter, by assigning columns differently on different pages. In such a case, you may have very little on the master pages, possibly only page numbers. Figure 12.4 shows a pair of pages from an annual report, and Figure 12.5 shows the master pages from which they were created. The items included on these master pages are the company logo at the top of both pages, the line at the bottom, and the page numbers.

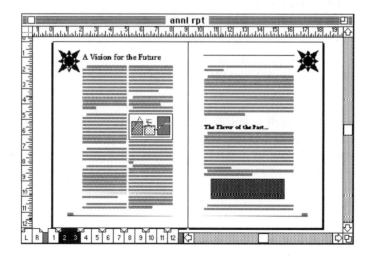

Figure 12.4
The text and figures were added on the regular pages.

Figure 12.5
Repeating
elements,
column guides,
and ruler
guides were
placed on the
master pages.

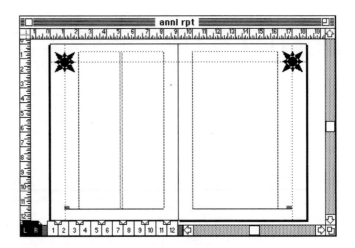

Even though the number of columns changes from left pages to right pages, the overall look remains consistent. Use of the repeating logo element and rules, as well as a consistent type style, ties it all together. Remember that you can change any regular page without affecting the others. Then if you decide the changes were a mistake, you can put back the guides and redisplay the master page elements.

Text and graphics for the report are best created in other programs and imported into PageMaker. You can, however, use PageMaker's Story Editor to check spelling and for final text editing. You can check the spelling in a single story or in all of the stories in your publication at once. Simple charts such as the bar graph in Figure 12.4 can be assembled right in PageMaker by using the Rectangle tool and filling with a pattern. (These obviously won't have a high degree of accuracy as they would if brought from another program.)

Programs generally used for outlining and desktop presentations, such as Symantec's MORE 3.0, Aldus Persuasion (available in a Windows versions, too), or Microsoft PowerPoint (also available in a Mac version), can also produce charts and graphics for PageMaker, as can integrated programs, such as MS Works, WordPerfect Works, or ClarisWorks. These applications let you set up pie charts, bar charts, and all sorts of other interesting graphs. Figure 12.6 shows a tree chart assembled from an outline created in MORE and saved as an EPS file. Figure 12.7 shows a pie chart created in ClarisWorks, ready to place in a PageMaker publication.

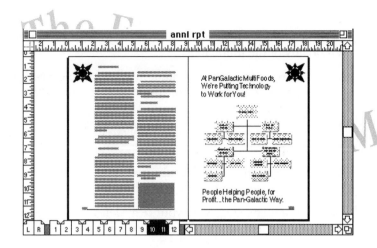

Figure 12.6
Tree chart
placed in an
annual report.

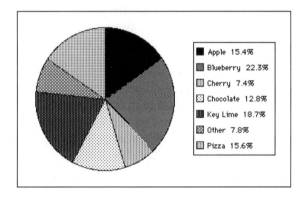

Figure 12.7
One of the
many kinds of
charts you can
bring into
PageMaker.

# Preparing Text to Import

Programs such as WordPerfect, WriteNow 3.0, and Microsoft Word have
much in common with PageMaker's text handling functions, so you can
easily format text in any of these programs and import the text into
PagcMakcr with little or no need for additional formatting. PageMaker
has a special affinity for Microsoft Word and will accept not only its style
sheet definitions, but its index entries as well.

There are several ways to save time in formatting imported text. You can do any of the following:

- Format text as you write it in a compatible word processing program such as WriteNow, MacWrite, WordPerfect, or Microsoft Word.

- Set type specifications to apply to unformatted type before you import it.

- Bring in unformatted text, select it, and apply an existing style or create a new one for it.

- Enter style tags with your text, define the styles in PageMaker, and check **Read tags** when you place the text.

When you're preparing text to import, you can do much of your formatting in advance. Practically every word processor lets you define bold and italic type. You can also set tabs so your text and formatted tables will import into PageMaker in the correct position on the line. In most word processors, you can specify a first line indent just as you can in PageMaker. If you're using some other word processor and you want first line indents, simply insert a tab. PageMaker recognizes the left margin as a starting point and will accept hanging indents (to the left of the left margin), as well as normal indents. Just be sure to click on the **Retain formats** check box in PageMaker's **Place document** box. Otherwise your formatting will be lost.

Macs and PCs are becoming more alike due to diligent word processing vendors. Crossing platforms successfully while retaining formats used to be very difficult, but since Microsoft Word for DOS, Mac, and Windows are completely co-compatible, working on alien files is much easier. In addition, PageMaker recognizes WordPerfect for the Mac, DOS, and Windows, as well as all of the MS Word permutations. You no longer have to convert your files to ASCII or text files to bring them into PageMaker. In addition, PageMaker recognizes many integrated packages that cross platforms, such as ClarisWorks, MS Works, and WordPerfect Works (formerly BeagleWorks). Using the Place command with any of these programs brings your data into PageMaker almost flawlessly.

If you do have some incompatible programs that you want to share among PCs and Macs before bringing them into PageMaker, you can use DataViz' MacLink Translators/Plus for the Mac and MacLink/PC on the PC to convert almost every type of file to its equivalent version (and back again) without losing formatting or content.

**By the Way . . .**

*If you import a formatted story but forget to click on the Retain formats box, simply press ⌘+D (or **Ctrl+D** in Windows), and place the story again, this time checking both **Replacing entire story** and **Retain format**.*

Remember not to use carriage returns (that funny little backwards "P" symbol) at the end of each line. Every return comes in as a line feed. This is fine at the end of a paragraph or after a fixed line of text, such as those that occur in a title or a table. But if you insert extra line feeds in your text, you'll end up with strange line spacing in your finished manuscript. Also, watch out for extra spaces after a period; the bad habit learned by anyone who was taught to type before word processors came along. If you're bringing in text as an ASCII (text only) file from some other word processor or from a non-Macintosh computer, you can still save time by making sure the text is clean and that it has been checked for spelling and for stray carriage returns and spaces.

Many PC-based programs have the decidedly unpleasant (for Mac users) habit of placing an extra carriage return at the end of every line in ASCII files. PageMaker's Smart ASCII filter will strip these off without disturbing the ones you want left behind. Just be sure the Smart ASCII filter is installed before you begin to import ASCII text. Mac files, on the other hand, use only a line feed and not a carriage return.

Since ASCII text appears on the page pretty much unformatted, you'll save steps if you set the specifications in the Type specifications dialog box before you place it. If you forget, then place the I-beam cursor in the text, press ⌘+A (**Ctrl+A** in Windows) to Select All, and then enter your specifications in the Type specifications box. The text will change when you click on **OK**. Of course, both of these methods assume all the text is going to be set to the same specification. If you have heads and subheads, you'll lose them with either of these methods.

To preserve style differences when you're importing text from a word processor PageMaker doesn't recognize, use *tags*. Simply decide on names for the different styles such as subhead 1, subhead 2, text, and so on. Next, type these style names in front of whatever text they're supposed to apply to, enclosed in angle brackets. For example, **<text>** would precede this section. Style tags apply to all the text that follows until the next style tag. Then, before you place the text, define your styles on the Style palette, and check the **Read tags** box in the Place document dialog box.

# Handling Pictures

In a technical manual or how-to book, illustrations can often occupy as much space as the words that explain them. Generally, the text refers to the illustrations, and it's important to keep them as close together as possible. Therefore, you may find it helpful to place them as inline graphics. Remember, there's no size limit for an inline graphic. It can, at least theoretically, be a full page. However, when you're dealing with very large graphics, you may find that they cause major disruptions in text flow. PageMaker may be forced to create new pages to accommodate your story. If the text disappears, go to Story view by pressing ⌘+**E** (or **Ctrl+E** in Windows), and move the cursor to the missing words. When you go back to Layout view you'll find them.

### Watch Out!

*If you're using a large inline graphic, you may need to adjust the page margins and/or remove master page items to make room for it.*

# Making a Book List

You've set up a book template to create individual chapters, and you've saved each of these chapters under its own name, such as Chapter 1, Chapter 2, and so on. Now you're ready to put them together as a book. Building a book allows you to perform various important functions, like creating the table of contents and Index, working with the group of chapters as a single unit, rather than doing the job one piece at a time and compiling it manually.

Once your publication is in book form, PageMaker can automatically repaginate chapters, renumber pages, compile the table of contents and index, and print the entire book in the correct order (with just one Print command). Use the **Book** command from the **File** menu to compile separate publications into a book and make up a book list of your chapters. To make up a book list, follow these steps:

1.   Open the Book publication list dialog box shown in Figure 12.8. The name of the publication that's open will be automatically listed.

2.   Select additional publications to insert into the book list. (You can only insert one publication at a time.) Click on the **Insert** button to place them. Don't worry if they're not immediately placed in the right order, because you can move them.

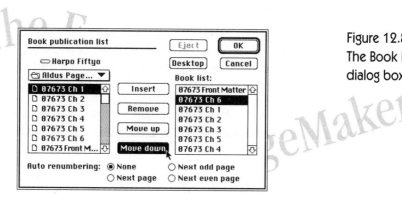

Figure 12.8
The Book List
dialog box.

3. To change the order, select the publication to move and click on **Move up** or **Move down**. Doing so moves the selection one notch up or down. To move one several spaces, you must click the button several times. Publications will be printed in the order in which they're listed, so you must arrange them in the correct order.

4. If you want to remove a publication from the list, select it, and click on the **Remove** button. PageMaker will delete it from the list.

   If you've already placed a publication and try to place it again, you'll see the Alert box shown in Figure 12.9. Simply click on **Continue**, or press **Enter** or **Return** to continue adding chapters.

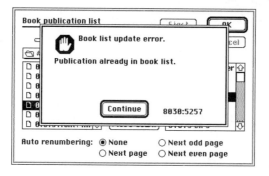

Figure 12.9
PageMaker
won't let you
insert the same
chapter twice.

5. When your book list is complete, click on **OK**, or press **Return** (or **Enter**) to close the box. When you open the Print document dialog box, you'll be able to select **Print all publications in book.**

You can create a book list in any publication you want to include in the book. Add as many publications as you wish. A publication can appear in more than one book, and can appear in more than one book list, but a publication can only hold one book list at a time. If you were creating an Annual Report to Stockholders and a Report to the Chairman of the Board, you might have many of the same publications in the two. To keep from getting confused, you could save the title page of each as a separate publication and assemble the appropriate book lists in them.

PageMaker always assumes that the open publication is part of the current book unless you select it from the book list and click on the **Remove** button. To copy a book list compiled in one publication into all others in the list, hold down ⌘ (Mac) or **Ctrl** (Windows) while you open **Book** from the **File** menu. The publication from which you copy must be named and saved, so PageMaker can follow its file path. If the publication into which you are copying the list already has one, the new list will replace the previous one.

The Book dialog box also lets you tell PageMaker how to automatically renumber pages. The Auto renumbering option you choose determines whether the first page of the next publication starts after the last page of the previous one (**Next page**), always on a right-hand page (**Next odd page**), or always on a left-hand page (**Next even page**). PageMaker will insert a blank page between chapters if one is needed.

### By the Way . . .
*PageMaker doesn't automatically renumber the pages until you perform a book operation, such as printing, generating an index, or compiling a table of contents. When you perform any of these tasks PageMaker will follow the options you choose.*

# Renumbering Without Losing Table of Contents Numbers

PageMaker lets you renumber pages from a given point without renumbering all the pages in the publication. For example, you may have set up a book with a separate publication for the title pages and other front material, and one for the table of contents as well as numerous chapters. The pages in the TOC have been set up with lowercase Roman numerals (i, ii, iii, and so on), and the first chapter is to start on Page 1. To renumber without losing the table of contents numbers, use the following steps.

1. Make sure your publications are in the correct order in the Book list. If they're not, correct the order by using the **Move up** and **Move down** buttons.

2. Close that publication, and open the chapter that is to start with Page 1.

3. Choose Page setup from the **File** menu.

4. Click on the **Restart page numbering** option, and close the box. When you print or perform any other "book" function, the pages will renumber.

### Watch Out!

*If you haven't placed page number markers (⌘+Option+P on the Mac or Ctrl+Shift+3 in Windows) on the left and right master pages of all your chapters, you won't see any page numbers.*

# The Table of Contents

Not all books include a table of contents, or TOC for short. Works of fiction seldom do. Anthologies always do. Other types of books like technical manuals and other nonfiction works usually benefit from having one. Short publications, like annual reports and similar documents, may or may not have one, according to the whim of the author.

PageMaker has eliminated much of the labor of producing a table of contents. You can generate one automatically for a single publication or for a whole book list. There are two basic steps in creating a table of contents:

- Specifying that a single paragraph or all paragraphs of a particular style be included in it.

- Using the **Create TOC** command from the **Options** menu to create the actual table and placing it as a story within the publication.

### By the Way . . .

*What PageMaker considers a paragraph for purposes of the TOC is what you might otherwise consider a chapter title or a first- or second-level subhead. (They're called paragraphs simply because they end with a carriage return.)*

You need to think about how detailed you want the TOC to be. In some types of publications, you might want only chapter headings. In a technical manual or how-to book, you might want to go all the way through a third or fourth level subhead. If you begin to plan the table of contents while you're creating the contents themselves, you can save time by marking the headings as you place them in PageMaker. When you tell PageMaker to assemble the TOC, it scans all of the marked headings and assembles them as a list, in Story Edit mode, along with their page numbers. There, you can revise and format them in any way you want. You can add dot leaders, tabs, and any other formatting information that you want to put there. Then, the TOC is placed as a new story.

## Marking Entries for the TOC

You can mark each of the paragraphs to go into the TOC in two ways: individually or as part of a paragraph style. To mark an individual entry, use the following steps:

1.  Use the **Text** tool to click an insertion point in the line you want to put into the TOC.

2.  Press ⌘+**M** (**Ctrl+M** in Windows), or choose **Paragraph** from the **Type** menu.

3.  Check the **Include in table of contents** option, and close the box.

The method above works fine if you're going through an existing publication. It's a lot easier, however, to decide first that you want a certain level of subhead in the TOC and to include it as you create your publication. This method also gives you a more consistent table of contents, as it captures all the heads at a given level, and doesn't tempt you to add extraneous items or overlook an important one. To include all the paragraphs, heads, or subheads in a particular style, follow these steps:

1.  Choose **Define styles** from the **Type** menu, or press ⌘+**3** (**Ctrl+3** in Windows) to open the Define styles dialog box. You'll see the list of styles on the scrolling menu.

2.  Choose the name of the style whose paragraphs you want to include in the TOC, and click on the **Edit** button to open the Edit style box.

3.  In the Edit style dialog box, click on the **Para** button to open the Paragraph specifications box.

4. Click on the **Include in table of contents** box, as shown in Figure 12.10.

5. Press **Option+Enter** (or **Return**) (**Ctrl+Alt+Shift+Enter** in Windows) to close all the boxes. All paragraphs using that type style will be included in the TOC.

**Paragraph specifications**

OK

Indents:
Left `.5` inches
First `0` inches
Right `0` inches

Paragraph space:
Before `0` inches
After `0` inches

Cancel

Rules...

Spacing...

Alignment: `Left`     Dictionary: `US English`

Options:
☐ Keep lines together      ☐ Keep with next `0` lines
☒ Column break before      ☒ Widow control `3` lines
☐ Page break before        ☐ Orphan control `0` lines
☒ Include in table of contents

Figure 12.10 Just click the check box in the Paragraph specifications dialog box to designate a TOC entry.

# The Table of Contents Publication

After you've identified all of the items that need to be entries in the TOC, you need to generate the publication that contains the list and place it within the book list. Although you could stick it in with the title page, dedication, and any other front material, it's better to keep the TOC as a separate publication so it can have its own set of page numbers. Start a new publication called TOC, and assemble your Book list in it.

Don't wait until the last minute to create the TOC. If it requires editing, make the changes in the publication(s), not just in the TOC. Otherwise, they won't match up, and you'll lose your revisions if you generate a new TOC later on. After you make changes in the publications, when you generate a new TOC, it will reflect the corrections.

### Watch Out!
*Page numbers within a book may not necessarily be sequential from one publication to the next. Check your page numbers before you begin to generate a table of contents or index.*

Use the following steps to create the table of contents publication:

1. Start a new PageMaker publication and title it **Table of Contents** (**TOC** in Windows). Give it as many pages as you think your table of contents will require.

2. From this new publication use the **Book** command from the **File** menu to link the publications you want the TOC to include.

3. Choose **Create Table of contents** from the **Utilities** menu. The dialog box shown in Figure 12.11 appears. If the present publication is part of a book list, the Include book publications box will automatically be selected.

4. You may change the title of the table of contents by deleting Contents from the Title field and entering whatever you want, up to 30 characters long. If you don't want a title at all, remove **Contents** from the box and leave it empty.

5. PageMaker will automatically place the correct page numbers for your TOC entries, but you need to specify how they should be displayed. If you don't want to use page numbers in the TOC, click on the **No page numbers** box. You may place the page number before or after the entry. The character combination ⌃**t**, as shown in Figure 12.11, is PageMaker's default, a right-aligned tab on the right margin with a dot leader pattern. When you're ready to compile the table of contents, click on **OK**.

6. PageMaker will search each page of your publication for TOC markers, compile the TOC for you, and give you a Place text icon. Place the table of contents as if it were any other story. Now you can edit it, change type styles, delete entries you've changed your mind about, and work with it in any way you like. Figure 12.12 shows a piece of an actual table of contents.

Figure 12.11
The Create
table of
contents
dialog box.

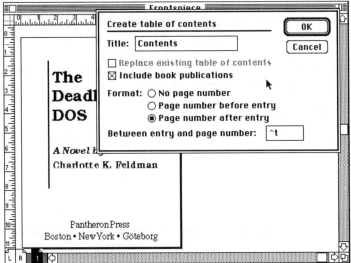

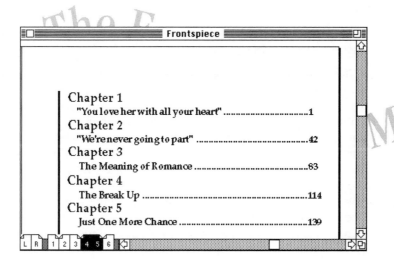

Figure 12.12
Looks like the
same old story.

Chapter 1
"You love her with all your heart" ....................................1
Chapter 2
"We're never going to part" ..............................................42
Chapter 3
The Meaning of Romance ...............................................83
Chapter 4
The Break Up ...................................................................114
Chapter 5
Just One More Chance .....................................................139

**By the Way . . .**
*If you haven't previously created a table of contents for this book, the*
*Replace check box in the Create TOC dialog box will be disabled. Other-*
*wise it is selected by default so that new versions will update the previ-*
*ous ones.*

The Create TOC command automatically assigns default styles to the
TOC title and entries. You can edit these styles just as you would any
others. The style names of TOC entries will have TOC in front of them—
for example, **TOC Headline**. TOC styles, by default, are based on the
style attributes of the original paragraph style for which they're named.
Thus, if you had level one subheads in 18-point Helvetica and level two
subheads in 14-point Helvetica italic, and designated them both as TOC
entries, you'd see some lines of 18-point and some lines of 14-point
type in the TOC publication. If you manually designate a TOC entry that
didn't have a style applied to it, it will appear in the TOC in whatever
the default "no style" font and size are.

If you edit a TOC style, you won't see the results of your changes
until you recompile the TOC. Don't change the TOC style names.
PageMaker searches for them and will re-create them and apply them
(unchanged) to your new table of contents, if you've edited the name
along with the style of any TOC style.

# Creating an Index

For any nonfiction book, the index is vitally important. It must be
accurate and complete. It's often the first place to which the reader
turns. A well-done index helps sell books and makes the browser more

likely to read the book. It makes the information in the book more useful and accessible.

The process of indexing a book is often tedious, especially when it must be done by hand. PageMaker makes indexing a great deal easier. You can define index entries as you write them, as you edit, or after the publication is finished. PageMaker will keep track of cross-references and establish up to three levels for an index entry. Once the index is complete, you place it in your document as you would any other story. You can view it and format it in Story Editor form before placing it in the publication. PageMaker also recognizes index entries created in Microsoft Word and will incorporate them when you place a Word document into a PageMaker publication, although imported index entries will lose cross-references, page ranges, and similar information.

### Watch Out!

*As in the table of contents procedure described earlier in this chapter, if you discover an error, such as a misspelling in the index, correct it in the publication itself, and not just in the index. Since the index is generated from the text, if you correct only the index, the text will still be wrong. If you then recompile the index, the misspelling will reappear.*

Index entries are defined any of several ways. The simplest way is to use a keyboard shortcut to index selected text with a page reference. Select the word to index and press either ⌘+**Shift+**; (semicolon) or **Ctrl+Shift+**; in Windows. This adds the selected word or phrase to the Index with its current page as a reference. It doesn't tag all occurrences of the selected word or phrase, only the one you've identified.

## Indexing Names

Some phrases, such as proper names or qualified keywords, need to be indexed last name first. To do so, follow these steps.

1. To index a proper name, select the whole name, and press ⌘+**Shift+Z** (**Ctrl+Shift+Z** in Windows). The name will appear properly in the index: last name first, then first name and page number.

   **Brown, James**          **43**

2. If the person's name or other key phrase to be inverted has more than two words or two words plus a title (Book of Kells, Dr. Irving R. Gerbil, Sir James Brown), you must **first** add nonbreaking spaces between the titles, first names, middle

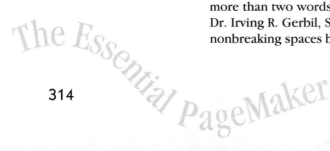

initials, or words not to be separated in the phrase. Doing so lets PageMaker see and index the entire phrase or name as only two words. To insert nonbreaking spaces, press **Option+ Spacebar (Ctrl+Shift+H** in Windows). This places a nonprinting character (^t) in the space, giving you:

**Brown, Sir James**          43
**Gerbil, Dr. Irving R.**       62
**Kells, Book of**           19

Thus, to prepare Nicolai von Stroganoff for indexing, delete the space between von and S, and press **Option+Spacebar (Ctrl+Shift+H** in Windows) to produce a nonbreaking space. Then you can press ⌘**+Shift+Z (Ctrl+Shift+Z** in Windows) to turn it around. Use nonbreaking spaces to format names with titles and middle initials such as Sgt. Elmo Pepper and Phipps P. Phipple. In these examples, the nonbreaking spaces would need to go between Sgt. and Elmo, and Phipps and P. Names with hyphens or apostrophes don't need special treatment. PageMaker handles them automatically, as it does titles after a last name such as Jr., II, and so on. The following examples need no custom characters:

**Fenelly-Kluggman, Rebecca**
**O'Reilly, Isadora**
**Lavendar, Lance Jr.**

If an academic degree follows a last name, it is always preceded by a comma. PageMaker, unfortunately, can't handle this, and entries such as Samuel Fullybright, Ph.D., must be typed in the Add index entry box in the form in which they should appear in the index, **Fullybright, Samuel, Ph.D.**

To index all the occurrences of a particular *keyword* (word you want to index), use the **Change** box.

1. Think of a word that you want to index for all of the occurrences.

2. In Story Editor, open the stories or publications you want to index.

3. Choose **Change** from the **Utilities** menu, and enter the word in the **Find what** box.

4. Then type a ^; (caret or **Shift+6**) and semi-colon in the **Change to** box. The caret semi-colon combination tells PageMaker to index the word. Typing ^z (caret + z) indexes the selection as a proper name, last name first, as above.

5. To carry out the find and change process, select **All publications**, and **All stories**, as shown in Figure 12.13, or search them one by one if you prefer.

6. Then click the **Change all** button, or if you want to index more selectively, use the **Find**, **Change & Find**, or **Find next** if you decide not to index a particular occurrence of the word. (The **Find** button changes to **Find next** after the first occurrence is found.)

Figure 12.13
This will index
the keyword
as Moose,
Talking.

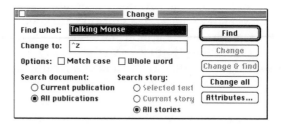

When a simple index entry isn't thorough enough, you need to create custom sub-entries, refer to a range of pages, or even create an index entry for a phrase that doesn't appear in the text. Some examples follow.

> **Smith, John, 12–49**
> **and Pocahontas, 33, 37**
> **response from King, 33**
> **leadership qualities, 17, 19, 42**
> **place in history, 48–49**

Index references can be customized in the Add index entry dialog box shown in Figure 12.14. Several choices, from the following list, must be made when entering a topic to be indexed. Some of these choices will be different if you select the **Cross-reference** option.

- *Page reference or Cross reference:* Page reference lets you define an individual index entry. Click on the **Cross-reference** button if you want to cross-reference this index entry with others.

- *Topic:* You may enter up to three index levels in the boxes. The first is the main entry, and the other(s) would be entered beneath it. For example, the index entries for lima beans might read:

> **Beans, 38–56**
> **Lima, 43–45**
> **cooking, 43–44**
> **growing, 45**

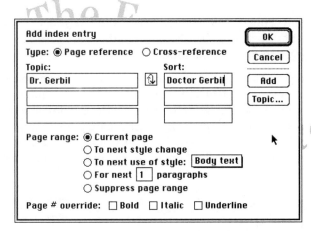

Figure 12.14
The Add index
entry dialog
box.

- *Promote/Demote:* The icon with the circling arrows is a button that enables you to change the hierarchy of levels of an index entry by promoting or demoting its level. Thus, the earlier entry could become:

**Beans, 38–56**
  **cooking, 43–44, 51–52**
  **Lima, 43–45**
    **growing, 45**

- *Sort:* Entries in these boxes tell PageMaker how to sort abbreviations and nonalphabet characters. To index *Dr. Gerbil* correctly, enter *Doctor Gerbil*. It will print as Dr. but be indexed as if it were Doctor.

- *Page Range:* This tells PageMaker what page range to assign to your entry.

- *Current page:* This means the entry is found only on that page.

- *To next style change:* This means the page range extends until the next type style occurs.

- *To next use of style:* Lets you select a style at which to end the page range.

- *For next paragraphs:* Lets you define a whole number of paragraphs the index entry spans.

- *Suppress page range:* This omits the page range from the index.

- *Page # override:* Lets you change the type attributes of a particular index entry to make it stand out. Otherwise, it will appear in PageMaker's default index type style.

- *Add:* Functionally the same as OK. It lets you add entries without closing the dialog box if there are several words you want to place in the index.

- *Topic:* This takes you to the Select topic dialog box, shown in Figure 12.15, which displays a list of current index topics. Move between sections by choosing the desired initial letter from the Topic section popup menu. Checking topics lets you avoid repeating index entries in slightly different ways and serves as a reminder as to whether you've previously included the topic.

Figure 12.15
The Select
Topic dialog
box.

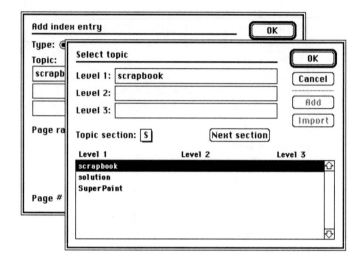

When you select the Cross-reference button, some of your choices are different. Figure 12.16 shows the Add index entry dialog box for cross-referencing. The Topic and Sort options are the same. The major difference is that you may select a way for the cross-reference to be entered. The Denoted by option gives you several choices. Select whichever seems appropriate.

The X-ref button gives you a box much like the Topic box. It's shown in Figure 12.17. Choose and place cross-references as you did with topics, using the X-ref box to select a topic to cross-reference your entry to.

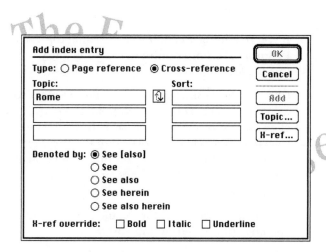

Figure 12.16
The Add index
entry box
for cross
referencing.

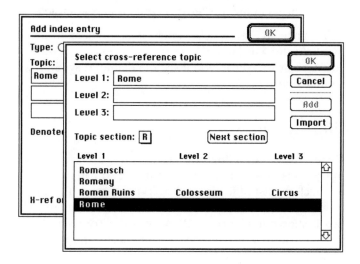

Figure 12.17
The X-ref box.

# Making an Index Entry

To make a simple index entry, follow these steps.

1.  Use the **Text** tool to select the word or phrase to enter. (It may be up to 50 characters long including spaces.)

2.  Choose **Index entry** from the **Utilities** menu, or press ⌘+; (semicolon) on the Mac or **Ctrl** l ; in Windows to open the Add index entry dialog box shown in Figure 12.14. The selected word or phrase will be entered in the first topic field.

3. If you're adding an entry to an existing topic, click on the **Promote/Demote** button to cycle the entry to the second or third field.

4. Click on the **Topic** button to open the **Select topic** box and locate the topic. Select it, and hold down ⌘ or **Ctrl** while you click on **OK**, or press Enter (or Return) to close the box. The selected topic will be displayed in the first field with your entry in the field below it. If you forgot to hold down ⌘ (Ctrl in Windows), your entry will not appear. Retype it into the appropriate field.

5. Specify the page range for the index entry and enter any special spellings (if needed) in the Sort field.

6. When you're done defining the index entry, click on **OK** or press Enter (or Return). The entry is complete.

To make an even quicker entry, if all the defaults are acceptable, just highlight the word to be entered, and press ⌘+**Shift**+; (semicolon). If you're in Story Editor, you'll see the diamond symbol, which indicates an index entry.

## Viewing the Index

Once you start defining index entries, PageMaker starts compiling the index. This means the index is available so you can consult it at any time to check the list of topics and cross-references. To find out what's been indexed, select **Show index** from the **Utilities** menu. The Show index box is shown in Figure 12.18. As with the Topics and X-ref boxes, you move through it by using the alphabetical popup menu under Index section.

Figure 12.18
The Show
index box.

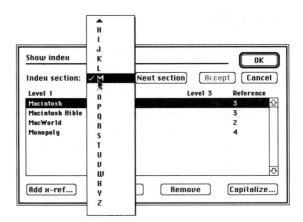

The Essential PageMaker

You can add cross-references within this dialog box, edit and remove entries, and accept the changes without closing the dialog box after each one. The following list gives you quick keyboard/mouse combinations for many of the edit functions. Note that whenever you see an **Option** key in the table, use the **Alt** key on Windows.

| Press | To Do |
|---|---|
| *Option+Add x-ref* | Deletes all cross-references since you opened the dialog box or clicked on *Accept*. |
| *Option+Remove* | Restores all cross-references you added since you opened the dialog box or clicked on *Accept*. |
| *⌘+Option+Remove* | Deletes all page references. To restore them press *Option+Remove*. |
| *⌘+Shift+Remove* | Deletes all cross-references. To restore them press *Option+Remove*. |
| *⌘+Option+Shift+Remove* | Deletes all index entries. To restore them press *Option+Remove*. |

# Compiling the Index

The last step in producing an index is to use the **Create index** command from the **Utilities** menu to compile the actual index from all the entries, and then to adjust the formatting, as needed, to produce a good-looking and easily readable index. Like the table of contents, the index is created as a story and placed within the publication. Since an index generally appears at the end of the book, you can just place it and let PageMaker add as many additional pages as are needed. Figure 12.19 shows the Create index dialog box. You can give your index a name if you want, by entering it in the box.

**Replace existing index** will be checked if you've previously created an index for this publication. Otherwise, it will be disabled. Use the **Format** button to bring up the Index format dialog box, shown in Figure 12.20. Index section headings are the A, B, and so on, which may be included at the head of each section of the index if you click on the box. You have the option of skipping any part of the alphabet that has no index entries.

Figure 12.19
The Create
index dialog
box.

Figure 12.20
The Index
format dialog
box.

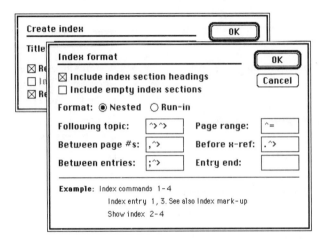

The strange symbols in the fields in the Index format box are called *metacharacters.* They are nonprinting characters that PageMaker inserts where you specify to leave spaces, tab across a line, and so on. When you adjust the formatting of index entries, you'll be able to preview the results immediately. The example at the bottom of the box changes whenever you change any of the metacharacter settings. The following chart of metacharacters will help you in formatting index entries.

| To insert | Use the Metacharacter |
| --- | --- |
| Carriage Return | ^p |
| Line break | ^n |
| Tab | ^t |
| Soft hyphen | ^- |
| Nonbreaking hyphen | ^[alt+126] |
| Computer inserted hyphen | ^c |
| Caret | ^^ |
| Unknown character | ^? |
| Nonbreaking space | ^s |

322

| To insert | Use the Metacharacter |
|---|---|
| White space or tab | ^w |
| Thin space | ^< |
| En space | ^> |
| Em space | ^m |
| En dash | ^= |
| Em dash | ^_ |

You can also use punctuation marks as shown in Figure 12.20. Commas between page numbers are helpful, as are semicolons between run-on entries. PageMaker will create and assign default styles when the index is created. You may edit these styles as you would any other. If you edit and rename an index style, PageMaker will apply the revised style the next time you create the index. However, you won't be able to see the changes unless you create the index again. Depending on the number of entries and the length of the chapters, it may take quite a while for PageMaker to completely compile the index. An Alert box with a thermometer like the one shown in Figure 12.21, will let you know how much progress is being made.

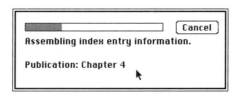

Figure 12.21
This process can take a long time.

To create the index after you've identified all the index entries, follow these steps.

1. Choose **Create index** under the **Utilities** menu. Give your index a name if you want, or delete the default name if none is wanted.

2. Click on the box to remove unreferenced topics. This removes index topics whose references have been deleted, topics imported from other publications not used as entries or cross-references, or topics you entered for which PageMaker found no matches.

3. Click on **Format** to verify formatting. The example in the Index format box reflects the current settings.

4.   Make changes or click on **OK**. To close the boxes, click on **OK**

What happens next depends on whether you started to create the index from the Story Editor view or the Page Layout view, and whether your index is new or replacing an existing index. PageMaker either:

- Opens a new Story window for the index if you're in Story view.

- Updates the existing Index window in Story view.

- Gives you a loaded Text icon so you can place the index as a new story in Layout view.

- Replaces the existing index and takes you to the first page of it in Layout view.

Figure 12.22 shows a portion of an index in Story view. The index entries have styles attached. You can edit these styles and reformat the index in any way you like. Place the index at the end of the last book chapter. PageMaker will create as many additional pages as it needs.

Figure 12.22
The index in
Story Editor.

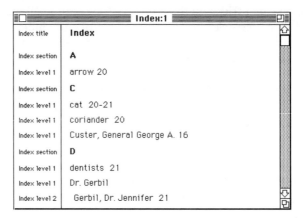

## Printing the Book

The job that seemed so endless and complicated has resolved itself into a series of fast and easy steps. You've created your book, complete with index and table of contents. You've checked to be sure the pages are properly numbered. You've checked the spelling and made sure that your graphics are correctly placed. Your publication is ready to print!

Before you start the print run, make sure you have plenty of paper on hand and that your printer is working well. Run a single test page and check for smudges. If all is well, use the following steps to print the book.

## Printing a Book

1. Open the first publication in the book.

2. Go to the Print document dialog box and select **Print all publications in book**, as shown in Figure 12.23.

3. Set any print options you want, as you learned in Chapter 9. PageMaker uses the print specifications in the current publication to print the entire book list, unless you click use paper settings of each publication.

4. Click on **OK**, or press Enter (or Return) to print. Check the printer every few minutes and add paper as needed.

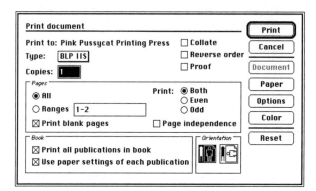

Figure 12.23
The final step is printing your book.

# Additional Tricks

Aldus Additions give you several other helpful functions when you must create a book master. You can also use these Additions for easier tasks, such as sending a file to a service bureau or just keeping track of your fonts and links.

Display pub info gives you a list of all of the fonts used in the publication, plus those available but not used. It also lists the links to graphics and text, and the file path to each, and gives you a list of all the styles defined in the publications, the styles these are based on, and the styles that follow. The list can be viewed on the screen or printed out to accompany a publication you are sending out for printing.

Build booklet takes care of the complex task of page imposition, making sure that your pages come out in the correct order when printed. To apply these, and other Aldus Additions, select them from the

Utilities menu and the Additions submenu. See the Aldus Addition guide for more information.

# The Bare Essentials

By the end of this chapter, you've learned everything you need to know to produce virtually any kind of a PageMaker publication, from a single-page flyer to an entire book. In this chapter, you learned all about working with longer documents. Specifically you have learned:

- How to plan and design a book or an annual report. You've learned about the importance of using style sheets and a book template to maintain a consistent look throughout the publication. You've seen some ways to make importing charts, text, and pictures easier.

- How to use the Book command to make a book list, and how to use the book list to link separate publications or chapters to create a continuous book.

- How to keep pages consecutively numbered throughout the book list, how to change page numbering to begin on designated odd or even pages, and how to keep TOC numbers separate from chapter page numbers.

- How to designate entries in a table of contents, and why you ought to create one as a separate publication.

- How to define index entries and cross-references, and how to format and create an index.

- How to print the entire book from the book list.

# The Essential PageMaker

# Chapter 13

## Chapter Preview

*Adding color to PageMaker publications*

*Spot color vs. process color*

*How color works*

*What you see isn't what you get*

*Using the Color palette*

*PageMaker's color libraries*

*Defining and editing colors*

*Making your own color library*

# Working with Color

Remember when you saw your first color computer screen? Remember the fun of going into a color paint program and splashing real colors across your screen, instead of just shades of gray? Color adds another dimension, whether it's on the computer screen or on a printed page. Black and white gets the message across, but color gives it emotion, action, and excitement. If black and white speaks, color sings! PageMaker 5.0, along with a color monitor and some means of color printing, lets you add as much or as little color as you want. You can even make process color separations, but, before you go wild with color there are a few things to think about.

The first of these is the cost factor. Adding colors to your pages will add to your print shop bill. If you add a *spot* color, it means that the page has to be printed twice, one pass through the printer for each ink. You also need a separate printing plate for each color on each page, and there's a charge for cleaning the press between colors and for the colored ink. Printing also takes twice as long, since the pages have to dry between colors. So, by the time you add it all up, you've added a lot to the price to add a second color to the page. Each additional color adds more—it's the same factors all over again—another set of plates, more ink and press charges, more time. . . .

Second, will using color add enough impact to the publication to justify the cost? If your publication is a newsletter or a single page flyer, the answer may very well be "no." If it's a catalog, and the merchandise in it is meant to appeal to the senses, then color will sell more product. It depends on what you're selling. A fashion catalog in black and white isn't very appealing. Neither is a catalog of gourmet foods. But if your products are electronic parts, pipe flanges, or something of that nature, color isn't important. You can spend your money more effectively elsewhere.

Third, assuming you decide in favor of color, how much color is enough? Do you need full-color photography? Or will adding a second or third spot color do the job? It depends on the effect you want to achieve. We've come to expect good color photographs in magazines, corporate reports, and other "fancy" printed pieces. Many magazines sell based on the quality of their artwork and photography. Publications such as *Architectural Digest*, *Travel*, and *National Geographic* have always been known for the quality of their graphics and printing. If your end result needs to fit into this category, there's no question that you'll be using process color.

### By the Way...

*Spot colors are printed with premixed inks, usually opaque ones. If you use process color, your job will be printed using four transparent inks, each needing a separate printing plate, and on some presses, a separate press run for each. But the four transparent colors combine to give you full color art or photography.*

Books like this one sometimes use one or more spot colors. They may also have a color signature bound in, especially if the book is about something that can best be shown in color. Cookbooks, books on art, travel, or interior design may use several color signatures, or may print all of the pages in full color. Children's books frequently use black plus one or two spot colors, sometimes overprinted to make a third.

*A signature is a set of pages treated as a group. Books are often broken into signatures that can be printed at once on one immense piece of paper, folded, and trimmed along three sides to create a "mini booklet." Many books use 32-page signatures, but this, of course, depends on the size of the page and printing press.*

# Spots Before Your Eyes?

Spot color is easier for the printer to deal with, but in some ways, it's more complicated for the designer than using full (process) color might be. For one thing, you have to choose a color, or find a way to define the color you have in mind. It's often a complicated procedure. You can't just say to the printer, for instance, "make the water blue and the boat red." What you think of as blue and red could be very different from the printer's notion of those colors. Fortunately, there are ways to define color. Unfortunately, there are many ways.

If you are using PageMaker, you are working with a computer and a video monitor. An 8-bit video can display 256 different colors. A 24-bit video supposedly is capable of showing as many as 16.7 million colors. The truth is, that's unrealistic. The human eye can perceive visible differences in only about two million colors. What the monitor actually displays depends on how well it's adjusted, and how well you see.

People see colors differently, even under the same conditions. And when you change the conditions, you change the colors drastically. Consider the light conditions under which you normally read a book or a magazine. If you're in your office, you are probably sitting underneath a fluorescent light. If you're at home in an easy chair with a good reading lamp, the bulb is an incandescent one. It may be pure white frosted, or it might even be tinted pink, or some other "flattering" color. (Check the shelves in the hardware store or supermarket. You'll find warm and cool bulbs, cameo pinks, and more.) You may be reading outdoors, perhaps at the beach under bright sunshine. Each of these different lighting conditions affects the colors you see. Sunlight intensifies blues. Fluorescent lights intensify reds. Incandescent lights give a warmer cast to most colors. If your office desk is near a window, you get a mix of fluorescent light and sunlight. So, as simple a thing as where you sit affects your color perception.

When we talk about color, we also have to define the kind of color we're talking about. Color on the video screen is not the same as color on the printed page, and neither of these works in the way we usually think. Let's go back to the beginning. When you were in kindergarten,

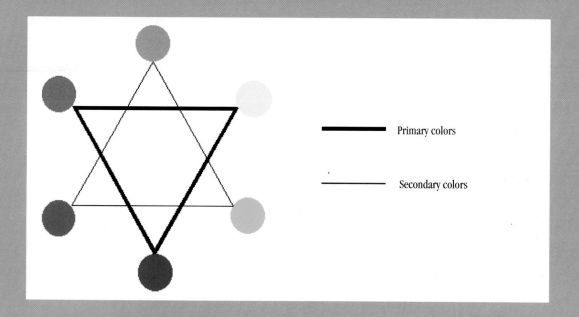

Color Plate 1
A basic color wheel.

Primary colors

Secondary colors

Color Plate 2
The numbers shown
create a pure yellow.

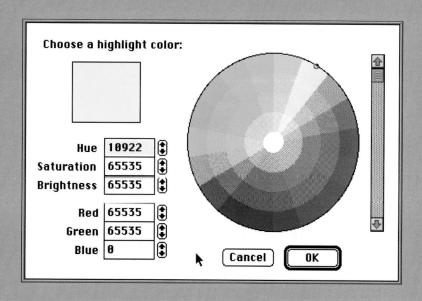

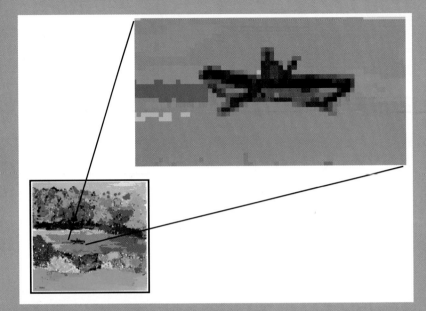

Color Plate 3
A man in a boat
looks like a blob of
colored pixels at
400% magnification.

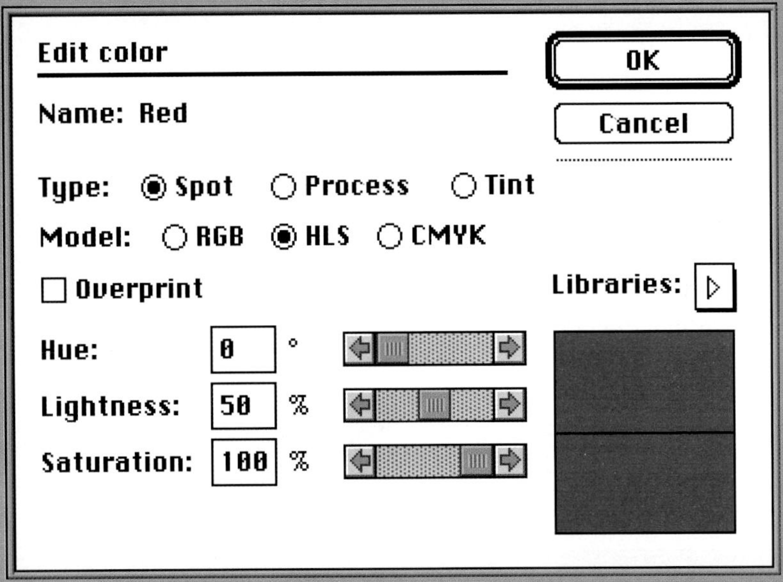

**Edit color**      **OK**

**Name: Red**      Cancel

**Type:** ◉ Spot    ○ Process    ○ Tint

**Model:** ○ RGB    ◉ HLS    ○ CMYK

☐ **Overprint**      **Libraries:** ▷

**Hue:** `0` °

**Lightness:** `50` %

**Saturation:** `100` %

Color Plate 4
Red is located at 0
degrees on the
color wheel.

Color Plate 5
The separations in Figure 13.3 come
together to print these colors.

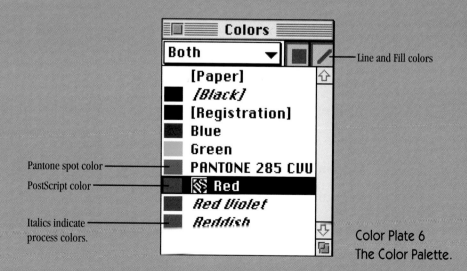

Line and Fill colors

Pantone spot color

PostScript color

Italics indicate
process colors.

Color Plate 6
The Color Palette.

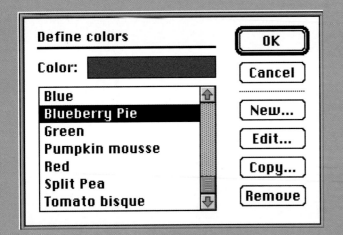

Color Plate 7
From this box you can define your own colors.

**Define colors**

Color:

Blue
**Blueberry Pie**
Green
Pumpkin mousse
Red
Split Pea
Tomato bisque

OK
Cancel

New...
Edit...
Copy...
Remove

Color Plate 8
Editing colors involves adjusting the ratio of each primary color.

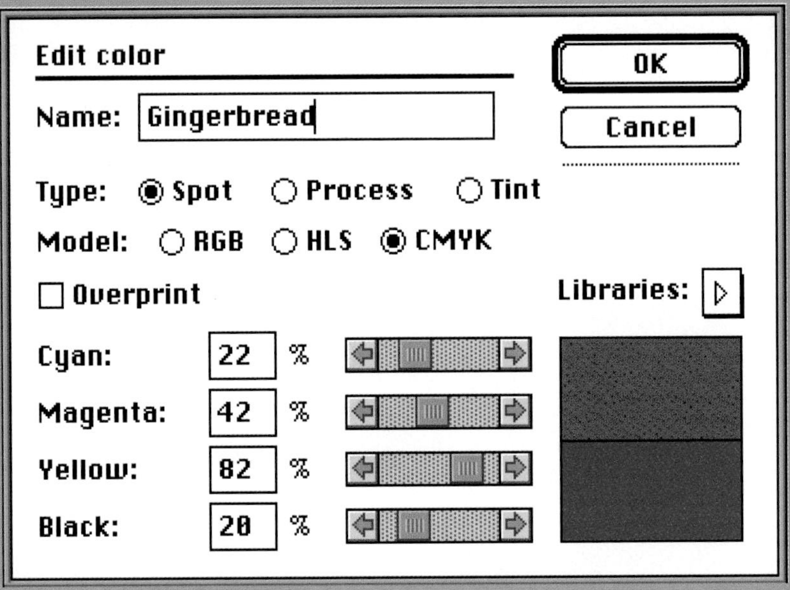

**Edit color**

Name: Gingerbread

OK
Cancel

Type:  ● Spot    ○ Process    ○ Tint
Model:  ○ RGB    ○ HLS    ● CMYK

☐ Overprint                          Libraries: ▷

Cyan:       22  %
Magenta:    42  %
Yellow:     82  %
Black:      20  %

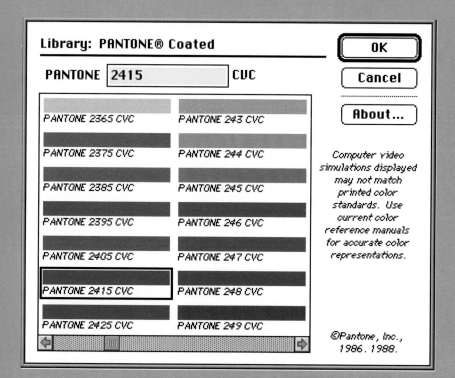

**Color Plate 9**
The library opens to the color closest to the one you have created.

**Library: PANTONE® Coated**

PANTONE `2415` CVC

OK

Cancel

About...

Computer video simulations displayed may not match printed color standards. Use current color reference manuals for accurate color representations.

PANTONE 2365 CVC
PANTONE 2375 CVC
PANTONE 2385 CVC
PANTONE 2395 CVC
PANTONE 2405 CVC
PANTONE 2415 CVC
PANTONE 2425 CVC

PANTONE 243 CVC
PANTONE 244 CVC
PANTONE 245 CVC
PANTONE 246 CVC
PANTONE 247 CVC
PANTONE 248 CVC
PANTONE 249 CVC

©Pantone, Inc., 1986. 1988.

**Color Plate 10**
When you select Tint, the box changes slightly.

**Edit color**

OK

Cancel

Name: `Pale Berry`

Type: ○ Spot  ○ Process  ● Tint

Base Color: `Blueberry Pie`

☐ Overprint

Libraries: ▷

Tint: `35` %

Color Plate 11
Using brown tones gives this music cover an "old" feeling.

Color Plate 12
This menu cover uses three colors plus black.

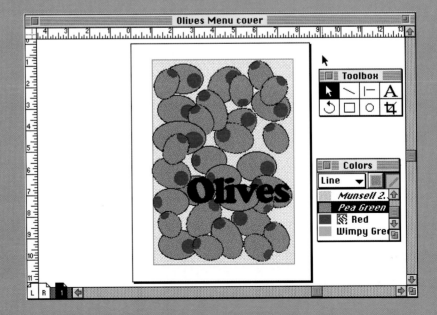

REYNOLDS

# WORLD

What began as an idea, now stands sturdy

and strong, always  embracing the change

of time with innovation and responsiveness.

**125 Years of Growth**

Color Plate 13
This striking design was only two process colors. The word "World" is
actually the same hue as the tree, although it appears lighter.

*Courtesy of Graphica Design and Communications Group*

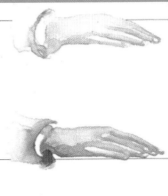

## Making yourself stand out

*(continued from front page)*

Internships and part-time work in your field show that you take initiative and have learned skills in the work place as well as in the classroom.

The most important part of having experience is to let prospective employers know how their companies can benefit from the skills you've learned.

The two most common ways to showcase your skills and talents is through the resumé and during the personal interview.

If you think they were important experiences, but they don't seem directly related to your field, include them and use your cover letter to explain why they are relevant.

- **Don't embellish.** If a project or award was a team effort, say so.

- **Proofread, proofread, and proofread.** Spelling and grammatical errors give the impression that your work will be careless and sloppy.

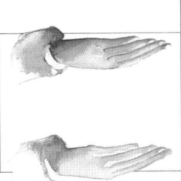

### NCR Career Contact

Editor:     Monica Valento
Director:   Anne Holaday
Published by NCR Corporation

An Equal Opportunity Employer

Copyright 1991 by NCR Corporation.
All Rights Reserved. Printed in U.S.A.

Member of the Dayton and International Association of Business Communicators

Comments may be sent to: NCR Career Contact, Editorial Services, Stakeholder Relations Division, NCR Corporation, WHQ-5, Dayton, Ohio 45479

Resumes and questions about NCR may be directed to: Director Recruitment and College Relations Personnel and Education NCR Corporation, WHQ-2 Dayton, Ohio 45479

**IABC Gold Quill Award Winner 1991**

**Color Plate 14**
Don't be afraid to combine graphics in unusual ways—it adds interest.

*Courtesy of Graphica Design and Communications Group*

Color Plate 15
Red, blue, and
black on white
make an attention-
grabbing book
cover.

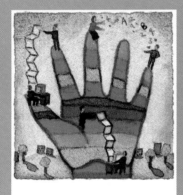

**NCR System 3000 is**

**designed to simplify**

**information processing,**

**helping you extend the**

**power of computing to all**

**levels of your organization.**

Color Plate 16
Small, colorful illustrations can
draw a reader's eye to a message.

*Courtesy of Graphica Design and*
*Communications Group*

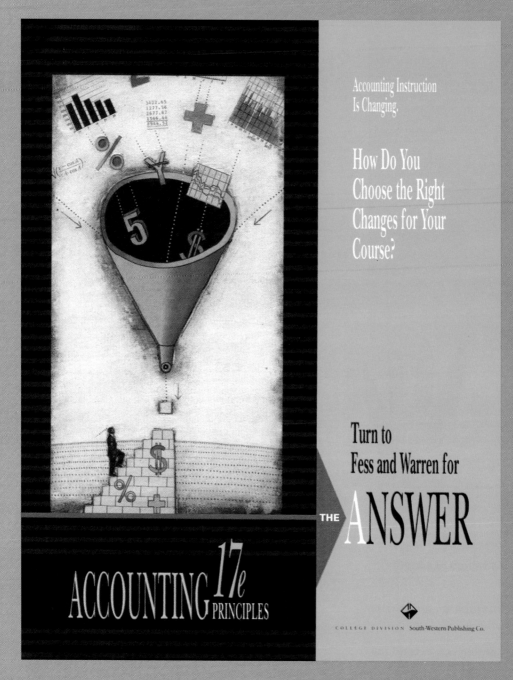

**Color Plate 17**
This brochure cover's design uses several eye-leading tricks. Notice the red arrow that points to text, and the reverse-color "A." The yellow funnel draws the eye up to the white text at the top.

*Courtesy of Graphica Design and Communications Group*

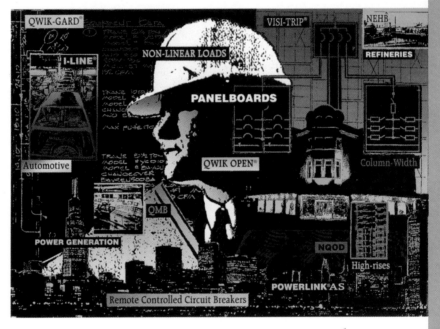

**PANELBOARD PRODUCTS**
NQOD
NEHB
POWERLINK®
I-LINE®
QMB

Innovative Solutions

**SQUARE D**
*We Respond.*
GROUPE SCHNEIDER

Color Plate 18
Notice how the very busy artwork contrasts with the sparse text and plentiful white space for an effective overall design.

*Courtesy of Graphica Design and Communications Group*

NCR System 3000 is designed to help you embrace the future—whatever the future may bring.

### Performance You Can Rely On

NCR System 3000 is designed for superior reliability and service-ability. Attention to reliability begins with extensive design simulation and continues with stringent testing during manufacturing. At high-end computing levels where fault resistance is vital, redundancy of critical components is provided through advanced features. Built-in features, such as remote diagnostics and the system's microprocessor design, complete the picture. All of this combines to promote end-to-end data integrity, helping protect data from transient errors and data loss.

### NCR People and Technology—A Sound Investment

NCR regards its people and its information as its most valuable resources. From our engineering designers to our field service representatives worldwide, we represent a superior product with a vision for tomorrow. We made a commitment to open systems a decade ago and pioneered the way for many others. Today we're coupling our vast knowledge, honed by years of experience, with our vision for an open computing environment.

We understand that no organization can flip a switch and change its computing environment overnight. However, NCR System 3000 is designed to give you a variety of economical choices...the stepping stones to embracing a total Open, Cooperative Computing environment.

Color Plate 19
Don't be afraid to use striking artwork at a large size.

*Courtesy of Graphica Design and Communications Group*

## HOUSE OF LORDS FAVORITES

**Reuben.** Rye bread grilled with sliced corned beef, Swiss cheese, sauerkraut and 1000 Island dressing. **4.95**

**BLT.** Served on double decker toast. **4.75**

**Club Bristol.** Sliced ham, smoked turkey, sliced bacon, American & Swiss cheeses served double decker style. **4.95**

**English Beef Sandwich.** Hot roast beef served with cream cheese, horseradish and red onions on grilled rye with horseradish sauce. **5.25**

**Steak & Mushroom Pita.** Marinated strips of beef with mushrooms, tomatoes & onions stuffed into pita bread and topped with a sour cream dill sauce. **5.25**

**Corned Beef & Swiss.** Deli corned beef thinly sliced and served with Swiss cheese on rye bread. **4.95**

**Meatloaf Sandwich.** Our specially prepared meatloaf is served hot on a French roll. **5.25**

## THE PUB'S LIGHTER SIDE

**Albacore Tuna Sandwich.** Served on whole wheat with tomato, onion, alfalfa sprouts and colby cheese. **5.25**

**The Pub's Grilled Cheese.** We melt Swiss and cheddar cheeses and top them with sliced tomato and red onion rings, served on grilled wheat. **4.25**

**Spinach Melt.** Rye bread grilled with Swiss cheese, cheddar cheese, fresh spinach, tomato slices and black olives. **4.75**

**Vegetarian King.** Wheat bread with fresh avocado slices, alfalfa sprouts, tomato slices, cucumber and cream cheese. **4.75**

**Veggie Melt.** Diced red onions, cucumbers and tomatoes topped with sliced mushrooms, alfalfa sprouts, avocado slices, ranch dressing and melted cojack, served on a cheese crust. **5.50**

**Tuna Melt.** Our homemade albacore tuna salad on grilled whole wheat and topped with melted colby cheese. **4.75**

## PUB SIDES

**French Fries.** Served with or without our unique spicy seasonings. **1.45**

**Potato Salad 1.50**          **Pasta Salad 1.50**

**Cole Slaw  1.50**          **Cottage Cheese with Peach Wedges 1.50**

Color Plate 20
Black-and-white photographs are used on this menu, along with a yellow-tinted paper, to achieve an antique look. The entire piece looks mono-chrome at first glance, but the headings are actually green.

*Courtesy of Graphica Design and Communications Group*

*Companies with global vision are bringing engineering and manufacturing organizations closer together in order to improve the quality and manufacturability of their products.*

*Reducing time-to-market gives manufacturers an important competitive edge in the world market.*

Color Plate 21
Small images scattered throughout a publication can help provide a sense of continuity.

*Courtesy of Graphica Design and Communications Group*

*Rapid technological change is shortening product life cycles. Developing global strategies that integrate this new technology will enable companies to better satisfy customers and react quickly to changes in the market.*

*A competitive enterprise combines world-class technology with an understanding of customer requirements in different countries to open up new markets around the world.*

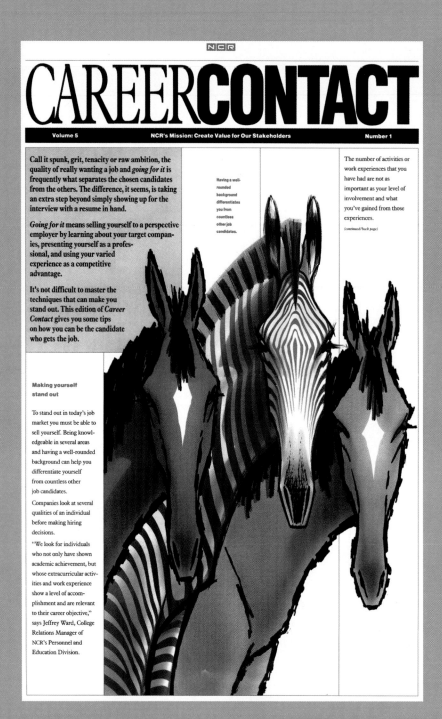

NCR

# CAREERCONTACT

**Volume 5** NCR's Mission: Create Value for Our Stakeholders **Number 1**

Call it spunk, grit, tenacity or raw ambition, the quality of really wanting a job and *going for it* is frequently what separates the chosen candidates from the others. The difference, it seems, is taking an extra step beyond simply showing up for the interview with a resume in hand.

*Going for it* means selling yourself to a perspective employer by learning about your target companies, presenting yourself as a professional, and using your varied experience as a competitive advantage.

It's not difficult to master the techniques that can make you stand out. This edition of *Career Contact* gives you some tips on how you can be the candidate who gets the job.

Having a well-rounded background differentiates you from countless other job candidates.

The number of activities or work experiences that you have had are not as important as your level of involvement and what you've gained from those experiences.

*(continued/back page)*

### Making yourself stand out

To stand out in today's job market you must be able to sell yourself. Being knowledgeable in several areas and having a well-rounded background can help you differentiate yourself from countless other job candidates.

Companies look at several qualities of an individual before making hiring decisions.

"We look for individuals who not only have shown academic achievement, but whose extracurricular activities and work experience show a level of accomplishment and are relevant to their career objective," says Jeffrey Ward, College Relations Manager of NCR's Personnel and Education Division.

**Color Plate 22**
A good layout is much more than just cramming text onto a page—this newsletter balances text, art, and blank space well.

*Courtesy of Graphica Design and Communications Group*

or somewhere around there, you learned to use paints. Mixing two primary colors gave you a secondary color. Red and yellow made orange. Blue and yellow made green, and so on. It made sense. You could even make up a color wheel, like the one in Color Plate 1, to show the relationships.

# RGB

When color television was invented, the people who developed the system for displaying color on the screen must have gone to a different kindergarten and gotten a different kind of paints. Instead of using red, yellow, and blue as the three primary colors, in video, the three primaries are red, green, and blue. When you mix red and green, you get yellow! That's because when colored lights are mixed, the result is the difference between the originals. Colored light is *subtractive*—and it doesn't matter whether you're talking about video monitors or the footlights of Broadway. Colored pigments, on the other hand, are *additive*; when you mix two of them together, the result includes hue from both. So for pigments, red and green make brown. And it doesn't matter whether you're talking about kindergarten paints or printers' inks.

You can experiment with this yourself if you have a Macintosh. Open the **Macintosh color picker** from the **color control panel**. Choose the brightest yellow you can find. Because one of the ways the Mac defines color is using the RGB (Red Green Blue) model, you'll be able to see how much of each is in the mix to make the bright yellow. Color Plate 2 shows the Mac's color picker set to the brightest yellow our monitor could display. As you can see by the numbers, it has equal parts of red and green, and no blue at all. And it's a shade that would make a lemon jealous! You could display a whole fruit basket on your screen, and all of the colors—lime green, cherry red, orange, plum, watermelon pink—would all be made up of little dots, or *pixels*, or red, blue, and green.

By the Way...
*You can experiment with colors in Windows, too. Choose **Color** from the **Control Panel**, then pick **Color palette**. A button will appear in the lower right corner of the dialog box that reads Define Custom Colors. Select it, and you'll see a screen roughly equivalent to the Mac one in Color Plate 2.*

The colors you see, however many there appear to be, are an optical illusion. On your video monitor, another dimension has been added. It's intensity. With 24-bit color, any pixel on the screen cannot only be

red, blue, or green but any combination of 256 different intensities of each of the three primaries. (The computer breaks the 24 bits into three groups of eight, one for each primary. Each eight bits can have 256 possible binary choices.) Zero equals black, or "color off." Your eye blurs them together and creates the impression of many colors. When the various intensities of each of the three colors are combined, you get a possible 256 cubed, or 16,777,216 different colors. This would be terrific, if you could see them. But as we said earlier, the human eye can't see anywhere near that many. And even if it could, the printing process can't reproduce more than a few thousand.

French impressionist painter Georges Seurat used the same illusion in his paintings, done in a style he called pointillism, using little dots of paint. From a distance, the dots in Seurat's works, like the pixels on your computer monitor, merge together, making an attractive and colorful painting. Up very close, there's not much to see. If you take a look at a piece of color art, greatly magnified, you can get the same effect. Color Plate 3 shows a 400% enlargement of a section of artwork. Notice that the individual pixels are squares of particular colors. The eye merges them so you see the man in the rowboat.

# HSB (or HLS)

Artists like to define color in a different way: The initials *HSB* stand for Hue, Saturation, and Brightness ( Aldus prefers to substitute Lightness for Brightness, but both mean the same thing.)

- *Hue* is a specific color, like red or green. It's defined by its location on a color wheel, assuming that red is at 0 or 360 degrees.

- *Saturation* is measured in percent. A very light shade of red would have a low saturation. You might think of saturation in terms of adding pigment to water to make paint. A 10% solution of red is a lot less saturated than a 90% solution.

- *Lightness*, *value*, and *brightness* are used interchangeably to define the difference between the color and black. The more black there is in the color, the less brightness. When the lightness is zero, the color is pure black. When the lightness/brightness is 100%, there's no black at all in the color. Color Plate 4 shows how red is defined in PageMaker's HLS terms.

# CMYK

To a typical PageMaker user, the color on the screen is much less important than the color that lands on the paper. What does print is almost never exactly what you saw on your screen. Printed colors look different from colors painted in light. If you're dealing with process color, you've got some of the same parameters as you did with the video screen. You're dealing with an optical illusion that blends dots of different colors to make you think you're seeing others. But instead of RGB, your color palette consists of Cyan (a vivid turquoise), Magenta (hot pink), and Yellow. These also combine to reproduce our fruit basket. Lime green is mostly yellow with a bit of cyan, watermelon pink is magenta, with small amounts of yellow and cyan, and so on.

But unlike the computer screen with 256 different intensities of each color, in process printing, you have only one intensity of cyan, one of magenta, and one of yellow. Instead, the printing process creates the *illusion* of intensities by applying a dot screen to the page and varying the number and size of the dots in each color. It's the same as printing halftones in each of the colors.

As you've probably realized, there's a fourth color involved in CMYK process printing. It's black, or blacK, as printers think of it. (They couldn't let B stand for Black because B stands for Blue in every other color system.) Theoretically, if you mix cyan, magenta, and yellow together, you'll get black. But what you really get is a muddy reddish brown. So black was added as the fourth process color, allowing you to apply real black shadows, and to use black type and black lines on the page.

The "process" in process color originally referred to the plate-making process. In order to separate the full-color art into four process colors, it was photographed four times, with a different filter each time. Each filter blocked all but one of the four colors, and a screen was added to each of the separations to turn the images into dots. Each process color screen is rotated to a different angle so the dots, instead of printing on top of each other, form rosette patterns on the page when they're printed. Figure 13.1 shows an example. The angles of the screens affect how your eye sees the colors.

If even one of the screens is at the wrong angle, you'll get an ugly moiré effect instead of something you'd otherwise perceive as even color. If the screens are too coarse, you'll get the effect familiar to readers of color comic books, which makes the characters look as if they're afflicted with some sort of skin disease.

Figure 13.1
The screens
are printed in
order of
intensity;
yellow first,
black last.

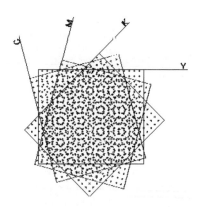

Figure 13.1
The screens
are printed in
order of
intensity;
yellow first,
black last.

PageMaker has made the color separation process simple. Instead of photographing your finished color pages, all you need to do is to open the **Print** dialog box, and then the **Color** dialog box as shown in Figure 13.2. Select the color separations you want printed and any spot colors you want plates made for. Then let PageMaker do the work. Figure 13.3 shows what the separations for the book cover in Color Plate 5 look like. In just a few minutes, you will have accurate color separations, ready to give to the printer. In the print shop, the separations are turned into printing plates, mounted on the press and run off.

Figure 13.2
The separa-
tions can be
printed on a
laser printer,
or directly to
film on an
imagesetter.

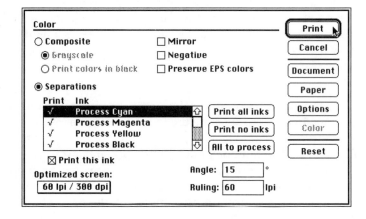

# What You See *Isn't Always* What You Get

The difficulty that most artists find in going from PageMaker, or from any kind of computer graphics program, to a printed page is that the colors just don't come out the way they looked on the screen. As we've seen, color perception is affected by the way it's viewed, by the ambient lighting conditions, and by differences in people's vision.

The video monitor can display many more colors than the printer can print, and those that the printer can handle may be quite different from their on-screen versions. Monitors go out of alignment. As they get older, they may suffer from various electronic problems that cause color shifts or dim the intensity of the monitor. People who use antiglare filters over the computer screen never see true color. The filter adds about 5–10% gray to the screen. Anyone who wears tinted eyeglasses or tinted contact lenses gets used to the differences in the colors she sees, but tinted eyewear can also make color matching difficult. And finally, there are a few colors that the printer can reproduce that the monitor just can't display properly. One of them is 100% Cyan, so you can imagine the difficulties encountered in trying to work with cyan as a process color.

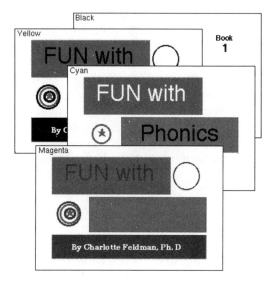

Figure 13.3
Notice the knockout (blank space) on the Cyan page for the Red letters.

Defining a spot color is even harder. Suppose you were designing a label for a bottle of ketchup. Your client wants a nice, red tomato on the label, but what he calls tomato red might be very different from what you call tomato red. If you go to the supermarket and look at the pile of tomatoes in the produce aisle, no two are the same shade of red. When you select a tomato and photograph it, you add variables relating to the light you shine on it, the temperature of the developer, and the age of the film. Scanning the photo adds more variables. Your printer's notion of tomato red may be even further away. Fortunately, there's a solution.

## Color Matching Systems

About thirty years ago, a system for consistent color matching was invented. It's called *Pantone*, and today it's an industry standard for defining spot colors. The Pantone PMS color-matching system lets you switch between electronic and print media, knowing that the PMS color you specify will exactly match the printed PMS samples in your sample book, and will be consistent every time you use it. Pantone moved into the world of desktop publishing as soon as it became apparent that this was a direction in which the industry was headed. Pantone color technology has been incorporated into PageMaker and into most high-end graphics programs.

Other color-matching systems have followed Pantone's lead. Now there are a half dozen or more different systems. PageMaker 5.0 supports all of the common ones. All work in more or less the same way. For each system, there's a book of color swatches, each with a different number. Some systems, including Pantone, publish different swatch books for coated papers and for special purposes. There are also different swatch books for the European market, using different color numbers. The printer has the inks to match these colors or the formulas for mixing them from other existing inks. Be sure to talk to your printer about color before you start a project. Find out which color-matching systems they prefer to work with, and why. If you choose and specify the colors you want to use according to their printed swatches, you are sure to be pleased with the result.

### Watch Out!

*If your swatch book is more than a year old, replace it. Ink colors will fade and shift as time goes by. If you leave your swatches in direct sun or exposed to bright office lights, they'll fade even more quickly.*

# Putting Color on the Page

One way that PageMaker makes it easier for you to use color is by giving you a Color palette with which to work. It functions much like the Style palette. Open it by selecting it from the **Window** menu. It's shown in Color Plate 6.

You'll notice that there are three items on it that you can't delete. These are (**Paper**), (**Black**), and (**Registration**).

- **Paper** refers to the paper color on which you'll be printing. If you plan to print a job on colored stock, you can set the paper color to match and preview the results on the screen. You can also use a "paper" colored object to cover up something on the screen that you don't want to print. The "paper" knocks out whatever is behind it, because PageMaker treats the "paper" object as if it were a spot color.

- **Black** is a 100% Process black, which also knocks out anything behind it. (See below for more information about knockouts.)

- **Registration** is an attribute rather than a color. If you designate something "registration," it will print on every page of the separation. Many designers use it to put the job number and the company name and phone number outside the print area, so they'll be able to look at separation negatives and immediately know which jobs they're part of, and so that the separations won't get lost or misplaced at the printer's.

The Color palette comes with three spot colors already installed: red, green, and blue. You can use these as they come, edit them, or remove them and replace them with colors you choose. If you import an EPS graphic that already has spot colors applied, they'll appear on the palette along with an EPS symbol. You can then apply these colors to other objects in the publication, too. If you create a tint, (a screened percentage of a spot color), it will also show in the color palette.

The Color palette also comes with Fill and Line popup boxes, so you can quickly designate a color for a line, fill, or both without having to go to the dialog boxes. If you've forgotten what color was assigned to a line or fill, you can check easily by looking at the palette.

# Working with Spot Color

Using colored lines and boxes as spot color blocks can brighten up a drab publication and add emphasis to type. Spot color can be defined as any area of color on the page that can be printed with one specific shade of ink. Spot color can include colored type, colored lines and filled shapes, and graphics in any one color. Spot color can also include tints of that color, as screened dot patterns rather than flat areas. If you have assigned a particular color (blue, for instance) to part of the page, you can also use one or more lighter shades of the same blue by specifying some percentage(s) of tint. Color is best handled on a color monitor, of course, but if you only have access to a black and white or grayscale screen, you can still assign colors in PageMaker and print the spot color overlays on your laser printer. The printer will then photograph these to make the color printing plates for the job.

Color can be applied to any single element: a text block or any kind of graphic. However, you can only assign one spot color per item. Layered items can have different spot colors, and you might put a tint of a second color over the first to make a third. You can, if you want, draw a shape and define its outline in one color and its fill in another. Colors are assigned through the Color palette.

To create a spot color, follow these steps:

1.  Select **Define colors** from the **Element** menu. The Define colors dialog box is shown in Color Plate 7.

2.  Click on **New** to open the Edit color box, shown in Color Plate 8.

3.  Type a name for the new color. (Unless you give it a name, you can't save it.)

4.  Click **Spot** or **Process** to specify the type of color.

5.  Choose a color model:

    Choose **RGB** if the publication will be "printed" as a color transparency for projection or an overhead transparency. Film recorders follow the RGB color model. Choosing RGB colors will also give you the most accurate screen display, but less accurate reproduction.

    Choose **HLS** if you are accustomed to working in that color model. (HLS is a color model used mostly by artists. The letters stand for Hue, Lightness, Saturation. It's also called HSV, for Hue, Saturation, Value.)

    Choose **CMYK** if you're printing with process color, or if there's any chance that your spot colors will end up as part of a process color printing job.

6.  Type numbers in the boxes for percentages of the hues shown, or move the sliders around until you get something close to the color you want. If you're using the CMYK color model, the values you enter in the boxes affect the way the colors will be separated. If you've used either of the other models to specify a process color, it will be converted to the approximate CMYK values when the separations are printed.

7.  Check **Overprint** if you want the color to print on top of any other colors it overlaps on the page. Otherwise, it will "knock out" the color behind it, so the top color prints and the color(s) under it do not. Knockouts are PageMaker's default. Specify **Overprint** only if you don't want the colors to knock out.

8. Click **OK** to close the box, or press **Option** (Mac) or **Alt** (Windows) while you click on **OK** to close all open dialog boxes at once. (If you want to add more colors, click **New** again instead of closing the Define colors dialog box.)

Your colors will appear on PageMaker's Color palette, as shown in Color Plate 6, and in the Fill and Line dialog box or any other dialog box that lists colors. Figure 13.4 shows how colors can be applied to a type style. Note that process colors are not listed in italics as they are on the Color palette.

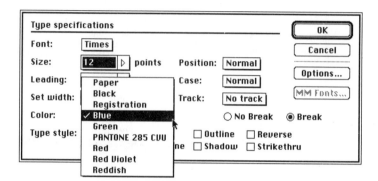

Figure 13.4
To create a type style with a color applied, use the Type specifications dialog box, and choose the color from the popup menu.

## Specifying Colors from a Library

You can have a lot of fun making up new colors, but it's not as much fun trying to convince your print shop that Blueberry Pie is a particular shade of blue. If you want to be sure that the colors you specify are the colors you'll get, you must use one of the color matching systems. Be sure you and your print shop are using the same color-matching system. It makes no sense for you to specify Pantone colors if they only use Toyo (or possibly even an obscure standard that PageMaker doesn't support).

If you've defined a color that you like (following the steps given earlier in this chapter), PageMaker can help you find its closest library equivalent. Select the color to match and open the **Edit color** dialog box. Click on the **Libraries** popup menu shown in Figure 13.5. Select the library you want to use, and it will open to the closest match to your color. Color Plate 9 shows PageMaker's best Pantone match for our Blueberry Pie. If you're satisfied with the match, click on **OK**. If not, you may see another choice in that library that you prefer. Select it instead, and click on **OK**. If you don't see what you want, click on **Cancel**, and try a different library, provided your print shop is willing to work with it.

Figure 13.5
Clicking the
arrow opens
the list of
available color
libraries.

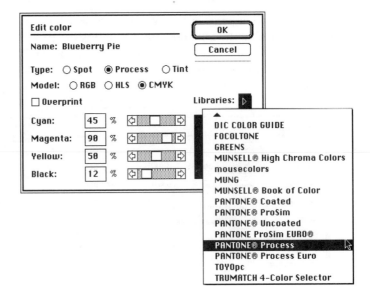

## Specifying Tints

*Tints* are simply screened percentages of your spot or process colors. To specify a tint, again open the **Edit color** dialog box, as shown in Color Plate 10. Select **Tint**. Enter a percentage for the tint, or move the slider until you get the percentage of tint that you want. PageMaker lets you specify 1% increments up to 100%. Give the tint a name that indicates its base color. Click on **OK** when you're done.

You can also use the 10% gradations of fill patterns to quickly apply a tint. Select the color for fill and any of the attributes from the **Fill** submenu of the Element submenu. All tints will print correctly on PostScript printers, but Fill attribute tints may look different on the screen and may print differently to a non-PostScript printer. Tints lighter than 20% may not print well or may be too light to see, depending on the printing process. Check with your printer before specifying a very light tint.

Be sure to select **the Overprint** option in the Edit color dialog box if you're applying a tint over something else. Otherwise, the area of the tint will knock out whatever is behind it. Color Plate 11 shows how a tint might be used to enhance a graphic. In this figure, we applied a spot color to the graphic itself and the lettering, and another to the other graphic elements on the page. Then we placed a tint of the second spot color behind everything. It made the face too dark, so we added a paper-colored oval between the tint and the face to knock out the tint in that one area.

## Applying Colors

Now that you've created or assigned a bunch of colors to your publication, you need to apply them to the objects and text you want to color. It's quite simple, with the Color palette. Select the object or text block to color. You can colorize imported graphics, including monochrome or grayscale TIFF images. Text blocks must be selected with the Text tool, and not the pointer. Then click on the color you want the object or words to be. That's all. Applying color to boxes and ovals is only slightly more complicated, since the line and fill can be defined as two separate colors or as one. At the top of the Color palette, you can select Fill, Line, or Both. The color you apply will go on accordingly. Color Plates 11 and 12 show some examples of spot color use.

## Copying Colors

If you've specified colors or created custom colors in one PageMaker publication and want to use the same ones in another publication, you can save a great deal of time by copying the colors from one palette to the other. To do so:

1. Choose **Define colors** from the **Element** menu, and click on the **Copy** button.

2. Doing so opens a dialog box that lets you locate the PageMaker publication you want to copy from. When you find it and select it, click on **OK**.

3. The colors will be added to the palette in the active publication.

If you want to copy a single color, the easiest way is to draw a block in that color and drag it from one publication to another, or cut and copy it. If you'll be working with the same colors frequently, set up a template that includes the appropriate color palette.

# Creating a Custom Color Library

If you often work with a particular combination of spot colors, you may find it saves you time and effort to put them into a custom color library. Your custom library can hold as many as 100 colors and display them just as the commercial ones do. There are two ways to do this. You can create a library as an editable text file, or as a noneditable binary file. To set up a custom color library in a text file, first locate a file called **Sample.ACF**. (If it's missing, you can use any file with the extension **.ACF**. In the example below, the Crayon library file is shown.) Chances are, you'll find it in a folder called **Color**, but this may be different in your installation, so a file finding utility might be helpful. Open **Sample.ACF** in a word processor, and you'll see a listing like this:

**ACF 1.0**
**Crayon**
**LibraryVersion: 1.0**

**Copyright: ©Aldus Corp.**
**AboutMessage:**
**Names: Partial**
**Rows: 4**
**Columns: 4**
**Entries: 62**
**Prefix:**
**Suffix:**
**Type: Process**
**Models: CMYK RGB**
**PreferredModel: RGB**
**Data:**
**0 0.15 0.3 0**
**65535 55705 45875**
**Apricot**
**1.0 0.1 0.1 0**
**0 58982 58982**
**Aquamarine**
**0.15 0.7 1.0 0**
**55705 19661 0**
**Bittersweet**
**0.71 0.70 0.21 0**
**19005 19661 51773**
**Blue**

Use this file as a basis to create your own library. Immediately, save it with a new title. Give it a name you'll recognize, and save the file as a text file in the **Color** folder or directory, making sure that it has the extension **.ACF**. Now you can make changes to it.

- You must retain the first line of the file. ACF identifies the library in a way that PageMaker can recognize. (It stands for Aldus Color File.)

- Change the name **Crayon** (or **Sample**, or whatever appears on the second line) to the title you want to use for your custom library. This name will appear in a **Libraries** popup menu, after you select **New** or **Edit** in the Define colors dialog box. It must be less than 31 characters long, to fit on the menu.

- You may, if you want, assign a version number and add copyright information. If not, skip these two lines.

- You may, if you choose, type additional information about the library to appear in the About box. Enter it after the words **AboutMessage:**, or skip this line, if you want.

- Color names may have prefixes and suffixes. Enter **Full** after **Names:** if you want the full color name displayed. Enter **Partial** to show the name only, without prefixes or suffixes.

- To define how many swatches will be visible in the color library at once, enter values for Rows and Columns. These may be any number from 1 to 10. As you increase the number of colors, the size of individual swatches gets smaller.

- Enter the maximum number of colors in your custom library following **Entries:**. You needn't enter the colors all at once. There will be placeholders for unassigned color entries.

- If you want to add a prefix or suffix to the names of the colors in your custom library, enter it after **Prefix:** and/ or **Suffix:**. It must be 11 characters or less in length. If you don't want to use an additional identifier, skip this line.

- Enter **Spot** after **Type:** if you are defining a library of Spot colors, or enter **Process** if the library will be used to specify colors for process printing.

- Models refers to how colors are defined and displayed. Use CMYK if you want to define colors by their percentages of Cyan, Magenta, Yellow, and blacK. You can also enter RGB to define a color by its screen definition. The preferred model determines the default setting for how the color model is shown in the Edit color dialog box.

### By the Way . . .

*To define a color by its screen definition on a Macintosh, the easiest way is to open the **Color picker**, and locate the color you intend to use on the Mac's color wheel display. Copy down the values for RGB. Enter these values in the RGB windows in PageMaker's **Edit color** dialog box, and you'll end up with precisely the same color.*

Under **Data:**, you will actually define and name the colors for your library. If you know what the CMYK percentages should be, you can enter them. Note that they must be expressed as decimals, rather than as percentages. Thus, 100% Cyan, 10% Magenta, 10% Yellow, and 0% Black is entered as 1.0  0.1  0.1  0. Leave a space between each set of numbers, and list color values in the order C,M,Y,K. If you know the RGB numbers for your color, enter them on the line below the CMYK colors. In the RGB color model, 65535 is equal to 100% for Red, Green, and Blue. Type the name of the color on the next line. Leave a blank line before you enter the data for the next color. If you don't know the correct values for a particular color, insert any reasonable numbers as place holders, give the color a name, and continue. When you're ready, open PageMaker, open your custom color library , and edit the colors.

Creating your custom color library as a binary file is easier. Open a PageMaker publication that has all of the colors that you want to include in your custom palette, or use the Define colors dialog box to add them to the Color palette. When the palette has all of the colors you want to include in the custom library, open the **Aldus Addition Create color library**, from the **Utilities** menu. You'll see a dialog box like the one in Figure 13.6. Give your new library a name and a file name with the **.bcf** extension. Click on **OK** when done to save it.

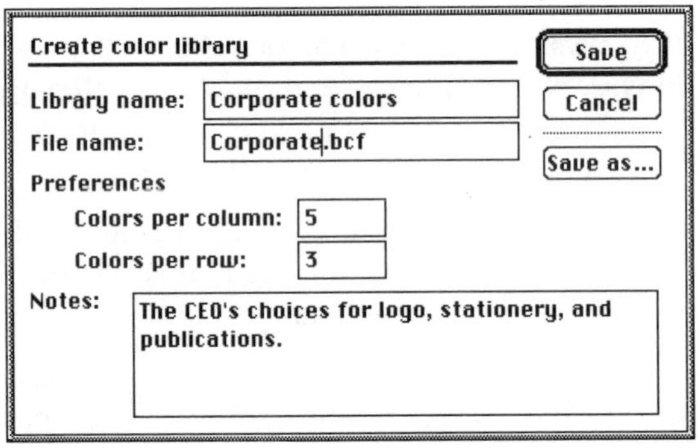

Figure 13.6
Use the Aldus
Addition to
create a
custom color
library.

# The Bare Essentials

In this chapter, you learned about working with color in PageMaker. You learned what the considerations are for choosing color, and how to apply them to your PageMaker publications. Specifically, you learned:

- The reasons for choosing spot or process color. Spot color is printed with opaque colored inks. Process color combines black with three transparent inks to produce many colors.

- There are different ways of describing color. The video monitor assigns color in percentages of red, green, and blue (RGB). Process printing uses percentages of Cyan Magenta, Yellow, and blacK (CMYK). Artists prefer to use the HSV, or HLS (Hue, Saturation, Value or Hue, Lightness, Saturation) model. PageMaker supports all of these.

- Process colors require separations. You learned to make color separations easily by selecting them from PageMaker's Print color box.

- You learned that Color Matching Systems, such as Pantone and Focoltone, let you specify exact colors and help bridge the gap between what you see on the screen and what the printer gives you.

- The Color palette makes it easier to apply color to text and graphics. You learned to add colors to the palette by creating them or by selecting them from a library.

- You learned to create your own custom color libraries with an Aldus Addition.

## Chapter Preview

*Tricks for getting started*

*Tips that help you find your way*

*Tricks for making PageMaker jump through hoops*

*Organizing your PageMaker tools*

*Printing tips*

# Tips and Tricks

hen you look at a printed page, you can't always tell whether it was produced by an amateur or a professional. That's especially true if it's a PageMaker page. You know that the columns will be straight, anything that's supposed to be centered on the page will be, and so on. Electronic DTP, unlike rubber cement paste ups, always comes out clean and straight.

The way to tell the beginners from the old pros, though, is according to how long the job takes them. The more you do, the faster you'll be able to do it. That's true of anything from piano playing to page layout to brain surgery. In this chapter, we'll reveal some of the tricks and shortcuts "real world" PageMaker users have invented. Not all will be useful to you, but some certainly will, and others may spark your imagination to invent your own newer and better ways of doing the job.

Thanks go to the folks at *MacUser* and *MacWorld* for providing consistently excellent articles through the years on PageMaker tips and tricks.

# Tricks for Getting Started

The next few paragraphs describe tips and tricks for setting up templates and other vehicles to streamline your work. PageMaker supports the creation of dummy files that contain all of the layout components you need to create multiple versions of a document. The next few paragraphs show you how to use templates to create repetitive publications. Other setup tips are included that assist you in preplanning your documents.

## Create and Use Templates

Busy design shops often find themselves creating the same kinds of publications over and over again for different clients. Since paper sizes and margins remain the same, they save time by using templates for the various pages. Opening a letterhead template would give you a standard page with a grid and placeholders for the company name, address, and logo. A business card template would have the page divided into appropriately sized blocks with crop marks, grid, and placeholders.

Whenever you set up a page that could be used more than once, save it as a template. If a client has a particular set of colors and type styles that are used on everything they do, save those as a template, too. Then, if you're doing a three-fold brochure for them, for example, open the brochure template, and copy the style and color palettes from their corporate template.

## Change PageMaker's Default Setup

You can change PageMaker's default Page setup to one that relates more closely to the way you use the program. If, for example, you always use it for a four-page newsletter, with a particular set of margins, configure the Page setup dialog box to those settings. To do so, choose **Page set-up** from the **File** menu without choosing New. Enter the settings you want to make standard. Click on **OK**. Now, to start a new newsletter, all you need to do is to type ⌘+N and **Return** (Mac), or **Ctrl+N** and **Enter** (Windows). You don't have to wait for the dialog box to appear.

## Create a Dummy Document

If you use PageMaker to produce recurring long documents that always look the same but contain different information, you can create a dummy for your document and let PageMaker do the work of composing new versions when you need them. PageMaker has a powerful feature called *linking and updating* that you can use to generate new versions of old layouts. Here's how:

1. Create a series of dummy text in your word processor and name their files **Story 1**, **Story 2**, **Story 3**, and so forth. You can create dummy graphics in a graphics program in the same manner.

2. Open a new PageMaker document, and select the **Links** command from the **File** menu (press ⌘+= on the Mac and **Shift+Ctrl+D** in Windows). When the dialog box appears, click on the **Options** button. When the Link Options dialog box is displayed, turn on the **Update automatically** option and the **Alert before updating** option.

3. Use the **Place** command from the **File** menu to place the dummy stories and graphics in the layout you want to use. Add any spot colors and other layout objects, to complete the document.

4. Save the PageMaker document as a template, and quit the program.

5. Go to your word processing program, open the dummy text files, and delete their contents. Enter the real text you want to use. You can also rename the dummies as **Story 1.old** and name an actual file as **Story 1**, and so forth. Be sure to always save the live text with the same name as the dummy files so that PageMaker can find the correct files.

6. Open the PageMaker template you just created. When the program asks you if you want to update the linked files, click on **Update**.

7. Each time you want to create a new report using your template layout, simply change your dummy files, and PageMaker will update the document using the new materials.

# Tips That Help You Find Your Way

The following set of tips and tricks let you use PageMaker's keyboard shortcuts to assist you in navigating around your document.

Table 14.1 displays a list of shortcuts you can use to view your publications in different ways in PageMaker.

## Table 14.1　Viewing Shortcuts

| To Select This View: | Do This: |
| --- | --- |
| To view every page with the same view | Select ⌘+**Option**+ (**Ctrl+Alt+** in Windows) *your view selection* from the **Layout** menu. |
| To see Fit to Window view | Select **Shift+page** icon on bottom left of pasteboard. |
| To create a thumbnail slide show of your document | Set every page to Fit to Window (⌘+**Option+Fit to Window** on the Mac and **Ctrl+Alt** in Windows); select **Shift+Option+Goto Page** command (**Shift+Ctrl** in Windows) from the **Layout** menu. Click the mouse to stop the slide show. |
| To view the total pasteboard | Select **Show Pasteboard** from the **View** menu, or you can press **Shift+Fit** in window from the **Layout** menu. In Windows, you can press **Shift+Ctrl+W.** |
| To shift between Actual Size and 200% view | Select ⌘+**Option+Shift+Click** (**Ctrl+Alt+Shift+Click** in Windows) in the Actual Size view. Use this keystroke combination again to toggle back. |
| To shift between 200% and 400% views | Select **Shift+200% view** from the **View** command on the **Layout** menu. |

The Option, Shift, and ⌘ keys (Ctrl, Alt, and Shift in Windows) also provide other functionality in PageMaker beyond toggling commands. For instance, if you want to shift rapidly between a tool, such as the Text or Ellipse, and the Pointer, press the ⌘+**Spacebar** key combination (**Ctrl+Spacebar** in Windows).

If you have selected a blown up view, such as 200%, and have lost your place in your document, PageMaker provides a grabber hand, like those in painting programs, that allows you to physically move the pasteboard around until you find where you want to be. To invoke the grabber hand, press the **Option** key (**Alt** in Windows) while dragging on the pasteboard.

If you have created a complex graphic with multiple layers and you want to select one of the layers without disturbing others, PageMaker provides a handy key combination. Simply press the ⌘ key (**Ctrl** in Windows) while clicking on the object, and PageMaker moves sequentially down and up the layers.

# Tricks for Making PageMaker More Graphically Aware

There are some tasks at which PageMaker is not very good. These procedures typically have to do with the graphics side of your desktop publishing effort. Here are some tricks for making PageMaker perform these acts of graphic legerdemain.

## Grouping Objects in PageMaker

PageMaker does not have a Group command that lets you select a set of objects and manipulate them as a single object, as you can do in most object-oriented graphics programs. Objects can be grouped in PageMaker, however. Here's how to get PageMaker to create a group of objects.

1. Create a graphic in a graphics program, or select a piece of clip art. Make sure that it contains no text.

2. Use the **Place** command from the **File** menu to place the graphic into a PageMaker document.

3. Enter any text you want to insert with the graphic using PageMaker's **Text** tool.

4. Use the **Shift** key to select both objects (**Shift+click**) (see Figure 14.1).

Figure 14.1
Note that each object is still separate.

Handles for one object

Handles for second object

5. **Copy** or **Cut** the selected items to the Clipboard, and then **Paste** them into your Scrapbook (see Figure 14.2).

Figure 14.2
The Scrapbook
is a fine
repository for
your graphic.

6. Use the **Place** command and import the now single graphic from the Scrapbook back into your PageMaker document (see Figure 14.3).

A single set of handles for the entire group

Figure 14.3
PageMaker
places the
Scrapbook file
as a single,
multipage PICT
file.

# Controlling Graphic Effects Within Your Documents

When you begin to experiment with borders, spot color, different sorts of headers, and other more jazzy effects in your PageMaker documents, you'll come upon one of the more frustrating graphic phenomena— reversed text disappears from your pasteboard, just when you want to use it. There are several ways to avoid losing text within your graphic elements.

PageMaker supports the ability to color your text, and especially the ability to white-out text so that it appears reversed when shown on a black or shaded background. The traditional way to do this is to reverse the text and drag it on top of a shaded or black box drawn with the Rectangle tool. The problem with this method, is that, often, you lose the location of your text or it slides off the box whenever you add new text to your document. These problems occur because the box and the text are not connected, and the reversed text graphic (the box and text) are not linked to the text they head up.

A solution to this problem is to create an inline graphic element consisting of reversed text within paragraph rules. As you remember from earlier discussions, inline graphics follow along with their linked paragraphs, thus solving the problem of sliding missing headings.

To create this type of graphic element, perform the following steps:

1. Select the heading text your want to reverse, and select the **Paragraph** command from PageMaker's **Type** menu (or press ⌘+**M** on the Mac or **Ctrl+M** in Windows). Note that the text is inverted, indicating its selection.

2. Click on the **Rules** button to bring up the Paragraph rules dialog box.

3. Create a 6-point rule above the heading's paragraph and a 12-point rule beneath the paragraph. Click on the radio button of your choice to make the rule extend the width of the column or of the text (see Figure 14.4).

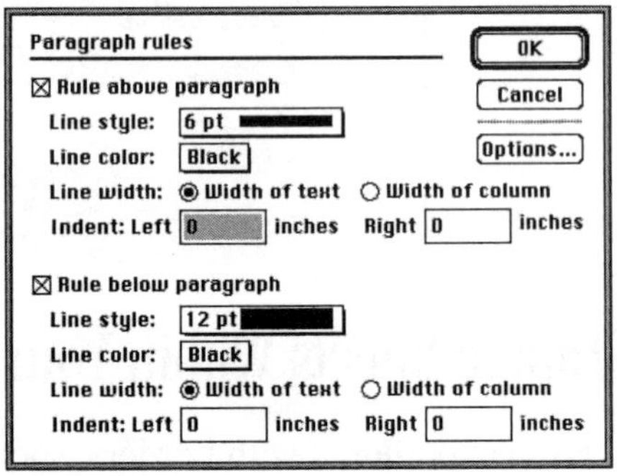

Figure 14.4
The rules above and below the paragraph create the black box for the reversed text.

Paragraph rules

☒ Rule above paragraph
Line style: [6 pt ▬▬▬]
Line color: [Black]
Line width: ⦿ Width of text   ○ Width of column
Indent: Left [0] inches   Right [0] inches

☒ Rule below paragraph
Line style: [12 pt ▬▬▬]
Line color: [Black]
Line width: ⦿ Width of text   ○ Width of column
Indent: Left [0] inches   Right [0] inches

[OK]
[Cancel]
[Options...]

4. Click on the **Options** button to invoke the Paragraph rule options dialog box. Change the contents of the text box for Top and Bottom baselines to **0**, and close the box by clicking on the **OK** button (see Figure 14.5). Close the Paragraph rules and Paragraph specifications dialog boxes by clicking on the **OK** button.

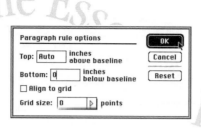

Figure 14.5
The 0 picas
instructions
for Top and
Bottom base-
lines move the
rules on top of
the text.

5. Select the **Type specs** command from the **Type** menu (or press ⌘+**T** on the Mac and **Ctrl+T** in Windows).

6. Check the **Reverse** text check box from the Type style section of the Type specifications dialog box. Set the Position of the text to **Subscript** on the Position pull-down menu (see Figure 14.6). Click on the **Options** button to invoke the Type options dialog box.

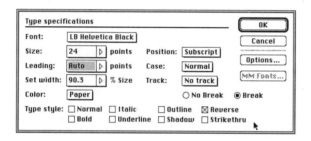

Figure 14.6
Use the Type
specs dialog
box to center
the text
vertically in
its rules and
reverse its
color.

7. In the Type options dialog box, change the Super/subscript size text box to read **100%** of point size. Also change the Subscript position text box to a lower percentage. For this 18-point type, select **17%** or one-half of the default 33.3 percent (see Figure 14.7). Click on the **OK** button of the Type options and Type specs dialog boxes to close and return to the highlighted paragraph.

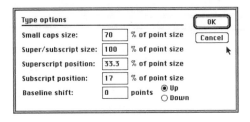

8. Create a style for your reversed text inline graphic so that you do not have to go through steps 1–7 again.

By the Way . . .

*If you do not feel like going through all of the above steps to create reversed text in a black box, you can use the old, tried and true method with a slight variation. Create your black box and text block. Place a bullet (**Option+8** on the Mac and **Ctrl+Shift+8** in Windows) after your reversed text. You'll be able to locate and manipulate your invisible text block since the bullet does not disappear like the rest of the text until you move the text on top of the black box. Of course, since the bullet is black, only black boxes hide the bullet, any other shade doesn't work.*

# Aligning the Tops of Two Graphic or Text Objects

PageMaker does not provide alignment tools to ensure that objects and paragraphs properly align to each other. Here is a trick using the powerful scripting language that Aldus provides with PageMaker through the Aldus Addition called Run Script.

1. Select **Edit Story** from the **Edit** menu, or press ⌘+E (**Ctrl+E** in Windows).

2. Enter the following script into the story editor. Note that the lines starting with double hyphens are notes and are ignored by the macro engine when running the script.

   **--align tops of scripts**
   **redraw off**
   **--get rid of guides on the page**
   **deleterulerguides**
   **--put a guide at the top of last object in drawing order**
   **guidehoriz last top**
   **--select the first object in the drawing order**

**select 1**
**--move the select object to the guide**
**move top guide 1**
**--turn redraw back on**
**redraw on**
**--end script**

3.  Export the story editor's contents as a text only file, and give it the name **Align Tops** (**ALINTOPS** in Windows).

4.  Select the first object that you want to align, and press the key combination ⌘+**B** (**Ctrl+B** in Windows) to move the object to the back. This makes the graphic *first* in the drawing order.

5.  Select the other object to which you want to align the first object, and press the key combination ⌘+**F** (**Ctrl+F** in Windows) to move it to the front. This makes the graphic *last* in the drawing order.

6.  Select the **Run script** command from the **Aldus Additions** submenu of the **Utilities** menu (see Figure 14.8).

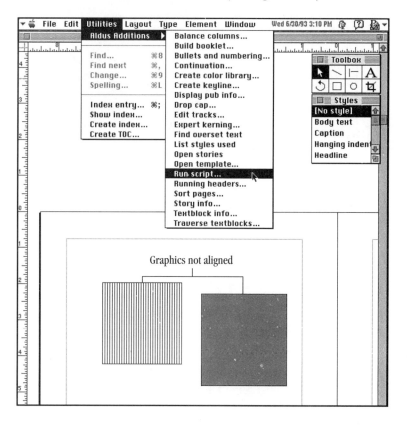

Figure 14.8
Use the Run
Script Aldus
Addition to
align your two
graphic
objects.

7. The script rapidly draws a new guide and aligns your graphics (see Figure 14.9).

Figure 14.9
The graphics
are aligned
using the Snap
To Guides
feature of
PageMaker.

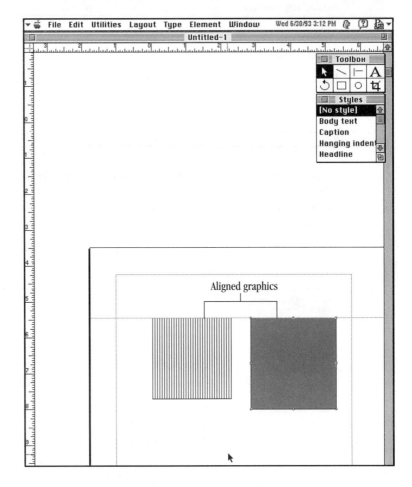

## Creating Complex Equations

PageMaker does not provide an equation editor used in word processing packages to assist you in writing complex mathematical equations more easily and correctly. Here's a trick for laying out mathematical equations correctly using the Paragraph specifications and Type specifications dialog boxes.

1. Type the following two lines of text. On the Mac, use the key combination **Option+W** to create the [Alt+228] symbol. On Windows, use the Symbol font for sigma.

**[Alt+228] x2**
**y2 + x2**

2.  Change the type size to 24 points (see Figure 14.10).

$$\Sigma x2$$
$$y2 + x2$$

Figure 14.10
The raw
equation.

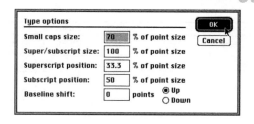

**Type options**

| | | |
|---|---|---|
| Small caps size: | 70 | % of point size |
| Super/subscript size: | 100 | % of point size |
| Superscript position: | 33.3 | % of point size |
| Subscript position: | 50 | % of point size |
| Baseline shift: | 0 | points  ● Up  ○ Down |

**OK**   **Cancel**

Figure 14.11
Use the Type
options dialog
box to arrange
the text in the
correct
position.

3.  Highlight the [Alt+228], and select the Type specs from the
    **Type** menu (⌘+T on the Mac and **Ctrl+T** in Windows).
    Enlarge the symbol to 72 points. Set the Position text box to
    **Subscript** using the pull-down menu. Click on the **Options**
    button to invoke the Type options dialog box.

4.  In the Type options dialog box, change the Subscript size to
    **100%** of point size and the Subscript position to **50%** of the
    point size. Click on **OK** in both boxes to close this dialog box
    and the Type specifications dialog box (see Figure 14.11).

5.  Select each of the '2' and using the Type specifications dialog
    box, move them into a Superscript position, to square the
    variables.

6.  Position the cursor on the second line of text ($y^2 + x^2$) and
    select the **Paragraph** command from the **Type** menu (⌘+M on
    the Mac and **Ctrl+M** in Windows). Set the Left Indent text box
    to move the line to the right far enough so that it is away from
    the sigma symbol (for 24-point text, 0.656 inches works well).

7.  Click on the **Rules** button to invoke the Paragraph rules dialog
    box. In this dialog box, create a 2-point rule above the selected
    paragraph the width of the text. Click on the **Options** button.
    When the Options dialog box is displayed, change the distance
    above the baseline for the rule to **0.3 inches**. Close the dialog
    boxes.

8.  Place the cursor on the first line of the formula ([Alt+228] $x^2$)
    and select the **Paragraph** command (⌘+M on the Mac and
    **Ctrl+M** in Windows) from the **Type** menu. Click on the

**Spacing** button to invoke the Spacing attributes dialog box. When the box appears, change the Autoleading specification to a lower number than the default 120%. With this font size, **40%** is good. This moves the first line closer to the paragraph rule above the second line.

9. Place a **Tab** after the sigma or space the squared variable over until it is aligned with the second variable of the denominator. The equation is now complete. (See Figure 14.12.)

Figure 14.12
The equation is now displayed correctly.

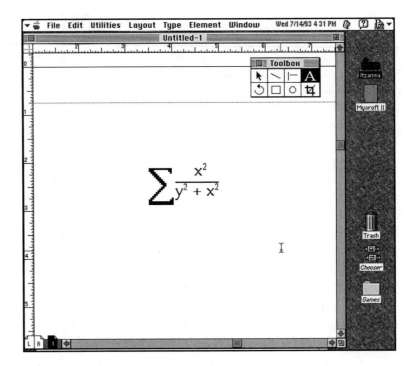

## More Graphic Tips and Tricks

Here are a few individual tips and tricks to make your graphic manipulation tasks easier.

- If you have successfully kerned a pair of letters, highlight the kerning, copy it, and paste it into another identical pair.

- You can create an automatic page number for individual pages by creating an automatic page number on the pasteboard in the same manner as you do on Master pages (for example, press the key combination ⌘+**Option**+**P** on the Mac or **Ctrl**+**Shift**+**3** in Windows). PageMaker creates an automatic page number called **PB** on the pasteboard. Format the PB placeholder as you want it to look. Leave the placeholder on the pasteboard until you need it to number added pages. Then, just copy it, and paste it on your page where you want the page number to appear. PageMaker numbers the page in the correct order with the rest of your document.

- You can constrain your toolbox tools by using the Shift key when making a selection. Using Shift with the object tools (Ellipse and Rectangle) lets you draw perfect circles and squares. Using Shift with the Line tools constrains their angles to 45 degrees. Using Shift with the pointer constrains your ability to drag an object to 90 degree angles.

- You can place identical objects on top of each other by either dragging the objects on top until the composite graphic disappears, or by using the **Paste special** command (**Option+⌘+V** on the Mac; no Windows equivalent) that duplicates an object directly on top of the original. Layering identical objects is useful when you want to create an object with a different color from a border object, or when you want to control overprinting and/or knockouts when using spot colors.

- You can perform mathematical slight of hand with PageMaker. To convert a fraction to a decimal, use the **Indents/tabs** command from the **Type** menu. When the ruler appears, create a tab mark at the fraction you want to convert. The correct decimal equivalent appears in the Position box. The bigger the page view, the more precision in the decimal (see Figure 14.13).

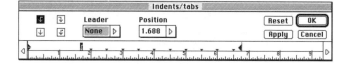

Figure 14.13 Use the Tab ruler to perform fraction to decimal conversions when measuring in inches.

# Making Your PageMaker Document Have More Pizzazz Through the Use of Clip Art and Textures

Catalogs and software stores have libraries of interesting textures to use behind pages of print or graphics. Some include marble, granite, and similar "natural" textures. Others feature shadings, star bursts, metallic effects, and even full page images. Look for Artbeats backgrounds on CD-ROM. They'll add pizzazz to annual reports, ads, package designs, and other publications.

If you have a flatbed scanner or hand scanner, you can also create your own textures. Try scanning fabrics, pieces of carpeting, marble floor tiles, wallpaper swatches, or anything you see that has an interesting texture. You can make a neat background by using an office copier with the top open to print a totally black (toner covered) sheet. Crumple it up, and then smooth it out again and scan it. You'll end up with something resembling marble. Turn it into granite by using it as a dithered Paint image instead. Use a darkroom program, such as Adobe Photo-Shop or Aldus Digital Darkroom, to do further image manipulation. Figure 14.14 shows some examples created in this way. (This sheet was scanned using a video camera and Computer Eyes software. The crumpled paper was lit from the side, creating deep shadows.)

Figure 14.14 These variations were created in Aldus Digital Darkroom. The original scanned page is behind them.

Clip art libraries are good sources of inspiration for creating your own logos and graphics. Borrow small bits of a larger graphic. Distort or stretch an image. Make a woman into a little girl by shrinking and then changing the face and hairstyle as needed. Add color to black-and- white clip art. A solid tone behind a line drawing looks great. But if color isn't an option, try a gradient in gray. Aldus SuperPaint lets you apply gradients to images and to type. Figure 14.15 shows what a simple gray gradient can do to make your words and pictures stand out.

**Clean Up Pollution**

Figure 14.15 Using the gradient makes this graphic much more interesting than using a plain gray.

Don't be afraid to experiment with type. Although your creations may not be suitable for headlines or body copy, they may make interesting logos or illustrations. In Figure 14.16. we took a rather ordinary type face (Helvetica Bold) and applied a variety of textures to it. The results are eye-catching.

Texture
Texture
Texture
**Texture**
Texture

Figure 14.16 You could use these as graphics or as attention-getting headlines.

Using unusual papers can give your work a much more expensive "look and feel." Companies such as Paper Direct have sample kits with hundreds of different kinds of paper, including parchments, metallic flecked, and translucence, as well as preprinted pages with color gradients, border designs, and much more. Using a preprinted gradient can give you a two-color brochure from your laser printer or office copier. (For more information, call 1-800-A-PAPERS.)

# Organizing Your PageMaker Tools

These tips and tricks enable you to work smarter with PageMaker. The tips include how to figure out what fonts your PageMaker documents require, how to speed up your PageMaker processes, how to count lines of type within your document, and other miscellaneous tips.

# Converting PageMaker Pages to
# an Alien DTP System and Back

Sometimes, you may want to convert PageMaker documents into alien formats, such as Quark Express. Aldus markets an add-on called PageMaker Import Xtension ($25) that will convert PageMaker files into Quark Express files. You cannot convert Quark files into PageMaker files.

Another way to transfer PageMaker documents into other DTP formats and vice versa, is to convert each page into a PostScript file using the Print command. When you select Print, you are provided the option of printing to a PostScript file. Then, take these PostScript files and place them into the DTP program as full-page graphics. You cannot modify the pages, but you can use them in other format documents.

## Increasing the Processing Speed in PageMaker

PageMaker can seem to take forever to redraw a page or place an object. Although the speed of processing is subjective, the program does slow down when it is given a complex task. One way to speed up processing is to place PageMaker's dictionaries into your Mac's System folder or into a separate Windows subdirectory. This lets PageMaker open faster, since it does not have to search for these files. (If you're using Windows, you could create a subdirectory under your PageMaker directory and call it DICTNRY.) Place an empty folder in your PageMaker folder and call it **Dictionaries in System folder** to remind yourself where you placed those files.

## Locating Your Proper Fonts

When running a font/DA manager program, such as MasterJuggler or Suitcase 2, you can quickly find which fonts you need to install for the proper display of PageMaker documents. First, close all of your installed fonts. Then, open your PageMaker document. The Fonts submenu will display dimmed names for fonts used in the document. Quit PageMaker, and turn on or install the grayed-out fonts.

## Time-Saving Tools of the Pros

A good way to save time when you're working in PageMaker is to use all of the preprogrammed keyboard shortcuts that Aldus has included, but, most of us have a hard time remembering them all. PageMaker's on-screen help files have lists of shortcuts. Figure 14.17 shows the Layout command's help screen. To help you get acquainted with the shortcuts, print screen shots of the shortcut help files and tack them up where you can refer to them as you work. Before long, you'll have them all memorized.

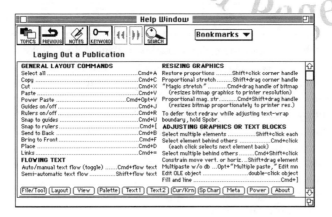

Figure 14.17 PageMaker provides keyboard equivalents for many popular commands.

If there are operations that you repeat frequently, which don't have shortcuts, consider using a macro program like CE Software's Quickeys to generate a macro. Quickeys macros can automate procedures that may otherwise take several keystrokes or mouse clicks. For example, you could create a macro to select a color from the Pantone library, by recording the sequence of opening the Element menu, selecting Define Colors, clicking the New button, and then opening the library list to Pantone.

Another time-saver for Macintosh users is Articulate Systems Voice Navigator. The Voice Navigator package includes voice recognition software that lets you train your Mac to respond to spoken commands, and a microphone that sits on your desk. (You can also use the Mac's own microphone, if your Mac has one.) You can record sets of commands for PageMaker and for any other applications you use frequently. It's much faster to tell the computer what to do in words than to stop typing and reach for the mouse. The initial set up procedure takes time, and must be repeated by each person who uses Voice Navigator, since it responds to the pitch and timbre of the voice. Commands are spoken and recorded several times. The software takes an "average" of the way the word is pronounced each time and compares your spoken command to the average. If it decides that it recognizes the command, it performs the appropriate action. Voice Navigator comes with a stack of commands for PageMaker, so all you need to do is record them (three times each) and you're in business.

## Using Color Calibrators

Many professional artists make a point of keeping their monitors calibrated for more accurate color. As of this writing, calibration devices are available only for Macintosh monitors, and are quite expensive ($2,700 for one that works with a 20" Trinitron display).

You can accomplish the same thing more easily and much less expensively (if you have a good eye for color matching) by using a swatch book and the color libraries in PageMaker. Make a PageMaker document that has blocks of red, green, and blue from the Color palette. Then, go into the color libraries to find the closest matches for these colors. The easy way is to press the ⌘ on the Mac (or **Ctrl** in Windows) key which selects the color from the Color palette. Open a library, and you'll be taken to its closest match for the color you have chosen. If it's not close enough, try another library until you find as perfect a match as possible. My 13" Apple Hi Resolution RGB monitor matches DIC 157 P (Red), DIC 224P (Blue), and DIC 643 P (Green). Yours may align better to a different library or to slightly different shades in the DIC library.

After you have located a good match, enter the name of the color on the PageMaker page. When you've found all three colors, check them against their printed swatches in that library. (If you're matching to a color library whose swatch book you don't have, your printer may be able to supply one, or at least tell you where to get it.) Adjust your monitor as necessary so they match perfectly. Next time you want to check the color calibration, open that PageMaker file, and hold the swatch up against the screen. It should match. If not, again adjust your monitor until it does.

# Printing Tips

The single most important printing tip is to make friends with your print shop. Shop around until you find a printer who meets your standards for price and quality. Then, talk to the printer before you begin a job that will be printed in the shop. Find out exactly what you need to supply, in what format, and how far in advance of your deadline. Talk about costs, too. If you have a low budget, say so. The printer may be able to suggest ways that you can economize on the job and still get the look you want.

When you send files on disk to a printer or service bureau, be sure that the disk is properly labeled, and includes your name, phone number, and the name of the job. You may find it helpful to include a ReadMe file readable using TeachText on the Mac if there's information that the printer or service bureau may need to know, such as font and link data.

# Hardware Helper

If you have a non-PostScript color printer, you may not be happy with its color output of PageMaker pages. Relatively low-cost color printers give you a taste of what it's like to be able to print real color, but it is impossible to get a color page without "banding," a sort of striped effect that spoils the look of the graphics. Impossible *unless* you have Freedom of Press, that is.

Freedom of Press Classic is an application that does for your page what ATM does for type. It eliminates jagged edges and leaves you with smooth, razor-sharp type and graphics on a color or black and white inkjet or laser printer. It's fully compatible with ATM, and with PostScript Type 1 and TrueType fonts. It's available for both Macintosh and Windows and supports all of the popular "low-end" printers including Apple, Canon, GCC, Hewlett-Packard and other QuickDraw and PCL compatibles. It also works with "portable" printers, turning an Apple StyleWriter or PC notebook printer into one that can handle PostScript. It automatically configures itself to whatever printer or fax software you are using.

A "sister" program, Freedom of Press Pro, turns a Canon CJ10 color bubble jet copier into one that can print PostScript at near imagesetter quality. Either version of Freedom of Press lets you preview your color graphics on a lower cost printer with good enough resolution to let you see something fairly close to the finished product. Since inkjet printers use the CMYK color model, your process color proofs will be reasonably accurate.

Freedom of Press has another use that's important in a busy design shop or art department. If your computer has a fax/modem, you can use Freedom of Press to send faxes. Your clients will see clean, crisp type, and screened graphics instead of the usual semilegible fax pages. They'll be able to approve faxed proofs instead of needing to see a printed copy first, so you'll save the cost of messengers, express mail, or overnight delivery. Even grayscale photographs come out crisply screened. If you send faxes of artwork, you *need* Freedom of Press.

# The Bare Essentials

This chapter has described some tips and tricks used by the "pros" culled from experience and literature searches through relevant magazines, such as *MacUser* and *MacWorld*. We discussed ways to let you work smarter in PageMaker and covered several areas, including moving around the document, working with graphics, PageMaker organization, and printer tips and tricks. Here is a review of what we described.

- Create a dummy template for your repetitious PageMaker documents and then change the linked files to fit the new data you want to publish.

- Use keyboard shortcuts to toggle your document views so that you can rapidly switch to the proper view whenever you want.

- Use Aldus Additions' Scripting tool to make manipulating graphics easier.

- Use the various Type specification dialog boxes to create inline reversed text-based graphics.

- Use the power of the Clipboard and Scrapbook to group text with graphics into a single graphic object.

- Use the various Type and Paragraph commands to properly format equations.

- Use clip art and textures to enhance your PageMaker documents.

- Use the Shift and Spacebar keys to constrain your Toolbox tools.

The Essential PageMaker

- Use the power of your Mac and System 7 to organize your PageMaker program files.

- Use the Print command to transfer incompatible files between DTP systems by converting the files to PostScript and importing the PostScript files as full-page graphics.

- Place your PageMaker System files in the System folder to speed up processing.

- Use Freedom of the Press, Voice Navigator, Quickeys, and other third-party software to create shortcuts that speed up your work.

- Use adjunct hardware and software to calibrate your monitor to fit your imagesetter or color printer's color requirements or print on non-PostScript printers with almost imagesetter quality.

# Installing PageMaker

I f you haven't installed PageMaker yet, and you're wondering how to get started, read this appendix. It'll tell you about PageMaker's requirements and will walk you through the installation process.

## Hardware Requirements

PageMaker is a very versatile and complex program that requires a lot of RAM and a lot of hard disk space.

## Computer Type

Although it is available for Windows, the majority of users run PageMaker on a Mac. It is technically possible to run PageMaker on a Mac Plus or on a Classic or Classic II. Many people do and their patience is rewarded with great-looking pages. It takes a great deal of patience, however. PageMaker runs very slowly on a Plus because the computer needs to go back to the disk for information frequently. The program runs somewhat faster on an SE, and quite well on any of the Mac II's, Performas, Centris, or Quadras. If you have the choice, use a fast, color-capable Mac with PageMaker for best results. It's to your advantage to be able to view pages in color, even if you're not intending to produce colored publications.

### By The Way...

*If you've got the money to spend, A IIfx or Quadra with a double-page HiRes monitor and a 1,200 dpi Linotronic would be ideal. If you don't have that kind of a computer system, rejoice in the fact that you'll have more time to study your page layouts and mentally improve them while you're waiting for PageMaker to do something.*

If you're an IBM-compatible computer user, you can run PageMaker through Windows. Technically, PageMaker will run on any computer that will run Windows 3.1 (a 286 or better), but performance will be slow, slow, slow on anything less than a 486 with plenty of RAM (see Memory later in this appendix).

# Monitor

Some monitors are better than others for use with PageMaker. Certainly, if you're doing anything with color, you need a color monitor to be able to see it. A full-page vertical monitor is especially well suited for forms design and for laying out posters or other tall pages. A two-page display, like SuperMac's 21" Platinum, is excellent for book and magazine design. The Radius Pivot, in both color and 256 gray or monochrome models, gives you the best of two worlds: it rotates from vertical (portrait) to horizontal (landscape) views.

Monitor performance can be improved with the addition of a video accelerator card. These come in various models with different features. Some give you 24-bit color; others provide multiple-resolution settings or faster screen redraws. Ask your dealer which will do the best job with your combination of CPU and monitor, and the type of publication on which you'll be working.

If you are considering investing in a new or additional monitor for use with PageMaker, here are some things to look for:

- Sharpness, especially outside of the center of the screen. You won't be happy squinting at a blurry screen.

- Ability to display an actual gray scale, rather than a "blue scale" photo.

- High refresh rate for less flicker in the images.

- A larger screen.

- More accurate color display. (You'll never see all 16.7 million colors, but it would be nice to see the same blue every time you use Pantone 2745CV.)

No two monitors come from the factory with exactly the same color settings. If you work on more than one computer, or if you are part of a work group with several other people, it's a good bet that you're not seeing the same publication the same way on your various screens at the same time. Colors even shift from day to day on the same monitor! When accurate color is important, consider investing in a display calibrator. SuperMac's SuperMatch Display Calibrator uses an electronic sensor that attaches to your screen with a suction cup, plus software that lets you calibrate all the Macs in your studio or design shop to display exactly the same colors. It also lets you correct color drift and even lets your display simulate various lighting conditions that affect color viewing. The entire process takes about three minutes and should be done at the start of every workday.

If you're running PageMaker for Windows, keep in mind that because it's a Windows product, your display is limited by the number of colors and resolution of your Windows 3.1 video driver. If you purchase a special monitor and video card, make sure to ask the dealer for a Windows 3.1 driver that will do your new hardware justice, because the drivers that ship with Windows will probably not be adequate.

# Memory

Ideally, you'll have more RAM installed than you need for PageMaker and your System files, so you can run PageMaker and your word processor and paint programs all at once.

On a Macintosh, you must be able to give it a minimum of three megabytes (3MB) of random-access memory (RAM). If you'll be doing complex graphics, working with large TIFF files, or building long publications, you'll need to give PageMaker at least 4MB of RAM, and perhaps as much as 6MB! On an IBM-compatible, you'll need at least 4MB to get started (3MB might do, but most IBM-compatible computers' RAM must be upgraded in multiples of 2 or 4), and 8MB to get rolling at top speed.

If you have extra hard disk space, consider using virtual memory. With a Macintosh, you can use System 7's Virtual Memory or Connectix Virtual, which also runs with System 6.0.7 and which many users find to be faster and more reliable. Figure A.1 shows the About the Macintosh box on the author's Macintosh IIsi, with PageMaker, Microsoft Word, and SuperPaint, all running at once. As you can see, I've added 5MB of additional RAM as virtual memory. Without it, I'd be unable to open the word processor or graphics program.

For Windows users, you can set up a swap file (in other words, virtual memory) by choosing the 386 Enhanced icon from the Control Panel and selecting either a temporary (slow) or permanent (faster) swap file. Make the swap file as large as you can afford—at least 2MB for starters.

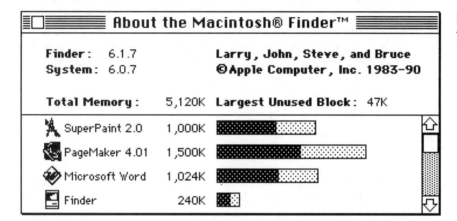

Figure A.1
This Mac is full!

If you don't have enough RAM to run several large applications, and you haven't installed Connectix Virtual or System 7 (or room for a swap file in Windows 3.1), one possible solution is to look for smaller applications. Instead of Microsoft Word 5, for example, use a leaner word processor like WriteNow or LetterPerfect (for the Mac) or Write (for Windows). They'll do the job, and demand a lot less memory. As for graphics programs, Zedcor's DeskPaint and DeskDraw are remarkably versatile applications which are actually desk accessories. They use very little disk space and require only 35K of RAM for both. Yet they handle 256-color work and save images as PICT or TIFF for importing into PageMaker publications. In Windows, take advantage of the built-in paint program Paintbrush or a small shareware drawing program.

# Printers

Ideally you will have a PostScript laser printer, or perhaps even an imagesetter. Less ideally, you could use a non-PostScript (QuickDraw or PCL) printer with Adobe Type Manager or TrueType. If you don't have access to any of these, but only to a dot-matrix printer or "near letter-quality" printer, plan on making many trips to the service bureau to print sample pages.

PostScript printers for both Mac and Windows machines require the installation of printer description files, which give PageMaker information it needs about the type of printer you are using. When you install PageMaker, you'll see a list of PPD (PostScript Printer Description) files. Choose the one(s) that you're likely to use. If you'll be sending work to a service bureau, install their PPD file, too. The Linotronic 100/300 PPD is helpful because the Linotronic is one of the printers most commonly used by service bureaus. If your printer (or your service bureau's favorite printer) isn't on the list, check with Aldus and/or the printer manufacturer, to see if there's a PPD file available for it. If not, or if you've customized your printer with additional fonts or more memory, you'll need to create a custom PPD for it. See the Aldus Commercial Printing Guide for instructions.

### By the Way...

*The PDX files used by previous versions of PageMaker are no longer required. The Custom PPD files replace them.*

Aldus supplies the new Adobe PSPrinter driver (as well as a new universal driver for non-PostScript printers) for both Macintosh and Windows. You'll need to install the driver before you print; Chapter 9 covers the installation. The new drivers should work with your other applications, but you may not want to delete your LaserWriter driver (or your other older driver) until you're sure the new driver is compatible with all of your applications.

### Watch Out!

*There's a conflict between the PSPrinter driver and Super Laser Spooler. If you normally use SLS, remove the spooler or disable it from the LaserQueue DA's menu.*

# Software Requirements

PageMaker 5.0 for Macintosh will run happily under either System 7, or System 6.0.7 or 6.0.8. Obviously, if you have not upgraded to System 7, you will not be able to take advantage of such features as Publish and Subscribe or Balloon help. PageMaker 5.0 for Windows will run under Windows 3.0 or 3.1, but without version 3.1, you will not be able to take advantage of features like OLE (object linking and embedding) or TrueType.

PageMaker will run without any other programs (except, of course, Windows for the Windows version). You need nothing to use it except the fonts that come with your Mac or with Windows. On the other hand, you won't be able to do much in the way of page design without a graphics program, and you will have a difficult time doing any serious writing without a word processor.

Which programs are compatible with PageMaker? PageMaker supplies filters which convert the output from virtually all Mac and PC word processors into a format that it can read. As for graphics, which program to buy depends on what kind of drawings you want to produce. Aldus FreeHand is recommended by many artists, especially those who do a great deal of color work on the Mac. Aldus SuperPaint is also a good choice. It's easy to use and lets you save your work in PICT or as a bit map. Engineers prefer Aldus Intellidraw which is particularly good for precision drawings. If you're a Windows user, try CorelDRAW!: it includes both a drawing and a painting module, as well as some other handy utility programs that make it easier to work with graphics.

# Extras

If you're using a scanner, a program such as Aldus Digital Darkroom or Adobe PhotoShop is a great help. These let you retouch your photos, adjust contrast, and make other helpful changes.

Adobe Type Manager is technically not a necessity, but it's hard to do without. It gives you good-looking type on the screen, and on a non-PostScript printer. When you're trying to adjust the spacing on a headline, or to show a client on the screen what the page is going to look like printed, you need ATM. If you're a Windows 3.1 user, however, you're exempted—TrueType provides all these benefits to you.

Clip art libraries and extra type fonts are nice to have, too, and are a big help for desktop publishing. You can find all kinds of clip art, including PCX, PICT, EPS, and TIFF images. Your software dealer should have a good selection of clip art libraries and will also have additional type fonts. You can buy these either as TrueType fonts, or as PostScript files. Look also on bulletin boards, user groups, and on-line services for more fonts and clip art. You're expected to pay the minimal cost of shareware distributed in this manner. But much of it is "postcard ware," for which the author asks only for a postcard from your hometown. Some is "smile ware." If you like it, smile.

# Before You Go Ahead, Back Up

The first thing you should do to your PageMaker disks is to make sure they're locked (write-protected). Aldus usually ships disks locked, but you still need to check. Locking a disk protects it against being accidentally erased, or having something else written onto it that doesn't belong there, like a virus. PageMaker (both Mac and Windows versions) ships on six high-density 3.5" floppy disks, which have locking tabs, as shown in Figure A.2. To lock a disk, slide the plastic tab up, so the hole is uncovered.

Figure A.2
Locking a disk.

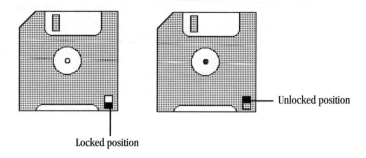

Locked position                    Unlocked position

Of course, disks are prone to other kinds of damage, too. That's why you should make backup copies before you install the program. Aldus allows you to make one copy of your PageMaker disks for this purpose. To make backup disks, you'll need a blank, formatted disk for each disk you're copying. You'll need six new, blank high-density disks.

### Watch Out!
*Make just one copy of your disks, for backup only. You are not allowed to make copies for your friends, co-workers, or relatives. That's software piracy and it's illegal!*

To format (initialize) a disk on the Mac, stick it into the disk drive. If it's blank and hasn't been used before, you'll get a series of dialog boxes asking if you want to initialize it and asking that you give it a name.

To copy a disk on the Mac after you've formatted it, make sure both disk icons are present on the desktop. To copy a document onto another disk, drag its icon to the location where you want to place the copy, and the Mac will copy it. If you only have one disk drive, you'll need to remove disks and replace them as a dialog box directs. Put the disk you want to copy to into the drive, and look for its icon on the screen. Then eject the disk, and put the original disk back in the drive. Select the material you want to copy, and drag it to the icon for the destination disk.

### Watch Out!

*Be sure that you name the backup disks exactly as PageMaker has; that is, if the first Aldus disk is called "Disk 1," your first blank disk should also be called "Disk 1," not PM #1, or any other variation. The Aldus Installer looks for disks by the names by which it knows them. It won't recognize an incorrectly labeled disk, and you won't be able to install the program.*

In Windows, you can format the new disks and copy the PageMaker disks to them in one step. Just select **Copy Disk** File Manager's **Disk** menu. Specify the source and destination drives (they can be the same), insert the first PageMaker disk, and choose **OK**. Follow the prompts, then repeat the procedure for each disk.

Now, look for the registration cards and information that came in the PageMaker box. You should find a set of stickers with the serial number for your copy of PageMaker. Stick one of these stickers on Disk 2, of both your backup and original sets. (Why not on Disk 1? PageMaker will ask you to enter the serial number while Disk 1 is in the drive. If you put the label on it, you won't be able to read the number.) Put the original disks in a safe place and use the copies to install PageMaker.

### By the Way . . .

*If you can't find the stickers, don't panic. The serial number is also on the bottom of the box. You must enter the correct number or the program won't load. It's a form of copy protection.*

# Installation

The Aldus Installer, provided with PageMaker, will copy the various files onto your hard disk. Some of these files are always needed; others are selected for copying depending on what word processor and printer you're using. The Template and Tutorial files are optional. The Aldus Installer utility will do most of the work for you. It will create the needed folders (or directories) and will install and decompress the program and all of the files you've selected. You can relax and flip through this book while you wait, and be there to answer questions and swap disks when the Installer asks you to. The complete installation takes about 15–20 minutes, depending on the speed of your computer and which options you are installing.

Before installing PageMaker 5.0, turn off any virus-protection software. Since PageMaker adds to your system files, it will trigger some antivirus programs, stopping the installation. (You can scan the disks for viruses first if you want.) Then quit any open applications, so the installation program will have your computer's full attention and resources.

**By the Way . . .**
*If you need a lot more room, you will have to do some disk management before you can install PageMaker. Remove any unnecessary files and store them on floppies. Run a defragmenting program, such as Norton Utilities Speed Disk, for better results.*

## Mac Installation

Follow these steps to install PageMaker on the Mac.

1. Put your copy of Disk 1 in the drive. If it doesn't open automatically, double-click on the icon. If the Utilities folder doesn't open automatically, double-click on it.

2. Double-click on the **Aldus Installer/Utility** icon. This will open the Main window. You'll also see three other windows. Installer History and Installer Diagnostics are empty files in which the Installer will make notes about the system tests and the progress of the installation. Read Me contains up-to-the-minute information on PageMaker that's not included in your PageMaker manuals.

**By the Way...**
*You might find it helpful to print a copy of the Read Me file for reference. Click on the window to select it, and choose **Print** from the **File** menu to print a copy. (Be sure your printer's turned on.)*

3. Select one of these installation options:

   - *Easy Install:* Installs PageMaker 5.0, all of the Aldus Additions, color libraries, and the most commonly used printer files and import/export filters.

   - *PageMaker 5.0:* Installs the program and lets you select any Additions, color libraries, printer files and import/export filters you want to install.

   - *Templates:* Installs the PageMaker 5.0 template scripts, a set of predesigned pages on which you can base your own publications.

- *Tutorial Files:* Lets you learn by doing. Use these with PageMaker 5.0 Getting Started if you feel you need a workbook approach. Otherwise, delete them, as they just waste disk space.

- *Additions:* Lets you choose which of PageMaker 5.0's Additions to install. If disk space is limited, only add the ones you'll use. You can always free up some disk space and add more Additions later.

4. Click on **Install**. The Installer will run some diagnostic tests to make sure you have enough memory and the right system and finder versions. The results will be displayed in the Diagnostics window. This file will automatically be saved on your hard disk, and you can open it and read it at any time, using the Teach Text application included with PageMaker.

5. Depending on which installation options you've selected, you may be asked to choose files to install. Figure A.3 shows how printer descriptions are chosen. To select only one from the scrolling menu, click on it. To select additional files, hold down **Shift** as you click. You can select as many as you want, as long as you hold down **Shift**. Click on **OK** or press **Return** when ready.

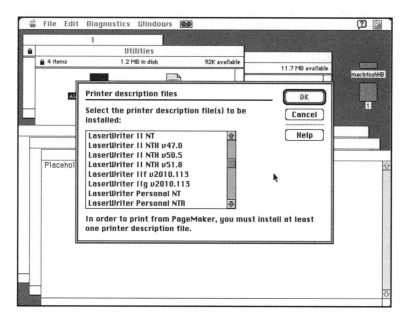

Figure A.3 Choose as many printers and/or imagesetters as you're likely to use. If your printer or service bureau adds a new one, you can install it later.

6. Next, you'll be asked where to install the program. PageMaker creates and names its own folder. Assign it to whatever hard disk or disk partition you want. The program will tell you if there's not enough space available to install on that disk.

7. The final dialog box in this series asks you to personalize your copy of PageMaker. Enter your name, company, and the serial number of your copy of PageMaker, as shown in Figure A.4. The serial number is on the sticker you put on Disk 2, on the registration materials, and on a sticker on the bottom of the PageMaker box. Copy it exactly as written, with hyphens and all the numbers. Omit any letters at the beginning of the serial number. It will repeat what you've typed and ask for verification. If you don't have the correct serial number, PageMaker will not install. Click on **OK** when done.

Figure A.4
Use the Tab key to scroll from one field to the next. Be sure to enter the serial number exactly as it's written.

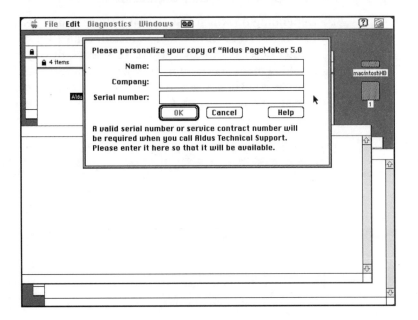

8. Now PageMaker will begin the installation. If there's not enough room on the disk, you'll get a message to that effect, and you'll be asked to cancel the installation. If you need only a little more space, try again, asking for fewer filters and PPDs.

By the Way . . .
*On the Mac, Disk 1 sometimes fails to eject. If this happens, press* ⌘*+Shift+1 to eject it.*

9. You'll be asked for a series of disk swaps as the Installer assembles all the necessary data. You can watch the progress on the thermometer, shown in Figure A.5, and in the Installer History window. When finished, you'll get a message that the installation was successful, and you'll be returned to your desktop, complete with a new PageMaker folder. There will also be a new Aldus folder inside your System folder, containing the PPDs, dictionary, filters, and other files. Do not remove or rename this folder and do not remove any of the files or folders in it. If you do, PageMaker will not work properly.

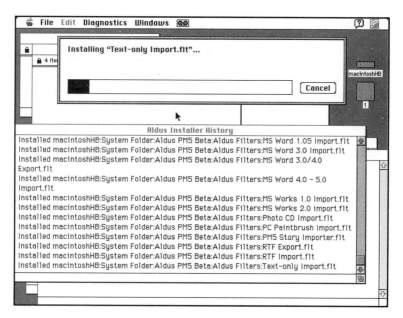

Figure A.5
Since watching the thermometer is boring, use this time to fill out the registration card.

10. Finally, you will get a message that installation was successful. Before you open PageMaker, turn your antivirus software back on and restart the computer. Doing so loads the printer drivers and other necessary files.

## Installation (Windows)

Here's how to install PageMaker for Windows.

1. Start Windows at the DOS prompt (type **WIN** and press **Enter**.)

2. Place PageMaker 5.0's Disk 1 in your drive A (or B drive if it won't fit into A.)

3. Open the **File** menu and select **Run**. The Run dialog box appears.

4. Type **A:\ALDSETUP** in the Command Line box (or **B:\ALDSETUP** if the disk is in drive B), as in Figure A.6. Then select **OK** or press **Enter**. After a few seconds, the Aldus Setup Main Window appears (Figure A.7).

Figure A.6
Start the Aldus
Setup program
with the File
Run command.

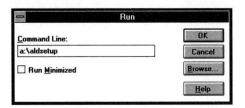

Figure A.7
The Aldus
Setup Main
Window.

5. If asked, confirm that you want shared files to go in a directory called **C:\ALDUS**, or change its designation to some other drive or directory.

6. Click on an installation option. To pick more than one, hold down **Ctrl** while you click on the extra ones. Then choose **Setup** to continue. Here are the options available:

- *Install everything:* Installs it all—PageMaker 5.0, Aldus Additions, color libraries, the tutorial, printer files, and import/export filters.

- *PageMaker 5.0:* Installs the minimum needed to get by—the essential program files plus a few Aldus Additions, printer files, import/export filters, and color libraries. Use this option if you are extremely short on disk space.

- *Tutorial:* Installs the PageMaker 5.0 tutorial, which you can use with PageMaker 5.0 Getting Started as a disk-and-workbook self study. If you're already an experienced PageMaker user, don't bother.

- *Additions:* Lets you choose which of PageMaker 5.0's Additions to install. If disk space is limited, only add the ones you'll use. You can always free up some disk space and add more Additions later.

- *Printer files:* Installs PPD (PostScript printer description) files for the printer(s) you select. If you're planning to print out work on a PostScript device, make sure you choose this option. Note that this is separate from installing the new printer driver, which you'll learn about in Chapter 9.

- *Dictionaries:* Installs dictionaries for checking hyphenation and spelling. If you spell-check your work in your word processor before bringing documents into PageMaker, you may find this feature unnecessary.

7. Choose the drive and directory that PageMaker 5.0 will be installed to and click on **OK**, or just press **Enter** to select the default, C:\PM5.

8. If you selected Install everything or Printer files, you'll be asked to choose the PPDs you need for your PostScript printer (see Figure A.8). Pick them from the list, and then choose **OK**, or just press **Enter** if you don't have a PostScript printer.

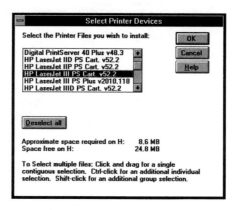

Figure A.8
Select the appropriate PPDs for the printers you'll be using for your work.

9. When asked (as in Figure A.9), input your name, company name, and serial number, and then choose **OK**. Remember, you put your serial number sticker on disk 2.

10. Follow along with the on-screen instructions, changing disks whenever prompted.

Figure A.9
Personalize
your copy of
PageMaker
with your
name and
serial number.

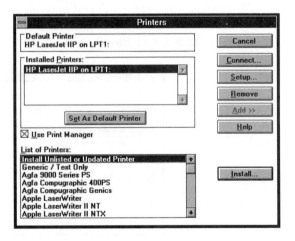

11. At the end of the installation, the Printers dialog box appears to remind you to install the new printer driver. If you want to do this later, choose **Cancel**. You'll find instructions in Chapter 9. To do it now, go on to step 12.

12. If it's not there already, insert the last installation disk in drive A (or the drive that it fits into).

13. Choose **Add**[Alt+A] from the Printers dialog box. The box expands, as shown in Figure A.10.

Figure A.10
Install the new
printer drivers
through the
Printers dialog
box.

14. Choose **Install Unlisted or Updated Printer** from the list (it's at the top), and then select **Install**.

15. When prompted for the location of the printer driver, type the drive letter of the installation disk if it's not correct on-screen, then choose **OK**.

The Essential PageMaker

16. Choose the driver you want from the Add Unlisted or Updated Printer dialog box. If your printer isn't listed, choose the one that's closest. Then choose **OK**.

17. Choose **Close** to close the Printers box. Click on **OK** in response to the confirmation messages.

18. At the Aldus Setup Main Window, click on **Exit**.

# Upgrading from Earlier Versions of PageMaker

Even though PageMaker 4 publications are compatible with PageMaker 5.0, if you have been working on a project in PM 4, it's a good idea to finish it with the earlier version. When you install PageMaker 5.0, you needn't immediately remove the earlier version of the program. Give yourself a few days to learn to use it, before you remove PM 4 from your hard drive.

There may be one or two PageMaker 4 files you'll want to save and use with PM 5. The PageMaker 4.0 or 4.2 User dictionary contains words you've added to PageMaker's dictionary and hyphenation resource. If you'd like to continue to use the words you have added, drag a copy of the file **ALDUSN.udc** from the **Proximity** folder inside your **Aldus** folder, into the new **Aldus PM 5** folder. (If you can't find it, look inside the USEnglish folder, or whatever language you've installed.) In Windows, copy the ALDUSN.UDC file to the new PM5 directory.

# Problems?

If there's anything you're not sure about during the installation, each dialog box includes a Help button. Clicking on it will bring up a screen with the answers to most questions.

If you have difficulty with the Installer, try turning off all your INITs and extensions when you restart (Mac only). Using an INIT manager or Startup Manager makes this easier, but if you don't have one, you can temporarily remove them from your System folder (System 6) or restart while holding the **Shift** key down (System 7).

If you find your Mac hard drive seems to be filling up faster than it should after you've been running PageMaker for a while, check to see if it's filling up with temporary files. PageMaker creates a temporary file whenever it does a "mini-save" in an unsaved publication. These temporary files sit on the disk with your System folder, in an invisible folder marked, appropriately, **Temporary Files**. You won't see it unless you use Fast Find, or some similar program to look for it. If your system crashes or does an "unexpected shutdown," the Temporary folder reappears in the Trash as **Rescued Items**. You can go into the folder, drag out the unsaved publication, and reopen it. The first such rescued publication will be labeled **ALDTMP001**, and those that follow will be **ALDTMP002**, and so on. If you don't need them, empty the trash and they'll go away. If you have a lot of crashes and forget to empty the trash for a while, you'll find a very full Trashcan. This can also slow down your whole system, if files get fragmented. Get into the habit of emptying the trash and defragmenting disks on a regular basis.

And that's all there is to it! Now you're ready to open PageMaker and explore the world of desktop publishing.

# The Essential PageMaker

# Index

## Symbols

>>>, special effects character, 112
? (question mark) wild card
 character, 148
^ (caret) wild card character, 148
≈≈≈, special effects character, 112
100% command (Set width menu), 89
12-point Times, type font default, 118
80MB hard drives, PageMaker 5.0
 Mac/Windows versions, 56

## A

Abeliene character typefaces, 9
About PageMaker 5.0 command
    Apple menu, 21
    Help menu, 21
Actual size view, 35
adding
    pages, 91-93
    spot colors on monochrome
     monitors, 16
additive pigments, 331
address lists, 263
addresses for dummy newsletters, 60
adjusting text blocks, 106-107
Adobe
    Font Downloader, 222
    Multiple Master Fonts, 8
    Super ATM, 8
Adobe Illustrator EPSF graphics
 programs, 10
Adobe Photo-Shop, 360
    converting graphics formats, 178
    digital image processors, 174
Adobe Systems, PostScript, xix

ads, 266-268
    blats, 271
    camera-ready, 272
    considerations, 277-279
    layout, 268-272
    magazine/newspaper, 272-277
    position, 269
advertising, 266-272
AGFA Pro Sets imagesetter, 57
ALDTMP01 temporary file (Mac), 41
Aldus
    Digital Darkroom, 11, 174, 360
    Filters, 97
    FreeHand, EPSF graphics, 10
    Import Xtension, 362
    Installer utility, 375-376
    IntelliDraw, 169
    Persuasion, 302
    program group, 21
    Setup Main Window, 380
    SuperPaint, xvii, 360
    TrapWise, 239
Aldus Additions, 48-50
    access via CompuServe, 50
    Create color library, 344
    menu, Open template command, 73
    Open template Addition, 245-246
    Open Templates utility, 287, 292
    Run script command, 354-355
    template scripts, 287
*Aldus* Magazine, 3, 50
algorithms computing hyphens, 157
alien formats, converting PageMaker
 files, 362
aligning graphics/text objects, 354
alignment, 113-114
Alignment command (Type menu), 70,
 108, 131

America Online
  templates, 245
  TrueType fonts, 217
annual reports, 244, 258-261, 301-309
ANSI character sets, searches, 151
Apple
  Font Utility, 221
  ImageWriter printers, 56
  LaserWriter printers, 56
  LaserWriter Pro printers, 12
  menu
    About PageMaker 5
      command, 21
    Chooser DA, Mac printer
      setup, 209
  Personal LaserWriter LS, 215
  StyleWriter printers, 8
  System 7 Publish and Subscribe
    feature, 98
  TrueType fonts, 8
application icons, 21
Apply icon, moving text blocks, 132
applying colors, 341
Artbeats backgrounds, 360
Articulate Systems Voice
  Navigator, 363
Arts & Letters, Windows drawing
  programs, 170
ASCII text files, importing data to Table
  Editor, 259
assigning styles, Story Editor, 143-144
ATM (Adobe Type Manager), 8,
  217, 373
attributes, changing/finding
  text by, 149
Auto-flow text icon, 100
auto-leading, 122
Autoflow (automatic text flow), 100,
  103-104
Autoflow command (Layout menu),
  100, 103
Autoflow icon, 103
automatic
  kerning, 126-129
  line drawing, 251

links, EPS files, 196
mini-saves, 41
page numbering, 358-359
tiling, 232
Avery MacLabelPro, mailing lists, 292
awards, 290-291

B

backgrounds, Artbeats, 360
backups for PageMaker disks, 374-375
banners, 61-62, 85-89
  dummy newsletters, 4, 60
  logos, 62-64
Barneyscan color scanners, 176
baseline leading, 122-124
BBSs (Bulletin Board Systems), label
  templates, 294
Bézier curves, 171
bids on printing, 17
binderies, desktop, 225
binding
  publications, 227
  systems (mechanical/thermal), 225
bit-mapped illustrations, Paint
  pictures, 169
bitmapped fonts, Mac/PC screen
  display, 7
Bitstream Speedo fonts
  (Windows), 218
Black and white mode, Image
  control, 202
blats, 271
bleeds, 64
blue grid lines (column lines), 31
BMP files, 169
body copy leading, 121
boilerplates, 84
Bold
  font styles, 6
  Italic font styles, 6
Book command (File menu),
  306-308, 312
book lists, 306-308, 311-313
book templates, 306-308
Bookman serif typefaces, 7-9

books
designing, 297-300
dummies, 299-326
printing, 324-325
trim size, 298
borders
on awards, certificates, and
diplomas, 290-291
Zapf Dingbats symbol set, 291
boundaries of graphics, 191-192
Box Drawing tool, 29
brochure templates, 347
brochures, 273-274
bumper stickers, 294
business cards, 254-255
business stationery, 253-263

## C

Caere Typist, 175
calendar templates, 287
calendars, 287-289
camera-ready
ads, 272
pages, 17
Cannot find dialog box, 198
Canvas (Deneba), 169
draw programs, 10
Paint programs, 169
caret (^) wild card character, 148
Cascade command
(Window menu), 55
cascading publications, 55
catalogs, 257-258, 262
CE Software Quickeys, 363
centered type, 114
certificates, 290-291
CGM (computer graphics metafile)
.CGM files, object-oriented art, 170
objects, 63
Change & Find button, 316
Change all button, 316
Change all function, 148
Change and Find function, 148
Change command (Utilities menu), 315
Change function, Story Editor, 148-152

changing
pages, 26-27
text by attributes, 149
characters
invisible, 151-152
special effects, 112
typefaces, 9
wild cards
caret (^), 148
question mark (?), 148
charts
Aldus Persuasion, 302
ClarisWorks, 302
importing with .PIC filters, 170
Microsoft
Excel, importing as
graphics, 260
PowerPoint, 302
MORE 3.0 (Symantec), 302
MS Works, 302
PIC files, 170
WordPerfect Works, 302
checking spelling, 154-156
Chooser DA (Apple menu), Mac
printer setup, 209
Cicero type measuring units
(European), 120
Claris MacDraw Pro, 169
ClarisWorks
charts and graphs, 302
importing text, 304
cleaning laser printers, 231
clip art, 10, 359-361
borders on awards and
certificates, 290
libraries, 360, 373
Clipboard
importing graphics, 178
placing corporate logos in templates, 249
CMYK (Cyan, Magenta, Yellow, blacK)
color model, 333-334
CMYK printing, 236
codes, special characters, 150-151

collating two-sided printing, 226
color
  calibrators for monitors, 364
  libraries, 339-344
  matching
    DIC library, 364
    systems, 336
  printing, 236-242
  process, 236, 333
  scanners, 176-177
  separations
    improvements, 47
    printing, 238-239
  spot, 330-331
color control panel, Macintosh color
 picker, 331
Color dialog box, 334
Color palette, 331, 336-341
colored blocks and lines, 81-83
colors, 330-336
  applying, 341
  copying, 341
  matching, 16
  paper, 227-231
  printing, 14
  process, 236, 333
  publications, 15-16
  spot, 236, 337-339
ColorScript printers (QMS), 56
ColorTag system (Letraset), 224
Column Break icon, 193
column guidelines, 32
column guides, 66
Column guides command (Layout
 menu), 33, 66-67, 274
Column guides dialog box, 67
column lines, 31
columns, multiple, 33
commands
  100% (Set width menu), 89
  About PageMaker 5
   (Apple menu), 21
  Alignment (Type menu), 70, 108
  Autoflow (Layout menu), 100, 103

Book (File menu), 306-308, 312
Cascade (Window menu), 55
Change (Utilities menu), 315
Column guides (Layout menu), 33,
 66-67, 274
Control Palette (Window menu), 50
Copy Disk (Disk menu), 375
Copy To (Edit menu), Windows, 87
Create index (Utilities menu), 321
Create Table of contents
 (Utilities menu), 312
Create TOC (Options menu), 309
Custom (Leaders menu), 112
Cut (Edit menu), 105
Define colors (Element menu), 15,
 237, 338, 341
Define styles (Type menu),
 136-137, 310
Display (Story menu), 152
Display pub info
 (Utilities menu), 325
Edit original (Edit menu), 185
Edit Story (Edit menu), 143, 354
Editions (Edit menu), 163
Exit (File menu), 41
Export (File menu), 146, 260
Fill (Element menu), 29
Get Info (File menu), 75
Hyphenation (Type menu), 157
Image control (Element menu), 202
Indents/tabs (Type menu),
 108-110, 359
Indents/tabs ruler
 (Layout menu), 111
Index entry (Utilities menu), 319
Insert pages (Layout menu), 91
Leading (Type menu), 122
Line (Element menu), 28, 183, 274
Link info (Element menu), 161, 195
Link options (Element menu), 163
Links (File menu), 160, 348
Lock guides (Layout menu), 34
Multiple paste (Edit menu), 251
New (File menu), 22, 64
None (Element menu), 81, 90, 200

Open (File menu), 24, 247

Open template
 (Aldus Additions menu), 73

Page setup (File menu), 66, 210,
 309, 347

Paper (Element menu), 81, 183

Paragraph (Type menu), 107, 310,
 352, 357

Paste (Edit menu), 105

Place (File menu), 85, 100, 188,
 262, 348-350

Place File (File menu), 170

Preferences (File menu), 38, 143

Print (File menu), 212-213, 232, 376

Remove pages (Layout menu), 91

Remove transformation
 (Element menu), 54

Revert (File menu), 40, 141

Run (File menu), 379

Run script
 (Aldus Additions menu), 355

Save as (File menu), 39-40, 74,
 93, 246

Set Width (Type menu), 8

Show index (Utilities menu), 320

Show pasteboard (Layout menu),
 26, 35

Snap to guides (Layout menu),
 34, 80

Snap to rulers (Layout menu),
 34, 80

Sort pages (Utilities menu), 282

Spelling (Utilities menu), 154

Style (Window menu), 135

Text wrap (Element menu), 189-191

Tile (Window menu), 26, 55

Track (Type menu), 125

Type specs (Type menu), 68,
 118, 353

Type style (Type menu), 8

Zero Lock (Layout menu), 31

commercial printers, 226-227

company logos, 249

company phone directories, 263

compiling indexes, 321-324

compressing
    files for print shops, 272
    saved files, 39-40

compression utilities
    CompactPro, 272
    PKZIP, 272
    StuffIt, 272

CompuServe
    Aldus Additions access, 50
    label templates, 294
    templates, 245

Computer Eyes (Digital Vision),
 176, 360

Computer Eyes (Digital Vision)
 scanner, 11

computer-generated metafiles,
 see .CGM files

computers, types for running
 PageMaker, 368-369

Connectix Virtual, System 6.07 virtual
 memory, 56

considerations for fonts, 218-219

contrast, images, 205

Control Palette, 50-53
    flipping objects horizontally/
     vertically, 53
    handles, 51
    hot spots, 51
    Printer-resolution scaling, 180
    Proportional Scaling, 180
    reflections, 50
    skewing, 53

Control Palette command (Window
 menu), 50

Control panel window, 209

control panels
    Color palette, 331
    Windows Font, 220
    TrueType fonts, 218

controls, images, 201-205

copy, 267

Copy Disk command (Disk menu), 375

Copy master guides command (Layout
 menu), 91

Copy styles feature, 140
Copy To command (Edit menu),
 Windows, 87
copying
    colors, 341
    linked files, 41-42
    style sheets, 139-140
copyright bugs/forms, 18
CorelDRAW!
    .PCX files, 169-170
    draw program, 10
corporate logos, placing in templates
 with Clipboard, 249
Courier monospaced fonts, 6
cover-ups, 182-184
Create index command (Utilities
 menu), 321
Create Table of contents command
 (Utilities menu), 312
Create TOC command (Options
 menu), 309
crop marks, 15
Cropping tool, 29, 86, 181-184
cross-platform compatibility of
 TrueType fonts, 8
cross-referencing indexes, 316
curves, Bézier, 171
custom color libraries, 341-344
Custom command (Leaders menu), 112
customized clip art, 10
customizing
    boundaries of graphics, 191-192
    templates, 249
Cut command (Edit menu), 105

## D

databases, 261-265
DataShaper (Elseware Corporation),
 263
DataViz, MacLink Translators/Plus for
 the Mac, 304
datelines, 88
defaults
    leading, 121
    linking, 197-198

Page setup, 347
pair kerning (12 points), 127
printers, selecting in Windows,
 210-211
publications, 71
settings, PageMaker, 108
styles, 135-136
tab settings, 111-112
type fonts (12-point Times), 118
Define colors command (Element
 menu), 15, 237, 338, 341
Define styles command (Type menu),
 136-137, 310
defining grid lines, 66
Delphi
    label templates, 294
    templates, 245
Deneba Canvas, 169
design axis criterion, Multiple Master
 fonts (Adobe), 8
designing
    ads, 268-272
    books, 298-300
    original forms, 250
desktop binderies, 225
DeskWriter (Hewlett-Packard), 215
destination programs (OLE), 98
Diagonal Line Drawing tool, 28
DIC library color matching, 364
dictionaries, 153-156
    adding frequently used terms, 154
    PageMaker
        System folder (Mac), 362
        Windows subdirectories, 362
Digital Darkroom (Aldus), 360
digital image processors, 174
Digital Vision Computer Eyes, 176
dingbats, 203
diplomas, 290-291
directories, 262-263
disadvantages
    non-PostScript printers, 216
    soft fonts, 216
discounts when printing, 17

Disinfectant, 242
Disk menu, Copy Disk command, 375
disks, submitting for printing, 17
display ads, 267
Display command (Story menu), 152
Display master items command (Layout menu), 91
Display pub info command (Utilities menu), 49, 325
distorted graphics, repairing, 181
documents
  dummies, 347-348
  multiple open, 55-56
dot patterns, 81-83
downloadable fonts, 217-222
drafts, printing, 213
drawing
  lines
    automatically, 251
    horizontal, 251-252
  logos, 63
drawing programs
  Arts & Letters, 170
  Canvas, 10
  CorelDRAW!, 10
  Harvard Graphics, 10, 170
  Lotus Freelance, 170
  MacDraw Pro, 10
  Micrographfix Designer, 170
drivers, printer, 54, 208-210
drop caps, Aldus Additions, 48
DTP (desktop publishing), xvii-xix, 2
dummies
  books, 299-326
  documents, 347-348
  imposition, 92
  newsletter, 4, 60-61
  page, 270
  sketches, 4
  text, see greeking

## E

Eastgate Fontina, 219
Edit All Stories addition, Aldus Additions, 48

Edit menu
  Copy To command, 87
  Cut command, 105
  Edit original command, 185
  Edit story command, 143, 354
  Editions command, 163
  Multiple paste command, 251
  Paste command, 105
editing
  graphics, 184-185
  OLE objects, 185
electronic cover-ups, 182-184
electronic white out, see masking
Element menu
  Define colors command, 15, 237, 338, 341
  Fill command, 29
  Image control command, 202
  Line command, 28, 183, 251, 274
  Link info command, 161, 195
  Link options command, 163
  None command, 81, 90
  Paper command, 81, 183
  Remove transformation command, 54
  Text wrap command, 189-191
Elseware Corporation, DataShaper, 263
embedded objects, 98-99
ems, kerning spaces, 127
EPS files
  automatic links, 196
  encapsulating, 172
  object-oriented art, 170-173
  PostScript printers, 172
EPSF (Encapsulated PostScript Format) graphics programs, 10
excess label space, 293-294
existing publications, 24
existing styles, 135-137
Exit command (File menu), 41
exiting PageMaker, 41-42
Export command (File menu), 146, 260
export filters, 97, 147
exporting stories, 146-166
eye-leading, 5

392

## F

families of fonts, 6
fast saving, 37
faxes, 294-295
    Freedom of Press, 366
    multipage, 295
    typefaces, 9
file extensions (Windows) publications
 and templates, 39
File Manager placing files in
 PageMaker, 178
File menu
    Book command, 306-308, 312
    Exit command, 41
    Export command, 146, 260
    Get Info command, 75
    Links command, 160, 348
    New command, 22, 64
    Open command, 24, 247
    Page setup command, 66, 210,
        309, 347
    Place command, 85, 100, 188, 262,
        348-350
    Place File command, 170
    Preferences command, 38, 143
    Print command, 212-213, 232, 376
    Revert command, 40, 141
    Run command, 379
    Save as command, 39-40, 74,
        93, 246
files
    ASCII text, 259
    BMP
        Paint (Windows), 169
        Publisher's Paintbrush, 169
    .CGM, 170
    compressing
        for print shops, 272
        saved, 39-40
    EPS
        automatic links, 196
        encapsulating, 172
        object-oriented art, 170-173
        PostScript printers, 172

formats, PICT/PICT2, 170
graphics, 178-179
greeking
    Lorem Ipsum, 300
    SampleText, 72
    TEXT.TXT, 72
linked, copying, 41-42
PageMaker, converting to alien
 formats, 362
.PCX, 169-170
.PFB, 220
.PFM, 220
PIC, charts and graphs, 170
placing in PageMaker, 178
PPD (PostScript Printer Descrip-
    tion), 238
restoring with Open dialog box, 41
SampleText, 300
temporary, 41
TEXT.TXT, 300
WIN.INI, 218
.WMF, 170
Fill command (Element menu), 29
Fill menu, None command, 200
Fill palette, 200
film negative printing, 234-235
filters
    export, 97, 147
    image, 177
    import, 97, 147
    .PIC, 170
    Smart ASCII (PageMaker), 305
final copies
    laser printers, 223
    printing, 222-226
Find boxes, special character codes,
    150-151
Find function, Story Editor, 148-152
finding text by attributes, 149
finished size of publication, 227-231
finishes of paper, 227-231
first line indents, 110
Fit in window view, 34
flat scanners, 174
flatbed scanners, 360

flipping objects with Control
  Palette, 53
floppy disks, service bureau printing,
  239-241
flow options for text, 99-100
flush left indents, 108
flyers, 273-274
Font Downloaders, 221-222
font lists, printing, 14
font managers
  Master Juggler, 219
  Suitcase 2.0, 219
font types, PostScript printers, 216
Font Utility (Apple), 221
font/DA managers, 362
Font/DA mover, 221
Fontina (Eastgate), 219
fonts, 6, 119-120, 216-222
  bitmapped, Mac/PC screen
    display, 7
  Bitstream Speedo, 218
  considerations, 218-219
  downloadable, 217-222
  families, 6
  installing, font/DA managers, 362
  Intellifont scalable, 217
  monospaced
    Courier, 6
    Monaco, 6
  Multiple Master (Adobe), 8
  PCL bitmap, 217
  permanently downloading, 221
  PostScript, 7
  printing problems, 240
  proportional
    Helvetica, 6
    Times, 6
  resident, 218
  screen, 218
  soft, WIN.INI files updates, 218
  styles, 6
  TrueType (Microsoft/Apple), 8
    America Online, 217
    cross-platform compatibility, 8

Windows Fonts control
  panels, 218
  type defaults, 12-point Times, 118
  Zapf Chancery, 291
force-justified type, 114
formal letterheads, 254
formats
  converting
    alien to PageMaker files, 362
    graphics, 177-178
  files
    PICT/PICT2, 10, 170
    TIFF, 201-205
formatting imported text, 304
forms, 248-250
four-color process printing, 16
free rotation
  graphics, 47, 53-54
  text, 47, 53-54
Freedom of Press Classic, 365
Freedom of Press Pro, 365
French folds in greeting cards, 285
frequently used terms, adding to
  dictionary, 154
functioning of laser printers, 214
functions
  Change, 148-152
  Change all, 148
  Change and Find, 148
  Find, 148-152
Futura sans serif typefaces in
  headlines, 9

# G

galleys, xviii
GCC Personal Laser Printers, 215
Get Info command (File menu), 75
Grabber Hand icon, 36
grammar checking, 96
graphics, 10-13, 200-201
  boundaries, customizing, 191-192
  converting to different formats, 177
  distorted, repairing, 181
  editing, 184-185

EPSF, 10
importing, 177-178
importing Microsoft Excel charts
  as, 260
improving performance, 350-361
independent, 185
inline, 185-189
inline elements, 351-354
linked, 194-199
logos, 62-64
manual kerning, 129
modifying, 179-181
object-oriented, 169-171
objects, 354
placing, 178-179
repositioning, 179
resizing, 179-181
graphics files, placing graphics from,
  178-179
graphics language, QuickDraw
  (Mac), 215
graphics programs
  Adobe Illustrator, 10
  Aldus FreeHand, 10
  shareware, 11
graphs
  Aldus Persuasion, 302
  ClarisWorks, 302
  importing with .PIC filters, 170
  Microsoft
    PowerPoint, 302
    Works, 302
  MORE 3.0 (Symantec), 302
  PIC files, 170
  WordPerfect Works, 302
gravure printing, 229
Gray mode, Image control, 202
grayscale limitations, laser printers, 12
greeking, 72
  Lorem Ipsum file, 300
  SampleText file, 72
  TEXT.TXT file, 72
greeting cards, 285-287
grid lines, 31, 66

grids
  layout, 31-34
    margins, 32-33
  grippers, 64
grouping objects, 350-351
guidelines
  columns, 32
  horizontal/vertical, 33-34
guides, ruler, 79-81
Guides and rulers submenu (Layout
  menu)
    Lock guides command, 34
    Snap to guides command, 34, 80
    Snap to rulers command, 34, 80
    Zero Lock command, 31
gutters, 32, 61

# H

hairline rules, 64
halftones, scanning, 11
Hammermill Laser Plus laser output
  paper, 230
hand scanners, creating textures,
  174-175, 360
handles
  Control Palette, 51
  resizing, 179
  window shade, 102
handouts, 273
hanging indents, 108
hard copies, proofreading, 213
hardware
  PageMaker requirements, 368-372
  tips for improving performance,
    365-366
Harvard Graphics
  draw programs, 10, 170
  .PCX files, 169
headings, styles in TOCs, 310-311
headlines, 129-132
  placing, 130-131
  tombstoning, 131
  typefaces, 9
Help menu, About PageMaker 5
  command, 21

Helvetica
   proportional fonts, 6
   typefaces, 6-9
      Helvetica DemiBold, 6
      Helvetica Light, 6
      Helvetica Thin, 6
Hewlett Packard
   DeskWriter printer, 56, 215
   LaserJet printers, 57
   PaintJet printers, 57
HiJaak (Inset Systems), 178
horizontal guidelines, 33-34
horizontal lines, 251-252
hot links, 194
hot spots, Control Pallette, 51
HotShot Graphics (SymSoft), 178
HP LaserJet 4si printer, two-sided
  printing, 226
HSB (Hue, Saturation, Brightness) color
  model, 332
hyphenation, 156-159
Hyphenation command (Type
  menu), 157
hyphenation zones, 158-159

## I

icons
   Aldus Installer/Utility, 376
   Apply, 132
   Autoflow, 100, 103
   Column Break, 193
   Grabber Hand, 36
   jump over, 193
   L page, master pages, 78
   Master page, 26, 66
   page number, 26-27
   PageMaker application, 21
   Place graphic, 178
   Printers, 209
   R page, master pages, 78
   Template, 247
   Text flow, 191
   Text wrap, 191
identical objects, layering, 359

illustrations, 169, 306
image control, TIFF formats, 201-205
Image control command (Element
  menu), 202
image filters, 177
images
   contrast, 205
   controls, 201-205
   converting
      HiJaak (Inset Systems), 178
      HotShot Graphics (SymSoft), 178
      The Graphics Link Plus+
        (Harvard Graphics), 178
   lightness, 205
   photographic, printing, 11
   PICT, 169
   scanned, 173-177
   storing object-oriented
     graphics, 170
   TIFF scaling, 177
   *see also* graphics
imagesetters, 233-236
   AGFA Pro Sets, 57
   Linotronic, 57
   PostScript laser printer compatibil-
     ity, 234
   printing guidelines, 235-236
   resizing Mac graphics, 234
   right-reading emulsion down
     negative, 235
import filters, 97, 147
Import Xtension (Aldus), 362
importing
   graphics, 177-178
   text, 97-101, 303-305
imposition dummy, 92
improving graphics performance,
  350-361
indents, 108-111
Indents ruler, 112
Indents/tabs command (Type menu),
  108-110, 359
Indents/tabs ruler command (Layout
  menu), 111

The Essential PageMaker

independent graphics, 185

Index entry command (Utilities menu), 319

indexes, 258, 313-325
> compiling, 321-324
> cross-referencing, 316
> keywords, 315
> making entries, 319-320
> metacharacters, 322-323
> viewing, 320-321

indexing names, 314-318

inks
> coverage in publications, 227
> previewing choices, 15
> process colors, 329
> specialty, 224-225
> spot colors, 329

inline graphics, 185-189

inline graphics elements, 351-354

Inner Media Collage, xvii

Insert pages command (Layout menu), 91

inserting text, 106

Installer History window, 379

installing
> fonts, font/DA managers, 362
> PageMaker, 375-383
>> on Mac, 376-379
>> on Windows, 379-383
> printer drivers (Mac), 209

instant printing, 13

IntelliDraw (Aldus), 169

Intellifont scalable fonts, 217

interpreters, PostScript, 172

interpreting words, Aldus Filters, 97

invisible characters, 151-152

Italic font styles, 6

Itek printing, 228

## J

jaggies, 169

jump over icon, 193

justified type, 114

## K

Kells character typefaces, 9

kerning
> automatic, 126-129
> em space, 127
> manual, 126-129
> pair, default, 127
> tips, 358-359

key combinatiions
> listing, 348-349
> Mac
>> Alignment (⌘+I), 108-110
>> Autoflow stop (Shift+⌘), 103
>> automatic page number (⌘+ Option+P), 69
>> background (⌘+B), 184
>> Bullets (Option+8), 354
>> cancelling text placement (⌘+Z), 104
>> centered type (⌘+Shift+C), 114, 131
>> Change box (⌘+9), 150
>> closing nested dialog boxes (Option+Return), 116
>> Control Pallette (⌘ +' ), 50
>> Cut (⌘+X), 105
>> Define Styles (⌘+3), 136-137, 310
>> duplicate footers (⌘+C), 70
>> Edit command (⌘+E), 354
>> fast-saving (⌘+S), 37
>> force-justified type (⌘+Shift+F), 114
>> foreground (⌘+F), 184
>> Guides option (⌘+J), 34
>> hyphenation (⌘+H), 157-158
>> index enrtries (⌘+;), 319
>> indexing proper names (⌘+Shift+Z), 314
>> justified type (⌘+Shift+J), 114
>> left align (⌘+Shift+L), 114
>> Links command (⌘+=), 160, 348

magnified view (⌘+option), 35
New command (⌘+N), 22, 64
Open command (⌘+O), 24
page numbers (⌘+Option+P),
  281, 299
Paste (⌘+V), 105
Place box (⌘+D), 85
Print (⌘+P), 213
Quit command (⌘+Q), 41
right-aligned type
  (⌘+Shift+R), 114
rulers (⌘ + ]), 80
Select All (⌘+A), 305
Show Pasteboard view
  (⌘+0), 35
Story Editor (⌘+E), 143
Story view (⌘+E), 150, 306
Style pallette (⌘+Y), 135-136
toggling Toolbox (⌘+6), 27
toggling views (Option+⌘), 35
Type Specs (⌘+T), 68, 118
zooming out (⌘+0), 26
Mac/Windows
add pages after (Alt+A), 92
add pages before (Alt+B), 92
add pages between (Alt+W), 92
back layer (Ctrl+B), 82
front layer (Ctrl+F), 82
guides (Ctrl+U), 80
pair kerning, 128
Spelling box (⌘+L), 154
Windows
Alignment (Ctrl+I), 108-110
Autoflow (Shift+Ctrl), 103
automatic page numbers
  (Ctrl+Shift+3), 69
background (Ctrl+B), 184
Bullets (Ctrl+Shift+8), 354
cancelling text placement
  (Alt+Backspace), 104
centered type (Ctrl+Shift+C),
  114, 131
Change box (Ctrl+9), 150
Control Pallette (Ctrl +' ), 50

Cut (Ctrl+X), 71, 105
Define Styles (Ctrl+3),
  136-137, 310
duplicate footers (Ctrl+C), 70
Edit command (Ctrl+E), 354
fast-saving (Ctrl+S), 37
force-justified type
  (Ctrl+Shift+F), 114
foreground (Ctrl+F), 184
Guides option (Ctrl+J), 34
hyphenation (Ctrl+H), 157-158
index entries (Ctrl+;), 319
indexing proper names
  (Ctrl+Shift+Z), 314
justified type (Ctrl+Shift+J), 114
left align (Ctrl+Shift+L), 114
Links command
  (Shift+Ctrl+D), 348
magnified view (⌘+option), 35
New command (Ctrl+N), 22, 64
Open command (Ctrl+O), 24
page numbers (Ctrl+Shift+3),
  281, 299
Paste (Ctrl+V), 70, 105
Place box (Ctrl+D), 85
Print (Ctrl+P), 213
Quit command (Ctrl+Q), 41
right-aligned type
  (Ctrl+Shift+R), 114
rulers (Ctrl+Shift+Y), 80
Select All (Ctrl+A), 305
Show Pasteboard view
  (Ctrl+0), 35
Story Editor (Alt+E, E), 143
Story Editor (Ctrl+E), 143
Story view (Ctrl+E), 150, 306
Style pallette (Ctrl+Y), 135-136
toggling Toolbox (Ctrl+6), 27
toggling views (Ctrl+Alt), 35
Type menu (Alt+T), 114
Type Specs (Ctrl+T), 68, 118
zooming out (Ctrl+0), 26
keywords in indexes, 315
knockouts, printing, 15
Koala MacVision, 176

## L

L page icon, 78
label templates, 292-294
large volume printing, 226-230
larger pages, printing, 231-232
laser output paper, Hammermill Laser Plus, 230
laser printers, 214-216
  cleaning, 231
  final copies, 223
  functions, 214
  grayscale limitations, 12
  master pages, 230
  PostScript, 7, 56
  small runs in printing, 13
LaserWriter Printer Driver (Mac), 209
LaserWriter printers (Apple), 56
LaserWriter Pro printers (Apple), 12
layering identical objects, 359
layering elements, master pages, 81-83
layout, 3-5
  ads, 268-272
  grids, 31-34
Layout menu
  Autoflow command, 100, 103
  Column guides command, 33, 66-67, 274
  Copy master guides command, 91
  Display master items command, 91
  Indents/tabs ruler command, 111
  Insert pages command, 91
  Lock guides command, 34
  Remove pages command, 91
  Show pasteboard command, 26, 35
  Snap to guides command, 34, 80
  Snap to rulers command, 34, 80
  Zero Lock command, 31
Layout view, toggling with Story Editor, 145
leaders, 112
Leaders menu, Custom command, 112
leading, 120-124
Leading command (Type menu), 122

left margin indents, 110
left-aligned type, 114
Letraset ColorTag system, 224
letterhead templates, 347
letterheads, 254-255
letterpress printing, 229
libraries
  Aldus Addition Create color, 344
  clip art, 360, 373
  color, 339-340
  custom colors, 341-344
  shareware, templates, 72
  texture, 359-361
Library of Congress copyright forms, 18
light tables, 232
lightness of images, 205
LightningScan Pro 256 (ThunderWare), 174
line breaks, 114
Line command (Element menu), 28, 183, 251, 274
Line Drawing tools, 28
lines
  drawing automatically, 251
  horizontal, 251-252
  skewing, 53
Link info command (Element menu), 161, 195
Link options command (Element menu), 163
linked files, copying, 41-42
linking
  and updating new layout versions, 348
  automatic, EPS files, 196
  defaults, 197-198
  graphics, 194-199
  text, 159-166
linking programs, OLE, 98
links
  hot, 194
  OLE, 98
Links command (File menu), 160, 348

Linotronic imagesetters, 57
Linotronic printers, 12
locking the zero point, 31
logos
    corporate, placing in templates
        with Clipboard, 249
        with Scrapbook, 249
    draw programs, 63
    graphics, 62-64
London character typefaces, 9
Lorem Ipsum greeking file, 300
Lotus Freelance Windows drawing
    programs, 170
lustre of paper, 224

## M

MacDraw, 169
MacDraw Pro (Claris), 10, 169
Macintosh color picker, 331
MacLabelPro (Avery), mailing lists, 292
MacLink Translators/Plus
    (DataViz), 304
MacPaint paint program, 10, 169
MacPaint II paint program, 169
macro programs, 363
*MacUser* magazine, 346
MacVision (Koala), 176
*MacWorld* magazine, 346
magazine ads, 272-277
magic stretch, 181
mailing indicia, 90
mailing labels, templates, 93
mailing lists, MacLabelPro (Avery), 292
Main program group, Program Manager
    Control Panel window, 209
making index entries, 319-320
manual
    kerning, 126-129
    text flow, 99
    tiling, 232-233
manual only hyphenation, 157
manual plus algorithm hyphenation,
    158
manual plus dictionary hyphenation,

157-158
Manutius, Aldus, 21
margin lines, 66
margins, 31-33
masking, 81
master copies, printing, 230-233
master page icons, 26, 66
master pages, 78-79
    laser output paper, 230-231
    layering elements, 81-83
    newsletters, 63
    removing elements, 91
master templates, 78-79
MasterJuggler, 219, 362
mastheads, 61-62, 83-84
matching colors, 16
mathematical tricks, 359
mathematical equations, 356-358
measuring units of type, 120
mechanical binding systems, 225
memory requirements for PageMaker
    5.0, 56, 370-371
metacharacters in indexes, 322-323
Micrografix Designer, , 169-170
Microsoft
    Excel, importing charts as
        graphics, 260
    PowerPoint, charts and graphs, 302
    TrueType fonts, 8
    Word, importing text, 303
modems, 294
modifying graphics, 179-181
Monaco monospaced fonts, 6
monitors
    color calibrators, 364
    monochrome, adding spot
        colors, 16
    PageMaker, 369-370
monospaced fonts
    Courier, 6
    Monaco, 6
MORE 3.0 (Symantec), charts and
    graphs, 302
moving text blocks, Apply icon, 132

MS Works
    charts and graphs, 302
    importing text, 304
multilayered transparencies, 283-285
multipage faxes, 295
multipage publications, 66
multiple columns, 33
Multiple Master Fonts (Adobe), 8
multiple open documents, 55-56
Multiple paste command (Edit
 menu), 251

## N

name tags, 140-141
names, indexing, 314-318
NCR (No Carbon Required) paper, 250
negatives, 255
nested indents, 108
New command (File menu), 22, 64
new styles, 137-138
newsletters
    dummy, 60-61
    master pages, 63
    planning production, 58-59
    titles, 61-64
newspaper ads, 272-277
non-PostScript printers, 215-216
nonbreaking spaces, indexes, 315
None command
    Element menu, 81, 90
    Fill menu, 200
normal indents, 108
Norton AntiVirus for the PC, 242
numbering
    pages, 68-71, 358-359
    transparencies, 279

## O

Object Packager, 98
object-oriented art
    .CGM files, 170
    EPS files, 170-173
    .WMF files, 170
object-oriented graphics, 169-171

objects
    CGM (computer graphics
     metafile), 63
    embedded, 98-99
    flipping horizontally/vertically with
     Control Pallette, 53
    graphics, aligning, 354
    grouping, 350-351
    identical, layering, 359
    OLE, editing, 185
    PICT, 63
    text, aligning, 354
    WMF (Windows metafile), 63
oblique font styles, 6
OCR (Optical Character Recognition)
 Typist, 175
offset printing process, 227
OLE (Object Linking and
 Embedding), 98
OLE objects
    editing, 185
    spreadsheets, 261
100% command (Set width menu), 89
onscreen indents, 110-111
Open command (File menu), 24, 247
Open template Addition, 245-246
Open template command (Aldus
 Additions menu), 73
Open Templates utility, 287, 292
opening
    existing publications, 24
    PageMaker, 20-22
    Story Editor, 143
OPI (Open Pre-press Interface)
 PostScript file convention, 47
options for printing, 223-224
Options menu, Create TOC
 command, 309
original forms, 250
orphans, 114-115
outline type style, transparencies, 281
Oval Drawing tool, 29
overhead transparencies, 278-281
overlays, 15, 283
overriding styles, 141-142

## P

page dummies, 270
page number icons, 26-27
Page setup command (File menu), 66,
  210, 309, 347
Page setup defaults, 347
PageAhead, 263
pages
  adding, 91-93
  automatic numbering, 358-359
  changing, 26-27
  large, printing, 231-232
  master, 78-79, 91
  numbering, 68-71
  renumbering in TOCs, 308-309
  tiling, 232
  zero point, 31
paint programs
  Canvas, 169
  MacPaint, 10, 169
  MacPaint II, 169
  PC Paintbrush for Windows, 10
  SuperPaint, 10, 169
Painter for Windows (Fractal), .PCX
  files, 169
pair kerning default (12 points), 127
Palatino serif typefaces, 9
Pantone PMS color-matching
  system, 336
paper
  colors and finishes, 227-231
  lustre, 224
  NCR (No Carbon Required), 250
  previewing choices, 15-17
  special printing types, 224
  types for publications, 227-231
  vellum, 224
Paper command (Element menu),
  81, 183
Paragraph command (Type menu),
  107, 310, 352, 357
Paragraph Rules feature, 115-116
paragraphs, 107-116

parts lists, 263
Paste command (Edit menu), 105
pasteboard, 25-26
patterns, screening, 204-205
PC Paintbrush for Windows, 10
PCL bitmap fonts, 217
PCL page description language, 216
PCL printers, 216
.PCX files
  CorelDRAW!, 169-170
  Harvard Graphics, 169
  Micrografix Designer, 169
  Painter for Windows (Fractal), 169
  PC Paint, 169
  PC Paintbrush, 169
permanently downloading fonts, 221
Perpendicular Line tool, 28, 201, 251
Personal Laser Printers (GCC), 215
Personal LaserWriter LS (Apple), 215
.PFB files, 220
.PFM files, 220
Photo-Shop (Adobe), 360
photocopying, 13
photographic images, printing, 11
photographs, image control, 201-205
photos, scanned, 11
.PIC filters, charts and graphs, 170
PIC files, charts and graphs, 170
PICT format, 10, 170
PICT images, 169
PICT objects, 63
PICT2 format, 170
picture blocks, dummy newsletters, 60
pink grid lines (margins), 31
pixels, 331
PKZIP compression utilities, 272
Place command (File menu), 85, 100,
  188, 262, 348, 350
Place File command (File menu), 170
Place graphic icons, 178
placing
  files in PageMaker with File
    Manager, 178
  graphics from graphics files,
    178-179

headlines, 130-131
inline graphics, 186-189
longer sections of text, 102-106
stories, Story Editor, 145-148
text, 98-99
planning books, 297-298
planning guidelines for publications, 2-3
PMS (Pantone Matching System), color matching, 16
Pointer tool, 26-27, 104, 146, 179-181
points, type measuring units (USA), 120
positioning of ads, 269
positioning graphics, 178-179
posters, 275
PostScript (Adobe Systems), xix
file conventions, OPI (Open Pre-press Interface), 47
fonts, 7
Windows printer drivers, 211
PostScript interpreter, 172
PostScript laser printers, 56
imagesetter compatibility, 234
PostScript printers, 215
EPS files, 172
font types, 216
laser printers, 7
WIN.INI file, 220
PostScript printing, 215
power nudges, 52
PPD (PostScript Printer Description) files, 238
pre-made templates, 72, 244-250
pre-press process improvements, 47
Preferences command (File menu), 38, 143
press run charges, 230
previewing
ink choices, 15
paper choices, 15
Print area option, printing, 223
Print command (File menu), 212-213, 232, 376

printer drivers, 54, 208-210
Mac, 209
PageMaker, 372
Universal, 211
Windows, 209-211
Printer-resolution scaling, Control Palette, 180
printers
Apple ImageWriter, 56
changing types for publications, 211-212
defaults, 210-211
Hewlett Packard PaintJet, 57
Hewlett Packard DeskWriter, 56, 215
Hewlett Packard LaserJet, 57
HP LaserJet 4si, two-sided printing, 226
laser, 214-216
cleaning, 231
final copies, 223
grayscale limitations, 12
master pages, 230
PostScript, 7
LaserWriter (Apple), 56
LaserWriter Pro (Apple), 12
Linotronic, 12
Mac setup, Chooser DA (Apple menu), 209
non-PostScript, 215-216
PageMaker requirements, 371-372
PCL, 216
Personal Laser Printers (GCC), 215
Personal LaserWriter LS (Apple), 215
PostScript, 215-216
QMS ColorScript, 56
QuickDraw (Mac), 216
SCSI, 215
StyleWriter (Apple), 8, 56
Printers icon, 209
printing, 13-15
bids, 17
books, 324-325

camera-ready pages, 17
CMYK, 236
color, 236-242
crop marks, 15
disk submissions, 17
drafts, 213
film negative, 234-235
final copies, 222-226
font lists, 14
four-color process, 16
gravure, 229
imagesetter guidelines, 235-236
instant, 13
Itek, 228
knockouts, 15
large volume, 226-230
larger pages, 231-232
letterpress, 229
linked graphics, 199
master copies, 230-233
master pages, 230-231
methods for publications, 227
offset process, 227
options, 223-224
overlays, 15
paper choices, 17
photographic images, 11
plates, 228
PostScript, 215
preparing floppy disks, 239-240
problems with fonts, 240
process color separations, 238-239
publications, 16-18
registration marks, 15
service bureaus, 14
small runs, 13-16
spot colors, 14-15, 328
spot separations
techniques, 227
thermographic, 254
tips, 364-366
to disk, 240-241
trapping, 15, 238
two-sided, 226
utilities, Aldus TrapWise, 239

printing plates, 228
printing presses, 229
printshops, 229
problems with PageMaker, 383-384
process color, 236-239, 333
process color separations,
 improvements, 47
process colors
    inks, 329
    printing, 14
processors, digital image
    Adobe PhotoShop, 174
    Aldus Digital Darkroom, 174
productions, planning newsletters,
 58-59
Program Manager, Main program
 group, Control Panel window, 209
programs
    destination (OLE), 98
    draw
        Canvas, 10
        CorelDRAW!, 10
        Harvard Graphics, 10
        MacDraw Pro, 10
    graphics
        Adobe Illustrator, 10
        Aldus FreeHand, 10
        shareware, 11
    graphics, logos, 62-63
    linking, OLE, 98
    macros, 363
    PageMaker 5.0 requirements, xx-xxi
    paint
        Canvas, 169
        MacPaint, 10, 169
        MacPaint II, 169
        PC Paintbrush for Windows, 10
        SuperPaint, 10, 169
    source (OLE), 98
    Table Editor 2.1, 117
proof copies, 212-213
proofreading hard copies, 213
proportional fonts
    Helvetica, 6
    Times, 6

proportional leading, 123
Proportional Scaling, Control Palette, 180
PS Group It (Aldus Additions), 49
PS Ungroup It (Aldus Additions), 49
Publish and Subscribe feature, System 7 (Apple), 98
Publisher's Paintbrush, BMP files, 169
pull quotes, 61

## Q

QMS ColorScript printers, 56
question mark (?) wild card character, 148
QuickDraw graphics language (Mac), 215
QuickDraw Printers (Mac), 216
Quickeys (CE Software), 363
quitting PageMaker, 41-42

## R

R page icon, master pages, 78
ragged right indents, 108
Rectangle tool, 90
reference-point proxy, 51
reflections, Control Pallette, 50
registration marks, 15
Remove pages command (Layout menu), 91
Remove transformation command (Element menu), 54
removing master page elements, 91
renumbering pages in TOCs, 308-309
repairing distorted graphics, 181
replacing stories, 105-106
reports
    annual, 244, 258-261, 301-309
    sales, 244, 258-261
repositioning graphics, 179
resident fonts, 218
resizing
    graphics, 179-181
    handles, 179
    Mac graphics for imagesetters, 234

restoring files, 41
return address blocks, 89
reusing templates, 347
Reverse order option, printing, 223
Revert command (File menu), 40, 141
reverting publications, 40-41
RGB (Red Green Blue) color model, 331-332
right indents, 110
right-aligned type, 114
right-reading emulsion down negative, 235
Roman font styles, 6
rotation
    graphics, 53-54
    text, 53-54, 131-132
Rotation tool, 29, 53
ruler guides, 66, 79-81
rulers, Indents, 112
Run command (File menu), 379
Run script command, Aldus Additions, 354-355

## S

sales reports, 244, 258-261
SAM (Symantec Anti-Virus for the Macintosh), 242
SampleText file, 300
sans serif typefaces, 7
    Futura, 9
    Helvetica, 7-9
Save As command (File menu), 39-40, 74, 93, 246
saved files, compressing, 39-40
saving
    fast, 37
    images in PICT format, 10
    publications, 37-41
    templates, 74
saving as, 37
Scaling option, printing, 223
scaling TIFF images, 177
scanned images, 173-177
scanned photographs, 11, 201-205

scanners, 373
   color, 176-177
   Computer Eyes, 11
   flatbed, 174, 360
   hand-held, 174-175, 360
scanning halftones, 11
Scrapbook
   importing graphics, 178
   placing company logos in templates, 249
screen fonts, 218
Screened mode, Image control, 202
screening patterns, 204-205
script templates, 246
scripts, Aldus Additions, 49
SCSI (Small Computer Systems Interface), 215
SCSI Printers, 215
Searches, ANSI character sets, 151
self-mailers, 89-90, 273
semi-automatic text flow, 99, 103
serif typefaces, 7
   Bookman, 7-9
   Palatino, 9
   Times Roman, 7
service bureaus
   preparing floppy disks for printing, 239-240
   printing, 14
   printing costs, 239
   problems with printing fonts, 240
Set Width command (Type menu), 8
Set width menu, 100% command, 89
setting up templates, 347-348
settings, PageMaker defaults, 108
shadow type style, transparencies, 281
shareware
   graphics programs, 11
   libraries, 72
Show index command (Utilities menu), 320
Show Pasteboard command (Layout menu), 26, 35
Show Pasteboard view, 35

signatures, 330
size considerations of printing presses, 229
skewing lines, 53
slugs, leading, 122
small caps type, 125
small runs in printing, 13-16
Smart ASCII filter (PageMaker), 305
Snap to guides command (Layout menu), 34, 80
Snap to rulers command (Layout menu), 34, 80
soft fonts
   drawbacks, 216
   WIN.INI files updates, 218
software requirements for PageMaker, 372-373
Sort pages command (Utilities menu), 282
source programs (OLE), 98
spacing paragraphs, 113
special character codes
   Change boxes, 150-151
   Find boxes, 150-151
special effects characters, 112
special printing paper types, 224
specialty inks, 224-225
specifications for paragraphs, 107-116
specifying type, 118-125
Spell Checker, 153-156
spell checking, 96, 154-156
Spelling command (Utilities menu), 154
spot color, 330-331
spot colors, 236, 337-339
   adding on monochrome monitors, 16
   inks, 329
   printing, 14, 328
spot separations, printing, 15
spray fixatives, multilayered transparencies, 284
spreadsheets, OLE objects, 261
standards of color matching, 16

starting
    PageMaker from Windows, 20-22
    publications, 22-24
stock certificates, 290
stories
    exporting, 146-166
    replacing, 105-106
    word processors, 96-97
Story Editor
    assigning styles, 143-144
    Change function, 148-152
    Find function, 148-152
    PageMaker, 97
    placing stories, 145-148
    toggling views with Layout, 145
    word processing, 144-145
Story Editor view, 142-148
Story menu, Display command, 152
stuffers, 273
StuffIt compression utilities, 272
Style command (Window menu), 135
Style palette, 135
style sheets, 134, 138-140
styles, 134-142
    assigning with Story Editor, 143-144
    defaults, 135-136
    existing, 135-136
    fonts, 6
    headings in TOCs, 310-311
    name tags, 140-141
    new, 137-138
    overriding, 141-142
StyleWriter printer (Apple), 8, 56
subdirectories, Windows, PageMaker
 dictionaries, 362
subscript, 124-125
Suitcase 2.0, 219, 362
Super ATM (Adobe), 8
SuperPaint, 10, 169
superscript, 124-125
Symantec MORE 3.0, 302
symbol sets, Zapf Dingbats, 291
System 6.07 virtual memory, Virtual
 (Connectix), 56

System folder (Mac), PageMaker
 dictionaries, 362
system requirements PageMaker 5.0,
 56-57

## T

Table Editor, 116-118, 259
tables, 116-118
tables of contents, 60
tabs, default settings, 111-112
tags, 305
Targa video card (Truevision), 176
.TBL files, Table Editor, 117
Template icon, 247
templates, 38, 245-249
    book, 306-308
    brochure, 347
    calendar, 287
    file extensions (Windows), 39
    label, 292-293
    letterhead, 347
    mailing labels, 93
    master, 78-79
    pre-made, 72, 244-250
    publication defaults, 72-74
    reusing, 347
    saving, 74
    script, 246
    setting up, 347-348
    shareware libraries, 72
    sources, 245
    word processor, 74-75
temporary files
    Mac, ALDTMP01, 41
    Windows, .TMP extension, 41
text
    Autoflow, 103-104
    finding and changing by
     attributes, 149
    flow options, 99-100
    importing, 97-101, 303-305
        ClarisWorks, 304
        Microsoft Word, 303
        MS Works, 304

WordPerfect, 303
WordPerfect Works, 304
WriteNow 3.0, 303
inserting, 106
linking, 159-166
objects, aligning, 354
placing, 99, 102-106
rotation, 47, 53-54, 131-132
threading/unthreading, 104-105
text attributes, 97
text blocks
adjusting, 106-107
dummy newsletters, 60
moving with Apply icon, 132
text boxes, Text tool, 188
text files
placing, 98
tab-delimited, Table Editor, 117
text flow
options, 190, 193-194
semi-automatic, 103
Text flow icon, 191
Text rotation tool, 132, 286
Text tool, 29, 83, 87, 90, 106, 112,
187-188, 310, 319
text wrap, 189-194
Text wrap command (Element menu),
189-191
Text wrap icon, 191
TEXT.TXT file, 300
texture libraries, 359-361
textures, creating with scanners, 360
The Graphics Link Plus+ (Harvard
Graphics), 178
thermal binding systems, 225
thermographic printing, 254
thermometers, 247
threading text, 104-105
threefold flyers, 273
thumbnails, 300
ThunderWare LightningScan
Pro 256, 174
TIFF format image control, 201-205
TIFF images, scaling, 177
Tile Auto option, 232

Tile command (Window menu), 26, 55
tiling, 232-233
time-saving tools, 362-364
Times proportional fonts, 6
Times Roman serif typefaces, 7
tints, 236, 340-341
titles of newsletters, 61-64
.TMP extension temporary files
(Windows), 41
TOCs (tables of contents), 309-313
toggling views, Story Editor/Layout
view, 145
tombstoning headlines, 131
Toolbox, 27-30, 359
top of caps leading, 123
Track command (Type menu), 125
tracking, 125-129
transparencies, 279-285
trapping, 238
trim size of books, 298
TrueType fonts (Microsoft/Apple), 8
America Online, 217
cross-platform compatibility, 8
Windows Fonts control panels, 218
Truevision Targa video card, 176
twelve on fourteen type size/leading
height, 121
two-sided printing, 226
type
default font, 12-point Times, 118
measuring units, 120
small caps, 125
specifying, 118-125
styles and sizes, 120
Type 1 fonts, PostScript, 7
Type menu
Alignment command, 70, 108
Define styles command,
136-137, 310
Hyphenation command, 157
Indents/tabs command,
108-110, 359
Leading command, 122
Paragraph command, 107, 310,
352, 357

Set Width command, 8

Track command, 125

Type specs command, 68, 118, 353

Type style command, 8

typefaces, 6

    character, 9

    design guidelines, 9

    faxes, 9

    fonts, 6

    Helvetica, 6

    sans serif, Helvetica, 7

    serif

        Bookman, 7

        Times Roman, 7

    weights, 7

types of paper for publications, 227-231

Typist (Caere), 175

typography, 6-9

## U

Universal Printer driver, 211

unlinking, 166

unthreading text, 104-105

upgrading PageMaker from earlier versions, 383

upgrading to PageMaker 5.0, 57

utilities

    Aldus Installer, 375

    compression

        CompactPro, 272

        PKZIP, 272

        StuffIt, 272

    Open Templates, 287, 292

    printing, Aldus TrapWise, 239

Utilities menu

    Change command, 315

    Create index command, 321

    Create Table of contents command, 312

    Display pub info command, 325

    Index entry command, 319

    Show index command, 320

    Sort pages command, 282

    Spelling command, 154

## V

vellum paper, 224

vertical guidelines, 33-34

video cards, Targa (Truevision), 176

video digitizers, 176

View submenu, Layout menu, Show pasteboard command, 26, 35

viewing indexes, 320-321

views

    Actual size, 35

    Fit in window, 34

    Show Pasteboard, 35

    Story Editor, 142-148

Virex, 242

Virtual (Connectix), System 6.07

 virtual memory, 56

virtual memory, 56

viruses, 241-242

Voice Navigator (Articulate Systems), 363

## W

weights of typefaces, 7

widows, 114-115

wild card characters

    caret (^), 148

    question mark (?), 148

WIN.INI file

    font downloading, 220

    soft font updating, 218

Window menu

    Cascade command, 55

    Control Palette command, 50

    Style command, 135

    Tile command, 26, 55

window shade handles, 102

Windows

    default printer, 210-211

    drawing programs

        Arts & Letters, 170

        Harvard Graphics, 170

        Lotus Freelance, 170

        Micrographfix Designer, 170

file extensions
publications, 39
templates, 39
Font control panel, 218-220
metafiles, Table Editor, 117
printer drivers, 209-210
subdirectories, 362
windows
Aldus Setup Main, 380
Installer History, 379
.WMF files, object-oriented art, 170
WMF (Windows metafile) objects, 63
word processing, Story Editor, 144-145
word processors, 96-97
grammar/spell checking, 96
templates, 74-75
text attributes, 97
WordPerfect, importing text, 303

WordPerfect Works
charts and graphs, 302
importing text, 304
words, interpretation, Aldus Filters, 97
write-protecting PageMaker disks, 374-375
WriteNow 3.0, importing text, 303
WYSIWYG (What You See Is What You Get), 219

## X-Z

Zapf Chancery font, 291
Zapf Dingbats symbol set, borders, 291
Zero Lock command (Layout menu), 31
zero point, 31, 79
zooming out, 26